STRUCTURED PROGRAMMING

AND PROBLEM SOLVING

WITH ALGOL W

RICHARD B. KIEBURTZ

Department of Computer Science
State University of New York at Stony Brook

PRENTICE-HALL, Inc.

Englewood Cliffs, New Jersey

Library of Congress Cataloging in Publication Data

KIEBURTZ, RICHARD B.
Structured programming and problem solving with
ALGOL W.

Includes index.
1. ALGOL (Computer program language). 2. Electronic digital computers—Programming. 3. Electronic
data processing—Problem solving. I. Title.
QA76.73.A24K54   001.6′424   75-4685
ISBN 0-13-854737-8

Printed in the United States of America

10 9 8 7 6 5 4 3 2 1

PRENTICE-HALL INTERNATIONAL, INC., *London*
PRENTICE-HALL OF AUSTRALIA, PTY. LTD., *Sydney*
PRENTICE-HALL OF CANADA, LTD., *Toronto*
PRENTICE-HALL OF INDIA PRIVATE LIMITED, *New Delhi*
PRENTICE-HALL OF JAPAN, INC., *Tokyo*

CONTENTS

	Page
Preface	vii
Glossary of terms	xi
CHAPTER 1 INTRODUCTION: WHAT IS COMPUTING?	1
1.1 Algorithms	2
Example 1.1.1	2
Example 1.1.2	3
Example 1.1.3	3
Example 1.1.4	4
1.2 How are algorithms formulated?	4
Example 1.2.1	5
Example 1.2.2	5
Example 1.2.3	6
Example 1.2.4	8
Exercises for Chapter 1	15
CHAPTER 2 USING COMPUTATIONAL VARIABLES	19
2.1 Assigning values to variables	19
Example 2.1.1	20
2.2 Some distinctions between algorithmic and algebraic notations	21
2.3 Precedence rules for arithmetic operators	22
2.4 Getting values in and out of the computer	23
2.5 Programming versus calculating	24
Example 2.5.1	25
Example 2.5.2	26
Exercises for Chapter 2	29
CHAPTER 3 PROGRAMMING THE COMPUTER TO MAKE DECISIONS	33
3.1 Conditional expressions	33
3.2 Relational and logical expressions	34
Example 3.2.1	35
3.3 Conditional execution of alternate algorithm steps	37
Example 3.3.1	38
3.4 Devising algorithms to solve problems	39
Example 3.4.1	40
3.5 Comments and their use	47
Example 3.5.1	47
3.6 Blocks and compound groups of statements	48
Example 3.6.1	49
3.7 Handling multiple alternatives	52
Example 3.7.1	52
3.8 Making programs readable	54
Exercises for Chapter 3	56

		Page
CHAPTER 4	REPEATING COMPUTATIONS	61
4.1	Computations that cannot be done in a single sequence of steps	61
	Example 4.1.1	62
4.2	Getting the initial values right	64
4.3	How do you know that an algorithm is correct?	65
4.4	How many times should we repeat?	68
	Example 4.4.1	70
4.5	Nested iterations	73
	Example 4.5.1	73
	Exercises for Chapter 4	78
CHAPTER 5	TELLING THE COMPUTER ABOUT THE DATA	83
5.1	Data types	83
5.2	Structured data types	84
5.3	Declarations	85
5.4	Representing data with arrays	87
	Example 5.4.1	87
	Example 5.4.2	95
5.5	Analyzing character strings	103
	Example 5.5.1	103
5.6	Sorting	106
	Exercises for Chapter 5	114
CHAPTER 6	GETTING INFORMATION IN AND OUT OF A COMPUTER	119
6.1	Record-oriented input	120
6.2	Interpreting the input	121
6.3	Output	125
6.4	Constructing tables	127
	Example 6.4.1	128
6.5	Using the computer to generate reports and catalogs	133
	Example 6.5.1	135
6.6	Teaching the computer to draw	137
	Example 6.6.1	139
	Example 6.6.2	147
	Exercises for Chapter 6	152
CHAPTER 7	COMPUTATIONS WITHIN COMPUTATIONS	155
7.1	Block structure	155
7.2	Communicating data to procedures	158
	Example 7.2.1	159
	Example 7.2.2	160
	Example 7.2.3	160
	Example 7.2.4	161
7.3	Side effects	162
	Example 7.3.1	163
7.4	Recursion	167
	Example 7.4.1	169
	Exercises for Chapter 7	174

		Page
CHAPTER 8 SOLVING HARD PROBLEMS		179
8.1 Top-down problem solving		179
Example 8.1.1		180
Example 8.1.2		193
8.2 Using trial and error methods		201
Example 8.2.1		203
Exercises for Chapter 8		214
CHAPTER 9 SIMULATING THE REAL WORLD		221
9.1 Simulating deterministic processes		
Example 9.1.1		222
9.2 Growth of populations		227
Example 9.2.1		228
Example 9.2.2		230
9.3 Probabilistic simulations		236
Example 9.3.1		237
Exercises for Chapter 9		244
CHAPTER 10 NUMERICAL COMPUTATION		249
10.1 Computing with floating-point numbers		249
10.2 Evaluation of functions		254
Example 10.2.1		256
Example 10.2.2		262
10.3 Finding roots of equations		265
Example 10.3.1		272
10.4 Solving systems of linear equations		273
Example 10.4.1		276
Exercises for Chapter 10		278
CHAPTER 11 HOW DOES THE COMPUTER WORK?		283
11.1 Organized complexity		283
11.2 Shift registers		291
11.3 The accumulator		293
11.4 Other arithmetic operations		295
11.5 How the computer communicates with the outside world		299
11.6 Managing the computer		304
11.7 Compilers		305
APPENDIX		309
Table A10.5.1 Character encodings		356
Index		359

PREFACE

This book is an introduction to problem solving by computational methods. If it helps you to learn how to specify the requirements for a solution, how to formulate, one step at a time, a procedure to follow in generating a solution, and how to describe that procedure so that it may be understood by others, then it will have succeeded in its purpose.

In browsing through the book, you can get some idea of the types of problems for which people have found computational solutions to be useful. These encompass many more activities that one might suspect at first, and of course, only a sampling can be presented here. It is no surprise that many problems arising in science, engineering and applied mathematics are susceptible to solution by computation. One is also prepared to believe that computing systems are useful for keeping business records, although the computation that is done is of a somewhat different nature than is the case in scientific applications. It is perhaps more surprising that activities requiring complex decisions can be analyzed as computational problems, and it certainly is not obvious without considerable study how computation is able to create pictures, translate languages, predict outcomes of elections, do medical diagnosis or discover proofs of mathematical theorems. It would require more and thicker volumes than this one to investigate all of the applications mentioned, but this book will introduce you to the principal computational techniques used in all of these applications.

You will also discover that this book is not much concerned with computing machines themselves, although you will certainly learn to run programs on some digital computer if you use this book as the text for a course. If your curiosity is aroused about what lies behind the panels on the box, (and it very likely will be) you can jump ahead to Chapter 11, which contains a brief description of some functional modules commonly used in digital computers, and a very sketchy description of how they are put together. This chapter is only a concession to your curiosity, however. If you really want to learn more about how computers work, you will have to read another book on that subject after you finish this one.

One of the principal ways in which this book differs from most introductory computer texts is that it emphasizes a more disciplined approach to the design of computational procedures. There are good reasons for this, although they are not always immediately apparent until your experience with computing gets beyond an introductory course. As in other endeavors, it is pretty easy in computing to discover satisfactory solutions to

simple problems. That is what we mean when we say that a problem
is simple. But when one is called upon to solve a problem which
is not simple, the computational procedure required may be
lengthy, complex, and therefore difficult to understand or to
describe.   It is at that point that the problem solver will see
the need for some discipline to guide the organization of his
effort, and to help divide the problem into simpler parts. If
you learn such an approach to designing computational procedures
at the outset, it will become a habitual tool, available for use
when needed.

     Since this book will require a slightly larger investment of
your time   to learn a disciplined approach to computing, it will
not be the right introduction for everybody.   In fact, the
quickest and easiest way to gain the ability to use a computer is
to learn to use an interactive computing system using the BASIC
language, or something similar. And this is quite satisfactory
for the computing needs of many people. But if you ever have the
occasion to tackle complex computational problems, or large
problems which require the coordinated effort of several persons
to design a computational procedure, the effort spent in learning
a computing discipline will be well rewarded.

     A decision which must be faced by the author of any textbook
on computing is the choice of a suitable language in which to
describe computational procedures. English seems at first to be
a good choice since anybody who is able to read this book already
knows it. But attempts to describe computations in English have
not been totally successful.   It lacks precision, contains
ambiguities and is therefore not easily translatable into a
program for a computer.   And a program for a computer is
required, eventually, if the computational procedure is to yield
a solution to the original problem. On the other hand, there are
many languages designed for the specific purpose of programming
computers.   These languages have precision, are unambiguous, and
are more or less intelligible to human beings. They are easily
translatable into computer programs; in fact, the translation is
done by the computer itself! But there are so many of them;
FORTRAN, COBOL, ALGOL, BASIC, PL/1, SNOBOL, LISP are the names of
but a few of the most widely used. And every computer programmer
has his own personal favorite.   If the author selects one of
these, then his text will only be used by other instructors who
favor the same programming language.

     Another option for the description of computations is the
use of a graphical language called flowchart language. It has
the advantages of precision, freedom from ambiguity, and is
reasonably universal, although variations do exist. At first it
seems to provide an ideal compromise between a natural language
(English) description of procedures and a description in terms of

a programming language. But it too has some drawbacks. It is not easily translatable into computer programs. The computer cannot do the translation from flowchart language directly. Instead, the programmer must provide an intermediate step, by translating the flowchart language into some programming language that can be read by the computer. This step turns out to be nontrivial in practice, particularly for the novice programmer, and so, much of the advantage of the flowchart language is lost. Flowcharts are very useful to people because they are fairly readily understood, but a flowchart has no value if it does not faithfully represent the actual computer program.

As you will see, this author has decided in favor of a choice of a particular programming language, ALGOL W. It will be used as a communication language to describe procedures, and as a programming language by means of which you will actually transmit your computational procedure to the computer. In order to render computations more readily understandable, the programming language will be freely augmented with comments in English. Also, English will be used in the preliminary stages of describing a problem and considering alternate strategies for its solution. In preliminary stages, lack of precision is no handicap, as the concepts themselves remain to be clarified as well as the language.

ALGOL W has facilities that are needed to support a disciplined approach to program structure, and this is the principal reason for its choice here. It also provides rather elegant diagnostic facilities to help you in following the course of a computation carried out by the computer. However, we shall not need nor shall we have time to explore in detail all of the facilities provided by the programming language. You are being given a large tool box from which you can select just those tools that are helpful to the job at hand.

Since this is principally a book about problem solving with the aid of a computer, the body of the text does not contain many digressions on the details of usage of the programming language. To help you with the grammar, punctuation and idiomatic expressions that you will need to write programs in ALGOL W, this book contains an Appendix, which is a manual for a subset of ALGOL W. The Appendix is extensively cross-indexed to help you to find what you want from it at the time that you are actually writing an ALGOL W program.

A dialect of a flowchart language is also introduced as an aid to visualization of the logical structure of programs. This language, called iteration graphs, helps one to see clearly what choices must be made in the course of a computation as well as indicating program steps which are to be repeated a number of

times.   Iteration graphs are a useful way to represent programs
in their inception, allowing one to fill in the details as they
are needed.

Another principal goal of this book is to teach you to
compose procedures and to program them for the computer in such a
way that another intelligent human being can read and understand
your programs.   A benefit of investing some effort to make
programs intelligible is that you are more likely to understand
them yourself.   This may sound facetious, but it is asking too
much of a computer to expect it to produce correct answers by
following a program about which the programmer himself is
uncertain.

Since this book attempts to do much more than just to teach
you a programming language, the ideas presented in it have been
gathered from many sources. It is typical after one has been
introduced to a new idea and has thought about it for awhile to
adopt the idea as one's own, as if it were orphaned from its
original source.   At the time of this writing, the author still
recalls that many of his ideas about programming were gleaned
from the work of Robert W. Floyd, Edsger Dijkstra and Niklaus
Wirth. With the passage of time, I suppose the ideas will seem
to become my own, and I hope that you also will see fit to adopt
some of them for your own.

GLOSSARY OF COMPUTING TERMS

accumulator--a register in the arithmetic unit of a computer

accuracy--in numerical computations, accuracy refers to the closeness with which a calculated value approximates the exact result one is trying to compute

algorithm--a list of instructions for performing a task or computing a result; given in elementary steps that can be carried out without further instruction

array--an indexed set of variables, possibly multiply indexed

assignment--an elementary computational step that gives a new value to a variable

binary--having only two possible values

bit--a single, binary unit of information

block--in a programming language, a bracketed textual context containing declarations of variables and a sequence of statements

byte--an information storage unit corresponding to a single character

character--an element of a designated set of symbols, usually consisting of the letters of the Roman alphabet, the Arabic numerals, and a number of punctuation symbols

comment--annotation within the text of a computer program, that is not interpreted as part of the program

compound group--a bracketed sequence of statements in a program, not containing any declarations of variables or procedures

computation--the process of executing a computer program

computer--an electronic, digital computer

conditional--depending on the computed value of a logical expression

data structure--any ensemble of data items with a prescribed mechanism for reference declaration--annotation in a program that is interpreted as defining attributes of variables or of a procedure

dimension--the number of elements along each coordinate of an array

execution sequence--the sequence of program steps actually executed during a specific computation

expression--an item in the text of a program composed of identifiers and operator symbols, and describing an evaluation

floating-point number--a number represented by a modulus and an exponent of the radix of the number system. This representation allows the point in a fractional number to be shifted, by adding or subtracting from the exponent the number of places shifted

grammar--a context-free grammar used to give a formal description of the syntax of a language

identifier--in the text of a program, any sequence of symbols used to name a variable, constant, label, or procedure

initialization--the process of giving initial values to program variables

instruction--one of a fixed set of orders that can be interpreted by a computer

invocation--the process of beginning execution of a program or procedure

iteration--repetition. However, the concept is generalized to include sequential execution of a list of instructions, and to include (conditional) non-execution, or repetition zero times

iteration graph--a graphical notation developed to describe iterative algorithms

logical--taking values from the set (true, false)

machine language--not a language at all, but the use of machine instructions to specify a program

memory--the internal data storage of a computer

nested--embedded within a surrounding context

operator--any of a specified set of computational operations

precedence--an order of priority of application that may be defined upon a set of operators

precision--the amount of information (number of bits or number of decimal digits) that is given in the approximation of a real number

procedure--a subsidiary algorithm declared in a program text

program--an algorithm given as a sequence of instructions that can be interpreted by a computer

programming language--a formally defined language for the specification of algorithms, and which can be translated or interpreted by a computer

record--a package of one or more items of data in a specified format

recursion--the computational process of re-invoking a program or procedure prior to its completion. Intermediate results of computation are stacked up so that they will not be lost

register--a cell for storage of data in a computer

relation--a binary relation defined on the possible values of a type of data

scope--the textual context in which a definition or declaration is valid

statement--an imperative sentence in a programming language, interpreted as one or a sequence of instructions by a computer

stepwise refinement--the process of algorithm composition by specification in successively finer levels of detail

string--a sequence of characters treated as a single data item

subscript--the index of an element of an array

substring--a designated subsequence of a string

type, or data type--a defined class of data objects

variable--a named object that can hold a value from a designated data type, and can receive new values by assignment

verification--the process of establishing the correctness of an algorithm

word--a unit of data corresponding to the capacity of a register
   of the memory of a computer

STRUCTURED PROGRAMMING

AND PROBLEM SOLVING

WITH ALGOL W

Chapter 1

INTRODUCTION: WHAT IS COMPUTING?

Nearly every person today knows of the existence of large computers and knows enough of their application that he has in mind some opinion as to what computing is all about. If pressed for an answer, our man on the street might tell you that computing is "the way they make out paychecks. You know, they put all the numbers into the computer and it figures out how much to deduct for income tax, how much for social security, for health insurance, for union dues, and it makes out your paycheck for the amount that's left." Or he might tell you, "Computing is the way they design things these days. If an engineer is designing a bridge, he has all of his complex calculations done on a computer instead of using a slide rule as he used to." Another interviewee may reply, with a tone of bewilderment, "Computing? Why computing is how everything is controlled nowadays. When I get in my car in the morning, the engine is run by a computer. My telephone calls are routed by another computer. The company I work with makes men's clothing. All of the patterns are produced by computers, and the cloth is cut by computer controlled machines. You know, they even sent a computer to the moon with the astronauts. Why, the world just wouldn't run without computing!" Yes, nearly everyone has some idea about the applications of computers today, but many fewer people would be able to give you a very clear picture of just how computing is brought to bear on all of these diverse applications.

Just what is computing all about? First, of all, it is concerned with elementary operations which are very simple indeed. In fact, the simplicity of the elementary operations performed by a computer sometimes leads people to underestimate the complexity of computing. One opinion sometimes heard from scientists (usually grey-haired ones) who know very well how computers work, is that "A computer is really no more than a very large, very fast calculating machine." In view of the sophisticated applications of computing of which even the layman is vividly aware, one cannot believe that this characterization as a large, fast calculator tells the whole story. Yet there is an element of truth to it, for on the level of the tiny components of which a computer is made, the individual operations performed are each very simple, as we shall see in Chapter 11 (which you may read at any time you are interested).

But the level of the elementary operations is too primitive a place to start if we want to gain an understanding of computing as quickly as possible. For the immense capabilities of computers are gained by the organization of these elementary operations; by composing simple functions to obtain capabilities of very much greater complexity. We shall do better to begin our study on a much higher and somewhat more abstract conceptual level dealing with the logical organization and composition of familiar operations.

1.1 Algorithms

Computer science is the study of computational procedures and of methods by which to design and apply these procedures to real problems. An algorithm is a computational procedure, usually given in the form of a list of instructions, and which is unambiguous, deterministic, finite and given in terms of elementary instructions that can themselves be carried out. In addition, we usually desire that our algorithms should be effective, that is, that they should accomplish the goal we had originally set out for them, but it turns out that the question of determining whether or not an algorithm is effective is so difficult that we would not want to make that requirement part of our definition of an algorithm. To illustrate the requirements imposed by the definition, we shall consider a few examples.

Example 1.1.1 -- Receipe for buckwheat pancakes

a. Place in a large bowl 1 cup of buckwheat flour, 1 teaspoon of baking soda, and some salt.
b. Add 1 tablespoon of melted shortening and 1 egg, and mix with the dry ingredients.
c. Add some water and mix into a thick batter.
d. Put two tablespoons of shortening in a frying pan and heat until the shortening begins to smoke.
e. Pour some batter into the hot frying pan and cook until bubbles appear through the pancake. Turn, and cook until golden brown.

Now this receipe might well be sufficient to guide an experienced cook to success in making buckwheat pancakes, but to a novice it is just not specific enough and his pancakes will very likely prove to be inedible. Most receipe books contain receipes given very much like this one, however, and the reason that people are able to use them is that a common bond of knowledge exists between the writer of the receipe book and the cook who uses it. This knowledge is gained by having been taught to cook, or else by years of experience in cooking, remembering successes and failures and the means by which they were achieved. In communicating receipes and procedures for doing other tasks, we usually take for granted that the person with whom we are communicating has a "common knowledge" of the rudiments of the task we are explaining, and we do not give instructions in sufficient detail to be followed by an absolute novice. When you start communicating with a computer, you will be shocked to

discover that the computer is an absolute novice, has learned
nothing from past experience, and that computational algorithms
must be specified in every detail, leaving nothing to be
interpreted by "common knowledge".

Example 1.1.2 -- Instructions for finding a summer cottage

    a. Go north on Route 3 for about six miles until you pass
       the general store on your left; then turn off at the
       next intersection.
    b. Go along until you pass a big, spreading oak tree by the
       road; then in about a quarter of a mile, look for a dirt
       road on the right.
    c. Follow the dirt road until the third, or maybe it's the
       fourth mailbox, and turn down the driveway.
    d. Go down the driveway about 400 yards. It's a white cabin
       with green shutters -- you can't miss it.

    These instructions are ambiguous at several points. In (a),
they fail to mention which way to turn from the main road. In
(b), there is no assurance that the large oak tree specified as a
landmark will be unique; the countryside may be an oak forest.
In (c), our guide is specifically ambiguous when he cannot
remember which mailbox marks the driveway. The receipe ends with
a comment at the end of (d) -- "you can't miss it". This comment
accompanies many lists of ambiguous directions. While the human
searching for his friend's summer cottage may rely on his past
experience, knowledge of the area or other aids not explicitly
given in the list of instructions, the computer would not be able
to do so, and a computational procedure containing ambiguities
such as the ones in the example would not be sufficient. The
human may also have difficulty, but he is adaptable to unexpected
situations and will fall back on other methods such as
exploration or asking for more specific directions if he cannot
successfully resolve the ambiguities in the directions he was
originally given.

Example 1.1.3 -- A procedure for becoming a millionaire

    a. Withdraw all your money from your bank account.
    b. Do step (c) each day until you become a millionaire or a
       pauper.
    c. Go to the local racetrack and bet all your money on the
       daily double combination paying the highest odds.

    This is an example of a procedure which is nondeterministic.
That is, if the procedure is executed at different times, it will
not necessarily produce the same outcome even though the
instructions are explicit and unambiguous. We do not wish to
consider nondeterministic procedures as algorithms, although they

are sometimes entertaining to contemplate.

Example 1.1.4 -- A procedure for drying out a leaky rowboat

    a. Get a two-gallon plastic bucket.
    b. Stand in the rowboat and bail the water out as fast as you can until less than two gallons remains in the bottom.

This procedure is unambiguous, deterministic, and the elementary steps can be readily carried out. But in carrying it out, there will be some cases in which you never finish bailing, namely if the boat is swamped to begin with or if it has such a large leak that the water runs in faster than you can bail it out. One would say that this procedure was not finite because there are some cases to which it applies where its execution would never halt. This characteristic is also true of some computational procedures, and it is often difficult to detect. However, we would like to require of an algorithm that it should be finite, for only after its execution has halted can one talk about the result given by the procedure.

You should now have an idea as to what we shall study about computation. In order to apply computation to the solution of problems, we compose algorithms, specific computational procedures which are unambiguous, deterministic, finite in their execution and which are carried out in simple steps. If we are successful and our algorithms accomplish the tasks they were designed to do, then we will say they are effective. Remember that to be effective, an algorithm must work correctly on all initial values of the data for which it was designed, and not only for one particular test case.

1.2 How are algorithms formulated?

When faced with a problem to be solved or a task to be performed, how does one go about developing an algorithm for its solution? Will the algorithm as formulated always satisfy the conditions of unambiguity, determinism, finiteness and the ability to be carried out in simple steps? Naturally, there will be opportunities to make mistakes, but a few examples may help to give an idea as to how we go about the formulation of algorithms.

Example **1.2.1** -- Given a non-negative integer, list all pairs of non-negative integers which sum to the given integer.

This is the type of problem that one encounters in school at age six or seven, which is about the age that most children first seem to develop algorithms for the solution of problems. The principal source of difficulty in this problem is that the pupil is asked to list _all_ pairs that sum to the given integer, rather than just one pair or some pairs. So if he just puts into his list those pairs which immediately come to mind as having the required sum, he will not be certain that he has listed them all. He must adopt a systematic approach. But he has some information to guide him. By the time he is given a problem of this type, he will know that addition is commutative, so that he may list only ordered pairs and still be sure of meeting the requirements of the problem. He will also know that of the pairs which sum to a given number, the pair containing the largest integer will be that consisting of the given integer and zero. So an algorithm that he may discover or which may be suggested to him by his teacher is the following:

a. Begin the list with the pair consisting of the given integer and zero.
b. For as long as the two integers in the last pair listed differ by more than unity, repeat the sequence of steps (c--d).
c. Subtract one from the first integer of the last pair listed and enter the result as the first integer of the next pair.
d. Find an integer which, when added to the number found in the previous step, sums to the integer given originally.

Of course, our first-grade pupil does not state his algorithm this formally, but he will learn to go through a sequence of steps such as those listed above in the course of solving problems of this type.

Example **1.2.2** -- An algorithm for long division

Everyone has learned how to do long division of integers, accumulating the quotient one numeral at a time. We can give an algorithm for this procedure, perhaps not quite in the same form that you have learned it.

a. Call the dividend by another name, _remainder_. If the divisor is larger than the remainder, then write zero for the quotient and stop, otherwise go on to the next step.

b. Count the number of decimal places in the divisor and in the remainder. Form a decimal number consisting of the numeral 1 followed on the right by a number of zeros equal to the number of decimal places by which the remainder is longer than the divisor. Call this number the _multiplier_.

c. For as long as any numerals at all remain in the multiplier, repeat steps (d--e).

d. Multiply the divisor by the multiplier, and determine how many times this product can be successively subtracted from the remainder. Write the number of subtractions as the next numeral of the quotient (immediately to the right of any previously written partial quotient) and discard the old value of the remainder, replacing it by the result of the successive subtractions.

e. Erase the rightmost numeral of the multiplier.

This algorithm probably differs from the one you learned in elementary school in that it does not specify the positions in which various numbers are to be written on a piece of paper. Instead, the algorithm refers to various numbers by name, and the actual values of the numbers attached to some of the names will change from one step to another during the course of the calculation. The algorithm does not even have to be done with pencil and paper, but could also be carried out using an adding machine or an abacus. Incidentally, as given here, the algorithm may produce a non-zero quotient having a zero as the leftmost digit. Can you see why?

Example 1.2.3 -- Looking up a word in a dictionary

This is an example of a searching operation, one of the most common functions performed in any information retrieval system. We shall consider several algorithms for this example.

Version 1 -- Sequential searching

a. Given any word to be looked up, begin by opening the dictionary to the first page of entries.

b. For as long as the desired word does not appear on the page to which the dictionary is opened, and the page is not the last one, repeat step (c). Otherwise, proceed to step (d).

c. Turn to the next page.

d. If the word appears on the page, then give its definition, otherwise report that the word as given was not found in the dictionary.

This algorithm is correct, but it is not one that most of us would choose to use because of the number of individual page searches required. The large number of words listed in a dictionary makes it important to us to use an efficient search procedure. The efficiency can be improved by making use of the alphabetical ordering relation which is defined on words, and of the fact that words are listed in the dictionary according to this order.

Version 2 -- Binary searching

a. Given any word to be looked up, make a sheaf of all the pages of the dictionary and hold them whith your left hand. Open the sheaf to an arbitrarily chosen page.

b. For as long as the desired word does not appear on the page to which the dictionary is opened, repeat step (c). When the word does appear, proceed to step (d).

c. If the desired word occurs in order before the first word on the open page, then select all the pages in the sheaf before the open page, and hold them with your left hand as the new sheaf. Otherwise, if the desired word occurs after the last word on the open page, select as the new sheaf all the pages of the sheaf following the open page. Open the newly selected sheaf of pages to an arbitrarily chosen page. In the event that neither of the above conditions is satisfied, but instead the desired word occurs after the first word and before the last word on the open page (but does not appear on that page), then stop and report that the word is not to be found in the dictionary.

d. Give the definition of the word found on the open page.

In comparison to the algorithm of Version 1, this algorithm can be much faster on the average. If N stands for the number of pages in the dictionary, then the average number of pages to be inspected in a search can be reduced by the ratio of $N/2 : \log_2 N$ [1]. Another interesting feature of the Version 2 algorithm is that while it appears to be nondeterministic, it is not. For the eventual outcome of either finding the word and giving its definition or of reporting that the word is not in the dictionary, is

----

[1] Achievment of the reduction depends on the rule used to select an arbitrary division of the sheaf. Dividing it exactly in two each time enables the search reduction to be realized. However, so does a uniformly random selection of the division point.

completely independent of the particular choices of page sheaves made in steps (a) and (c).

Some dictionaries furnish still more information to guide an efficient search, in the form of index tabs. For a tabulated dictionary, one might use the following algorithm:

Version 3 -- Indexed binary searching

a. Given any word to be looked up, select as a sheaf the pages starting with the tab corresponding to the first letter of the desired word, and extending up to the following tab. Open the sheaf to an arbitrary page.

Steps (b--d) are the same as in version 2.

We see that the benefit of the index tabs is only to reduce the size of the initially chosen sheaf of pages to be searched. If there are R tabs and the number of pages between adjacent tabs is approximately the same for all tabs, then the number of pages to be searched will be reduced by approximately log R. This is only an improvement by a constant, and so is not nearly so important as the improvement obtained in going from sequential searching in Version 1 to binary searching in Version 2.

The reason for referring to Versions 2 and 3 as binary searching algorithms is that in step (c) a binary choice is made to determine which of the two alternatives to use as the next sheaf. It is the division of the search space into two parts at each repetition which makes the algorithm efficient and which leads to the estimate of approximately log N as the average number of pages to be searched.

Example 1.2.4 -- The missionaries and the cannibals

In the wilderness of the island of New Guinea, three missionaries and three cannibals are traveling together when they encounter a broad river. They have with them a small canoe which can carry a maximum of three people at a time. The missionaries do not trust the cannibals, and so they establish the following conditions for the river crossing.
   i) A missionary must occupy the canoe on each trip across the river.
   ii) On either bank of the river, cannibals must not outnumber missionaries (unless there is no missionary on a particular bank).
Can you help the missionaries devise a scheme for ferrying the party across the river?

This is an example of a decision-making problem, in which there are several constraints imposed at each step of a solution. It is not obvious at the outset that there exists even one solution satisfactory to the missionaries, or whether there may be several.

A starting point for analysis might be to list all the possible configurations of missionaries and cannibals on the two banks of the river. In this problem, the number of configurations is finite. The order in which they are enumerated is arbitrary; it merely furnishes us with a means of indexing the configurations. We use "X" to stand for a cannibal and "O" to stand for a missionary.

Index	Right bank	Left bank
1	XXXOOO	-
2	XXXOO	O
3	XXXO	OO
4	XXX	OOO
5	XXOOO	X
6	XXOO	XO
7	XXO	XOO
8	XX	XOOO
9	XOOO	XX
10	XOO	XXO
11	XO	XXOO
12	X	XXOOO
13	OOO	XXX
14	OO	XXXO
15	O	XXXOO
16	-	XXXOOO

Of the sixteen possible configurations, only numbers 1, 4, 5, 6, 8, 9, 11, 12, 13, and 16 are acceptable to the missionaries. Configuration 1 is the one from which the problem starts, and number 16 is the desired goal.

Possible loadings of the canoe can also be enumerated. We give only those boatloads that contain at least one missionary, since that condition has been made a requirement.

Load index	Canoe loading
a	O
b	OO
c	OOO
d	XO
e	COX
f	CXX

What is really of interest in this problem is the dynamic behavior of the configurations, that is, the way in which they can be changed from one to another by prescribing sequences of canoe loads back and forth across the river. To keep track of all possibilities, we shall require two tables, one to determine the changes of configuration resulting from right bank to left bank trips, and the other to account for transportation in the opposite direction. The columns of each table represent configurations, specified by an index from one to sixteen, and the rows of each table represent the possible canoe loadings, indexed from a to f. In each square of each table may appear a number giving the index of the configuration that would result if the initial configuration corresponding to the column was modified by making a canoe trip in the specified direction, using the loading corresponding to the row. The entries given in the tables can easily be checked by drawing little diagrams on paper. However, the use of the tables will help us to keep track of this information without figuring it out all over again each time we may wish to simulate a river crossing.

Table RL

	Configuration index															
	1	2	3	4	5	6	7	8	9	10	11	12	13	14	15	16
a	2	3	4	-	6	7	8	-	10	11	12	-	14	15	16	-
b	3	4	-	-	7	8	-	-	11	12	-	-	15	16	-	-
c	4	-	-	-	8	-	-	-	12	-	-	-	16	-	-	-
d	6	7	8	-	10	11	12	-	14	15	16	-	-	-	-	-
e	7	8	-	-	11	12	-	-	15	16	-	-	-	-	-	-
f	10	11	12	-	14	15	16	-	-	-	-	-	-	-	-	-

Table LR

	1	2	3	4	5	6	7	8	9	10	11	12	13	14	15	16
a	-	1	2	3	-	5	6	7	-	9	10	11	-	13	14	15
b	-	-	1	2	-	-	5	6	-	-	9	10	-	-	13	14
c	-	-	-	1	-	-	-	5	-	-	-	9	-	-	-	13
d	-	-	-	-	-	1	2	3	-	5	6	7	-	9	10	11
e	-	-	-	-	-	-	1	2	-	-	5	6	-	-	9	10
f	-	-	-	-	-	-	-	-	-	1	2	3	-	5	6	7

Tables RL and LR give all possible configurations, but we already know that some of them are unacceptable to the missionaries. Since we have no wish to generate unacceptable solutions, the tables could be pared down somewhat by listing only those columns corresponding to the acceptable configurations. Also, those table entries indicating unacceptable configurations may just as well be replaced by an "x". The pruned tables are:

Table RLA

	Configuration index									
	1	4	5	6	8	9	11	12	13	16
a	x	-	6	x	-	x	12	-	x	-
b	x	-	x	8	-	11	-	-	x	-
c	4	-	8	-	-	12	-	-	16	-
d	6	-	x	11	-	x	16	-	-	-
e	x	-	11	12	-	x	-	-	-	-
f	x	-	x	x	-	-	-	-	-	-

Table LRA

	1	4	5	6	8	9	11	12	13	16
a	-	x	-	5	x	-	x	11	-	x
b	-	x	-	-	6	-	9	x	-	x
c	-	1	-	-	5	-	-	9	-	13
d	-	-	-	1	x	-	6	x	-	11
e	-	-	-	-	x	-	5	6	-	x
f	-	-	-	-	-	-	x	x	-	x

At this point, we have not yet made any attempt to formulate an algorithm for the missionaries, but have developed a systematic way to represent the various possibilities that are available in the generation of a solution. And in the course of developing this systematic representation it has been possible to discover a surprising amount about the form that a solution might take. From tables RLA and LRA one can see, for instance, that canoe loading f (one missionary and two cannibals) will never be used, and that there are two possible configurations (4 and 13) from which only a single canoe loading can enable the constraints to be satisfied.

A solution, if one does exist, could be expressed in the form of a sequence of canoe loadings to be utilized on successive trips back and forth across the river. Thus, dacccb would represent the following sequence: a missionary and a cannibal cross from right bank to left; the missionary returns alone; three missionaries cross from right to left; all three return; they cross again; two missionaries return. This example illustrates something about these sequences that may be useful in developing an algorithm. When a letter appears doubled in a sequence, it indicates that a canoe load has crossed the river in one direction, then returned with exactly the same load. Such trips are redundant and will contribute no progress toward a solution. Therefore, we could restrict our attention to sequences containing no doubled letters.

A brute force algorithm by which to search for a solution would be the following. Enumerate all possible river crossing sequences somehow or other. Then, testing each sequence in turn, determine whether or not the sequence is acceptable, by seeing if it leads to legal configuration transformations according to tables LRA and RLA. The search would continue until a sequence was found which produced a transformation from configuration 1 to configuration 16.

For instance, to test the sequence dad, first apply loading d to configuration 1 using table RLA, which tells us that configuration 6 will result. Next, using the table for return crossings, LRA, apply loading a to configuration 6, obtaining configuration 5. Lastly, when loading d is applied to configuration 5 in table RLA, it is found to produce an unacceptable configuration, and so the sequence dad is rejected.

The astute reader will see that if some sequence, such as dad, fails to produce a transition to an acceptable configuration, then no other sequence having dad as its first three letters can be acceptable either. As soon as it is determined that dad is not an acceptable sequence, one can proceed to cross out of the enumeration all untried sequences having this beginning. The amount of effort spent in testing sequences can be reduced drastically by this simple expedient.

12

Finally, if an enumeration of sequences is to be used to guide the search for a solution, how might one give such an enumeration? An easy way is to first give all sequences one letter long, in alphabetical order: a, b, c, d, e. (Note that canoe load f has already been found not to lead to acceptable configurations.) Next all two-letter configurations are given: aa, ab, ac, . . . ed, ee; then three-letter sequences, and so on. By searching an enumeration of sequences ordered by length, one will be assured of finding a solution involving the minimum number of canoe trips, if any solution exists.

Completing the specification of an algorithm to solve the missionaries and cannibals problem will be left as an exercise. If you attempt to carry out the algorithm yourself in order to find a concrete solution, you will soon discover that one can save much time by generating only those sequences of a given length that have already been found to have acceptable prefixes, instead of generating all sequences of that length, and crossing out the very large number of unacceptable ones.

This last example is typical of many decision-making problems. If they are to be solved by an algorithmic approach, then the solution involves the generation of a succession of seemingly plausible candidate configurations and a series of tests imposed on each of these candidates to determine whether or not it is actually acceptable. It is characteristic of such problems that the number of conceivable candidates for solution is very large, so the key to an effective algorithm is often to discover some means of limiting the generation of proposed solutions to those which already satisfy some of the required conditions. In the example just given, a first step towards this type of algorithm was to determine a means of enumerating proposed solutions, even though they seemed not to possess any natural order, or means of enumeration.

We have considered four examples of algorithm composition to try to gain some idea of what might be the essential constructions used in algorithms. Although it is, of course, too early to give a definitive list on the basis of these four examples, one can observe that each made use of the ability to test conditions and to determine further action on the basis of the outcome of the test, that each used repetition or iteration of some sequence of basic steps, and that the second and third, at least, made use of a name for some entity (the remainder, a sheaf of pages) whose value changed during the course of execution of the algorithm, but which was treated in the same way upon each iteration of the basic steps. These constructions will be formalized and used continually when we begin programming computations for a computer.

Algorithms constitute systematic procedures that can be used to solve whole classes of problems, rather than being restricted to obtain specific, one-time-only answers. From the examples given, it should be evident that nearly everyone makes use of algorithmic methods in carrying out tasks at least some of the time, and some people make use of algorithmic methods in nearly everything they do. These persons are referred to by their acquaintances as being "highly organized". The reason that we are not more aware of the use of algorithmic methods in carrying out everyday tasks is that people seldom bother to write down the algorithms they have learned or devised for their own use; they only know them informally. It is only when we are dealing with a formal system, and can rely on no common bond of experience or ingenuity to interpret informal algorithms, that we are faced with the need to write down algorithms in a formal notation.

Up to now, the algorithms we have neen using as examples have concerned tasks carried out by humans, so it has been possible to state them in informal English, readily understood by humans. Faced with the prospect of communicating with a computer, it will be necessary to learn a new language, a formal notation in which meanings are precise and unambiguous and which can, therefore, be translated by a computer into the myriad electrical signals which govern its own internal workings. Fortunately, many years of development have provided us with formal programming languages that are relatively intelligible and easy to learn.

Exercises for Chapter 1

1.1 Give an algorithm for selecting items in a supermarket from your grocery list. This can be thought of as a matching problem, for the sequence in which items appear on the grocery list will not agree with the sequence in which they are shelved along the aisles of the store.

1.2 An exercise given to elementary school children is that of matching lists of words to form compound words. For instance, given the list:

1. break   a. plane
2. air   b. fold
3. hard   c. bird
4. blind   d. ware
5. blue   e. fast

the corresponding list of compound words would be indicated by the pairs of indices, 1e, 2a, 3d, 4b, 5c. Give an algorithm for matching lists of this kind, giving as a result a list of pairs of indices corresponding to the compound words formed.

Notice that the algorithm you have constructed is very likely unable to handle cases in which some of the possible constructions are not unique. For instance, suppose we dissect the words bargain, peacock, horsefly, doughnut, and carboy to make this pair of lists:

1. bar   a. nut
2. pea   b. fly
3. dough   c. gain
4. horse   d. boy
5. car   e. cock

Unless you have composed an algorithm that can back up to try other choices than the first ones that seem to make sense, it will probably fail to complete the resynthesis of these lists. An elementary school child would also have trouble, but if you were asked to match the lists yourself, you would employ a more sophisticated algorithm, possibly augmented by _ad hoc_ methods.

1.3 Give an algorithm for the addition of two decimal integers. Next, give an algorithm for the addition of a list of decimal integers. How do you keep track of the carry? Is your algorithm for adding a list the same one you would actually use with pencil and paper?

1.4 Give an algorithm for checking the accuracy of multiplication of decimal numbers, by the sum-of-nines method. (The sum-of-nines method forms a check numeral from each of the multiplicand and the multiplier. The check

numeral is the modulo 9 sum of the digits of the given
number. To form this check numeral, you merely accumulate
the sum, retaining only the excess over 9. For example, the
check numeral formed from 78 is 6, since 7 + 8 = 15, which
is greater than 9, and 15 - 9 = 6. The product of the check
numerals, modulo 9, must agree with the check numeral of the
product.)

Will the same algorithm be effective when the digits of
the numbers are summed modulo some digit other than nine,
such as seven? Explain why the algorithm works.

1.5 Give an algorithm for making change for a customer in a
store. The result of the algorithm should tell how many
bills or coins of each denomination to return, and should
return the fewest possible pieces of money. Thus, an
algorithm that always gives only pennies in change is not
acceptable.

1.6 Give an algorithm for locating a house in a strange city if
you have the street address. Try to include all details
that are actually significant, such as determining which way
along the street the house numbers increase.

1.7 Complete the specification of an algorithm for the
missionaries and cannibals problem (Example 1.2.4) by giving
a sequence of steps by which trial solutions are to be
generated and tested until a satisfactory solution is found.

NOTES

NOTES

Chapter 2

USING COMPUTATIONAL VARIABLES

The language that we are going to use to describe algorithms for the computer is called ALGOL W. It was developed at Stanford University as a dialect of another programming language, ALGOL 60, to incorporate several additional features believed to be especially desirable. Some of these features make the language relatively simple for students to learn and to use. Even though you may have a need to use some other programming language sometime in the future after you have completed this course, you will find that many of the basic concepts which you will learn in ALGOL W will also apply to the other language. Of course, the specific notation may be different, but learning a new notation is not a very difficult task.

In this programming language, one can write ordinary decimal numbers and expressions of arithmetic, such as 3.1416, 7 + 5, 1/2, and 9.3*18. The arithmetic operations of addition, subtraction, multiplication and division are represented by the symbols +, -, * and /. Parentheses can be used, just as in expressions of ordinary arithmetic, to indicate the scope of the operators. The expression 2 * (3 - (4 + 4)) will make sense in this language, and the computer will evaluate the expression to the number -10. Negative numbers are indicated by placing a minus sign before the number.

The examples of the last chapter showed that one also wants to be able to express <u>variables</u>, which may take different values at different steps during the course of a computation, just as is done in mathematical notation. In ALGOL W, variables can be given names. The names may be as long or as short as you like, and may contain numerals as well as letters, but each name must begin with a letter and must not contain any blanks or punctuation marks, except for an underbar. Thus, "FRANK", "HARRY", "X", "A1", "A2", "A3", "DECEMBER25", and "LARGEST_FACTOR" are all acceptable names, but "2BY2", "U.R.STUCK", and "FIRST OF JANUARY" are not. A name is attached to a variable and a variable can have a value, but how can it be given one?

2.1   Assigning values to variables

The most direct way to give a value to a variable is by assignment. Assignment is the operation you are familiar with from algebra, when you say "let X have the value 2" or "let S be the square root of 5." In ALGOL W, we don't use the word "let" to denote assignment, but there is a special symbol, ":=" which is used for the assignment operator. The symbol ":=" can be read as "is assigned the value", in reading ALGOL W programs.   We would

19

write X := 2, or S := SQRT(5). Once a value has been assigned to a variable, then that value may be referred to in subsequent expressions just by referring to the variable by name. The variable will retain the same value until another assignment is made to it, or until it receives a new value by one of the other means to be discussed. Thus, if we write C := (7-4) / 2, followed subsequently by the expression C * 8, the latter expression will be equivalent to 1.5 * 8, and will be evaluated to 12.

Assignment of a value to a variable is a way by which you can specifically state that you want to have an expression evaluated now and to remember this value for reference later. The assignment statement implies a certain order in which its component operations are to be done. The evaluation of the expression to the right of the := is to be done first, then the variable on the left is to be looked up and to receive the new value. It is important to keep this order in mind.

Not only can values be used over again by making repeated references to the variables, but the variables themselves can be reused by making subsequent assignments of new values. Sometimes this is a good idea, and sometimes it is not. As was seen in the examples of the last chapter, it is very helpful to be able to assign a succession of values to a variable in a repeated step of an algorithm. Each value that the variable receives is processed in exactly the same way. It is a potential source of confusion, however, to use the same variable name to represent values of completely unrelated entities which are referred to in different parts of a computation. In fact, it usually helps our understanding of an algorithm given as a program written in a programming language, if distinct variable names are used to represent conceptually distinct quantities, and if the variables are given descriptive names rather than being given abstract, symbolic names. This is particularly true if the algorithm involves the use of a large number of quantities that must be represented by variables. Consider the following simple example.

Example 2.1.1 -- Computation of sales tax.

Version 1: using abstract names for variables

```
A1  :=  .07;
A2  :=  A1 * X;
Y   :=  X + A2
```

Version 2: using descriptive variable names

```
TAXRATE    :=  .07;
SALESTAX   :=  TAXRATE * NETPRICE;
TOTALPRICE :=  NETPRICE + SALESTAX
```

It sometimes happens that after initially composing an algorithm, one may put it aside for several days in order to do other work, and upon returning to the task of completing and checking the algorithm, one is faced with the problem of trying to recall his thoughts of the previous few days. Imagine having to do this if you have written your algorithm in the cryptic style of the first version of the example, and imagine how much easier the task might be if you had made use of the descriptive power available to you by giving variables names such as those used in Version 2.

2.2 Some distinctions between algorithmic and algebraic notations

In conventional algebraic notation, there is no notion of immediate evaluation of expressions and so it is possible to state equations or other relations involving variables which represent unknown quantities. For example, the pair of simultaneous linear algebraic equations

$$5x + 8y = -1$$
$$3x - 2y = 13$$

is such an example, in which the variables x and y represent unknowns. The equations can be satisfied if there exist real numbers such that when substituted for the variables x and y in each equation, the resulting arithmetic expressions on the two sides of each equation evaluate to common values. The order in which evaluation is to be carried out is not prescribed. In algorithmic notation, there is no such notion of an unknown or an unevaluated variable. Evaluation proceeds by a prescribed sequence, and each expression must be capable of being evaluated at the step in the algorithm at which it is encountered. In an algorithm, one does not state the conditions of a problem in hope that a solution exists; instead, one states an explicit procedure for constructing a solution. Thus, if a solution to the pair of simultaneous equations given above is desired, we must first do a little algebraic manipulation to eliminate variables. We can obtain a pair of equations, each containing only a single variable:

$$5x + (4*3)x = -1 + (4*13)$$
$$(3*8)y - (5*(-2))y = (3*(-1)) - (5*13).$$

Collecting terms in the same variable and dividing by the coefficient of each variable, one obtains

$$x = \frac{-1 + (4*13)}{5 + (4*3)}$$

$$y = \frac{(3*(-1)) - (5*13)}{(3*8) - (5*(-2))}$$

From explicit equations such as these, one obtains values for the unknowns x and y which will solve the equations by the simple operation of assignment. Thus, an algorithm for obtaining a solution to the original pair of simultaneous equations is arrived at:

```
X  :=  (-1 + (4*13)) / (5 + (4*3));
Y  :=  ((3*(-1)) - (5*13)) / ((3*8) - (5*(-2)))
```

In the notation of ALGOL W, there is no convention of implied multiplication if a numerical coefficient is written immediately to the left of the variable name. Thus, 5y has no meaning in ALGOL W, although in algebraic notation the meaning of 5y is understood to be shorthand for 5*y. Also, one can only use linear notation in ALGOL W. Fractions cannot be expressed by writing the numerator above the denominator, but instead must be written as a numerator followed by the division operator followed by a denominator.

2.3 Precedence rules for arithmetic operators

There are, however, some conventions which exist in the notation of ALGOL W which are not usually used in algebra. The most important of these conventions is one adopted to reduce the number of parentheses required in order to write an expression which has the form of a polynomial. In a polynomial, each term may consist of a variable raised to a power and multiplied by a coefficient which may itself be a fraction. In evaluation of a polynomial expression, the powers, products, and fractions which make up each term must be evaluated before the various terms are summed together. Accordingly, ALGOL W associates with each of its arithmetic operators a priority, indicating whether the operation indicated by that operator is to be performed before or after other kinds of operations. The precedence rules are:

first: raising to a power (the operator symbol is a double asterisk, "**");

second: multiplication or division;
third: addition or subtraction.

For example, the polynomial expression $5x^3 + 8x^2 - 2x + 12$ would be written in ALGOL W notation as:

        5*X**3 + 8*X**2 - 2*X + 12.

Evaluation of the expression would proceed from left to right, subject to the priority indicated by the underbars in the following sequence:

    5*X**3 + 8*X**2 - 2*X + 12

    5*X**3 + 8*X**2 - 2*X + 12

    5*X**3 + 8*X**2 - 2*X + 12

Of course, there will be expressions one wishes to write in which the order of evaluation of operations given by the precedence rules is not what is desired. In such cases, parentheses can be used to indicate the desired order of evaluation, and the innermost parenthesized expressions will be the first to be evaluated.

2.4   Getting values in and out of the computer

        Quite obviously, if a computer is to do anything more interesting than to execute fixed computations and to keep the outcome a secret unto itself, there must be some way to communicate values of data items to a computer, and to have the results reported back. In ALGOL W programs, input and output of values to the computer can be called for by using the built-in procedures READ and WRITE. Values to be read must be supplied on a sequence of punched cards to follow a program deck (assuming that your computer uses card input) and the values to be output will be printed following the listing of your program.

        To utilize a READ instruction, the program must contain variables which are to hold the values that are to be read from the data cards. The effect of a READ is very much like the effect of one or more assignment statements, except that the values to be assigned are not obtained by evaluation of expressions appearing in the program, but instead by interpretation of the data cards supplied to the card reader. For instance,

```
READ (A, B, C)
```

will direct the computer to examine the data cards until it
locates three values, assigning the first value found to variable
A, the second to B, and the third to C. In case three appropriate
values are not found on the data cards, the computer will be
unable to complete the instruction, and will print a message on
your output that begins with the prefix

```
RUN ERROR . . .
```

A WRITE instruction is less likely to cause trouble, for it
does not depend on the availability of data supplied at the card
reader, and can fail only if a program has become so verbose that
the number of lines written exceeds the maximum number specified
by you, the programmer. In the list of items to be written, one
can include not only variables, but any expression which can have
a value, including constants and messages. Thus one might give
the instruction

```
WRITE (A, B, "PRODUCT =", A*B)
```

This statement would cause the printing of four items in a single
line across a page of the output: the value currently held by A,
the value currently held by B, the message PRODUCT = and the
value of the expression A*B. For instance, the sequence of
ALGOL W statements

```
A := 7;
B := 3;
WRITE (A, B, "PRODUCT =", A*B)
```

could produce the line of output:

```
      7                    3  PRODUCT =              21
```

For more details on such matters as how the spacing in
controlled, see section A10.3.3 of the Appendix, or look ahead to
Chapter 6.

2.5   Programming versus calculating

The examples that we are about to consider are essentially
trivial computations which could easily be done on a hand-held
electronic calculator (or more painfully, without one), with
perhaps a pencil and scratchpad handy in order to record
intermediate values. Yet the computations as we shall describe
them illustrate some of the aspects of programmed computation

24

that make it so powerful. First of all, the use of program
variables eliminates the need for the scratchpad; this form of
memory is replaced by the memory capability of the computer.
Also, one does not have the problem that sometimes arises when
the scratchpad becomes crowded with figures, that of recalling
which figure to use in the next step of calculation. Since each
variable is identified by a unique name, rather than by its
currently held value, the values held in the computer's memory
cannot become confused during the execution of a particular
calculation.

Secondly, the sequence of instructions executed by a hand
calculator must be remembered by the user if the calculation is
to be repeated on some additional set of data. To use the
computer, the sequence of instructions is written down once and
given to the computer before the calculation is done the first
time. The set of instructions constitutes a program for the
computer, and is a particular representation of an algorithm. It
can be remembered by the computer in order to do the programmed
calculation on one set of data after another, without
intervention by the programmer.

There is a price to be paid by the human for the use of this
powerful capability of a computer to store programs. Programming
requires a greater level of intellectual abstraction than does
the use of a hand-held calculator. When using a calculator, each
instruction is interpreted immediately, and its result is
available to help the user decide what should be the next step of
the calculation. But in composing a program, the user must
anticipate what the computer will do when it executes his program
sometime in the future. He does not have intermediate results at
hand to guide his choice of the next program step, but must be
able to grasp the significance of each program step that he has
written, as it may be applied to any data he may wish to provide.

Example 2.5.1 -- Currency conversion

As every tourist who has visited a foreign country has
found out, the first week he is away from home he is
troubled by the difficulty of translating prices given in
the local currency of the country he is visiting into an
equivalent price in his 'home' currency. Suppose, for
instance, that one wishes to program a computer to convert
Japanese yen to American dollar values. This program
requires the ability to obtain a value, the price in yen
which is to be converted, then to multiply by a constant
conversion factor, and to output the result. In ALGOL W
such a program segment would be

```
READ (PRICE);
WRITE ("PRICE IN YEN IS", PRICE);
WRITE ("EQUIVALENT DOLLAR VALUE IS", .00358 * PRICE)
```

where .00358 is the yen-to-dollar conversion factor.

The capability to do this trivial sort of programmed calculation, multiplication by a stored constant, has been built into many of the electronic hand-held calculators, earning their manufacturers the everlasting gratitude of countless American tourists.

In the program of Example 2.5.1 it appears that a redundant statement has been included, namely the instruction which calls for the value of PRICE to be written on the output record immediately after it has been input. However, the statement is not at all redundant. First, remember that a hand-held calculator does the same; a value entered on the keyboard is displayed so that the user can confirm that the entry was made correctly. Also, the output may contain the only record of the computation that a user, or the client of a user has to show. If the data cards used in a computation are unavailable, then the only way to relate a result to the values that were input will be to have called for the input values to be printed on the computation record. This should always be done.

A somewhat less trivial sort of calculation is one which requires the generation of intermediate values, and the use of these values in several different parts of the ensuing calculation. By using a program variable, an intermediate value can be computed once and saved for multiple future references, and need not be recomputed each time that it is needed.

Example 2.5.2 -- Calculating the per unit cost of manufactured items

A small business manufactures bookshelf kits for installation on a wall. There are three kits in its product line, consisting of

Kit 1: 4 shelves, each 3 feet long, and 12 mounting brackets;
Kit 2: 3 shelves, each 6 feet long, and 15 mounting brackets;
Kit 3: 3 shelves, each 1 1/2 feet long, and 6 mounting brackets.

26

The manufacturer employs a labor force of three persons, with a payroll of 150 dollars per day; he buys shelving and brackets in large lots at a fixed price per lot. His problem is to calculate, from his labor cost, materials costs, and the number of units of each kit produced in one day, the cost of manufacture of a kit of each type.

Let us introduce program variables to be used as follows,
FEET_OF_SHELVING will represent the number of linear feet of shelving purchased;
COST_OF_SHELVING will represent the total price paid to purchase shelving;
NUMBER_OF_BRACKETS will be the number of brackets purchased;
COST_OF_BRACKETS will be the purchase price of the lot of brackets;
LABOR_COST will be the daily payroll of the business;
N_OF_KIT1, N_OF_KIT2, N_OF_KIT3 will represent the number of kits of each type produced in one day.
Other variables will also be introduced, but their use will be clear from the context of the program segment.

Since the amount of materials purchased, and the cost, may vary from one purchase to the next, these quantities will be read as data. After reading these values, the remaining program steps evaluate the unit costs of materials and labor, and then add these to obtain a cost per kit produced.

```
READ (FEET_OF_SHELVING, COST_OF_SHELVING, NUMBER_OF_BRACKETS,
    COST_OF_BRACKETS);
WRITE (FEET_OF_SHELVING, COST_OF_SHELVING, NUMBER_OF_BRACKETS,
    COST_OF_BRACKETS);
COST_PER_FOOT := COST_OF_SHELVING / FEET_OF_SHELVING;
COST_PER_BRACKET := COST_OF_BRACKETS / NUMBER_OF_BRACKETS;
LABOR_COST := 150;
READ (N_OF_KIT1, N_OF_KIT2, N_OF_KIT3);
WRITE ("DAY'S PRODUCTION IS", N_OF_KIT1, N_OF_KIT2, N_OF_KIT3);
LABOR_COST_PER_UNIT := LABOR_COST / (N_OF_KIT1, + N_OF_KIT2
                                    + N_OF_KIT3);
KIT_1_UNIT_COST := 12 * COST_PER_FOOT
                 + 12 * COST_PER_BRACKET
                 + LABOR_COST_PER_UNIT;
KIT_2_UNIT_COST := 18 * COST_PER_FOOT
                 + 15 * COST_PER_BRACKET
                 + LABOR_COST_PER_UNIT;
KIT_3_UNIT_COST := 4.5 * COST_PER_FOOT
                 + 6 * COST_PER_BRACKET
                 + LABOR_COST_PER_UNIT;
```

```
WRITE ("COST PER UNIT FOR KIT 1 IS", KIT_1_UNIT_COST);
WRITE ("                          KIT 2 IS", KIT_2_UNIT_COST);
WRITE ("                          KIT 3 IS", KIT_3_UNIT_COST)
```

In the program segment above, the variables COST_PER_FOOT, COST_PER_BRACKET, and LABOR_COST_PER_UNIT are used to hold intermediate values that are used several times. The algorithm is inelegant, but that is largely because we have not yet learned any more elegant ways to describe repetitive calculation. It should be noted that in the three WRITE instructions at the end of the segment, the long strings of blanks that appear within the quoted messages of the second and third output lists are inserted to ensure that the printed results will be aligned in a column under the result printed by the first WRITE instruction, but without repeating the lengthy prefix of the message.

Finally, the reader should be warned that the program segment given here, while correct, is not quite a complete ALGOL W program, and will therefore not be accepted by the computer without being embedded in a block (see section A8.1.1 of the Appendix).

Exercises for Chapter 2

In each of the following problems, identify the computational variables that will be needed, give them appropriate names and compose an algorithm in the form of an ALGOL W program segment.

2.1 An hourly employee is paid at the rate of $4.37 per hour, for the number of hours actually worked each week. From his gross pay, 6% is deducted for payment of social security tax, and 14% is withheld as income tax. He also has union dues of $3 per week deducted from his pay. Give an algorithm to determine the gross pay, social security tax payment, withholding tax payment, and take home pay of an hourly employee. The number of hours worked during a week is to be supplied as data to the algorithm.

2.2 One form of consumer loan is the discounted installment loan. It works this way. On a loan of $1000 face value, at 6% annual interest, for a duration of 18 months, the interest is calculated in advance by multiplying 1000 by .06, then by the period of the loan, 1 1/2 years. This yields the interest owed, $90, and it is immediately deducted from the face value; the borrower never sees it. He instead receives the difference of $910 as the principal amount of the loan. Repayment is made in equal monthly payments whose amount is the face value of $1000 divided by the duration of the loan in months.

a) Devise an algorithm which takes as data the face value, interest rate in percent, and duration in months, and which calculates the total amount of interest to be paid, and the actual principal amount of a discounted installment loan.

b) Since the face value of a discounted installment loan is repaid in equal monthly payments, the balance outstanding declines each month. It is not hard to show that the _average_ balance over the duration of the loan is given by the formula

$$\text{Average unpaid balance} = \text{Face value} * \frac{1 + \text{Duration in months}}{2 * \text{Duration in months}}$$

Calculate the rate at which simple interest would be paid on the average balance over the duration of the loan in order to produce the same total dollar amount of interest as is produced by the discounted installment loan.

2.3 The plot plan for situating a building on a lot is shown below. All corners are right angles except for the two front corners of the lot which are obviously not. The zoning regulations decree that not more than 30% of the area

29

of the lot can be built upon. Can you devise a computational algorithm to determine what fraction of the area of the lot will be occupied by the building?

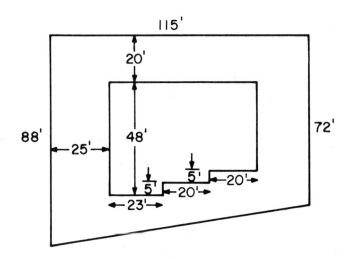

2.4 When rational numbers are expressed as fractions, it is often difficult to compare them. (Is it obvious by inspection that 24/91 is greater than 17/65 ?) Devise a computational algorithm to determine which of two rational fractions is the larger.

2.5 A mathematician is out for a walk when it begins to rain. He realizes that while he remains outside, the amount of rain falling on his head will be proportional to the density of raindrops in the air, to the velocity with which they are falling, to the upwards projected area of his head, and to the duration of his exposure. If he runs for shelter, he can reduce the length of time he remains outdoors. On the other hand, if he runs, he will be struck on the front by raindrops and will receive a wetting from his own action that is proportional to the density of raindrops, his running speed, his projected frontal area, and to the time it takes him to reach shelter.

    The time to reach shelter is proportional to the distance to reach it, and inversely proportional to his speed afoot. Can you help him by giving a computational algorithm to compute the total amount of rain he will encounter, if given the initial values of the other parameters as inputs? (This simple problem can, of course, be solved analytically; it is complicated to some extent if you add a wind that gives the raindrops a horizontal component of velocity.)

2.6 Corporate and municipal bonds are issued under the following
     terms. Each bond carries a redemption value, an amount of
     money to be paid upon maturation of the bond. In addition,
     the bond pays interest in equal amounts to be collected
     quarterly. The nominal rate of interest is the sum of four
     quarterly interest payments divided by the redemption value
     of the bond. However, bonds are traded like other
     securities, and the nominal interest rate may differ from
     the prevailing rate of interest for comparable securities at
     the time a bond is sold. To compensate for this, bonds are
     bought and sold at values discounted or increased relative
     to the redemption value, so that the net worth of the bond,
     which is the sum of all remaining interest payments plus the
     redemption value, is equivalent to the net worth of a
     hypothetical bond whose redemption value is the sale price,
     and whose nominal interest rate is the interest rate
     prevailing at the time of the sale. Define algebraic
     variables to stand for (a) redemption value, (b) nominal
     rate of interest, (c) sale price, (d) prevailing rate of
     interest, (e) time until maturation, (f) net worth. Give an
     algebraic equation equating the net worth of an actual bond
     to the net worth of a hypothetical bond. Solve the equation
     for the sale price.

          Give a computational algorithm to calculate the selling
     price of a corporate bond, given its redemption value and
     nominal interest rate, and the prevailing rate of interest
     on bonds at the time of sale. Use the algorithm to
     determine the sale price of a $1000 bond collecting interest
     at 6% per year, which is 12 years from maturation, if the
     prevailing rate of interest is 9%.

NOTES

Chapter 3

PROGRAMMING THE COMPUTER TO MAKE DECISIONS

In the last chapter we saw that computer programming languages allow one to evaluate expressions and to assign values to variables. An algorithm may consist partly of sequences of assignment statements giving a succession of values to individual program variables. But there will be many problems for which the algorithm we wish to use will contain several alternatives for evaluation. In such cases, the computer must make decisions as to which or algorithm steps to execute, based on conditions of the data. The programming language must provide means for stating the conditions governing such a decision.

3.1   Conditional expressions

The most obvious way to employ decision-making capability in an algorithm is by formulating an expression whose evaluation depends on some condition of the data. This is common practice in mathematics as, for instance, in the definitions of the simple functions,

Maximum:
$$\max(x,y) = \begin{cases} x, & \text{if } x > y, \\ y, & \text{otherwise;} \end{cases}$$

Minimum:
$$\min(x,y) = \begin{cases} y, & \text{if } x > y, \\ x, & \text{otherwise;} \end{cases}$$

Modified Difference:
$$x - y = \begin{cases} x - y, & \text{if } x > y, \\ 0, & \text{otherwise.} \end{cases}$$

Expressions evaluating to these functions can also be written in ALGOL W using the notation of conditional expressions;

```
max:    IF X >= Y
        THEN X
        ELSE Y;
```

33

```
min:    IF X >= Y
           THEN Y
           ELSE X;

Modified Difference:
        IF X > Y
           THEN X - Y
           ELSE 0;
```

The syntax of conditional expressions is defined in Section A7.7.1 of the Appendix.

3.2   Relational and logical expressions

The condition that is tested in making a decision as to which alternative to evaluate in an ALGOL W conditional expression is itself given by an expression. Between the keywords IF and THEN appears an expression which will evaluate to either TRUE or FALSE; we call this a logical expression.

The simplest kind of logical expression simply states a relation which may or may not hold between two quantities. If the quantities are numeric, then the possible relations are strict inequalities '>', '<', reflexive inequalities '<=', '>=', equals '=' and does not equal '¬='. If the quantities are non-numeric as, for instance, the addresses of houses, then it makes no sense to talk about inequalities which derive from a total ordering of values, but the relations "equals" and "does not equal" are still meaningful. One can conceive of other useful relations such as the membership relation between objects and sets, but no such relations happen to be defined in the ALGOL W programming language.

A relational expression is evaluated to a truth value, TRUE or FALSE, depending on whether or not the two quantities given in the relational expression satisfy the given relation. If variables or numerical expressions are written to represent the related quantities, then the values of these variables or expressions are first obtained, then examined to determine whether or not the indicated relation holds for these values.

Relational expressions are the most obvious, but are not the only kind of logical expression. One sometimes wishes to base a decision on whether or not several relational conditions hold simultaneously or on whether at least one of several possible conditions hold. Consider the following:

34

<u>Example 3.2.1</u> -- Parcel post dimensions

The United States Postal Service imposes restrictions on the maximum size and weight of a package to be sent by parcel post. The weight must not exceed 44 pounds, and the sum of the length plus the girth must not exceed 72 inches. Suppose that for parcels of rectangular cross-section, the dimensions are given as values of the variables A, B and C, and the weight as the value of WGHT, in units of inches and pounds, respectively. However, the dimensions are not necessarily given in order of greatest length. Give an algorithm to determine whether or not such parcels are acceptable.

To calculate the postal dimension, one needs to know which of the three dimensions is the largest, for the formula penalizes girth more than it does length. We can give a single expression for the postal dimension, However, by making use of conditional expressions.

```
POSTALDIMENSION := IF (A >= B) AND (A >= C)
                      THEN A + 2*(B+C)
                   ELSE IF B >= C
                      THEN B + 2*(A+C)
                   ELSE
                      C + 2*(A+B)
```

In the first line of the expression, two conditions are tested to find out whether A is the largest of the three dimensions. If it is, then the expression A + 2*(B+C) is evaluated and becomes the value of the conditional expression. Otherwise, if one or the other of the conditions tested in the first line is false, the expression on the second line is not evaluated, but instead the expression following the first ELSE will be evaluated and becomes the value of the conditional expression.

This second alternative is only evaluated having determined that A cannot be the largest of the three dimensions. Referring to the expression following the first ELSE, we find it to be

```
      IF B >= C
         THEN B + 2*(A+C)
      ELSE
         C + 2*(A+B)
```

which is another conditional expression nested within the larger one. Knowing that either B or C is the largest dimension, the condition B >= C is tested. If it is true, then B must be the largest dimension, and the expression B + 2*(A+C) will be evaluated, becoming the value of the nested conditional expression and thereby of the larger expression as well. However, if B >= C is false (recalling that (A >= B) and (A >= C) have also been found to be false), then it must be that C is the largest dimension. Therefore, no further testing is required, and C + 2*(A+B) can be evaluated. Notice that only one of the three component arithmetic expressions, A + 2*(B+C), B + 2*(A+C), C + 2*(A+B) is actually evaluated. The values of the relational expressions are used to determine which one it is to be.

Finally, a second step involving a test of two conditions will determine acceptability of the parcel.

IF (POSTALDIMENSION <= 72) AND (WGHT <= 44) THEN accept
ELSE reject.

In ALGOL W it is possible to form expressions involving logical quantities such as relational expressions by the use of three logical operators. These are the symbols ¬ (not), AND, OR. ¬ is a unary operator; it negates the truth value of the logical constant, variable or relational expression immediately following it, while AND and OR are binary operators. There is a precedence of evaluation of these operations, with the operation of ¬ being performed first, followed by AND, then OR, and finally by the relational operators. Parenthetical brackets can be used to specify explicitly the order and scope of evaluation of these operations, just as is the case with the arithmetic operations. As a consequence of the precedence of logical and relational operators, it is necessary to use parentheses to specify the logical conjunction or disjunction of two or more relational expressions. For example, the form

X > 0 AND Y = 1

will not be acceptable in ALGOL W. A correctly formed expression would be

(X > 0) AND (Y = 1)

Rules defining the logical operations are most easily given in terms of constants, TRUE and FALSE

¬TRUE = FALSE
¬FALSE = TRUE
TRUE AND FALSE = TRUE
TRUE AND FALSE = FALSE

```
FALSE AND TRUE = FALSE
FALSE AND FALSE = FALSE
TRUE OR TRUE = TRUE
TRUE OR FALSE = TRUE
FALSE OR TRUE = TRUE
FALSE OR FALSE = FALSE
```

Values of logical expressions can be assigned to logical
variables for reference in a later step. A logical variable can
in turn be used as a term in a conditional expression, or can be
tested in an _if_ clause (see sections A7.2, A7.3, and A7.7.1 of
the Appendix for a complete description of the grammar of logical
expressions). Although a logical variable can be assigned the
value of a relational expression the logical variable should not
be thought of as shorthand for that relational expression, but
merely as a record of the value that relation had at a particular
point in the program. For instance, suppose that IS_POSITIVE is
the name of a logical variable, and N is an integer variable.
Consider the sequence of statements

```
N := 1;
IS_POSITIVE := N > 0;
READ (N);
IF IS_POSITIVE THEN . . .
```

At the second statement, the relation N > 0 is evaluated and
found to be TRUE, which is the value assigned to IS_POSITIVE. At
the third statement, N is given a new value, which might be
positive, negative, or zero. At the fourth statement, the _if_
clause tests the value held by the logical variable IS_POSITIVE,
which no longer has anything to do with the current value of N,
which has been reset by the read instruction. The value of
IS_POSITIVE at the fourth statement is a record of the condition
N > 0 at the second statement. A logical variable used to store
the truth value of a condition for use in governing a decision to
be made in a subsequent step of the algorithm is called a _flag_.

3.3 Conditional execution of alternate algorithm steps

Relational or logical expressions can not only be used to
control the choice of which expression to evaluate, but of which
algorithm steps to execute. Identification of the choices to be
made is so important in composing algorithms that there have been
invented several informal notational aids to keep track of these
alternatives when one is in the pencil-and-paper stage of
algorithm composition.

One such scheme, called _iteration graphs_[1] will be presented in this and the following chapter, and then used in the remainder of the book. An iteration graph is composed of several types of rectangular boxes, with informal descriptions of algorithm steps written inside. The basic box is simply a rectangle

in which is written the description of a single step, or a sequence of several steps.

A binary choice of steps is designated by a rectangle containing a triangle at the top, in which is written the conditional or logical expression upon whose outcome the choice is to be made.

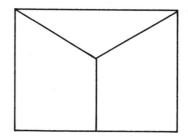

The lower part of the rectangle is divided into two boxes. In the leftmost is written the algorithm step to be performed in case the condition is satisfied, in the rightmost the step to be performed in case the condition fails. A simple example will illustrate the scheme.

Example 3.3.1 -- The shopper's dilemma

A music lover, shopping during his lunch hour, discovers a turntable on sale that is just what he needs to complete his stereo system. However, it is a few days until his next payday, and he is uncertain as to how to pay for the purchase. If the balance in his checking account is sufficient, he would prefer to write a check in payment, but otherwise he will have to charge the purchase to an account on which he must pay carrying charges.

----

[1] The form of iteration graph presented here is due to I. Nassi and B. Shneiderman, ACM SIGPLAN Notices, vol. 8, no. 8, pp. 12-26, Aug. 1973.

An informal description of the choice of action that will be made by our shopper can be given by a decision box in the notation of iteration graphs:

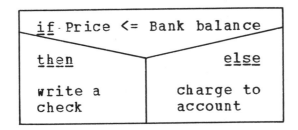

If we were to try to describe the consequence of the shopper's purchase on his financial records, we might be able to make use of an ALGOL W program segment. For instance, if the consequence of writing a check is a reduction in the balance of the checking account, and the consequence of charging a purchase is an increase in indebtedness, a program segment describing these effects could make use of a conditional statement,

```
IF PRICE <= BALANCE THEN
    BALANCE := BALANCE - PRICE
ELSE
    DEBT := DEBT + PRICE
```

Notice that the conditional statement corresponds directly to the decision box, once the two actions to be governed by the specified condition have been expressed as ALGOL W statements.

3.4 Devising algorithms to solve problems

The payoff of our study of algorithms will come when we are able to invent algorithms to obtain solutions to real problems. It would be nice if there were some straightforward, easily explained procedure to follow so that one could move from the statement of a real-world problem to the construction of an algorithm for its solution. Life is not so easy. Problem solving requires considerable application of intelligence, careful attention to details, and often a sequence of trials and errors. There is, however, a method for developing an algorithm by means of a sequence of partial specifications, proceeding from a description of the solution, in intellectually manageable steps. This process has been given a variety of names by various authors; we shall call it stepwise refinement.[2] The best way to illustrate the process may be by example, and the only way to

---

[2] N. Wirth, "Programming by stepwise refinement", Communications of the A.C.M., vol. 14, p. 221, 1971.

39

learn it is to try for yourself.

Example 3.4.1 -- Shall I rent or buy a house?

A man and his wife have just been transferred to a new
locality, and he is faced with the choice of whether to buy
or to rent a home. After consulting a real estate agent, he
finds two possibilities which interest him. There is a
comfortable apartment for rent, including utilities, for
$300 per month. Alternatively, there is a house for sale
for which he will have to put up a down payment of $6000,
monthly payments of $290, and a utilities bill which will
average $60 a month. He would prefer to buy the house, but
it appears at first glance to be too expensive. However, he
consults his accountant who advises him that of the monthly
house payment, $110 goes to pay local property taxes and
$140 goes to pay the interest on the mortgage. Under
federal income tax law, the amounts he pays in interest and
in local taxes may be deducted from his gross income before
he figures his federal tax. His problem is now more
complicated than before, and the answer to the question of
which alternative is more economically advantageous is by no
means obvious. Can we devise an algorithm to help the man
figure out the net cost of owning a house?

At first glance, if the income tax is not considered,
it looks as though our friend will pay $50 per month, or
$600 per year more to purchase a house than to rent an
apartment, when the utilities payments are taken into
account. In addition, he will lose the interest he could
get if the amount of his down payment were invested in a
savings bank -- 6% of $6000, or $360 per year.

Now, let us develop an algorithm to compute the net
cost of buying, relative to that of renting, when the income
tax is taken into account. What we will do is to calculate
the expendable income that the man will have left over after
taxes and after paying his housing expenses under each
option. The man's salary will have to be known, as will
other information required to calculate his income tax. The
parameters used in making the calculation under each of the
alternate options will be:

SAVINGS_INTEREST -- the interest he expects to receive
             from his savings account;

LOCALTAX -- the local property taxes he expects to pay
         each month which are a deductible expense
         under the income tax law;

MORTGAGEINTEREST -- the interest paid on his mortgage each month, which is also a tax deductible expense;

PAYMENTS -- monthly payments for housing;

UTILITIES -- anticipated monthly payment of utilities bills.

Next, let us describe the tasks to be performed. Our client is basically interested in knowing what will be his expendable income remaining after taxes and after deducting his housing expense. This can be specified as

Principal task: compute expendable_income;

this is to be done in case of
   a) purchase of a house,
   b) rental of an apartment.

Before expendable income can be computed, however, the gross income and the income tax must be known. These requirements lead us to define

Subtask 1: compute GROSS_INCOME; and
Subtask 2: compute INCOME_TAX.

Subtask 1 can be carried out directly, since the constituent parts of gross income are known,

GROSS_INCOME := SALARY + SAVINGS_INTEREST

Subtask 2, on the other hand, is somewhat more complicated. Income tax is not computed directly as a function of gross income, but instead is a function of the so-called taxable income obtained by subtracting authorized exemptions and deductions from the gross income. This leads to the definition of

Subtask 2.1: compute TAXABLE_INCOME; and
Subtask 2.2: compute INCOME_TAX from TAXABLE_INCOME.

Let us develop an algorithm segment to accomplish Subtask 2.1, the computation of taxable income. A married couple is allowed a personal exemption of 750 dollars for each person, to be deducted from gross income.

ADJUSTED_INCOME := GROSS_INCOME - 2*750

Certain expenses are also allowed as deductions from income prior to tax computation. Two alternative methods are provided for the computation of deductions, one based on an itemization of actual expenses, and the other based on a standard estimate. The taxpayer may employ whichever method yields him the greater advantage.

```
ITEMIZED DEDUCTION := 12*(LOCALTAX + MORTGAGE_INTEREST)
                      + OTHERDEDUCTIONS;
STANDARD_DEDUCTION := .15 * GROSS_INCOME
```

A conditional statement is used to indicate the choice to be made on the basis of the relative values obtained in the two preceding statements.

```
IF ITEMIZED_DEDUCTION > STANDARD_DEDUCTION THEN
    DEDUCTION := ITEMIZED_DEDUCTION
ELSE
    DEDUCTION := STANDARD_DEDUCTION
```

Finally, Subtask 2.1 will be completed by

```
TAXABLE_INCOME := ADJUSTED_INCOME - DEDUCTION
```


Now that we know how Subtask 2.1 will be carried out, calculation of income tax is to be done according to a graduated schedule, as shown in the diagram of Fig. 3.4.1. Those who earn more are expected to pay a higher percentage of their income in taxes (unless they have claimed very large deductions). Therefore, the computation of tax must take into account the rate of taxation, depending on income. Let us assume that the taxable income is at least as great as the value of BASE1 but not as great as BASE3. Since income in the range from BASE1 to BASE2 is taxed at a lower rate than is income in the range from BASE2 to BASE3, it is necessary first to determine which tax formula applies, and then to do the appropriate computation. ALGOL W provides the conditional statement as a means of designating such a choice (see Section A8.3.1 of the Appendix). A statement that will accomplish the tax computation is

```
IF TAXABLE_INCOME <= BASE2 THEN
    INCOME_TAX := BASETAX + RATE1*(TAXABLE_INCOME - BASE1)
ELSE
    INCOME_TAX := BASETAX + RATE1*(BASE2 - BASE1)
                  + RATE2*(TAXABLE_INCOME - BASE2)
```

This will complete the algorithm segment for Subtask 2..2, and therefore for Subtask 2 as well.

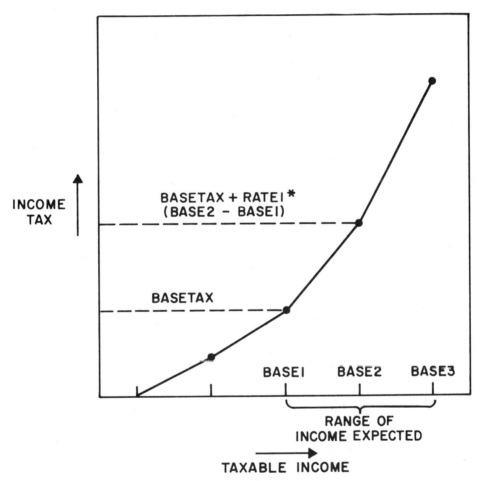

Fig. 3.4.1 Relation between income tax and taxable
            income when the tax rate is graduated

In terms of the results of performing the subtasks, the algorithm steps required to complete the principal task under conditions of either purchase or rental can be given by a pair of ALGOL W assignment statements,

```
NET_INCOME := GROSS_INCOME - INCOME_TAX;
EXPENDABLE_INCOME := NET_INCOME - 12*(PAYMENTS + UTILITIES)
```

These statements will be the final steps of an algorithm.

Having now completed the composition of program segments to perform each of the subtasks as well as the principal task, all that remains is to assemble the program segments into the required sequence. The sequence is dictated by the order in which the various subtask results are required. If the program segment for each subtask is substituted into the sequence in place of the subtask specification, each required value will be computed before it is needed in another step. Upon doing this substitution, the following program segment is obtained for the accomplishment of the Principal task:

```
GROSS_INCOME := SALARY + SAVINGS_INTEREST;

ADJUSTED_INCOME := GROSS_INCOME - 2*750;
ITEMIZED_DEDUCTION := 12*(LOCALTAX + MORTGAGE_INTEREST)
                          + OTHERDEDUCTIONS;
STANDARD_DEDUCTION := .15 * GROSS_INCOME;
IF ITEMIZED_DEDUCTION > STANDARD_DEDUCTION THEN
    DEDUCTION := ITEMIZED_DEDUCTION
ELSE
    DEDUCTION := STANDARD_DEDUCTION;
TAXABLE_INCOME := ADJUSTED_INCOME - DEDUCTION;

IF TAXABLE_INCOME <= BASE2 THEN
    INCOME_TAX := BASETAX + RATE1*(TAXABLE_INCOME - BASE1)
ELSE
    INCOME_TAX := BASETAX + RATE1*(BASE2 - BASE1)
                          + RATE2*(TAXABLE_INCOME - BASE2);

NET_INCOME := GROSS_INCOME - INCOME_TAX;
EXPENDABLE_INCOME := NET_INCOME - 12*(PAYMENTS + UTILITIES)
```

If values are now supplied for the constants which determine the amount of income tax, and initial values are supplied for the variables which represent data concerning our friend's personal finances, then we can carry out the steps of the algorithm to help him calculate his expendable income for each of the two alternate housing arrangements.

Suppose that the following assignments of values are made:

```
BASE1 := 8000;
BASETAX := 1280;
RATE1 := .22;
BASE2 := 12000;
RATE2 := .26;
```

and that our friend's salary is

```
SALARY := 16000
```

He is able to justify tax-deductable expenses other than the interest on a mortgage or local property taxes of

```
OTHERDEDUCTIONS := 500;
```

and the $6000 which he had available to use as a down payment on a house represents his entire savings.

Option 1 -- to rent an apartment

If the man decides to rent the apartment, then his $6000 will remain in the savings bank, drawing interest at 6%, and he will have

```
SAVINGS_INTEREST := 360;
LOCALTAX := 0;
MORTGAGEINTEREST := 0;
PAYMENTS := 300;
UTILITIES := 0;
```

as initial values of the data to use in calculating his expendable income. If the steps of the algorithm are executed using the intial values given above, the successive values calculated and assigned to each of the variables will be

GROSS_INCOME	16360
ADJUSTED_INCOME	14860
ITEMIZED_DEDUCTION	500
STANDARD_DEDUCTION	2000
DEDUCTION	2000
TAXABLE_INCOME	12860
INCOME_TAX	2483.60
EXPENDABLE_INCOME	10276.40

<u>Option 2</u> -- to buy a house

In the event that the man should choose to purchase the house, then his savings must be invested as a down payment on the purchase; however, his monthly payments become partially tax deductible. The initial values of the parameters are assigned as

```
SAVINGS_INTEREST := 0;
LOCALTAX := 110;
MORTGAGE_INTEREST := 140;
PAYMENTS := 290;
UTILITIES := 60;
```

Upon execution of the algorithm, the following values will be calculated

GROSS_INCOME	16000
ADJUSTED_INCOME	14500
ITEMIZED_DEDUCTION	3500
STANDARD_DEDUCTION	2000
DEDUCTION	3500
TAXABLE_INCOME	11000
INCOME_TAX	2040
EXPENDABLE_INCOME	9760

Before going on, follow the computational steps of the example, carrying out the indicated calculation by hand, to see if you can verify the values given above.

From the results of the two calculations, it is seen that it will still be less expensive for the man to rent than to buy, but the difference it will make to his expendable income is only $516.40 rather than the apparent difference in cost of $960. Furthermore, our model has not attached any value to the fact that of the monthly house payment, $40 goes toward the retirement of the mortgage, increasing the net worth of the man, if not his expendable income, by $480 in the course of one year. On a net worth basis, the added cost of purchasing his own house would amount to only $36.40 per year.

Even on this basis, the model we have used is over simplified, for it should take account of a probable rate of economic inflation of between 2 and 20 per cent per year. Inflation will increase the attractiveness of purchasing a house when properly accounted for. However, the example has already achieved its immediate purpose, which was to demonstrate that a seemingly complicated problem can often

be solved algorithmically by simply breaking down the
analysis of the problem into a sequence of small steps. You
can gain experience in doing this for yourself by trying
some of the exercises at the end of the chapter.

A final comment is in order. Since any expression appearing
in a step of an algorithm must be evaluated when that step is
executed, it is important that steps of an algorithm are listed
in proper order. The order in which steps are evaluated should
ensure that each variable is assigned a value before it is
referred to in any expression. In this way, because it is to be
executed in sequence, an algorithm differs from a definition
which is not to be executed.

3.5   Comments and their use

Even when a programmer is careful to give descriptive names
to the variables he uses, it is often difficult to read an
algorithm given as an ALGOL W program and understand its function
completely without some hints. There is a means of providing
hints in the form of comments in the text of a program. Comments
are distinguished from statments or expressions of the language
by the keyword COMMENT. A comment consists of this keyword,
followed by any string of symbols which does not include a
semicolon, and terminated by a semicolon. Thus, the pair
COMMENT ... ; forms a kind of bracket pair, the comment bracket.

Example 3.5.1   --   A comment

COMMENT COMMENTS IN ALGOL W ARE NOT PART OF THE ALGORITHM,
         AND ARE IGNORED BY THE COMPUTER.;

Of course, you must be careful not to forget to place a semicolon
at the end of a comment, for the computer will then ignore the
text of your algorithm from that point on until it encounters a
semicolon!

In reading a long program, it should be easy for a reader to
distinguish comments from the text of actual ALGOL W statements.
While the keyword COMMENT and the terminating semicolon allow the
computer to make the distinction without difficulty, this
convention is not always adequate for the human reader.
Therefore, we prefer a convention in which some additional
identifying symbols are to be embedded in a comment, in order to
catch the eye of a reader and alert him to the fact that he is
not reading program but prose. The text of short, one-line
comments can be bracketed by a string of four or five asterisks,

```
COMMENT ***** SHORT COMMENTS LOOK LIKE THIS *****;
```

Longer comments, which have the status of explanatory paragraphs,
can be enclosed in a box of asterisks. The asterisks must appear
between the opening COMMENT keyword and the closing semicolon.

```
COMMENT*******************************************************************
*  MULTI-LINE COMMENTS ARE NOT EASILY CONFUSED WITH THE SUR- *
*  ROUNDING PROGRAM TEXT, EVEN IF THEY SHOULD CONTAIN ALGE-  *
*  BRAIC EXPRESSIONS  --   SUCH AS                           *
*     X*(X*A + B) + C = 0                                    *
*  WHEN THE ENTIRE COMMENT IS BOXED IN ASTERISKS             *
*******************************************************************;
```

There are some places in the text of a computer program
where the insertion of comments is ordinarily very helpful. At
the beginning of a program, comments can be used to describe the
functions that the algorithm is designed to perform, and to give
a general description of the method of the algorithm. Next, it
is very helpful to use comments describing the program variables
and their intended uses. Within the body of the program text,
comments are generally helpful in describing the alternative
courses of action whenever a conditional statement indicates that
a decision is to be made in execution of the algorithm.

3.6   Blocks and compound groups of statements

Often, the alternate portions of an algorithm to be executed
depending on the outcome of a conditional test cannot easily be
expressed by single statements. It would be convenient to have
some means by which to package together a whole sequence of
statements to be executed as a group whenever that decision is
indicated. ALGOL W provides this capability with a pair of
reserved words, BEGIN and END, which can be used to bracket a
sequence of statements very much as parentheses are used to
bracket expressions, to indicate an order of evaluation.

With a bracketed sequence of statements, it would sometimes
be convenient to be able to introduce one or more new variables,
for use only within the bracketed statements. ALGOL W also
permits this. New variables are introduced by means of
declarations, about which more is said in Chapter 5 and in
section A5 of the Appendix. Declarations can appear between the
word BEGIN and the first executable statement of a bracketed
sequence. A statement sequence enclosed by BEGIN . . . END is
called a compound statement, and if declarations are also
enclosed, it is called a block. The following example
illustrates the use of blocks.

Example 3.6.1 -- Finding the intersection of a pair of line segments

Given a pair of straight line segments, how might we find out whether or not they intersect? One way would be to plot both line segments on a piece of graph paper and solve the problem by inspection. However, one can also represent a line by a linear algebraic equation, and we can devise a mathematical algorithm to test for intersection of the line segments. A suitable form for the equation of a line involves three coefficients,

$$Ax + By = C, \qquad (1)$$

where the variables x and y represent coordinates of points in a plane. Given any set of three coefficients, the pairs of points (x,y) which satisfy the equation lie on a straight line. If a line segment is specified by giving the coordinates of its endpoints $(\underline{u},\underline{v})$ and $(\underline{x},\underline{y})$, then substitution of these point into equation (1) gives us a pair of simultaneous equations that must be satisfied by any set of coefficients A, B, C which describe the line.

$$A\underline{u} + B\underline{v} = C,$$

$$A\underline{x} + B\underline{y} = C.$$

Since there are only two equations and three parameters are to be determined, one of the parameters may be chosen arbitrarily. We shall choose C to be the determinant of the matrix formed by the endpoint coordinates,

$$\text{Let } C = \begin{vmatrix} \underline{u} & \underline{v} \\ \underline{x} & \underline{y} \end{vmatrix} = \underline{u}\,\underline{y} - \underline{v}\,\underline{x}.$$

This choice makes C equal to the square of the distance from the origin of coordinates to the point on the line nearest the origin.

When this choice is made for C, solution of the equations for A and B yields

$$A = \underline{y} - \underline{v}, \text{ and } B = \underline{u} - \underline{x}.$$

Once the equations of two lines have been obtained, it is easy to locate their intersection. If there is a point (x,y) that lies on both lines, then the coordinates of that point must satisfy the equations of both lines. Therefore, to solve for the intersection, we must solve another pair of simultaneous, linear equations. In case the lines are parallel, however, the simultaneous equations will have no solution. Once an intersection of two lines has been found, we determine whether two line <u>segments</u> intersect by asking whether the point of intersection of the lines lies within both line segments.

Utilizing the method of stepwise refinement, let us first specify the major algorithm steps that are to be carried out, in the informal notation of an iteration graph.

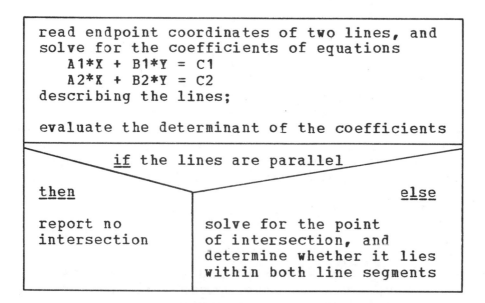

```
read endpoint coordinates of two lines, and
solve for the coefficients of equations
    A1*X + B1*Y = C1
    A2*X + B2*Y = C2
describing the lines;

evaluate the determinant of the coefficients
```

	if the lines are parallel	
then		else
report no intersection	solve for the point of intersection, and determine whether it lies within both line segments	

Since each of the informally described steps is itself fairly simple, we shall be able to translate this iteration graph directly into an ALGOL W program, without intermediate stages of refinement. This will be the fist complete program that has been given in an example; it will consist of a block, and all variables will appear in declarations prior to their appearance in executable statements. The declarations of variables as REAL is to indicate that they are to assume real number values in assignment or READ instructions.

```
BEGIN
COMMENT****************************************************
*   THIS ALGORITHM TESTS TWO LINE SEGMENTS, SPECIFIED    *
*   BY THE COORDINATES OF THEIR ENDPOINTS, AND           *
*   DETERMINES WHETHER OR NOT THEY INTERSECT.            *
*      LINE 1:   FROM (U1, V1) TO (X1, Y1)              *
*      LINE 2:   FROM (U2, V2) TO (X2, Y2)              *
*   BOTH LINES ARE TO BE REPRESENTED BY EQUATIONS        *
*   OF THE FORM A*X + B*Y = 0                            *
****************************************************;
```

```
REAL U1, V1, X1, Y1, A1, B1, C1, U2, V2, X2, Y2, A2, B2, C2;
REAL DETERMINANT;
COMMENT*****OBTAIN A, B, C COEFFICIENTS FOR BOTH LINES*****;
READ (U1, V1, X1, Y1);
WRITE ("ENDPOINTS OF LINE 1:", U1, V1, X1, Y1);
READ (U2, V2, X2, Y2);
WRITE ("ENDPOINTS OF LINE 2:", U2, V2, X2, Y2);
A1 := Y1 - V1;
B1 := U1 - X1;
C1 := U1*Y1 - V1*X1;
A2 := Y2 - V2;
B2 := U2 - X2;
C2 := U2*Y2 - V2*X2;
COMMENT***** EVALUATE THE DETERMINANT OF THE COEFFICIENTS
        ZERO DETERMINANT INDICATES PARALLEL LINES *****;
DETERMINANT := A1*B2 - A2*B1;
IF DETERMINANT = 0 THEN
    WRITE ("THE LINES ARE PARALLEL");
ELSE
    BEGIN
        COMMENT***********************************************
        *   FIND THE POINT OF INTERSECTION, AND DETERMINE *
        *   WHETHER IT LIES ON BOTH LINE SEGMENTS         *
        *   'ON_LINE_1' AND 'ON_LINE_2' ARE LOGICAL VARI- *
        *   ABLES USED TO REPRESENT THE CONDITION THAT THE*
        *   INTERSECTION LIES BETWEEN THE ENDPOINTS OF     *
        *   A LINE SEGMENT                                 *
        ***********************************************;
        REAL X,Y;
        LOGICAL ON_LINE_1, ON_LINE_2;
        X := (B2*C1 - B1*C2)/DETERMINANT;
        Y := (A1*C2 - A2*C1)/DETERMINANT;
        ON_LINE_1 := (U1 > X1) AND (X <= U1) AND (X >= X1)
                  OR (U1 < X1) AND (X >= U1) AND (X <= X1)
                  OR (V1 > Y1) AND (Y <= V1) AND (Y >= Y1)
                  OR              (Y >= V1) AND (Y <= Y1);
        ON_LINE_2 := (U2 > X2) AND (X <= U2) AND (X >= X2)
                  OR (U2 < X2) AND (X >= U2) AND (X <= X2)
                  OR (V2 > Y2) AND (Y <= V2) AND (Y >= Y2)
                  OR              (Y >= V2) AND (Y <= Y2);
        IF ¬ON_LINE_1 THEN
        WRITE ("INTERSECTION DOES NOT FALL ON LINE SEGMENT 1")
        ELSE IF ¬ON_LINE_2 THEN
        WRITE ("INTERSECTION DOES NOT FALL ON LINE SEGMENT 2")
        ELSE WRITE ("THE LINE SEGMENTS INTERSECT AT", X, Y);
    END;
END.
```

The logical expression to determine whether or not the intersection of the infinite lines falls between the endpoints of a given line segment is complicated because of the number of special cases to be considered. Each expression considers four alternatives. The first is the case that the x-coordinate of the first endpoint is greater than that of the second endpoint; the second is that the x-coordinate of the first endpoint is less; third is that the line is parallel to the x-axis but the y-coordinate of the first endpoint is greater than that of the second, and fourth is the remaining case of a line parallel to the x-axis and with the y-coordinate of the first endpoint less than that of the second.

One final caution concerning the example must be mentioned. The test for DETERMINANT = 0 will not yield the expected result in all cases. This is because the computer cannot actually handle real numbers, but only finite rational approximations to them. A better test would be DETERMINANT < (A1*B2 + A2*B1)*'-6. For an explanation, see Chapter 10.

3.7   Handling multiple alternatives

Now that conditional expressions and conditional execution have been introduced as a means of programming a computer to make decisions, these tools can easily be generalized to cases involving multiple decisions. The technique is simply to cascade the use of conditional tests.

Example 3.7.1 -- Computing income tax from a graduated scale

A page from the 1973 Federal Income Tax Forms contains the following table:

```
SCHEDULE X  --  Single Taxpayers

If the amount on                      Enter on
Form 1040,                            Form 1040,
line 55 is:                           line 18:

Not over $500   14% of the amount on line 55:

Over--          But not                                of excess
                over--                                 over--


$      500      $ 1,000       $      70 + 15%       $      500
$    1,000      $ 1,500       $     145 + 16%       $    1,000
$    1,500      $ 2,000       $     225 + 17%       $    1,500
$    2,000      $ 4,000       $     310 + 19%       $    2,000
$    4,000      $ 6,000       $     690 + 21%       $    4,000
$    6,000      $ 8,000       $   1,110 + 24%       $    6,000
$    8,000      $10,000       $   1,500 + 25%       $    8,000
$   10,000      $12,000       $   2,090 + 27%       $   10,000
      .               .               .                   .
      .               .               .                   .
      .               .               .                   .
$   90,000      $100,000      $  46,190 + 69%       $   90,000
$  100,000                    $  53,090 + 70%       $  100,000
```

How might we program an algorithm to perform the computation indicated by the table? A straightforward method would be to compose a conditional expression testing successively whether taxable income falls within each of the ranges specified by the table.

```
INCOMETAX := IF TAXABLEINCOME <= 500 THEN
                .14*TAXABLEINCOME
        ELSE IF TAXABLEINCOME <= 1000 THEN
                70 + .15*(TAXABLEINCOME - 500)
        ELSE IF TAXABLEINCOME <= 1500 THEN
                145 + .16*(TAXABLEINCOME - 1000)
        ELSE IF TAXABLEINCOME <= 2000 THEN
                225 + .17*(TAXABLEINCOME - 1500)
        ELSE IF TAXABLEINCOME <= 4000 THEN
                310 + .19*(TAXABLEINCOME - 2000)
        ELSE IF TAXABLEINCOME <= 6000 THEN
                690 + .21*(TAXABLEINCOME - 4000)
        ELSE IF TAXABLEINCOME <= 8000 THEN
                1110 + .24*(TAXABLEINCOME - 6000)
                .
                .
                .
```

```
        ELSE IF TAXABLEINCOME <= 100000 THEN
              46190 + .69*(TAXABLEINCOME - 90000)
        ELSE 53090 + .70*(TAXABLEINCOME - 100000)
```

When multiple conditions are tested by a cascaded conditional expression such as the one in the last example, the computer will test for the occurrence of each condition in exactly the order they are given. Thus, in the example, if TAXABLEINCOME exceeds 100000, the computer will make all of the indicated comparisons with lesser amounts before discovering that fact. In this particular application, we have reason to believe that a taxable income in excess of $100,000 is much less likely than a taxable income falling into one of the lower brackets, so that the relative inefficiency of the test for very high income does not worry us. In some other applications, however, we might wish to adopt a different strategy to avoid making more comparisons than necessary.

3.8   Making programs readable

Only rarely does one have occasion to write a computer program that will be read only by a computer, and never by another human being. Since a programming language is also a precise, formal language for the statement of algorithms, it seems natural that one should attempt to write algorithms so that they can be read and understood with a minimum of effort by the reader. As was pointed out previously, even if the reader is only yourself, you may not remember exactly what was in the back of your mind at the time that you first composed an algorithm, and it can be most useful to leave some hints for yourself in the form of a lucidly written program. We have already discussed the role of descriptive variable names and of strategically placed comments in making programs intelligible. There are some other rules to follow as well.

The control structure of an algorithm is organized into groups of statements that are executed in sequence. Such a group of statements can be written on successive lines of a page, and indented so that all statements of a group begin on a common left hand margin. If the group of statements happens to be bracketed by a BEGIN ... END pair, then the scope of the BEGIN ... END can be clearly indicated by writing each of these words on individual lines with the same indentation, and letting the group of statements that they enclose be indented three spaces further than the BEGIN and END. The program segment in the example of Section 3.6 illustrates this. In addition, one should indicate the scope of a conditional statement by indenting the statement or group of statements to be conditionally executed three spaces with respect to the left margin of the IF ... THEN clause. If multiple options are listed, then each ELSE should begin on a common left margin. When a statement or group of statements is to be repeated, the scope of the repetition can similarly be indicated by indentation.

Although it may seem relatively unimportant to adhere to fixed rules of style in the physical appearance of programs (particularly if editing can only be done by retyping or keypunching), the effort spent in making programs readable so that a minimum of external documentation is required for their explanation is well worthwhile. When you have gained more experience in composing algorithms, you may wish to try an exercise, formulating an algorithm to have your programs automatically edited for indentation by the computer!

In this chapter, several of the examples have been chosen to illustrate business applications. This is because algorithms for business applications tend to involve a great deal of decision making, rather than a great deal of computation. In other chapters, we shall investigate many examples of applications from other fields.

Exercises for Chapter 3

3.1 Using pencil and paper, follow the steps of the algorithm of Example 3.6.1 to determine whether or not there is an intersection of a pair of line segments whose endpoints coordinates are:

$$U1 = -2, \quad V1 = -3, \quad X1 = 4, \quad Y1 = 6,$$

$$U2 = 3, \quad V2 = 0, \quad X2 = 3, \quad Y2 = 8.$$

3.2 A computer dating service has solicited information sheets from potential customers of their service. The choice of a match is to be made on the basis of correlation of a list of personal interest preferences, but to guard themselves against suggesting unworkable matches, the dating service needs to screen potential pairs by physical, occupational, and social characteristics before considering them as candidates. Each pair is to consist of one male and one female; if the age of the male is under 26, then the female should not be more than one year older; the male should not be more than two inches shorter nor more than 10 inches taller than the female; if both are employed, then they should work the same part of the day; if both indicate religious preferences, they should agree; their places of residence should not be more than 20 miles apart. Give an algorithm to screen a pair of information sheets to see if the persons submitting them are potential dating candidates.

3.3 The director of a zoo is preparing a new enclosure in which several animals of various species are to be housed. To achieve balance, he wishes to limit the number of individuals in the enclosure to 50, of which not more than 25 will be birds, not more than 25 mammals and not more than 15 reptiles. It is also necessary to ensure that the carnivores do not devour the herbivores, so the largest carnivore is not to be larger in body weight than the smallest herbivore. Give the director a program segment to determine whether or not a given animal can be added to the group he has already selected.

3.4 (moderately difficult) From plane trigonometry, you know that if given any of the following sets of data about a triangle, it is possible to find the remaining sides and angles not given as data:

all three sides,
two sides and the angle between them,
two sides and the angle one of them makes with the
   remaining side,
two angles and the side between them,
two angles and the side opposite one of them.

Give an algorithm as an ALGOL W program that will accept as
input six values to be interpreted as the lengths of sides
and the angles of a triangle given in the order side 1,
angle 12, side 2, angle 23, side 3, angle 31, with all
angles specificed as interior angles. A zero value for
either a side or an angle will designate it as unknown. The
algorithm is to determine whether or not the data given
define a triangle, and if so, to determine the values of the
missing sides and angles.

3.5   A small manufacturing concern is converting its accounting
      operations to a computer-based system. The firm has both
      regular and part-time employees, all of whom are paid hourly
      wages. Each week the personnel clerk submits a report of
      the time each employee has worked, and of any vacation or
      sick leave he may have taken. For the plant as a whole, he
      reports the length of that particular work week, and the
      maximum number of hours of overtime authorized for any
      employee during that week.

      The task to be performed by the accounting system is to
      verify that the weekly employment record of each employee
      corresponds to the authorized figures (for instance, that an
      employee does not claim more vacation leave than he is
      entitled to), to prepare the paychecks after having
      calculated withholding tax and other deductions from gross
      pay, and to update the personnel record of each employee to
      reflect the week's transactions. The personnel record is to
      contain the hourly pay rate, the number of days accrued
      vacation leave, the number of days of vacation expended this
      year, the number of days of accrued sick leave, days of sick
      leave taken, total pay received during the current year,
      total withholding tax, total social security tax withheld,
      and total union dues deducted durin the year. Assume that
      withholding tax is deducted at a rate of 14% of total weekly
      wages, that social security tax is deducted at a rate of 6%
      of wages, but only on the first $9000 of wages earned during
      the year, and that union dues amount to $3 per week. Also
      assume that overtime is paid time-and-a-half, that ten days
      paid vacation is authorized per year, and that sick leave
      credit accumulates at a rate of one day for each twelve days
      actually worked.

List all of the program variables required to represent
(a) the weekly employment status of the plant as a whole,
(b) the weekly employment record of an individual employee,
(c) the cumulative yearly employment record of an individual employee.

Give an algorithm to compute the week's take-home pay for an individual employee, and to update his cumulative employment record each week.

3.6 The Albatross Boat Company manufactures a line of custom built pleasure craft. A buyer can choose his particular vessel by specifying combinations from the following list of characteristics:
   (a) Length can be from 15 to 75 feet, in increments of 1 foot;
   (b) Width can be from 5 to 25 feet, in increments of 1 foot;
   (c) Number of sleeping accommodations can be from 0 to 14;
   (d) Engine horsepower can be any one of (10, 20, 50, 100, 200, 300, 500, 1000).

The cost of an Albatross boat is $25 times the square of the length, plus $150 for each sleeping berth, plus $8 per unit of horsepower.

Some combinations of the specifications listed above would result in ludicrous boat designs, so certain constraints must be introduced. Specifically, the length of a boat must be at least three times, but not more than five times its width. The horsepower can be no greater than 0.6 times the product of length and width. And the number of sleeping berths cannot exceed 1/100 of the product of length and width. Should any of these constraints be violated, the customer is to receive one of the following notifications:
   THE DESIGN REQUESTED IS TOO WIDE FOR ITS LENGTH,
   THE DESIGN REQUESTED IS TOO NARROW FOR ITS LENGTH,
   THE DESIGN REQUESTED IS OVERPOWERED,
   TOO MANY SLEEPING ACCOMMODATIONS REQUESTED FOR A BOAT OF
   THIS SIZE.
Also, if a customer specifies a design parameter outside the range of values given by (a -- d), he is to receive notification.

Compose and test an ALGOL W program that can be used by the Albatross Boat Company to check the acceptability of lists of design parameters submitted by its customers, and to compute the cost of each acceptable design. The program should accept, on successive data cards, the specifications submitted by several customers, terminating when it encounters a set of data for which the length is specified as zero.

Chapter 4

REPEATING COMPUTATIONS

4.1 <u>Computations</u> <u>that</u> <u>cannot</u> <u>be</u> <u>done</u> <u>in</u> <u>a</u> <u>single</u> <u>sequence</u> <u>of</u> <u>steps</u>

Recalling the examples of Chapter 1, there were many algorithms calling for the repetition of a step or of a sequence of steps. In fact, there are many problems for which no algorithm can give an effective solution unless it provides some mechanism for repetition.

Repetition is a fundamental concept in controlling the execution of the steps of an algorithm, and there is a special notation for it in the informal language of iteration graphs. An iteration box contains a space with the shape of an inverted letter 'L', enclosing a smaller rectangular box.

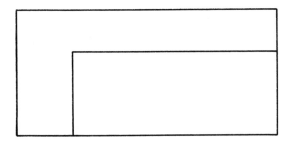

Within the inverted 'L' is written the condition controlling the iteration, and within the smaller box are written the algorithm steps to be repeated. By convention, the controlling test is performed before each execution of the controlled step, and so it is possible that the step appearing in the small box will not be executed even once, in case the controlling test fails immediately.

To illustrate the notation and the concept, let us form an iteration box that will cause a step called 'operation' to be executed N times, if N is a positive integer, and no times in case N is zero or negative.

```
while N > 0
    operation;
    N := N - 1
```

Of course, the controlling test can be given by an arbitrary logical expression, and iteration control is often not so simple as merely counting a fixed number of executions of the controlled step.

The following is a simple example of a problem for which some mechanism for repetition is required, and for which we shall use iteration, but not simply counting.

<u>Example</u> <u>4.1.1</u> -- Finding the greatest common divisor of a pair of positive integers

If we require an algorithm which uses as its primitive operations only the elementary arithmetic operations (addition, subtraction, multiplication, division) and comparison of integers, a convincing argument can be made that no algorithm which does not repeat any step can compute the greatest common divisor of a pair of integers of arbitrary size. On the other hand, Euclid's algorithm for finding the greatest common divisor is particularly simple, using only the operations of subtraction and comparison of integers. Euclid's algorithm is based on the observation that the greatest common divisor of a pair of positive integers, M and N, will also be a divisor of their difference, unless the difference is zero. The difference of M and N will always be smaller then the larger member of the pair, and if the difference is in fact, zero, then the common integer value of M and N is also their greatest common divisor. Thus, an obvious step to iterate is the replacement of the larger member of the pair by the difference. This step is iterated until the difference becomes zero. The algorithm must be finite since the sum of the two members of the pair is reduced at each iteration, and neither number can be reduced to zero.

A first attempt at describing the algorithm by the use of an iteration graph might recognize the iteration control condition and the task of the step that is to be repeated.

<u>while</u> M ¬= N

> replace the larger of (M, N) by their difference

In this description of the algorithm, the controlled step is not yet given in simple enough terms to permit a direct translation to an ALGOL W program segment. Forgetting about the iteration control for the moment, let us concentrate just on refinement of the controlled step. When it designates 'the larger of (M, N)', we realize that a choice has to be made, depending on the current values held by variables M and N. A different action is to be taken in each of the two alternate cases. We could describe the choice by a conditional box, and the actions to be taken in the two cases can be described by assignment statements.   Thus the box

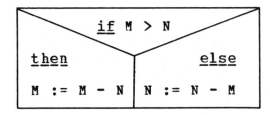

can be refined to

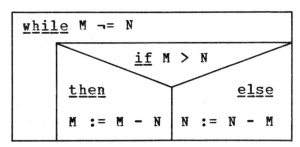

Substituting the conditional box for the controlled step in the original graph, we obtain an iteration graph describing the entire algorithm in elementary steps

GCD1:

```
┌─────────────────────────────────┐
│ while M ¬= N                    │
│     ┌───────────────────────────┤
│     │          if M > N         │
│     │ then              else    │
│     │ M := M - N │ N := N - M   │
│     └───────────────────────────┤
└─────────────────────────────────┘
```

     Translating the algorithm, to which we attach the label GCD1 as a means of naming it, into an ALGOL W program segment we obtain

```
GCD1:
    WHILE M ¬= N DO
        IF M > N THEN
            M := M - N
        ELSE
            N := N - M
```

The effect of the WHILE clause is to cause repetition of the statement that follows it until the condition M -= N is no longer satisfied. The answer, the greatest common divisor of the original values of M and N, appears as the final value of M (or N). Try carrying out the calculation yourself, with initial values M=63, N=48.

4.2   Getting the initial values right

In the last example, we assumed that the variables M and N had received initial values by some means or other before execution of the program segment GCD1 was begun. We also assumed that the values given were both positive integers. (How would the computation proceed if one of the values were zero or a negative integer?) In formulating complete programs, it is always necessary to specify how the initial values of variables are to be acquired, and if there is any doubt as to whether the initial values lie within the range for which the algorithm is defined, then these values must be checked.

One way to initialize the values of M and N used in the GCD1 algorithm would be to have these values read from some device that supplies inputs to the computer, such as a punched card reader or a communications terminal. In such a case, out-of-range values might be submitted, so the initial data must be checked for validity. These tasks can be accomplished by appending the following ALGOL W test as a prefix to GCD1,

```
READ (M,N);   WRITE (M,N);
IF (M <= 0) OR (N <= 0) THEN WRITE ("VALUE OUT OF RANGE")
ELSE . . .
```

In nearly every program segment whose execution is to be repeated a number of times, there are variables whose values must be initialized prior to beginning execution of the segment. It is easy to identify such variables from the text of the repeated segment, for they are characterized by the fact that the first reference to them occurs in the evaluation of an expression, rather than as the left-hand side of an assignment or in an input statement. Such a variable is said to be, in the personified vernacular of computer science, live on entry into the iterated program segment. Failure to properly initialize a variable that is live on entry is the commonest cause of error in formulating algorithms as computer programs.

Failure to initialize a variable commonly occurs because, in inventing an algorithm, we tend to focus our attention first on the steps to be iterated and simply forget to fill in an intended initialization step later. Or, in an algorithm containing many conditionally executed statements, it may happen that we have not correctly analyzed all possibilities, and that a statement initializing a variable, which ought to have been executed before an iterated program segment was executed, was in fact passed by due to the occurrence of an unforeseen combination of conditions. What happens to the execution of an algorithm when an uninitialized variable is referenced? This depends on the particular computer and programming language you are using, but quite commonly the computer proceeds as though the uninitialized variable _does_ have a value, perhaps one left over from a previous computation it has done for another user, and you get mysteriously wrong answers!

4.3   How do you know that an algorithm is correct?

This question is one of the most difficult, yet obviously most important questions one can ask about computing. All that we can provide are partial answers; they will be sufficient to establish the correctness of simple algorithms and of some complicated ones, but they will not succeed in every case. On the other hand, in an attempt to verify that an algorithm is correct, one is very often led to exposure of its weak points, or the potential errors in it.

There are two principal methods for attempting verification of an algorithm: testing, and logical analysis. By correctness of an algorithm, we do not mean only that a program is free of syntax errors. Syntax errors are really errors in the statement of an algorithm, and are easily checked by submitting a program to the computer. What we mean by correctness is that an algorithm when executed on any values of data, either computes a correct result or else reports that the data values are unacceptable.

Testing of programs on a few 'typical' sets of data is the most commonly used means of verifying correctness, but it suffers from an obvious flaw. Most algorithms are intended to work on such a large set of data values that it is impossible to test all combinations, and so testing is often confined to determining that a program works on the programmer's favorite example! Nevertheless, there are a few rules that can be given for developing adequate sets of test data. The first rule is that every statement of the program should be tested. Not every set of test data will do this. For example, in the example of GCD1, given in the preceding sections, the data (24, 4) would never cause the assignment N := N - M to be executed. If this statement had been inadvertently omitted from the program segment, the correct result would still be computed on the data (24, 4). In order to fully exercise a program, it is often necessary to furnish it with several sets of test data. In order to be certain than an ALGOL W program has had all statements tested at least once, one can make use of the execution flow summary (see section A11.1 of the Appendix), which will provide a count of the number of times each statement has been executed in a particular test.

Returning to the example of GCD1, a set of test data should include a pair of numbers relatively prime, a pair in which one divides the other, and a pair not relatively prime, but in which neither divides the other. Each set should be given in both orders, larger number first and larger number second. Thus a set of test data might be (5, 3), (3, 5), (4, 2), (2, 4), (6, 4), (4, 6) and (3, 3). These would test all normal states of the algorithm, that is, would test every instruction and test instructions in all relative orders of execution. But this amount of testing is still not sufficient. If there are other, abnormal sets of data that might be submitted to the algorithm for its consideration, then it should be tested on such sets. In the case of GCD1, it is intended that it should get its input from a card reader, rather than some more benevolent device which checks data values before submitting them, and so the additional test data (1, 0), (0, 1), (1, -1), (-1, 1) should be added.

The other principal method for verification of algorithms is based on systematic mathematical reasoning about the computation that an algorithm describes. In mathematical reasoning we are not handicapped by the inability to describe all possible input values; we are used to making statements prefaced with phrases such as 'for all positive integer values', or 'there exists a pair of integers such that . . .' Let's see how this technique works on GCD1.

The first thing to do is to rewrite the algorithm description, identifying points in the algorithm at which assertions can be placed about the values held by the program variables. In doing this, one is forced to realize that the execution of an algorithm is a dynamic process, and that the same algorithm steps may be repeated with several different sets of values of the program variables, as the evaluation progresses in time. In GCD1, we identify five points at which to make assertions:

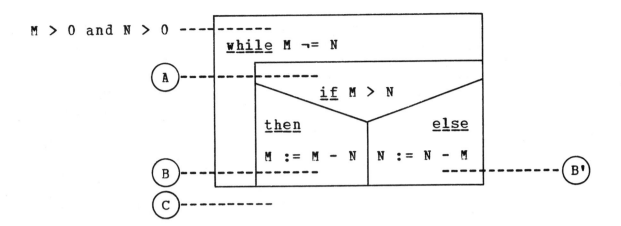

M > 0 and N > 0

while M ¬= N

if M > N

then   else

M := M - N   N := N - M

A

B   B'

C

Since this algorithm performs iteration, we shall use a
method of inductive assertion. This involves looking for a
hypothesis that will be true of the values at point A no matter
how many times the iterated statement is repeated. One way to
form such a hypothesis is to look for a condition that will
remain invariant from point A to either of points B or B', even
though some change in the values of the variables occurs as a
result of executing the intervening statements. For example, an
invariant condition might be 'M > 0 and N > 0'. If this were true
at point A, then in case M is the greater of M and N, the
assignment M := M - N will be executed, replacing the value of M
with a new value. The new value, however, is assuredly positive.
The value of N remains unchanged, and so the assertion remains
true. On the other hand, if the condition were false at A
because N was negative, then it would remain false at B, with N
still negative and M still positive (and larger). Thus the
hypothesis 'M > 0 and N > 0' is invariant from A to B. Since
(M ¬= N) at point A is guaranteed by the while clause, the
alternative to M > N at A is that M < N. In this case, the
invariance of the hypothesis from point A to point B' can also be
established by similar reasoning.

A more interesting hypothesis is that for any positive
integer constant G, the condition that 'G divides both M and N'
remains invariant from A to either of B or B'. If G divides both
M and N, then there are positive integers P and Q such that
M = G*P and N = G*Q. Thus, when M is replaced by M - N, the
common factor G can be extracted, and the new value of M will be
M = G*(P - Q). Thus G still divides both M and N at point B.
Similar reasoning demonstrates the condition to be invariant from
point A to point B' as well.

The utility of these invariant conditions lies in the
application of the inductive method. There are just two ways by
which values are obtained at point A. One is that M and N hold
their initial values at point A and that these initial values are

not equal. The other is that the values M and N held at point B
or at point B' were not equal after some number of repetitions of
the iterated statement, and that these values are inherited at
point A. Thus any condition which is invariant from point A to
both points B and B', and which can also be established to hold
for the initial values, must always hold at point A. As an
example of such a condition, let the constant G of the preceding
paragraph be any member of the set of common divisors of the
original values of M and N. This set of common divisors will then
remain invariant throughout execution of the algorithm! In
particular, when the algorithm terminates execution at point C,
with M and N having equal final values, the set of common
divisors will be the set of all factors of M, and the largest
factor, the final value of M itself, will be the greatest common
divisor.

    Lest it seem as if we are advertising logical analysis as a
panacea for solving all problems of algorithm verification, two
difficulties should be pointed out. First of all, there are some
algorithms for which verification by mathematical reasoning is
extremely difficult, perhaps even impossible, even though the
algorithm may, in fact, have all the desired properties.
Secondly, there is always a danger of acquiring a false sense of
confidence by generating a logically invalid verification, just
as one sometimes gives a false proof in mathematics, or composes
an incorrect algorithm in the first place! However, the very act
of going through a logical analysis of an algorithm will nearly
always increase your understanding of it, even if it is an
algorithm that you have composed yourself.

4.4   How many times should we repeat?

    Frequently, when repetition of an algorithm step is called
for, one can predict in advance exactly the number of repetitions
required. For example, n! can be evaluated with exactly n
multiplications. When an exactly predictable number of
iterations is required, it is helpful to use an iteration control
clause which counts the number of repetitions, instead of testing
to see whether a specified condition is satisfied. ALGOL W (and
most other, similarly conceived programming languages) has such
an iteration control clause, the FOR clause. It could be used to
accomplish the evaluation of n! as follows:


```
        FACTORIAL := 1;
        FOR I := 1 UNTIL N DO
           FACTORIAL := I*FACTORIAL
```

Of course, not every iterated step can be controlled by a FOR clause, but for those which can, its use offers the advantage, (compared to a WHILE clause) that the number of iterations is always bounded, even if other errors occur in the execution of the program. Also, there is much less chance that the controlling variable will be improperly initialized since its initialization is accomplished by a specific assignment within the FOR clause. The controlling variable is not actually accessible in the statement or compound group whose iteration is controlled by the FOR clause. Instead, there are two copies of the controlling variable which are made each time the FOR clause is executed. One copy, which is the one actually used to control the number of times that the iteration occurs, is inaccessible to the rest of the program. The other copy is the one called by the name of the controlling variable, and it is accessible to the program.

In order to get a more explicit understanding of the FOR clause, let us compare it with an exactly equivalent WHILE clause.

```
FOR I := 1 UNTIL N DO          I' := 1;  N' := N;
    <statement>                WHILE I' <= N' DO
                                   BEGIN
                                       INTEGER I;
                                       I := I';
                                       <statement>;
                                       I' := I' + 1;
                                   END
```

In the program segment on the right, the variables I' and N' are inaccessible to the programmer and never actually appear in his program. The variable I is declared locally in the block controlled by the WHILE clause, and does not exist in the program context surrounding the block. The program segment on the right can be taken to be a definition of the effect of the FOR statement on the left.

The reason that the designers of ALGOL W have resorted to this seemingly complicated ruse, is to ensure that the FOR clause will <u>always</u> produce a finite number of iterations. Thus, if the program contains an assignment to the (apparent) controlling variable, such as

```
FOR I := 1 UNTIL N DO
    BEGIN
        .
        .
        .
        I := I - 1;
    END
```

the assignment to I will have no effect on the number of times that execution of the group is repeated. Similarly, if instead of assigning a new value to I, the programmer attempted to increase the upper bound on the number of iterations, by including the statement

        N := N + 1;

within the group, it would have no effect on the number of iterations performed.

The FOR clause is quite flexible, as you can find out from section A8.2.2 of the Appendix. Both the initial value of the controlling variable and the size of the steps by which it is incremented can be set in the FOR clause, and it can be used for counting down by negative increments, as well as for counting upwards by positive increments. Thus, the factorial function could also be evaluated by:

        FACTORIAL := 1;
        FOR I := N STEP -1 UNTIL 1 DO
            FACTORIAL := I*FACTORIAL

In case the initial value assigned to the controlling variable is already out of the range of the count, as for instance, if N = 0 in the algorithm for the factorial function, then the statement under control of the FOR clause is not executed at all.

In some algorithms the number of iterations required is obvious, but in others, we can often figure out a fixed number of iterations that will be sufficient.

Example 4.4.1 -- Computing the square root of a number

One of the oldest problems of real-valued arithmetic is that of computing the square root. There is a very simple algorithm for this computation, usually attributed to Isaac Newton. Suppose N is any positive number whose square root is to be found, and suppose X is an estimate of the square root arrived at by some means, say initially by guessing. If X is actually greater than $\sqrt{N}$, then N/X will be smaller than $\sqrt{N}$, and conversely. The product of X with N/X is, of course N, so these two numbers serve as reciprocal estimates of $\sqrt{N}$. Newton's algorithm is to iteratively replace the estimate X with the mean of the reciprocal estimates, 1/2(X + N/X), until the difference of the reciprocal estimates, |X - N/X|, has been made as small as desired.

Since the algorithm itself is to be independent of the value of N whose square root is to be estimated, one is obligated to make the initial guess a constant value, and 1 is as good a choice as any. The desired accuracy might be expressed as a constant multiple of the original number, or as a specified number of significant digits to be given correctly. In the first version of the algorithm, we shall ask for the difference of the reciprocal estimates to be made less than 10^{-7} times the value of the estimate.

```
COMMENT***********************************************************
*     NEWTON1:  N IS THE NUMBER WHOSE SQUARE ROOT IS TO BE *
*         FOUND.                                           *
*         X IS THE CURRENT ESTIMATE OF THE ROOT.           *
*****************************************************************;
X := 1;
WHILE ABS (X - N/X) > 1'-7 * X DO
   X := .5*(X + N/X)
```

In the expression appearing in the WHILE clause, ABS is a built-in ALGOL W operator which takes the absolute value of a number (see section A7.1.6 of the Appendix).

There is one deficiency of the algorithm as given above. Although it will need only a few iterations to evaluate the root of a number not too far removed from 1, to take the root of a very large or a very small number will require a number of iterations that increases as $|\log_2 N|$. This is because when the reciprocal estimates are far apart, the new estimate which is found is just about half of the larger one.

The rate of convergence of the algorithm can be improved by selecting a better estimate than 1 before applying Newton's method. The initial value of the estimate can be preconditioned by multiplying it by some number chosen so that the estimate squared is still smaller than the large number whose root is desired. In fact, this preconditioning can be applied repetitively, until the square of the estimate is within some constant ratio of N.

An added benefit of preconditioning is that whenever it is known that the square of the initial estimate is within some given, fixed ratio of N, then we can also give a fixed bound on the number of iterations of Newton's procedure that will guarantee a specified number of significant digits in the result. Thus, it will no longer be necessary to control the iteration by testing the difference of the reciprocal estimates, but instead we can just iterate the procedure a fixed number of times. A modified form of the square root algorithm is

```
COMMENT**********************************************************
*       NEWTON2:  N IS THE NUMBER WHOSE ROOT IS TO BE FOUND. *
*                 X IS THE ESTIMATE OF THE ROOT OF N.        *
***********************************************************;
X  :=1;
WHILE N > 64*X*X DO
    X  := 8*X;
WHILE N < X*X/64 DO
    X  := X/8;
FOR I := 1 UNTIL 6 DO
    X  := .5*(X + N/X)
```

Notice that only one (or possibly neither) of the statements controlled by the WHILE clauses will be executed, for any specific initial value of X.

When Newton's procedure is begun in the last line of the algorithm, it is known that X squared must be within a factor of 64 of N. When begun with an estimate this close to the square root, six iterations of Newton's procedure will suffice to give a result accurate to seven significant decimal digits. The factor of 64 was selected arbitrarily; however, on many computers, which use an internal representation of numbers with a radix of 2, 8, or 16, multiplications or divisons of integers by powers of 2 can be carried out very quickly. This is a use of machine-dependent knowledge, however, and the specific selection of 64 as the factor is in no way crucial to the algorithm.

It is instructive to compare the efficiency of NEWTON1 with NEWTON2, insofar as we are able. For very large (or very small) values of N, the number of iterations of the preconditioning step by NEWTON2 will be $|\log_{64} N|$, which is 6 times smaller than the $|\log_2 N|$ estimate of the number of iterations that NEWTON1 will require. At first glance, it appears that NEWTON2 incurs some additional overhead when the value of N is within a factor of 64 of 1, for then the conditions of the two WHILE clauses must be evaluated although no preconditioning is actualy necessary. But because of the certain knowledge that X squared is within a factor of 64 of N when the last statement is begun, a simpler form of iteration control is used that requires less computation for its evaluations than does the WHILE clause of NEWTON1. So NEWTON2 appears to be superior for _any_ value of N (other than the very special case, N = 1).

4.5   Nested iterations

Since an iteration control clause can appear in a sequence
of algorithm steps just as a simple step might, there is the
possibility of including an iteration control clause within the
scope of a statement group controlled by a previous iteration
clause. When this happens, we say that the iterations are
nested.   Nested iterations, when properly used, enable some
fairly complicated algorithms to be stated quite succinctly.   The
following example is one in which we know of no better method
than trial and error to arrive at a solution.   It involves
computation with an iteration of trials, using the result of each
trial to improve the estimate of the desired solution.

Example 4.5.1 -- Mortgage loans

The terms of a mortgage loan differ from those of
simpler consumer or business loans in that the amount of
inerest paid in each monthly payment is calculated as a
fixed percentage of the unpaid balance (rather than as a
fixed percentage of the total amount borrowed), yet the
amount of the monthly payments is constant. Therefore, in
the first years of a mortgage, the payments are largely
devoted to interest, while during the last year, the
interest due is comparatively small and the payments are
mostly applied to retirement of the principal.

A problem faced by a mortgage banker is the following.
Given a rate of interest to be paid on the balance of the
principal outstanding, and given a duration over which the
mortgage is to be retired, how large should the monthly
payments be, per $1000 borrowed?

We don't know how to solve this problem directly, but
we can solve a somewhat different, although related problem.
Given a fixed rate of interest and a fixed amount of each
monthly payment, we can calculate the balance remaining
after some specified number of monthly payments has been
made.   This can be done by simply calculating the actual
amount to be paid in interest each month, subtracting this
amount from the total monthly payment to determine the
amount applied to reduce the balance, and thereby obtaining
the new balance to be used in the calculation for the
following month.   Letting BALANCE represent the unpaid
amount of the principal, RATE be the monthly rate of
interest, INTEREST be the actual interest to be paid in a
specific month, and DURATION be the number of months in
which the loan is to be repaid, the calculation of the final
balance remaining would be:

```
FOR TIME := 1 UNTIL DURATION DO
    BEGIN
        INTEREST := RATE*BALANCE;
        BALANCE := BALANCE - (PAYMENT - INTEREST);
    END
```

To gain a better understanding of the problem, one
might carry out the above calculation, using initial values
of RATE = .1, BALANCE = 1000, PAYMENT = 150. This yields the
following table, showing the accelerating rate at which the
balance is retired.

TIME	INTEREST	BALANCE	PAYMENT - INTEREST
1	100.00	950.00	50.00
2	95.00	895.00	55.00
3	89.50	834.50	60.50
4	83.45	767.95	66.55
5	76.79	694.74	73.21
6	69.47	614.21	80.53
7	61.42	525.63	88.58
8	52.56	428.19	97.44
9	42.82	321.01	107.18
10	32.10	203.11	117.90
11	20.31	73.42	129.69
12	7.34	-69.24	142.66

If, after execution of the above program segment, the final
value of BALANCE is not zero (or nearly zero), it means that
the value guessed for the equal monthly payments was not
correct. A positive final balance indicates that the
payments have been too small, a negative value that they
have been too large. What is needed is some way to
systematically improve the guess of a value for the monthly
payment. Then the calculation of the balance remaining
after repayment can be iterated until the desired goal is
achieved, that is, until a monthly payment is obtained that
will enable the balance to be reduced to zero in the desired
time.

Unfortunately, we may never be lucky enough to
calculate a payment that will leave the balance exactly zero
after the desired number of months. However, if the balance
remaining was very small, say give or take 10 cents per 1000
dollars of the original loan, few people would quibble. So
in the iteration control clause, we shall use this criterion
to determine when to stop the trial-and-error process.
Since it is immaterial whether the remaining balance is

74

positive or negative so long as it is less than 10 cents, we
shall use the condition of a negligibly small balance to
control the iteration of a trial-and-error search for a
solution.

At this point, a description of the partially
formulated algorithm by means of an iteration graph will be
helpful.

```
┌──────────────────────────────────────────────────┐
│ Set initial Balance to 1000;                       │
│ Guess a value for the monthly payment;             │
├──────────────────────────────────────────────────┤
│ while abs (Balance) > .10                          │
│   ┌──────────────────────────────────────────┐    │
│   │ calculate the final value of             │    │
│   │     Balance after repayment;             │    │
│   │ refine the estimate of the monthly       │    │
│   │     payment                              │    │
│   └──────────────────────────────────────────┘    │
└──────────────────────────────────────────────────┘
```

Next, we must face the problem of determining an
initial guess for the monthly payment, and a means of
refining that guess. In any month, the payment consists of
two parts, the interest, which is RATE*BALANCE, and the
remainder, called the amortization, which goes toward
retirement of the outstanding balance. In the first month,
the interest can be estimated exactly, for we know the
initial value of the balance is always to be 1000 dollars.
Therefore, let

        INIT_INTEREST := RATE*1000

The monthly payment should never be smaller than the value
of INIT_INTEREST, for if it were, the amortization would
always be negative! One can make a naive guess at an
initial value for the amortization, letting

        INIT_AMORT := 1000/DURATION

This value, which would be correct if the interest owed did
not decrease with time as the loan is repaid, will actually
be somewhat larger than the correct value, but that does not
matter. Having analyzed these components of the first
month's payment, let an initial guess for the payment be:

        PAYMENT := INIT_INTEREST + INIT_AMORT

Now, if the initial guess for PAYMENT is not correct, and the final value of BALANCE after calculating the repayment over the desired duration is not zero, a new value of INIT_AMORT (the first month's amortization) should be guessed. The new guess is to be larger if BALANCE has a final value between 0 and 1000, and smaller (but not negative) if BALANCE has a negative final value. The simplest function which accomplishes the modification of INIT_AMORT is

$$INIT\_AMORT := INIT\_AMORT * (2000/(2000 - BALANCE))$$

Since we had previously considered how to calculate the final value of the balance after repayment over a fixed duration, all that remains is to initialize the variables. Since the calculation can be done per $1000 of principal aount of the loan, the initial value of BALANCE will be 1000. This initialization must be redone before each recalculation of repayment, however, so the initialization of BALANCE must be placed at the head of the group of statements controlled by the WHILE clause. Since the WHILE clause will also require an initial value of BALANCE in its test the first time the iteration control is encountered, BALANCE must also be initialized in the prefix to the iteration.

Values for DURATION and RATE will be obtained from the input, and should therefore be checked for validity. It will also be convenient to give their values in units of years and percent per year, and so they must be converted to apply to a time unit of one month.

After translation from the iteration graph, making the refinements of steps that were described above, and appending declarations of the variables, the following ALGOL W program is the result.

```
COMMENT*****************************************************
*     MORTGAGEPAYMENT:                                     *
*         CALCULATES THE MONTHLY PAYMENT, PER THOUSAND DOL- *
*         LARS OF PRINCIPAL, REQUIRED TO REPAY A MORTGAGE.  *
*         RATE IS THE INTEREST RATE IN PER CENT PER YEAR.   *
*         DURATION IS THE LOAN DURATION IN YEARS.           *
*****************************************************;

BEGIN
    REAL RATE, BALANCE, INTEREST, PAYMENT, INIT_INTEREST,
        INIT_AMORT;
    INTEGER DURATION;
```

```
COMMENT*************************************************
*      BALANCE -- BALANCE OUTSTANDING EACH MONTH,      *
*                  INITIALLY 1000                      *
*      INTEREST -- THE INTEREST DUE EACH MONTH, DOLLARS *
*      PAYMENT -- AMOUNT OF EACH MONTHLY PAYMENT, DOLLARS *
*      INIT_INTEREST -- INTEREST DUE THE FIRST MONTH   *
*      INIT_AMORT -- AMOUNT OF THE FIRST MONTH'S PAYMENT *
*                  AVAILABLE FOR AMORTIZATION          *
*******************************************************;
READ (RATE,DURATION);
WRITE ("RATE =", RATE, "PER CENT.  DURATION =", DURATION,
       "YEARS");
ASSERT (RATE > 0) AND (DURATION > 0);
COMMENT***** CONVERT RATE, DURATION TO MONTHS *****;
RATE := RATE/1200;
DURATION := 12*DURATION;
BALANCE := 1000;
INIT_INTEREST := RATE*1000;
INIT_AMORT := 1000/DURATION;
PAYMENT := INIT_INTEREST + INIT_AMORT;
COMMENT*************************************************
*    OBTAIN A CORRECT VALUE FOR THE PAYMENT BY SUCCES-  *
*    SIVE TRIALS.                                      *
*******************************************************;
WHILE ABS (BALANCE) > .10 DO
   BEGIN
      BALANCE := 1000;
      FOR TIME := 1 UNTIL DURATION DO
         BEGIN
            INTEREST := RATE*BALANCE;
            BALANCE := BALANCE - (PAYMENT - INTEREST);
         END;
      COMMENT**** REFINE THE ESTIMATED PAYMENT****;
      INIT_AMORT := INIT_AMORT*2000/(2000 - BALANCE);
      PAYMENT := INIT_INTEREST + INIT_AMORT;
   END;
 WRITE ("THE REQUIRED MONTHLY PAYMENT IS:", PAYMENT);
END.
```

Exercises for Chapter 4

4.1 Instead of repeated subtraction, one could make use of the integer division functions, DIV and REM, in an algorithm for the greatest common divisor of two numbers. Give such an algorithm as an ALGOL W program.

4.2 compose an algorithm for the least common multiple of a pair of integers.

4.3 A well-known sequence in number theory is the Fibonacci sequence,

0, 1, 1, 2, 3, 5, 8, 13, 21, 34, 55, 89, 144, . . .

This sequence is defined by a recurrence relation, after specifying the first two terms:

$F_0 = 0$,
$F_1 = 1$,
$F_{n+1} = F_n + F_{n-1}$, for $n > 0$.

Compose an algorithm to compute and print the first 45 terms of the Fibonacci sequence.

4.4 Compose an algorithm to find all of the perfect squares that occur within a given interval of the positive integers.

4.5 What is the largest integer less than 100 whose square is the sum of the squares of two other integers? What is the second largest? Is there an integer less than 100 whose cube is the sum of the cubes of two other integers?

4.6 There are some sequences of values that can be generated in a regular manner and which tend to a limit. In some cases, the sequences are infinite, as is the sequence of reciprocal integers, 1/1, 1/2, 1/3, 1/4, 1/5, 1/6. . . . which tends to the limit 0 as the integers tend towards infinity. If a sequence is generated by substitution of successive arguments of a function, its limit can sometimes be used to compute values of the function that could not be calculated by conventional means. From the following functions, generate finite sequences that approach the limiting values of the arguments indicated, and from the sequence, estimate the value of each function at the limit point.

a) $\frac{\sin x}{x}$ as $x \to 0$;

b) $x \log_e x$ as $x \to 0$;

c) $\dfrac{\log_e x}{x-1}$ as $x \to 1$;

d) $\dfrac{e^{-x^2/2} - 1}{x^2}$ as $x \to 0$.

In each case, display the results in the form of a table of values of the argument and values of the function. Then give your estimate of the limiting value of each sequence.

4.7 Compound interest means that a bank will reinvest the interest payments it makes to depositors at regular intervals, and by crediting the interest payment to the depositor's account, that sum in turn is used as part of the balance on which interest is computed during the next interval. Compute the accumulation of funds in a savings account with an initial balance of $1000, drawing interest at the rate of 6% per year, over 20 years if the interest is compounded
    a) yearly;
    b) quarterly;
    c) monthly;
    d) weekly;
    e) daily.
Give the accumulation in the form of tables, showing the balance in the account initially and at the end of each year. If interest is compounded quarterly, what is the effect of reducing interest to 3% per year? Of doubling it to 12% per year? Is the balance after 20 years altered in direct proportion to the rate of interest paid?

Recently, some banks have advertised that they offer continuous compounding of interest. This does not mean that they run their computers continuously, at least not on interest calculations. There is a mathematical function, the exponential function e^x, that has the property that upon increasing x by a small amount, δ, the value of $e^{x+\delta}$ exceeds the value of e^x by an amount δe^x. Thus, if x is allowed to represent the rate of interest multiplied by the time in years since the original deposit, the value of $e^{rate*time}$ gives the factor of expansion of the principal using continuous compounding. (ALGOL W has a built-in function, EXP( ), which evaluates the exponential function.) The calculation is not made continuously, but only for those discrete time values at which one wants to know the balance. Calculate the accumulation of a 1000 dollar savings account over 20 years, at 6% interest compounded continuously. If interest was compounded yearly, what equivalent rate of interest would produce the same growth of the balance as does 6% interest compounded continuously?

4.8 An infinite sum has a value if the infinite sequence formed by the finite partial sums of the first n terms (n = 1, 2, 3, . . .) approaches a limiting value as n tends to infinity. Investigate the sequence formed by the finite partial sum of each of the following infinite sums:

a) $\displaystyle\sum_{n=0}^{\infty} \frac{1}{n!}$

b) $\displaystyle\sum_{n=1}^{\infty} \frac{1}{n}$

c) $\displaystyle\sum_{n=1}^{\infty} (-)^{n-1} \frac{1}{n}$

4.9 An infinite power series provides a means of specifying a function, since for each value of the argument, it defines an infinite sum. If the infinite sum has a value, then the value of the function is given by the sum for that particular value of the argument. If the sum does not have a value, then it may be that the function is undefined for that particular value of its argument, or it may simply be that the power series does not correspond to the function for that argument. Evaluate the infinite sums given by the following power series at values of the arguments of 0, 1/2, 1, and 2, and try to guess the function to which each series corresponds.

a) $\displaystyle\sum_{n=0}^{\infty} \frac{x^n}{n!}$

b) $\displaystyle\sum_{odd\ n=1}^{\infty} (-)^{(n-1)/2} \frac{x^n}{n!}$

c) $\displaystyle\sum_{n=1}^{\infty} \frac{(1-x)^n}{n}$

4.10 Newton's method can be extended to find integral roots other than square roots. The reciprocal estimates of the nth root of N become X, and N/X^{n-1}. Compose an algorithm to evaluate integral roots by Newton's method. Does it require more or fewer iterations to achieve comparable accuracy in evaluating the 5th root of two as it does to evaluate the square root of two? Compare the rates of convergence for

80

other powers and other arguments.

4.11 Use mathematical reasoning to verify that in any single evaluation by NEWTON2 of Example 4.4.1, at most one of the statements X := 8*X and X := X/8 that are controlled by the WHILE clauses will be executed, although whichever statement is executed may be repeated.

4.12 Compose an algorithm which will read a sequence of N integers (where N is to be read first, and must be positive) and will select and print the largest of the values read (not including N).

4.13 For the algorithm GCD1 of Example 4.1.1, verify by mathematical reasoning that when applied to initial values both of which are positive integers, execution of the algorithm always terminates.

4.14 For the algorithm MORTGAGEPAYMENT of Example 4.5.1, verify by mathematical reasoning that execution always terminates.

NOTES

Chapter 5

TELLING THE COMPUTER ABOUT THE DATA

5.1 <u>Data types</u>

Up to this point, we have described computations involving simple variables taking values that are integers, real numbers, or logical truth values. Any particular variable is only used to represent values of one of these types, however. One can associate with each variable a property or attribute describing the class of values that variable is allowed to take. This attribute is called the data type of the variable, and its use is to guide us (and the computer) in making proper interpretations of operations on the program variables. Data types can be simple or compound. The simple types are specified in the definition of the programming language, and never vary. Compound types are built up from the simple types by qualifying them with parameters; thus, there is no limit to the number of compound types that can be formed. The best way to explain this is by considering the data types of ALGOL W as examples.

ALGOL W has nine simple types. They are: <u>integer</u>, <u>real</u>, <u>long real</u>, <u>complex</u>, <u>long complex</u>, <u>logical</u>, <u>bits</u>, <u>string</u> and <u>reference</u>. Types <u>integer</u> and <u>real</u> describe integer and real numbers, respectively. The computer represents real numbers in floating point form. This is explained in detail in Chapter 10, but briefly, it means that the computer actually represents each real by a pair of integers, one of which is interpreted as the modulus, and the other as the exponent of the floating point number. This is similar to the use of scientific notation with the added convention that the modulus will always be written with the decimal point immediately to the left of the first significant digit, and the magnitude of the actual real number will be accounted for by multiplying the modulus by an appropriate power of 10. For example, 12,244.75 could be represented in scientific notation with this convention on placement of the decimal as $.1224475 \times 10^5$. The computer only keeps a fixed number of significant digits in the modulus of each floating point number, so there is a limit to the precision with which it can represent an arbitrary real number. It is for this reason that when we know that a computation can be done with integer values, we shall prefer to use variables of type <u>integer</u> rather than of type <u>real</u>. For in computations on integer variables, there is no loss of precision due to rounding the modulus to a fixed number of significant digits.

The data type <u>long real</u> also is used to represent real numbers. It differs from type <u>real</u> in that more significant digits are retained in the modulus. This provides greater accuracy in certain scientific applications in which small numerical errors tend to grow in size during the course of an extensive computation. The data types **complex** and **long complex** are provided to represent complex numbers, also for use in scientific applications. Data type **logical** is provided for logical variables, whose use we have studied in Chapter 3.

The data types **bits** and **string** describe sequences, or strings of binary bits and of characters (a character is any symbol that can be read by the computer), respectively. With binary bit strings one can play many interesting games. Most of them involve encoding numbers or other information in the form of patterns or sequences of bits, and manipulating the information by operations on bit strings. A bit string can represent a sequence of truth values or the membership of a set chosen from a finite universe.

With character strings, one can process textual information. The operations defined on character strings include comparisons, extracting a substring, and with some difficulty, reconstructing strings from individual characters.

In this book, the data type **reference** will not be explained in detail. Briefly, however, a reference variable is one whose function is to tell you where you may find other information. Suppose you had a variable that took for its values Library of Congress catalog numbers. Then you could use this variable as a reference to any library book, by assigning to the reference variable the number by which to locate the desired book. Within the computer, there is also an internal numbering system by which to locate other pieces of information, and an ALGOL W reference variable takes as its values these internal numbers.

5.2 Structured data types

In many cases, we shall wish to consider a whole set of variables, bound together in some structure, as a single entity. Examples of such structures are not hard to think of; matrices and vectors are examples, a list is another, and a family tree yet another. What these entities have in common is that for each, there exists some sort of mapping function that enables one to locate individual elements. This concept gives us a strong hint as to what is meant by a structured type. It is a mapping such that when given a value of a specified simple type as an argument, it yields a variable that is a member of the set onto which the mapping is defined. The referenced variable will itself be of a simple type which must be specified as part of the structured type definition.

There are two classes of structured types definable in ALGOL W and, of course, as many distinct instances of these types as you wish to define. The classes of structured types are arrays and records. A structure whose type class is array is an indexed set. Arrays may be singly or multiply indexed, but each individual element of an array must be of the same simple type. The indices of an array take integer values, and the mapping function is an obvious one, which picks out from the entire set of elements the particular one corresponding in sequence to the integer values given as arguments. If any value given as an argument lies outside the range defined for that particular index, then the mapping is undefined. The name for this structured type originates from the fact that when singly and doubly indexed sets (vectors and matrices, respectively) are written down on paper in the conventional representation, they appear as one and two dimensional arrays of elements. Extending this concept to n-indexed sets, one can conceive of a spatial representation as an array of elements laid out in n-dimensional space.

A structure of type record is a set of n-tuples of simple type variables. The number of elements of the tuple, and the types of the various elements (they can be mixed) are specified as part of the structured type definition. The set of n-tuples is not indexed; individual instances are referred to by the use of a reference variable. The mapping associated with a structured record type is from reference values to component n-tuples. Since reference is itself a simple type, it is possible to define reference variables as members of the n-tuples of a record structure. In this way, the n-tuples of a record class can be chained together to build linked data structures.

5.3 Declarations

The ALGOL W statements by which the data types of variables are defined are called declarations. If the language contained only simple data types, then it might be possible for the computer to determine the data type of each variable from the context of its use, although there would inevitably be cases in which real and integer variables could not be distinguished by their context, let alone long real variables. However, structured types require explicit definition, since these types require the specification of parameters in order to make them specific.

ALGOL W does not attempt to determine types on your behalf, but requires that you explicitly define the type of every variable by mentioning the variable name in a declaration.[1] Sometimes, you will find it annoying that the computer rejects your program for failure to declare the type of a variable, when you believe that a person of the meanest intelligence could have made a proper interpretation of the intended type from the context of use of the variable. But the requirement that variables be declared is really a blessing in disguise. At some time or other, you will make an error in typing the name of a variable, and will fail to detect the misspelling in reading over your program. The computer will not understand that you intended the variant in spelling to represent the same variable as one you had declared, and will send you a message marking the variant as an undeclared variable. This is doing you a favor, for if it did not send you such a message, it would proceed to compute, treating your misspelled variant as a new variable (probably not properly initialized), and might give you an erroneous result without notifying you. The undeclared variable message can prevent a trivial typing error from producing a more serious error of misinterpreting your algorithm.

A few examples of ALGOL W declarations are:

```
INTEGER I, J, K;
REAL X, Y, Z;
REAL ARRAY THREE_BY_THREE_MATRIX(1::3, 1::3);
STRING ARRAY NAMELIST (1::500);
LONG COMPLEX ARRAY POTENTIALGRID (-50::50, -100::100);
RECORD PERSON (STRING NAME; INTEGER AGE; LOGICAL MALE;
              REFERENCE (PERSON) FATHER, MOTHER,
              YOUNGESTOFFSPRING);
REFERENCE (PERSON) ADAM, EVE
```

A declaration consists of the simple type or structured type class name, followed by a list of the names of variables declared to have that type. In the case of array or record declarations, the type definition is completed by giving after the name of each structure, a parenthesized list of the parameters needed to complete the definition of the structure. For arrays, this is a list of pairs giving the upper and lower bounds of each index. For records, it is a list of the names and simple types of the variables that constitute an instance of a tuple belonging to the record class. Reference variables, while all belonging to the same simple type, are sorted into subsets according to the name of the record structure to which each reference variable refers. In the declaration of a reference variable, the record name is given in parentheses following the name of the reference variable.

----

(1) The sole exception to this rule occurs in the case of the control variable in a FOR clause. The appearance of an identifier following the keyword FOR causes the implicit declaration of a local variable of type integer.

One last point should be stressed. The order in which statements appear in a program is not necessarily the order in which they were conceived during the composition of the algorithm. Although declarations will appear in the text of a program preceding the algorithm step in which the declared variables are used, when composing a program you will ordinarily conceive the algorithm steps before writing out the declarations of all of the variables. Thus, when you do get around to giving the declarations, you will have in mind exactly the use to which each variable is to be put. Don't forget to tell your friends with comments! Commented declarations, telling the role of the principal variables, are just as important in documenting your algorithm as are comments on the executable statements.

5.4 Representing data with arrays

Arrays are extremely useful devices to have available in a programming language because the data of many diverse problems can be represented as indexed sets. Frequently, however, the problems that one faces do not dictate any unique form of representation of data; the choice of an appropriate data representation is one of the decisions to be made in the composition of an algorithm, and the choice can have a profound effect on the ease with which the remaining steps can be conceived, and upon the efficiency of execution of the final product.

Example 5.4.1 -- Finding the nth prime number.

The prime numbers are of central importance in number theory, and an obvious computational problem is to locate the nth prime in sequence. We shall first propose an algorithm for this problem that appears to be correct, but will be seen to fail because of the data representation chosen in it. A second algorithm, using a different representation of data will then be constructed.

The prime factorization theorem of number theory tells us that any positive integer can be represented as a product of prime factors, and that the factorization of a number into its prime factors is unique. We can use this knowledge to advantage in proposing a seemingly simple test of whether or not a number is prime. Since we know how to find the greatest common divisor of a pair of numbers (see Example 4.1.1), and we know that a given integer is prime if and only if the greatest common divisor of that integer with each smaller prime is unity, we can accomplish the test for primeness in a single application of the g.c.d. algorithm. He trick is this; keep a test integer which is the product of all previously found primes. Then a given number will be relatively prime with respect to all previously found primes if and only if the g.c.d. of the number with the product of previous primes is 1. In fact, we need not even test all integers for primeness, for since the first prime is 2, only the odd integers greater than 2 are possible candidates for primes. An algorithm to search through odd integers, counting primes found until the nth is reached (for n greater than 1) can be informally described by the following iteration graph

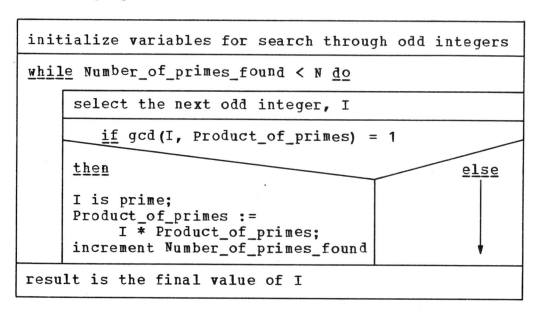

In this algorithm the variables needed will be integers N, I, Number_of_primes_found, and Product_of_primes. In translating the iteration graph to an ALGOL W program, if we decide to initialize the value of N, the index of the prime to be found, by a READ instruction, then the value received from the input should be checked to ensure that it is indeed a positive integer. We also include provision for the case N = 1, which is not covered by the iteration graph above, but which is valid as the index of a prime. The graph can be translated to:

```
BEGIN
    COMMENT**********************************************************
    *    PRIMES1:                                                   *
    *        N IS THE INDEX OF THE PRIME BEING SOUGHT,              *
    *        I IS AN INTEGER BEING TESTED FOR PRIMENESS,            *
    *        PRIMESFOUND RECORDS HOW MANY HAVE BEEN FOUND           *
    *        PRIMEPRODUCT RECORDS THE PRODUCT OF ALL ODD            *
    *              PRIMES FOUND PREVIOUSLY.                         *
    ***********************************************************;
    INTEGER N, I, PRIMESFOUND, PRIMEPRODUCT;
    READ (N);
    ASSERT N > 0;
    IF N = 1 THEN I := 2
    ELSE
        BEGIN COMMENT***** SEARCH ODD INTEGERS *****;
            I := PRIMEPRODUCT := PRIMESFOUND := 1;
            WHILE PRIMESFOUND < N DO
                BEGIN
                    I := I + 2;
                    IF gcd (I, PRIMEPRODUCT) = 1 THEN
                        BEGIN COMMENT*****I IS PRIME*****;
                            PRIMESFOUND := PRIMESFOUND + 1;
                            PRIMEPRODUCT := PRIMEPRODUCT * I;
                        END;
                END;
        END;
    WRITE ("PRIME", N, "IS", I);
END.
```

At the initialization step, a multiple assignment
statement is introduced. Multiple assignment allows a
common value to be assigned to several variables in a single
statement. The order in which the assignments are performed
is from right to left. In this algorithm, the program to
compute the function gcd has not been specified. However,
it can be filled in later if we are satisfied with the rest
of the algorithm. This will be a technique often used as it
enables us to concentrate our attention first on the
fundamental questions.

As it stands, it appears that the algorithm will be
effective, but if we were to submit it to the computer and
ask for the evaluation of several primes, we would discover
that it can only determine values for the first ten of them!
What has gone wrong? The difficulty is with the
representation of the values of all previously found primes
in the form of a product. The product of the first ten odd
primes is

$$3*5*7*11*13*17*19*23*29 \;\;=\;\; 3,534,515,985$$

which is already greater than the largest value than an ALGOL W variable of type integer can have. The specific limitation on the largest representable integer is due to the particular computer on which the computation is done, but the limitation of the algorithm is not. Using the largest computer in existence would only enable a few more primes to be evaluated by this algorithm. In trying to put all of the information about previously calculated primes into a single number, we have accumulated an amount of information that requires a very large number for its representation. The use of a product to represent all previously found primes is a form of information encoding. Encoding can be a useful way to represent information in the computer, but one must be aware of a practical limit on how much information can successfully be encoded into a single number.

Let us start over again to compose an algorithm to find the Nth prime. Perhaps a more suitable way to keep track of previously found primes will be to treat them as an indexed set of integers, and to define a singly-indexed array to represent this set. We shall also need an integer value to record the number of primes found so far.

```
INTEGER ARRAY PRIME (1::1000);
INTEGER PRIMESFOUND;
```

The size of the array limits our algorithm to the first thousand primes, but if this limit is too small, it can easily be set as large as it desired.

Next in the algorithm should come some steps that initialize PRIMESFOUND and if necessary, the first few elements of the table. These initialization steps will be filled in later when we know what values should be assigned. Right now, suppose that the table contains some primes already known, and that the Nth prime is desired. It might be that it is already in the table.

```
IF PRIMESFOUND < N THEN more primes must be computed
ELSE the Nth prime = PRIME(N).
```

To compute the additional primes will be an iterative procedure. It should be continued until the number of primes in the table includes the Nth:

```
WHILE PRIMESFOUND < N DO. . .
```

The sequence of steps to be iterated should produce the next prime, the one following the last insertion in the table of primes. To obtain this, it would be sufficient to start counting through all the positive integers, and test each against all of the primes already in the table. The first integer that passes the test will be the next prime to be inserted into the table. However, as was already noted in considering the previous algorithm, the only even prime is two, so only odd integers greater than one need be checked. Also, there is no point in reviewing candidates that have already been checked in the course of previous searches for primes. Thus, the first candidate that needs to be checked will be given by adding two to the value of the last prime entered in the table;

    I := PRIME(PRIMESFOUND) + 2.

    At this point in the evolution of an algorithm, it is useful to summarize the structure we have designed so far by giving an iteration graph.

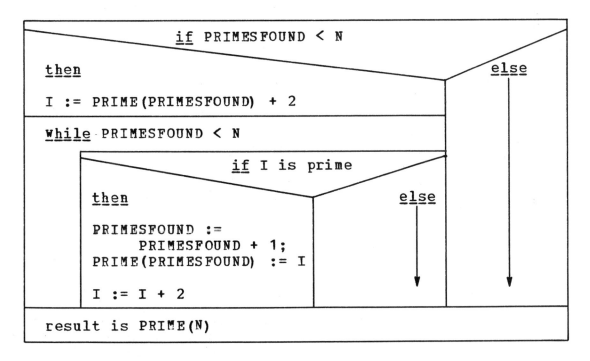

From the iteration graph it is apparent that the step remaining to be developed is the test to determine whether or not a particular value of the candidate I is prime.

Since no even integers have been considered as candidates, there is no point in testing any candidate to see whether it is divisible by two. The testing can begin with the second prime, which is 3. Also, a little thought will tell us that if a candidate passes the test of having no prime divisors up to a certain point in the table, then none of the remaining primes in the table can be a divisor either. It should not be hard to convince yourself that for any positive integer which is not a prime, at least one of its prime factors is less than or equal to its square root. With this fact in mind, we see that in testing a number to see if it has any prime factors (other than itself), it will be sufficient to test only those primes that are less than or equal to the square root of the number. If none of these primes is a factor, then the smallest prime factor must be the number itself.

Since it appears that the test 'I is prime', as given in the iteration graph above cannot be done by a single expression, we should perhaps modify the graph slightly, replacing

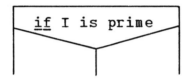

by

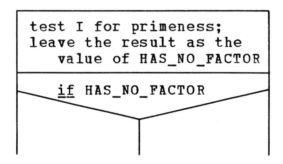

Turning our attention to the operation 'test I for primeness', we know from the preceding discussion that this test can be carried out by determining whether I can be divided by any of the primes starting with 3 and which are less than or equal to 1. In case any of these primes does divide I, then the test can be terminated, with the outcome that I is not prime. Otherwise, the test will be completed when the designated list of primes has been exhausted, and it has been found that none is a factor of I. Informally, the test can be represented as

test I for primeness:

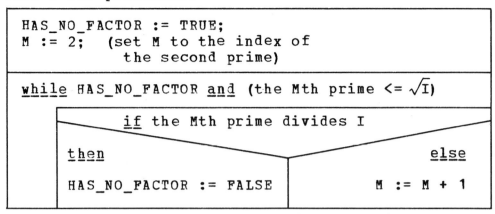

In translating this iteration graph into an ALGOL W program segment a few changes of form can be made. First of all, an easy way to tell whether the Mth prime is less than or equal to the square root of I, without actually evaluating the square root function, is to compare the square of the Mth prime with I itself. The iteration control clause can be written as

    WHILE HAS_NO_FACTOR AND (PRIME(M)*PRIME(M) <= I) DO

Secondly, ALGOL W contains an integer division function, REM, which evaluates the remainder in a division. A test of whether or not one integer divides another is to determine if the remainder is zero in an integer division. Thus, 'the Mth prime divides I' can be translated to

    I REM PRIME(M) = 0

Employing these modifications which take advantage of the programming language capabilities and allow all of the computation to be done using only integer arithmetic, 'test I for primeness' becomes the ALGOL W program segment

```
HAS_NO_FACTOR := TRUE;
M := 2;
WHILE HAS_NO_FACTOR AND (PRIME(M)*PRIME(M) <= I) DO
   IF I REM PRIME(M) = 0 THEN
      HAS_NO_FACTOR := FALSE
   ELSE
      M := M + 1;
```

Translation of the iteration graph describing the entire algorithm is now straightforward. Of course, in the translation, a program prefix must be added, in which variables are declared, some values are set initially, data are read and tested, and comments are inserted. This necessary but somewhat verbose portion of the program text may be as lengthy as the portion which translates the iteration graph.

```
BEGIN
    COMMENT*****************************************************************
    *     PRIME2:   GIVEN N, TO LOCATE THE NTH PRIME NUMBER              *
    *        N IS THE INDEX OF THE PRIME TO BE LOCATED,                  *
    *        I IS AN ODD INTEGER, A CANDIDATE FOR A PRIME,               *
    *        PRIME IS AN ARRAY RECORDING PRIMES ALREADY FOUND,           *
    *        M IS AN INDEX INTO THE ARRAY,                               *
    *        PRIMESFOUND IS THE NUMBER OF PRIMES ALREADY LOCATED,        *
    *        HAS_NO_FACTOR IS A LOGICAL FLAG USED TO RECORD THE          *
    *                OUTCOME OF TESTING I FOR PRIMENESS.                 *
    ******************************************************************;
    INTEGER N, I, M, PRIMESFOUND;
    INTEGER ARRAY PRIME (1::1000);
    LOGICAL HAS_NO_FACTOR;
    COMMENT*****************************************************************
    *  INITIALIZE THE TABLE OF PRIMES TO CONTAIN 2 AND THE FIRST *
    *  ODD PRIME.   INITIALIZE THE TABLE SIZE ACCORDINGLY        *
    ******************************************************************;
    PRIME(1)  := 2;
    PRIME(2)  := 3;
    PRIMESFOUND := 2;
    READ (N);
    ASSERT (N > 0) AND (N <= 1000);
    IF PRIMESFOUND < N THEN
        BEGIN
            COMMENT*******************************************
            *     SEARCH THE ODD INTEGERS, STARTING        *
            *     FROM THE LAST PRIME FOUND PREVIOUSLY     *
            ***********************************************;
            I := PRIME(PRIMESFOUND) + 2;
            WHILE PRIMESFOUND < N DO
                BEGIN
                    HAS_NO_FACTOR := TRUE;
                    M := 2;
                    WHILE HAS_NO_FACTOR AND (PRIME(M)*PRIME(M) <=I) DO
                        IF I REM PRIME(M) = 0 THEN
                            HAS_NO_FACTOR := FALSE
                        ELSE
                            M := M + 1;
```

94

```
        IF HAS_NO_FACTOR THEN
             BEGIN  COMMENT***** I IS PRIME *****;
                PRIMESFOUND := PRIMESFOUND + 1;
                PRIME(PRIMESFOUND) := I;
             END;
          I := I + 2;
       END;
    END;
  WRITE ("PRIME", N, "IS", PRIME(N));
END.
```

   If one can think of a satisfactory data representation, then
it is often possible to devise computational algorithms for tasks
that are not always obvious applications of computation.   For
instance, in doing algebraic operations on polynomials in one
variable, we are accustomed to spreading the calculations out
over a piece of paper in order to keep separate the terms of
different powers in the variable.   But another representation
might use indices to keep track of powers.   In manipulating
polynomials in a single variable, the variable name is of no
importance whatever, and need not be represented.   The individual
arithmetic operations are all performed on the coefficients of
the various powers, which are just numbers.   So it seems that
operations on polynomials should be able to be performed by
algorithms in which the only primitive operations required are
operations on numbers.

   Example 5.4.2 -- Multiplication of polynomials

      In representing polynomials in a single variable, the
name of the variable is of no importance, only the powers
appearing in the various terms and their coefficients need
to be remembered.   An easy way to represent a polynomial is
by a singly indexed array of numbers.   If the indices start
from 0, then the index of each element can represent the
power of the variable in a corresponding term of the
polynomial, and the value of each element is the
coefficient.   Since negative coefficients can be
represented, let us adopt the convention that the polynomial
is the sum of products of coefficients and powers of the
variable, then we won't have to worry about some terms being
added and others subtracted.   Various representations of an
abstract polynomial in one variable are

$$a_n x^n + a_{n-1} x^{n-1} + \ldots + a_1 x + a_0 \quad \text{(expanded pencil-and-paper representation)}$$

$$\sum_{i=0}^{n} a_i x^i \qquad \text{(pencil-and-paper representation in summation form)}$$

95

```
INTEGER ARRAY  A(0::N);   (ALGOL W  representation  as  an
                           array of coefficients).
```

To make these representations fit a concrete example, we
must give values to the coefficients;

$x^3 + 12x^2 - 9x + 22$ (expanded representation)

$$\sum_{i=0}^{3} a_i x^i,$$ where $a_0 = 22$, $a_1 = -9$, $a_2 = 12$, and $a_3 = 1$

(summation representation)

```
INTEGER ARRAY A(0::3);
A(0) := 22; A(1) := -9; A(2) := 12; A(3) := 1;
                         (ALGOL W representation).
```

Now let us think about the operation of multiplying two
polynomials in the same variable. When this operation is
carried out with pencil on paper, we are accustomed to
writing down successively a list of polynomials, each
obtained by multiplying the entire first polynomial by a
single term of the second. These intermediate polynomials
are then summed, using the rule that coefficients of terms
of similar power in the variable are added. As an aid in
keeping the terms of dissimilar powers separated, the whole
computation is spread out over the paper like this:

$$
\begin{array}{rrrrrr}
      & x^3 & +\ 12x^2 & -\ 9x & +\ 22 \\
      &   & 3x^2   &   & -\ 2 \\
\hline
 -    & 2x^3 & -\ 24x^2 & +\ 18x & -\ 44 \\
3x^5 + 36x^4 & -\ 27x^3 & +\ 66x^2 & & \\
\hline
3x^5 + 36x^4 & -\ 29x^3 & +\ 42x^2 & +\ 18x & -\ 44
\end{array}
$$

The calculation looks very much like the way we would do a
long multiplication of integers on paper, but in fact, it is
easier than multiplying integers because there is no carry
from one column to the next in adding polynomials. Thus, it
is not really necessary to follow any fixed order in
deciding which column to total first. Also, notice that as
soon as any of the coefficients of one of the intermediate
polynomials has been included in the summation of the column
to which it belongs, that coefficient is no longer needed.
This suggests that in an algorithm for the computer, where
it requires a little bit of effort to write down an
intermediate result and recall it later, that we might as
well incorporate these intermediate coefficients into the
final sum as soon as they have been found. This idea can be
expressed concisely in the mathematical summation notation

as

$$c_k = \sum_j a_{k-j} b_j$$

where polynomials being multiplied are represented by coefficients a_i and b_j, and c_k is the coefficient of the term of kth power in the product. In the informal summation notation, it is to be understood that the sum is carried out over all indices for which it makes sense. In a computational algorithm, we must be more specific.

Let us study polynomial multiplication in the pencil and paper representation, and attempt to identify the indices of terms in the summation of intermediate products.

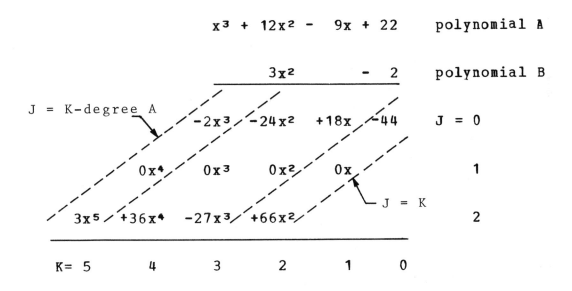

Here we have indicated by indices J and K the rows to be summed, corresponding to powers from 0 to the degree of polynomial B, and the columns, corresponding to powers from 0 to the degree of the product polynomial. The row indices over which a sum in each column is to be carried out would be from 0 to degree B if it were not for the diagonal sides of the trapezoidal array of coefficients. However, the equations of these diagonal lines can be given; the line on the right side is specified by pairs (J, K) which satisfy J = K, and on the left by pairs which satisfy J = K - degree A.

Therefore, from this simple analysis of the sum in diagrammatic form on paper, we can determine limits for the summation indices, obtaining

$$c_k = \sum_{\max(0,\,k-\text{degree A})}^{\min(k,\,\text{degree B})} a_{k-j}\,b_j$$

An ALGOL W program segment to carry out the multiplication is:

```
BEGIN
    COMMENT**********************************************************
    *   POLYNOMIAL MULTIPLICATION:                                 *
    *     MULTIPLIES A PAIR OF POLYNOMIALS WHOSE INTEGER           *
    *     COEFFICIENTS ARE REPRESENTED BY THE VECTORS 'A' AND*
    *     'B'.  THE RESULT IS REPRESENTED BY THE VECTOR 'C'. *
    *     THE DEGREES OF THE POLYNOMIALS ARE GIVEN AS THE          *
    *     VALUES OF DEGREE_A, DEGREE_B, AND DEGREE_C.              *
    ***************************************************************;
    INTEGER ARRAY A, B, C (0::50);
    INTEGER DEGREE_A, DEGREE_B, DEGREE_C;
    initialize A, B, DEGREE_A, AND DEGREE_B;
    DEGREE_C := DEGREE_A + DEGREE_B;
    ASSERT DEGREE_C <= 50;
    FOR K := 0 UNTIL DEGREE_C DO
        BEGIN
            C(K) := 0;
            FOR J := min(0, K - DEGREE_A) UNTIL
                min(K, DEGREE_B) DO
                C(K) := C(K) + A(K-J)*B(J);
        END;
    COMMENT***** OUTPUT RESULTS HERE *****;
END.
```

In the last example, we saw that the form of an algorithm for the computer could differ appreciably from a familiar pencil-and-paper algorithm for the same task, but that arraying intermediate results on paper can sometimes suggest an algorithm that we might not easily have discovered otherwise.

example 5.4.3 -- Evaluation of binomial coefficients.

From high school algebra, you are familiar with the binomial expansion, and probably remember that a formula for the coefficient of the rth power of x in the expansion of $(x + 1)^n$ is

$$\binom{n}{r} = \frac{n!}{r!\,(n-r)!}$$

where N!, read as 'N factorial', stands for the product 1*2*3*...*N. An obvious algorithm for the evaluation of $\binom{n}{r}$ is

```
INTEGER N, R, BINOMIAL;
READ (N,R);
BINOMIAL := 1;
FOR I := N STEP -1 UNTIL N - R + 1 DO
    BINOMIAL := I*BINOMIAL;
FOR I := 1 UNTIL R DO
    BINOMIAL := BINOMIAL DIV I
```

This computes the product n*(n-1)*(n-2)* . . . . *(n-r+1) first, then divides it by r!

But this algorithm is not much good except for small values of n. It cannot even evaluate

$$\binom{13}{13}$$

because it must first compute 13!, which is larger than the maximum integer representable on the computer. Of course, we have not taken advantage of all we know about the binomial coefficients. In particular, we know there is a symmetry, that

$$\binom{n}{r} = \binom{n}{n-r}$$

and so the above algorithm could be improved by inserting after the READ step, the conditional statement

```
IF R > N DIV 2 THEN R := N - R.
```

Then the number accumulated in the first iterated step will have the fewest possible factors. However, even this improvement does not help much, for

$$\binom{17}{8}$$

cannot be computed by the improved algorithm, although its value is 31310 which is much less than the maximum representable integer value of 2,147,483,647.[2]
It seems that the algorithm fails for large n by computing a numerator much larger than will be the final result, then dividing it by a succession of factors to reduce its size. Is there a different way to compute binomial coefficients?

----

[2] This is the maximum integer representable in the ALGOL W implementation for the IBM 360 or 370 series computers.

Suppose we consider a pencil-and-paper algorithm for expansion of a binomial by successive multiplications. If the expansion of $(x + 1)^{n-1}$ has been obtained, then to get $(x + 1)^n$, one more multiplication by $x + 1$ is performed. Writing out this multiplication by a pencil-and-paper algorithm, it looks like:

$$\binom{n-1}{0}x^{n-1} + \ldots \binom{n-1}{r-1}x^{n-r} + \binom{n-1}{r}x^{n-1-r} + \ldots + \binom{n-1}{n-2}x + \binom{n-1}{n-1}$$
$$\underline{ x + 1}$$
$$\binom{n-1}{0}x^{n-1} + \ldots \binom{n-1}{r-1}x^{n-r} + \ldots \ldots \ldots + \binom{n-1}{n-2}x + \binom{n-1}{n-1}$$
$$\underline{\binom{n-1}{0}x^{n} + \binom{n-1}{1}x^{n-1} + \ldots \binom{n-1}{r}x^{n-r} + \ldots \ldots \ldots + \binom{n-1}{n-1}x}$$
$$\binom{n-1}{0}x^{n} + \ldots \ldots + \ldots \left[\binom{n-1}{r-1} + \binom{n-1}{r}\right]x^{n-r} + \ldots \ldots \ldots \ldots + \binom{n-1}{n-1}$$

From this display, we can see a recurrence relation that is satisfied by the binomial coefficients:

$$\binom{n}{r} = \binom{n-1}{r} + \binom{n-1}{r-1}$$

The extremal coefficients, $\binom{n}{0}$ and $\binom{n}{n}$ are 1 for any n. Thus, the formula for the binomial coefficients in terms of factorial functions is a concise representation, but it does not provide the only means for their evaluation. The recurrence relation suggests a different form of iterative calculation.

When the iterative calculation of the binomial coefficients is carried out by hand, the results can be displayed in an attractive array that we know as Pascal's triangle.

```
                          1
                       1     1
                    1     2     1
                 1     3     3     1
              1     4     6     4     1
           1     5    10    10     5     1
        1     6    15    20    15     6     1
     1     7    21    35    35    21     7     1
  1     8    28    56    70    56    28     8     1
1     9    36    84   126   126 . . . . . .
```

However, if our purpose is to evaluate a single binomial coefficient, we should not try to duplicate Pascal's triangle, for that will require that a large number of coefficients must be remembered when we are ultimately interested in only one. By displaying Pascal's triangle in a somewhat less elegant form, it is easy to see which terms a given coefficient depends on.

```
n=0 |  1
  1 |  1   1
  2 |  1   2   1
  3 |  1   3   3   1
  4 |  1   4   6   4   1
  5 |  1   5  10  10   5   1
  6 |  1   6  15  20  15   6   1
  7 |  1   7  21  35   .   .   .   .
    |_____
   r= 0   1   2   3   4   5   6   7
```

The diagram above illustrates the succession of terms needed in the evaluation of $\binom{7}{3}$.

A logical way to compute the terms of Pascal's triangle is row by row. Within each row, the terms might be computed from left to right,

```
 1      6     15     20     15      6      1
 1      7     21     35
```

or from right to left,

```
 1      6     15     20     15      6      1
                     35     35     21      7      1
```

If the evaluation is done right to left, then the values of the preceding row which lie to the right of the element being computed need not be remembered, for they will not be

101

used again. The "old" values of elements of the preceding row could be crossed out and replaced by newly calculated elements, allowing the entire computation to use only a single row for remembering values,

<u>1</u>   <u>6</u>   <u>15</u>   35   35   21   7   1

The array shown above represents a partial computation of the seventh row of Pascal's triangle. The elements underlined are elements of row six which have not yet been replaced. The next element of row seven that will be calculated is the third. Its values will depend on elements two and three from row six, whose values still remain available in the array.

The conservation of space needed to remember intermediate values of the computation is unimportant in a pencil-and-paper calculation, for the amount of paper that could be saved is not worth the added effort of erasing. But in programming a computer to do the same computation, the amount of memory space may be limited, and it is worthwhile giving a little thought as to how it might be conserved. The algorithm we have just developed by considering examples can now be given as an ALGOL W program. In this case, we shall not go through the step of giving an iteration graph, because the iteration required is just to sequence through the rows and columns of Pascal's triangle, as represented by the diagram on the preceding page. We must take care that the unit values that occupy the borders of the triangle are properly set.

```
BEGIN
    COMMENT*****************************************************************
    *    PASCAL1:                                                         *
    *       EVALUATES BINOMIAL (N, R) BY CALCULATION OF THE NTH           *
    *       ROW OF PASCAL'S TRIANGLE.  AS EACH SUCCEEDING ROW             *
    *       IS COMPUTED, ITS VALUES REPLACE THOSE OF THE PRE-             *
    *       VIOUSLY COMPUTED ROW IN THE VECTOR 'PASCAL'                   *
    ******************************************************************;
    INTEGER ARRAY PASCAL (0::40);
    INTEGER N, R;
    READ (N, R);
    ASSERT (R >= 0) AND (N >= R) AND (N <= 40);
    PASCAL(0) := 1;
    FOR ROW := 1 UNTIL N DO
        BEGIN
            PASCAL(ROW) := 1;
            FOR I := ROW - 1 STEP -1 UNTIL 1 DO
                PASCAL(I) := PASCAL(I) + PASCAL(I-1);
        END;
    WRITE ("BINOMIAL COEFFICIENT (", N, R, ") EQUALS", PASCAL(R));
END.
```

5.5   Analyzing character strings

There are a great many computing applications which either
do not involve numbers at all, or in which numerical computation
comprises only a relatively small part of the overall task. Most
such applications involve analysis, storage, and transformation
of data represented by character strings.   To some extent, a
computer can also be programmed to interpret the data represented
by strings, although more frequently, the final interpretation of
such data is left to a human reader.

It is at first surprising that computations on character
strings are of much practical importance, because the algebra of
operations that can be performed on strings is so much less
powerful than the algebra of numbers. The basic operations on
strings are <u>selection</u> of a substring of one or more strings, and
<u>catenation</u>, whereby two strings are laid end-to-end to form a
longer string. Indeed, in the early days of computing, not much
attention was paid to string processing. However, the importance
of character strings as data representation is exactly that this
is the representation most often chosen by humans for most
transactions which are not intrinsically numerical, and for some
that are.

ALGOL W does not directly support all of the operations that
can be defined upon character strings, but it defines enough
operations that when they are used in conjunction with iterative
control, any definable string operation can be accomplished. The
ALGOL W string operations are selection of a fixed-length
substring,   (see section A7.5 of the Appendix), assignment
(including assignment to a substring), and comparison (see A7.2).
The following example will illustrate some of the basic uses of
these operations.

<u>Example 5.5.1</u> -- Picking words out of a line of text

A line of text is merely a string of characters, of
some predetermined length.   Normally, one or more blank
characters are used to separate words in the text, and a
word consists of any unbroken sequence of non-blank
characters. By this definition, we include a lot of 'words'
that would not be well-formed in any natural language, let
alone meaningful, but it would be asking too much of the
computer to make a judgment about which words were
meaningful in the English language and which were not.   To
keep the problem simple, we shall not even require that
punctuation marks or invalid characters be distinguished.
It is not hard to describe in informal terms an iterative
algorithm for extracting words. An iteration graph for such
an algorithm is:

```
┌─────────────────────────────────────────────────┐
│ read a new line of text                          │
├─────────────────────────────────────────────────┤
│ while not at the end of the line                 │
│   ┌───────────────────────────────────────────┐  │
│   │ scan across any blanks;                   │  │
│   │ copy a substring of non-blanks,           │  │
│   │    calling it WORD;                        │  │
│   │ print (WORD)                              │  │
│   └───────────────────────────────────────────┘  │
└─────────────────────────────────────────────────┘
```

Each of these informally described operations can be translated using the ALGOL W string operators, although some of these operations will not translate to single statements. To begin with, the strings that we intend to work with must be declared. Let us suppose that the string length of a line of text is not longer than 72 characters. This also restricts the length of a word, by the definition given above. The string variables needed are:

        STRING (72) TEXTLINE, WORD

In addition to the string variables, we shall need a marker to keep track of the position of individual characters within each string. Let these be designated as TP (for Text Pointer) and WP (for Word Pointer).

        INTEGER TP, WP

When a new line of text is read, but before any analysis is done, the Text Pointer variable must be initialized to mark the first character of the text string.

        READ (TEXTLINE);
        TP := 0

The use of the Text Pointer also suggests a means of performing the test to tell whether or not the end of the line has been reached. The condition "not at the end of the line" can be expressed by

        TP < 72

The operation "scan across any blanks" cannot be realized by the execution of any single, unconditional ALGOL W statement. The operation of scanning can be realized by iteratively incrementing the position of the Text Pointer. The iteration control should apparently test the condition that the character selected by the Text Pointer is or is not a blank. Since one cannot tell in advance how far to scan before encountering a non-blank character, the iteration control must be a WHILE clause. The statement

```
WHILE TEXTLINE (TP|1) = " " DO
    TP := TP + 1
```

increments the Text Pointer so long as the single character (substring of length 1) indexed by the Text Pointer is a blank. However, in case the statement is ever executed when the unscanned portion of TEXTLINE contains only blanks, the iteration will not terminate normally, but will be terminated by a substring indexing error when the value of TP reaches 72. To prevent this, the end-of-string test should be included as a termination condition for the iteration:

```
WHILE (TP < 72) AND (TEXTLINE (TP|1) = " ") DO
    TP := TP + 1
```

After executing the iterative statement that calls for scanning across blanks, the Text Pointer will either be positioned at the end of the string, or at a non-blank character, the beginning of a word. In the latter case, a copy is to be made of the word, into the string whose name is WORD. Once again, we face the condition that we do not have prior knowledge of the length of the word, and must therefore copy it character-by-character. The end of the word will be detected either by the occurrence of another blank character in TEXTLINE, or by the end-of-line condition. Before beginning to copy the word, it will be advantageous to set WORD to an all blank string, like beginning with a clean sheet of paper. We must also not forget to initialize the Word Pointer to indicate the initial character of WORD.

```
WORD := " ";  WP := 0;
WHILE (TP < 72) AND (TEXTLINE (TP|1) ¬= " ") DO
    BEGIN
        WORD (WP|1) := TEXTLINE (TP|1);
        TP := TP + 1;  WP := WP + 1;
    END
```

The last operation, that of printing WORD, is elementary.

```
WRITE (WORD)
```

When the ALGOL W program segments for the operations indicated by the iteration graph are joined together, the following program is the result.

```
BEGIN
    COMMENT***************************************************************
    *   FIND AND PRINT THE NON-BLANK 'WORDS' FROM AN INPUT STRING *
    ****************************************************************;
    STRING (72) TEXTLINE, WORD;
    INTEGER TP, WP;
    READ (TEXTLINE);
    TP := 0;
    WHILE TP < 72 DO
        BEGIN
            WHILE (TP < 72) AND (TEXTLINE (TP|1) = " ") DO
                TP := TP + 1;
            WORD := " ";
            WP := 0;
            WHILE (TP < 72) AND (TEXTLINE (TP|1) ¬= " ") DO
                BEGIN
                    WORD (WP|1) := TEXTLINE (TP|1);
                    TP := TP + 1;
                    WP := WP + 1;
                END;
            WRITE (WORD);
        END;
END.
```

5.6   Sorting

The simplest order that can be defined on the items of a
list is a total ordering, in which an ordering relation is
defined between values of every pair of elements on the list. If
the order of appearance of the elements on the list satisfies the
ordering relation among their values, then the list is said to be
sorted.   The entries in a dictionary are sorted by lexicographic
order; the words in this paragraph are not. Sorting a list is
one of the common operations performed, although it is by no
means as simple as inserting or deleting a single element. There
have been numerous algorithms developed for sorting, volumes
written on the subject, and thousands of years worth of
accumulated human effort spent developing and analyzing sorting
algorithms. We shall consider the topic very briefly.

In sorting a small set of fixed size, such as a bridge hand
of 13 cards, it may be possible to scan the entire set with a
single glance, and to improve the sequencing by making judicious
removals and reinsertions of elements without following any fixed
algorithm. But for the computer whose powers of observation are
more limited than our own, or even for ourselves if the set of
objects is too large to scan all at once, it is necessary to
employ a more systematic approach. We shall assume that the
largest scope of a single reordering operation is limited to the

comparison of two objects, interchanging their positions in the list if they are not already in proper sequence. Informally, this algorithm step can be described as follows:

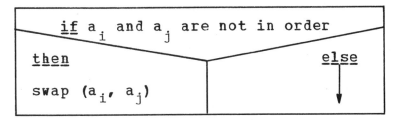

where the list is represented in an indexed set $\{a_i\}$, and the operation <u>swap</u> means to interchange the indices on the two elements.

To make the operation more precise in ALGOL W notation, suppose that the list is represented by the array A, and that the desired order is that the lesser value should have the lesser index. Then, if indices I and J have been selected so that I < J, the fundamental operation is:

```
reorder (I, J):
        IF  A(I) > A(J) THEN
          BEGIN
            TEMPORARY := A(I);
            A(I)  := A(J);
            A(J)  := TEMPORARY;
          END
```

in which TEMPORARY is the name of a variable used to hold one of the two values during the exchange, so that it will not be lost. For simplicity, we shall refer to this program segment by its name, <u>reorder</u>, in the development of the sorting algorithm instead of writing it out in full. However, the indices of the elements to be reordered will not always be I and J, so the actual indices will be given in parentheses after the name <u>reorder</u>.

Since one must begin somewhere, it seems that a suitable way to start a sorting algorithm might be to bring the last element to the head of the list, which is its desired position. If we knew how to do this, then the job of sorting the whole list would have been partially accomplished, for all that would remain to be done would be to sort the remaining list, which begins at the second element position. This idea suggests an approach to an iterative algorithm,

107

```
for I := 1 until LISTSIZE

    bring to position I the least element of the
    sublist extending from position I to position
    LISTSIZE
```

Next, we shall focus our attention on the task of locating
the least element of the specified sublist, and bringing it to
the head of that sublist. Having no prior knowledge of either
the value of the least element or of its position in the list, it
will be necessary to scan the whole sublist. One way to
accomplish this, using the operation reorder, is to begin at the
end of the list and work toward the top, comparing adjacent list
elements. Wherever the least element is initially encountered,
successive applications of reorder will sweep it along toward
ever lower indexed positions until it finally reaches the head of
the sublist. This process may be compared to that of an air
bubble rising in a glass of water, and gives the algorithm its
name, bubble sort. If the list is represented by the array

STRING ARRAY NAME (1::LISTSIZE)

then the iteration control needed to bring the least element to
the Ith position will be

```
for J := LISTSIZE step -1 until I+1

    reorder (J-1, J)
```

In composing the two iteration graphs, a slight improvement
in the iteration control can be made. To see what it is,
consider the case of a list of only two elements, LISTSIZE = 2.
Then the first iteration control is

for I := 1 until 2

However, only a single application of reorder is required to sort
a two-element list, and we realize that the range of the
iteration control variable is one greater than it would need to
be. By letting this range extend only as far as the head of a
sublist of length two, the iteration control of the bubble sort
algorithm is represented by the following iteration graph

```
for I := 1 until LISTSIZE - 1

    for J := LISTSIZE step -1 until I + 1

        reorder (J-1, J)
```

Before concluding this example by encoding the algorithm as
an ALGOL W program, it will be worthwhile to investigate the
dynamic behavior of its control structure, and to see if by
mathematical reasoning we can verify that it is correct. The
effect of the first iteration control is to partition the list
into an initial sublist on which sorting has been completed, and
a terminal sublist on which sorting is to be done.

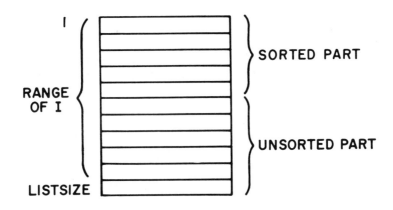

As a hypothesis, let us assume that the elements of the sorted
sublist are indexed in ascending order, and furthermore, that
every element in the sorted sublist is less than or equal to the
least element of the unsorted sublist in value. The operation
that is under control of the first iteration control is the
selection of the least element of the unsorted sublist, and its
transfer to the Ith position in the list. If this operation were
done, then the initial sublist extended by the Ith element would
have the property that we took as a hypothesis. Thus, by the
principal of mathematical induction, if the operation is applied
LISTSIZE - 1 times, the entire list will have the sorted
property, save possibly for the sublist of length one at the very
end. But since the value of the least (and only) element of this
sublist is greater than or equal to the value of all preceding
elements, the sorted property will in fact apply to the entire
list.

Having thus established that bringing the least element of a
terminal sublist to the head of that sublist is an operation that
will assure the success of the sorting algorithm, let us examine
the effect of the second iteration control. It applies the

109
```
```

operation <u>reorder</u> to a succession of element pairs, beginning with indices LISTSIZE and LISTSIZE - 1, and extending to indices I + 1 and I.

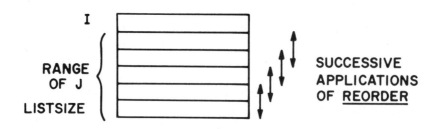

As a hypothesis, let us assume that the least element of the sublist headed by the index J occupies the head of that sublist. Since an application of <u>reorder</u> (J-1, J) will exchange the values of the J-1st and the Jth elements if the former is larger, performing this operation will ensure that the hypothesized property holds for the terminal sublist headed by the J-1st element. If J ranges from LISTSIZE down to I + 1, then the iteration over these indices in decreasing order will establish the hypothesized property for the terminal sublist headed by the Ith element.

One more property is required of a sorting algorithm. The set of values constituting a list must be left unchanged by the sorting operation; only their order of appearance in the list is to be altered. Obviously, the iteration control cannot establish whether or not the algorithm has this property. The <u>reorder</u> operation is the only one in the algorithm which changes the content of any cell of the list. The correctness of the <u>reorder</u> operation is easily verified by hand simulation on a couple of examples. That form of verification is sufficient for <u>reorder</u>, since it does not involve any iteration, and there are only two typical cases on which to try it, one in which the initial value of NAME(J-1) is greater in order than the initial value of NAME(J), and one in which it is not.

An ALGOL W program obtained by translation of the iteration graphs is

```
BEGIN
    COMMENT***********************************************************
    * BUBBLESORT:                                                   *
    *    SORTS A LIST OF CHARACTER STRINGS REPRESENTED              *
    *    BY THE ARRAY 'NAME'.  TO ADAPT THE ALGORITHM TO SORT       *
    *    A LIST OF ANOTHER TYPE, THE DECLARATIONS OF 'NAME' AND*
    *    OF 'TEMPORARY' MUST BE MODIFIED.                           *
    *       FIRST, THE ARRAY IS INITIALIZED BY READING INPUT.  *
    ***********************************************************;
    STRING ARRAY NAME (1::1000);
    STRING TEMPORARY;
    INTEGER LISTSIZE;
    READ (LISTSIZE);
    ASSERT (LISTSIZE > 0) AND (LISTSIZE <= 1000);
    FOR I := 1 UNTIL LISTSIZE -1 DO
        BEGIN
            READ (NAME(I));
            WRITE (NAME(I));
        END;
    COMMENT***** THE ACTUAL SORTING ALGORITHM BEGINS HERE *****;
    FOR I := 1 UNTIL LISTSIZE -1 DO
        FOR J := LISTSIZE STEP -1 UNTIL I + 1 DO
            IF NAME(J-1) > NAME(J) THEN
                BEGIN
                    TEMPORARY := NAME(J-1);
                    NAME(J-1) := NAME(J);
                    NAME(J)   := TEMPORARY;
                END;
    COMMENT***** SORTING IS DONE, PRINT THE RESULT *****;
    WRITE ("THE SORTED LIST IS:");
    FOR I := 1 UNTIL LISTSIZE DO
        WRITE (NAME(I));
END.
```

It is interesting to consider the efficiency of our sorting algorithm. Consider for the moment just the innermost iteration, the one that selects the least element of a sublist and sweeps it to the head of that sublist. This operation requres $N - 1$ applications of <u>reorder</u>. If no more than a pair of elements can be compared in a single operation of comparison, then it is not hard to prove (although we do not prove it here) that $N - 1$ comparisons are necessary just to select the least element from a set of size N. Since the bubble sort does not use more than this number of iterations of <u>reorder</u>, its efficiency cannot be improved upon by any algorithm that uses a basic comparison step like <u>reorder</u>.

How about the whole sorting algorithm; is its efficiency optimal? Surprisingly, the answer is no, it is not even close to optimal. A full consideration of optimal sorting algorithms is beyond the scope of this book, but it is not hard to show how to effect a minor improvement over the efficiency of bubblesort, thereby establishing the fact of its non-optimality.

The reason that the whole sorting algorithm is not optimal is that while no fewer than N - 1 steps are necessary to sort out the least element, this number of steps can actually do more than that in terms of progress toward getting the whole list sorted. Our algorithm, bubblesort, does not make any use of the additional progress which may have been made. But suppose the N - 1 reordering steps required to sort out the least element were executed in a different sequence. For simplicity, suppose that the list to be sorted contains an even number of elements. Then to begin with, carry out N/2 reordering steps,

FOR J := 2 STEP 2 UNTIL N DO reorder (J-1, J).

After these steps, we don't yet know which index is that of the least element, but we do know that the index is odd. In addition we know that the index of the greatest element is even! There are N/2 odd elements, so to complete sorting out the least element of the original list, just treat the odd indexed elements as a list, and sort out its least element using bubblesort. This requires N/2 - 1 more reordering steps for a total of N - 1 steps expended to get the least element of the original list. However, we can also sweep the list of even indexed elements, sorting in reverse order now, to move the largest element to the end of the list. This can be done with an additional N/2 - 1 reorderings, so that only 3N/2 - 2 reordering steps have been used to get the two extremal elements to the ends of the list. This is fewer steps, for bubblesort requires (N - 1) + (N - 2), or 2N - 3 reorderings to separate out the first two elements. Needless to say, the modified algorithm is not optimal either, but it serves to illustrate the possibility of improvement in efficiency.

If sorting is such an important operation, and all kinds of sorting algorithms have been developed and studied, why doesn't everyone use whichever algorithm has been found to be the most efficient? There are a number of reasons. First of all, not everyone has the same sorting problem. In some applications, there is additional knowldge available about the values of the particular set to be sorted, that may be brought to bear to yield an algorithm very efficient for sorting that particular set. This algorithm may not be at all efficient for sorting some other set, for which the assumptions about the range or distribution of values do not hold. The algorithms we have considered do not assume, nor do they take advantage of, any prior information about the values of elements to be sorted.

Also, there are other considerations of efficiency besides just the number of comparisons to be made. Some of these are machine-dependent, that is, they depend on the physical characteristics of the particular device on which the information is stored. Manufacturers of computing equipment spend money for the development of algorithms that take advantage of the characteristics of the devices they manufacture, and suggest to their customers that they use these algorithms for efficient sorting. The customer, once he incorporates these algorithms into his library of programs, may become understandably reluctant to change algorithms or to change to another manufacturer's equipment!

And finally, efficiency is a relative thing. The algorithms that are the most efficient, in that they require fewer comparisons of elements to sort a list, only display efficiency when the size of the list is large. On lists of only a few tens of elements, the difference between the most efficient algorithm and bubblesort is only a few tens or hundreds of comparisons, and at the speed of modern computers, that difference is irrelevant. In fact, the so-called optimal algorithm may actually take more time to sort a small list, because the algorithm itself will be much more complicated than bubblesort. The extra overhead of initializing extra variables and testing extra conditions may use more time than is saved on doing fewer comparisons of elements. In practice, the degree of concern about efficiency depends on the magnitude of one's task.

Exercises for Chapter 5

5.1 The fundamental theorem of arithmetic tells us that every integer can be written as a product of primes, and that the factorization of a number into prime factors is unique. Compose an algorithm to find the prime factors of a positive integer, and use it to obtain the prime factors of 204, 13915, 22019, and 27648.

5.2 Every integer can be expressed as the product of a pair of integers, and for integers greater than one, the pair is not unique unless the number is a prime. Devise an algorithm that will give all pairs of factors of any positive integer and try it on the integers 204, 13915, 22019, and 27648.

5.3 Given a sequence of n elements, it is easy to generate permutations of the sequence by interchanging elements. It is not quite so easy to generate <u>all</u> of the n! possible permutations of the sequence. Compose an algorithm that will generate and print all possible permutations of a sequence represented as a vector of length n. Try it out by generating the 120 permutations of the sequence 1, 2, 3, 4, 5.

5.4 The binomial coefficients are important in combinatorial theory because the number of distinct ways of choosing a subset of r objects from a set of n, is the value of $\binom{n}{r}$. Several interesting problems are of this type.

a) A political banquet is being held for 100 loyal supporters of the party. The head table will seat only 10. How many ways are there to compose the group that will be seated at the head table?

b) The same political banquet is being held in a hall that has ten tables, each seating ten persons. If the tables are all alike, how many ways are there to compose the makeup of persons assigned to various tables?

c) The aforementioned banquet is being held for 100 people, to be seated at 10 tables of 10 persons each, and all tables are alike but one, that one being distinguished as the head table. How many ways are there to distribute the party regulars at tables? (Do you see how difficult it is to be a politician?)

5.5 For some combinatorial problems, it is difficult to give solutions in terms of simple formulae, but it is possible to compose an iterative algorithm to generate solutions.

a) A hostess is holding a dinner for an important group of guests, all of whom are arriving as couples. She has a long rectangular table and wishes to seat her husband at the head of it, herself at the foot, and the guests along each side in equal numbers. An additional constraint is that men and women are to be seated alternately around the table, and that no lady is to be seated next to her escort. How many seating arrangements are there if the number of diners (counting the hostess and her husband) is 6? How many for 8, 10, 12, 13, 16, 18 or 22 diners?

b) The hostess, having discovered a source of difficulty when the number of diners is divisible by four, has purchased a round table. No place is distinguished, but she still wishes men and women to be seated alternately, with no lady seated next to her escort. How many seating arrangements are possible for parties of the sizes given in part (a)?

5.6 Compose an algorithm to divide one polynomial by another, giving as results a quotient and a remainder polynomial.

5.7
a) Devise an algorithm that when presented with two lists of names, each sorted in alphabetical order, will merge them into a single list that is sorted in alphabetical order. (This operation on lists is known as merging).

b) Modify your algorithm of part (a) so that any name that appears on both of the original lists will appear only once on the merged list. This corresponds to taking the union of sets. It is an operation that should be used, for instance, in merging lists for direct mail advertising in order to avoid duplicate mailings.

5.8 Give as an ALGOL W program, an algorithm for sorting a list by using a binary selection of the largest and smallest elements, moving them to the ends of the list at each iteration.

5.9 Compose an ALGOL W program to

a) Read in a list of names in the format

firstname $\left\{ \begin{array}{c} \text{middlename} \\ \underline{or} \\ \text{middleinitial.} \end{array} \right\}$ lastname

where middlename is optional, middleinitial is optional, and in case middleinitial is present, the period which follows it is optional;

b) Sort the list into alphabetical order by last name, or if last names are the same, by first name and middle name (or initial).

c) Print the sorted list in the format
   lastname, firstname, middleinitial

d) Include in the test data the names
   JACK S. PHOGBOUND
   JUBILITATION T CORNPONE
   JOHN Q.PUBLIC (no space after the period; must be accepted)
   ABNER YOKUM
   DAISY MAE YOKUM
   U. R. STUCK (invalid format for firstname; must be rejected)
   (Hint: if the acceptable names are transformed into the desired format for output prior to sorting, the sorting operation will be easier to program).

5.10 Compose an ALGOL W program that will

a) Read in a sequence of data records, each record of the form of a name, given as a string of up to 36 characters, followed by a real number, representing the height in inches and tenths, of the individual named. Reading should terminate when a data record containing a zero height is encountered;

b) Compute the average height from the sequence read in (a);

c) Compute and print a distribution of the number of heights falling into each six-inch interval from 36 to 96 inches;

d) Compute and print the median value of height, and list the names of those individuals (there may be more than one) having the median height.

5.11 Given a list of names of persons, and a binary symmetric relation of friendship (if A is a friend of B, then B is a friend of A), find two names that have the greatest number of friends in common.

5.12 Use mathematical reasoning to prove that the algorithm of Example 5.5.1 always terminates normally.

NOTES

Chapter 6

GETTING INFORMATION IN AND OUT OF A COMPUTER

Since a computer has neither eyes, ears, fingers, nor tongue, we must put forth more effort to communicate with it than we are used to in conversing with our fellow human beings. When we input information to ourselves from the printed page, an enormous amount of information processing is done by our eyes and by a large portion of our brain that is specialized for vision, and does no 'thinking' in the usual sense. This magnificient structure of nerve cells enables us to perceive letters of the alphabet from a physical stimulus that consists of tiny patterns of light focused on the retinas of our eyes. Even though the images of a few words of text constitute only a very small part of the total visual stimulus, our visual information processing system is so effective that we are able to perceive whole groups of letters without conscious effort, and in a time so short that to us it seems immediate. This marvelous visual perceptual system is the end product of evolution since life began, and is not available on the latest models of electronic computers designed by man.

Instead of supplying the computer with a printed page, one must resort to cruder and less flexible media for passing information. First of all, we must agree on a standard, finite set of characters that we will have our computer recognize. Then, these characters can be encoded in some form acceptable to the computer. Depending on the conceptual level on which you are examining the computer, you may think of the encoded equivalent of a character as being an integer number, a sequence of binary bits, or as a sequence of electrical signals. By means of the encoding, it is possible to transmit sequences of characters to the computer from a terminal resembling an electric typewriter or from a punched card reader. Encoded sequences can be transmitted over telephone lines, by radio, from the next room, or halfway around the world. But these are technical matters, and the point to remember now is that the entire perceptual ability of a computer is limited to accepting input sequences formed from a prescribed set of characters. Our communication with the computer is always subject to this limitation, although it can be partially overcome by devising algorithms to enable the computer to interpret the input sequences in a way we desire.

Another obligation we incur if we wish to communicate with the computer is that of putting our inputs -- character strings -- into machine readable forms. This means that we must enter all the information through a keyboard, either for direct transmission to a computer, or in order to punch rectangular holes in paper cards, later to be read by a card reader attached to the computer. It is the laborious task of retyping huge stores of information to get it into machine readable form that is the greatest obstacle to the formation of large computer-managed data bases, such as the card catalog of a library, or an index to the collections of a museum.

6.1 Record-oriented input

For most computing applications, one wishes to have the computer analyze and interpret a string of input characters, using agreed-upon conventions of meaning. When this is done, one need not worry about all of the details of how the interpretation is done; conversion is automatic. The agreed-upon conventions used in ALGOL W are quite simple. In an input statement, (READ or READON) there is a list of variables whose values are to be set by reading and interpreting an input string. The particular conversion algorithm to be used on each successive non-blank substring of input is determined by the declared data type of the variable whose value is being set. For integers, an input string is to consist of numerals, possibly preceded by a plus or a minus sign. For real or long real variables, an input string is to be an integer or a decimal number, possibly preceded by a sign and followed by an exponent in scientific notation. The exponent is set off from the modulus by an apostrophe, so that $3.5*10^{-4}$ would appear as 3.5'-4. Complex numbers are represented by a pair of real numbers (see Sec. A4.1 of the Appendix). Logical values are represented by the words TRUE and FALSE. String type variables are expected to receive values that are character strings, but since there is no agreement on where the value of a string is to start or stop within the sequence of input characters on a record, each data string must be set off by quotation marks, " . . . ". These standard conventions used for the conversion of ALGOL W input are among the simplest in general use.

There is one detail related to how the computer actually processes input that still shows up in the automatically converted input that most users employ. Since ALGOL W normally takes its input from 80-column punched cards, it is specified that each time the computer calls for input, there will be transmitted a sequence of exactly 80 characters. The sequence of characters is temporarily held in a place called a buffer while the characters are interpreted. When there is such a convention on how input is to be transmitted, we say that the input is logically divided into records. A record is a string of characters that is transmitted in response to a single input request. The records are of fixed length, in this case 80 characters, but in general, of any fixed length that is agreed upon ahead of time.

There are other conventions that can be used to transmit input to a computer. The simplest is character-by-character transmission in which special characters must be used to indicate the beginning and end of an input message. Usually, the convention used is selected to be compatible with the physical characteristics of the device transmitting the input. The computer really doesn't care; it requires a program to tell it how to process input in any case.

ALGOL W provides three instructions to request input. The instruction READCARD, followed by a parenthesized list of the names of strings that are to be used as buffers, requests input in the form of unanalyzed 80-character records to be transmitted into each of the variables named. Naturally, this instruction will only succeed if the variables named as buffers are themselves of type STRING, and with lengths of at least 80 characters.

If input conversion is desired, then the variables whose values are to be set by the input are listed in a parenthesized list following either the instruction READ or READON. These two instructions differ only in that READ takes notice of record boundaries in the input. Each time a READ instruction is executed, the computer calls for a new record to be input, and begins analysis of the input string there. On the other hand, if there is an input string in the input buffer that has not yet been fully analyzed (down to the 80th character) then the READON instruction will continue analyzing input until it finishes the contents of the string in the input buffer before calling for a new record to be transmitted. With either instruction, if the requested list of values is not found within the record being analyzed, then a new record will be requested and analysis will continue. When READON is used, the input is treated as if it were a continuous stream of characters; when READ is used, analysis of the input always begins on a new record. If the distinction between these instructions seems too subtle at this point, don't worry. Just pick one or the other of the instructions and stick with it in your programs.

6.2 Interpreting the input

If all input to the computer must be in the form of character strings, how does one input numbers in order to do numerical computations? Quite obviously, by representing numbers as strings of numerals, just as is done on a printed page. We have to learn in the primary grades of elementary school how to interpret these strings of numerals as numbers. In order for the computer to interpret them, someone must provide a computational algorithm for this task. Ordinarily, in composing computer

121

programs, one does not worry about providing such an algorithm; the programming language provides standard functions already implemented as computer programs to interpret several forms of numeral strings as numbers. However, just so that we can gain an appreciation for what is involved, let us go through the development of such an algorithm from the ground up.

Although for some scientific applications in which the computer is used in data collection, one will find it convenient to invent a special set of characters to be used as input to the computer, for the vast majority of general purpose computing, people use one of two standard sets of characters and encodings for computer input. The characters consist of the twenty-six letters of the Roman alphabet, in upper and lower case, the ten decimal numerals, between 20 and 30 special symbols and punctuation marks, and the blank space which is also an encoded character.

What we really mean by "interpreting the input" is a change of representation within the computer. So long as a number is represented as a string of numerals, one can only do operations with it that are defined on strings; these operations have nothing to do with arithmetic. In order to make use of the computer's arithmetic operations, a number must be represented within the computer in a standard form designated by the computer's designer. ALGOL W provides a pair of standard functions which can be used to translate between these representations for individual characters; if NUMERAL is a string of length one whose value happens to be one of the numerals "0" through "9", then the numerical representation of this value can be obtained by means of the expression
DECODE(NUMERAL) - 240
(The subtraction of 240 is obtained from the fact that the EBCDIC code for the numeral "0" is 240. The character encodings of the other numerals follow in sequence. See Section A10.5 and Table A10.5.1 of the Appendix for more details.)

Once it is known how to translate an individual numeral to its equivalent numerical representation, the arithmetic capability of the computer can be applied to form numerical values equivalent to strings of numerals. The idea is simple. If you scan a character string from left to right, proceeding one character at a time and decoding each numeral as it is found, then you will need to accumulate the value of the number built up so far. Each time another digit is found, the previously accumulated number should be multiplied by 10 and the newly found digit added to the result. When no new digit is found, the accumulated result will be the desired interpretation of the string of numerals. Initially, when no digits have been found, the accumulated result should be zero. An iteration graph describing this portion of the algorithm is

```
Accumulator := 0

while not end-of-number

        Accumulator := 10*Accumulator +
                       DECODE (Digit) - 240;
        advance Text-pointer to select next
                         digit
```

where Text-pointer is an index into the numeral string.

Although the iteration graph given above could be translated
into an ALGOL W program segment, and would yield correct results
for many numeral strings, it fails to check for numeral strings
that cannot be translated to a directly representable integer.
If translation of a number that exceeds the maximum representable
integer is attempted, the computer will balk at the attempt,
issuing a message that there has occurred integer overflow. If
we wish to check for this condition as the input string is
interpreted, then the magnitude of the accumulated value must be
checked before it is increased, each time another digit is about
to be appended. Upon including this test, the algorithm becomes

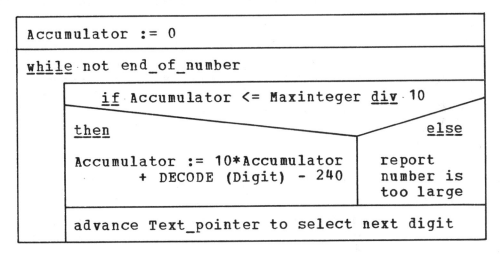

To complete the translation of the algorithm into an ALGOL W
program, some declarations must be given,

```
STRING (80) TEXTIN;
INTEGER TP, ACCUMULATOR
```

123

The first statement to be executed is to ask for an 80-character string to be input. Regardless of the actual input medium employed, the ALGOL W input facility takes input in the same way as if the computer were reading punched cards. If we do not wish the character string from a card to be interpreted by the built-in algorithms for that purpose, we use the instruction

READCARD (TEXTIN)

The iteration control clause "while not end-of-number" should include both a test that the end of the input string has not been reached (see Example 5.6.1) and that the next character to be analyzed is in fact a numeral. Since the numerals are encoded in ascending order as characters, this clause can be given by

WHILE (TP < 80) AND (TEXTIN (TP|1) >= "0") AND (TEXTIN (TP|1) <= "9") DO

In testing the magnitude of the accumulated result, there is a predeclared and preinitialized variable in ALGOL W called MAXINTEGER, whose value is that of the maximum representable integer. Thus the expression to be tested could be written as

ACCUMULATOR <= MAXINTEGER DIV 10

A final step in the ALGOL W program will be to print the result.

```
BEGIN
    COMMENT*****************************************************
    *   INTERPRET A STRING OF NUMERALS AS AN INTEGER NUMBER   *
    *****************************************************;
    STRING (80) TEXTIN;
    INTEGER ACCUMULATOR, TP;
    READCARD (TEXTIN);
    TP := 0;
    ACCUMULATOR := 0;
    WHILE (TP < 80) AND (TEXTIN (TP|1) >= "0")
                    AND (TEXTIN (TP|1) <= "9") DO
        BEGIN
            IF ACCUMULATOR <= MAXINTEGER DIV 10 THEN
                ACCUMULATOR := 10*ACCUMULATOR + DECODE(TEXTIN(TP|1)) - 240;
            ELSE
                WRITE ("NUMERAL STRING IS TOO LARGE TO BE REPRESENTED");
            TP := TP + 1;
        END;
    WRITE (ACCUMULATOR);
END.
```

The careful reader will note that the scheme used here to test for integer overflow is not foolproof! Although it will catch almost all numeral strings that would produce an integer too large to be represented, one could, knowing the value of MAXINTEGER, devise an input that would produce overflow of ACCUMULATOR, but that would not be detected as too large by the above algorithm. It is left to the reader to determine how, by trying to devise such an input.

The algorithm has been left in this state, almost but not quite perfect, to make a point. The point is this. Almost perfect algorithms may be fully satisfactory for your own personal use since you have no reason to sabotage a computation by malicious intent, and since you are in complete control of the inputs to be furnished to the algorithm. But as soon as you begin to advertise an algorithm as suitable for public use, or to incorporate it into a large group of programs that interact with one another in a manner not always predictable, the flaw in the almost perfect algorithm is very likely to be found out. The best programming practice is to proceed as though you will not have control over the inputs to be furnished, and not to be satisfied with almost perfect algorithms. As an exercise, try to correct the flaw in this algorithm.

6.3 Output

Now that we know something about how information is input to the computer, it will be easier to describe the output system as well. Output is pretty much the reverse of input. Data exist in the computer in internal forms that depend on the data type of each item. For output, these internal forms must all be converted to representations of the data items by character strings. The characters to be output are assembled in an output buffer, that you may think of as a variable of type string with sufficient length to hold one output record. When the buffer is filled or the output list is exhausted, the string is transmitted to an output device. If the output device is a typewriter terminal or a line printer, the output string is printed for the benefit of a human observer. The output device might also be one that provides storage for future reference of the data by a computer, in which case the output string will be represented by patterns of magnetization of metallic oxides on a plastic tape, a disc or a drum, or by holes in a card or a paper tape. We shall only consider printed output.

If the output device is a printer of some sort, then it will most likely print lines whose maximum length is fixed by the size of the type used and the width of its carriage or paper. This type of output device most naturally calls for record-oriented output in which the record length corresponds to the number of characters in a printed line. The standard ALGOL W output record length is 132 characters, the length of a line on the most commonly used line printers.

Just as with input, the conversion from internal representation to character representation for output is done automatically, using an algorithm appropriate to the data type of each output expression. The output instructions are WRITE and WRITEON. Each instruction is followed by a parenthesized list of expressions that may, of course, include variable names or constants as special cases of expressions. When the WRITE instruction is used, output begins on a new line; if WRITEON is used, it continues on the previous line, beginning a new line only when the previous one is filled.

Initially, when you compose and run your own computer programs, you may be quite satisfied merely to print the value of the variable that represents the result when the execution of the algorithm is completed. An instruction such as

WRITE (X)

will cause the value of the variable X to be printed by itself in a line of output. As you gain more experience in running programs on the computer, you will either encounter the problem of printing several values and forgetting in which order you had called for them to be output, or else you may feel that a single lonely number appearing on a large and otherwise blank sheet of paper does not do justice to the effort expended in producing it. In either case, you will wish to produce output containing some annotation. This is easily done.

One of the ways to have a comment printed is just to include the desired message, enclosed in quotation marks, in the list of expressions to be output. Thus, to dress up a naked number, one might ask to have printed an introductory message, such as

WRITE ("THE ANSWER IS:", X)

If the value of the variable X is 24, for instance, then this instruction will cause the following line to be printed:

THE ANSWER IS: 24

Or, if the purpose of the annotation is to identify which variables the printed values belonged to, the appropriate output instruction might look like:

```
WRITE ("A =", A, "B =", B, "C =", C)
```

Other uses of messages in the output are to identify unexpected or erroneous values of data that are encountered in the course of the computation as the algorithm tests data for validity. You may also wish to have printed on the output a title, a brief description of the problem for which you have composed your algorithm, the initial values of data used for the computation, your own name and the date, or other information relevant to the computing application.

As you gain more experience with planning the layout of computer-generated output, you will soon become aware of the fact that the width allocated by ALGOL W for printing of numerical values is sometimes excessive. Numerical output is allocated sufficient space in which to print the largest value that might be generated, plus two blank spaces following the printed number in order to ensure separation from a following print field. For real values, as many as 13 characters may be printed: a minus sign, seven decimal digits, a point, an apostrophe to indicate an exponent of ten, the sign of the exponent, and two decimal digits for the value of the exponent. A print field width of fourteen spaces, plus two trailing blanks, is allowed. For integers, a print field width of 14 characters is specified as the default option, but in recognition of the fact that in many cases, fewer characters will actually be printed, ALGOL W allows the width of the print field for integers to be controlled by a program variable. This variable is called INTFIELDSIZE. It is predeclared, and preinitialized to a value of 14, but its value may be changed by assignment within a program. For instance, the pair of statements

```
INTFIELDSIZE := 4;
WRITE ("THE ANSWER IS:", 24)
```

will produce the output line

THE ANSWER IS: 24

in contrast to the wider spacing obtained without modification of the variable INTFIELDSIZE.

6.4 Constructing tables

There are many computing applications in which the result is not expressed as a single number or even a few numbers, but as a whole table of values giving results applicable to a variety of cases. When humans prepare tables by hand, they usually use special forms, or lacking a suitable form, prepare one for

themselves by ruling lines on a piece of paper. The form
indicates the alignment of entries in the table. If a table is
to be prepared with a typewriter, the problem is complicated
slightly. Unless the typewriter is being used to fill in spaces
on a form, one may use tab stops on the typewriter to obtain
alignment of entries into columns. Constructing tables with a
computer is similar to using a typewriter for the task, in that
one must decide in advance on the spacings required to obtain
alignment, and incorporate these spacings into the output
instructions that will direct the printing of lines of the table.
The process is best illustrated by an example.

You have seen from a previous example (4.3.1) that a
computational algorithm can be devised to work out the monthly
payments required to pay off a mortgage at a given rate of
interest and extending over a given number of years. Now suppose
the banker, as a service to his customers, wants to show them how
much interest will be paid on a mortgage each year, and how
rapidly the balance of the principal amount is being reduced. We
shall not review the computation required to obtain the values,
but shall concentrate on providing a tabular output that can be
shown to a customer.

Example 6.4.1 -- Mortgage repayment tables

The body of the tables indicating the yearly progress
of mortgage repayment is to consist of lines on which are
listed the year, the amount of interest paid in that year,
and the balance remaining at the year's end. The dislay is
to be approximately centered on a page 60 columns wide. But
an equally important part of preparing tables is to provide
appropriate titles and column headings. A logical way to
proceed will be to write out a page in the way it is
intended to appear, and the to use this sample page as a
guide to the composition of output instructions.

```
+--------------------------------------------------------------+
|                        (Sample page)                         |
|                                                              |
|                                                              |
|   *****   M O R T G A G E   P A Y M E N T   T A B L E S  *****|
|                                                              |
|   LISTING THE INTEREST PAID AND THE BALANCE REMAINING        |
|   AT THE END OF EACH YEAR OF THE DURATION OF A MORTGAGE.      |
|                                                              |
|   PREPARED BY THE DIME SAVINGS BANK FOR MR. OWEN PLENTY.      |
|                                                              |
|   TERMS: PRINCIPAL AMOUNT:        30000 DOLLARS              |
|          RATE OF INTEREST:            7 PER CENT            |
|          DURATION:                   25 YEARS               |
|          MONTHLY PAYMENT:        208.70 DOLLARS             |
|                                                              |
|   NOTE:   THE MONTHLY PAYMENT DOES NOT INCLUDE LOCAL TAXES   |
|                                                              |
|              YEAR        INTEREST PAID      BALANCE          |
|              1973            2089            29581           |
|              1974            2076            29153           |
|               .               .               .             |
|               .               .               .             |
|               .               .               .             |
|              1998             88             2416           |
+--------------------------------------------------------------+
```

In preparing the sample page, it has been foreseen that
each numeric variable is allowed fourteen columns, plus two
following blank spaces by the automatic output conversion
routines of ALGOL W. This imposes a limit on how closely
spaced the columns of a table might be. For integer
variables it is possible to reduce the amount of space
required, by redefining the value of INTFIELDSIZE. Within
the fourteen columns allocated for each number, the actual
number will be printed as far to the right as possible.

Most of the lines of the title and introductory text
can be generated just by duplicating them in WRITE
statements, allowing for indentation where required. For
example, the principal title would be generated by

WRITE ("*****   M O R T G A G E   P A Y M E N T   T A B L E S   *****")

Lines in which a number is printed must allow for the
printing of the value of a variable between sequences of
text. Thus, the fifth through eighth non-blank lines could
be generated by the instructions

```
WRITE ("TERMS: PRINCIPAL AMOUNT:", PRINCIPAL, "DOLLARS");
WRITE ("        RATE OF INTEREST:", RATE, "PER CENT");
WRITE ("        DURATION:        ", DURATION, "YEARS");
WRITE ("        MONTHLY PAYMENT: ", MONTHLYPAYMENT, "DOLLARS")
```

Notice that the subtitles must be padded on the right with blanks so that each string is of the same length, in order that the units descriptors in the right column of the printed page will be aligned. Since each variable has its value printed in a field of fixed width, no misalignment can occur in printing these values.

The column titles of the table are printed in similar fashion,

```
WRITE ("        YEAR        INTEREST PAID    BALANCE");
```

but some care must be taken to secure the proper spacing of column titles to agree with the spacing of the columns of numbers. In order to determine the proper indentation of the lines of numbers in the table, one can count from the rightmost character of the year, back to the left margin. This is sixteen spaces, and since the number field itself requires fourteen, there must be an indentation of two spaces preceding the first number field. The output instruction to enter numbers in the table would be embedded in an iteration loop, such as

```
FOR YEAR := FIRSTYEAR UNTIL LASTYEAR DO
    BEGIN
       .
       .
       .
       WRITE ("  ", YEAR, INTEREST, BALANCE);
       .
       .
    END
```

For those parts of the table in which a blank line is called for to improve the appearance, one simply calls for the printing of a blank line, using the instruction WRITE (" ") with an output list consisting of a single blank character.

There is one more potential problem in creating a program for the banker to use. The fourth non-blank line contains the name of the bank and the name of the customer. If our program is to be designed for use by more than one bank, then the name of the bank will not appear explicitly in the program but will be the value of a variable of type string. The customer's name will also be held by a string type variable. The line shown on the sample page could be printed by executing the instruction

```
WRITE ("PREPARED BY THE ", BANKNAME, " FOR ", CUSTOMERNAME);
```

where BANKNAME and CUSTOMERNAME are the variables that hold the names of the bank and its client, respectively. However, string variables must be declared to be of some fixed length, and the names of various banks and customers will not all fit this fixed length.

To accomodate names of various lengths, these string variables would probably be declared with maximum lengths

```
STRING (44) BANKNAME, CUSTOMERNAME
```

In addition, one could use integer variables to keep track of the actual lengths of the strings representing the names of the bank and its customer,

```
INTEGER LENGTHBANK, LENGTHCUSTOMER
```

Now, when the initial data are supplied to the program, the names and their lengths will probably be set by an input statement like

```
READ (BANKNAME, LENGTHBANK, CUSTOMERNAME, LENGTHCUSTOMER)
```

The input record containing the data would look like

```
"DIME SAVINGS BANK" 17 "MR. OWEN PLENTY" 15
```

To print strings whose lengths depend on the data, one must use an iteration statement to print them character by character, for ALGOL W will not allow variables to designate length in a substring designator expression. Thus, a sequence of statements is necessary to print the line of output containing these names:

```
WRITE ("PREPARED BY THE ");
FOR I := 0 UNTIL LENGTHBANK - 1 DO
   WRITEON (BANKNAME(I|1));
WRITEON (" FOR ");
FOR I := 0 UNTIL LENGTHCUSTOMER -1 DO
   WRITEON (CUSTOMERNAME(I|1))
```

At this point it should be clear that we have not yet solved the problem. For part of the specification of the problem was that the table was to be printed on paper 60 columns wide, and if one happens to encounter a bank and a customer both having long names, they won't fit into such a line. For example a report prepared by Manufacturer's Hanover Trust for Mr. Nikita Sergeivich Khruschev will appear as:

PREPARED BY THE MANUFACTURER'S HANOVER TRUST FOR MR.   NIKI

Something must be done, or the public relations department of the bank will arrange to have its computer programmer replaced.

The problem can be solved with a little computation. An equally attractive display would be

```
    PREPARED BY THE MANUFACTURER'S HANOVER TRUST
       FOR MR.   NIKITA SERGEIVICH KHRUSCHEV
```

In order to have these lines printed with the indentation required to center them, we need to do a little arithmetic. The string "PREPARED BY THE " contains sixteen characters, and so the sum of 16 plus the value of LENGTHBANK plus twice the length of the indentation should total the length of a line, 60 characters. We can use an integer variable INDENT, and compute its value by

INDENT := (60 - 16 - LENGTHBANK) DIV 2

The first of the two lines containing names is printed by the following sequence of instructions, where the first instruction, IOCONTROL (2), is used to start a new print line when the WRITEON instruction is used.

```
IOCONTROL (2);
FOR I := 1 UNTIL INDENT -1 DO WRITEON (" ");
WRITEON ("PREPARED BY THE ");
FOR I := 0 UNTIL LENGTHBANK - 1 DO
   WRITEON (BANKNAME(I|1))
```

In execution of these instructions, the indentation and the name of the bank will be assembled into the output buffer one character at a time. A similar sequence of instructions can be used to write the line containing the customer's name, and the computer programmer's reputation with the public relations department of the bank will be secure for yet another fortnight.

6.5 Using the Computer to generate reports and catalogs

As you are no doubt aware, there is a growing use of computers to prepare reports and catalogs. Either the computer output itself is the finished product, or is reproduced by a photocopy process, or in more sophisticated applications, the computer may control a typesetting machine. The direct use of computer printout for reports has many limitations from the point of view of the printer's art, but it has one great advantage to recommend it: it is cheap, when only a small number of copies is required. Because of the limitations of only a single type font and size, often restricted to upper-case letters, the appearance of computer printout is monotonous, and special care must be taken to organize the display of information so that it will by intelligible to the human reader. Unfortunately, most computer programmers are not experienced in the graphic arts, and have themselves grown so used to reading computer printout that they tend to overlook its deficiencies as a medium for visual display of information. The standard for appearance of computer-generated reports is not very high.

Nevertheless, computer printout has found widespread acceptance. Typical of the types of reports prepared by computer are monthly financial statements, inventory reports, library catalogs, work schedules, and bibliographies. We can learn some principles of organizing information on a printed page that will help us to prepare readable reports.

The basic rules accepted by people who read one of the Indo-European languages are that clues as to what data are contained on a page are to be found in some sort of header at the top of the page, and if a page consists of several separate items appearing in a column from top to bottom, then clues as to the content of each item are to be found by scanning down the left side of the column. These rules are implemented in our practice of displaying titles at the tops of pages, of putting page numbers in an upper corner, of heading dictionary pages with the initial and final words that appear on each page, of indenting from the left margin in a column, and of aligning paragraph numbers and subtitles on the left column boundary.

There is one other important rule, and it is the hardest to implement successfully in computer printout. Titles and headings are to be made strikingly different in appearance from the body of text that they head. This last rule is of particular importance in newspapers in which an enormous amount of information is competing for the limited attention of the reader. There are some other general guidelines as well, all having to do with the physical appearance of the text. The ratio of the length to the height of a printed line should not be greater than about 35:1, or else the reader tends to lose track of which line he is on as his eye scans back from the right end of one line to the left end of the following one. If the line is interrupted by large spaces, this ratio should be lowered.

A few ways that people have found to make titles and headings stand out in printouts are to use extended spacings, to bracket titles in patterns of special symbols, usually asterisks, to enclose them in boxes constructed from asterisks, plus signs, or vertical and horizontal bars, to underline them, and to create large font letters by pictorial representation. Here are some illustrations.

Underlining: (This requires a printing device capable of overstriking)

THIS IS A TITLE

Extended spacing:

T H I S   I S   A   T I T L E

Bracketing with asterisks:

***** THIS IS A TITLE *****

Enclosing in a box:

```
+++++++++++++++++++++++++++
+                         +
+      THIS IS A TITLE    +
+                         +
+++++++++++++++++++++++++++
```

Using large font, pictorial letters:

```
XXXXX X  X XXX  XXX    XXX XXX    XX    XXXXX XXX XXXXX X    XXXX
  X   X  X X   X   X    X   X    X  X     X    X    X   X    X
  X   XXXX X  XX    X  XX   XXXX  X    X  X    X    X   XXX
  X   X  X X   X     X   X    X X X X  X     X    X    X   X
  X   X  X X XXX XXX    XXX XXX    X  X     X   XXX   X   XXXX XXXX
```

The techniques used to manage the display of titles constructed by any of these means (except underlining) are similar. In a later section, we shall investigate printing with pictorial letters. For now, however, we shall continue to be less concerned with the details of how to program the printing of a page of a report that with how to lay it out for ease of reading.

Example 6.5.1 -- Printing the semester time schedule

An example of a report that is usefully generated by computer is the time schedule of courses offered each semester at a university. The time schedule must be produced quickly, at low cost, for use by students and advisors in advance registration for the next semester. The information it is to contain is already under the management of a computer-based accounting system. An example of a page of a time schedule in use by one university, and printed from computer output, is shown in Table 6.5.1. This report relies for its success on a high degree of motivation by the reader to ferret out the information he requires, for it was not designed with much consideration for the human reader. We can improve it.

As it stands, the page of Table 6.5.1 does not make proper use of a tabular display of data, for its column headings are repeated so often that they get in the way of the information. Also, there is no visual means of distinguishing the column headings from items of information in the columns. One must read and interpret the headings, in order to determine that they are indeed headings.

On each page, information is grouped by academic course and by sections of that course. However, upon scanning down the left margin where one has been taught by experience to look for markings distinguishing the individual items of a table, the indices encountered first are the call numbers. These call numbers are used for internal bookkeeping purposes by the accounting system, and are of very little interest to the student who is looking up an entry for a particular course. They should not be given such a high priority in their placement on the page.

In Table 6.5.2 an alternate format is suggested for displaying exactly the same information. Since the courses are grouped in the time schedule according to their general academic subject area, this designation is the one that a reader would use as a coarse index in seeking a particular course. Therefore, the subject area of the first course appearing on the page is displayed at the top of the page, just as is done in dictionaries or telephone directories to indicate the range of content of a page.

The information display on the page is not strictly tabular, since successive lines may have differing information content, and since some lines will be used for prose comments. Nevertheless, the organization is sufficiently regular that a template of the information fields of each

```
CALL#    DPT    CRS    TITLE                              CRD

15630    HBW    111    INTRO HEBREW I                     3.0
         SEC TYP  DAYS        TIME        BUILDING      ROOM    INSTRUCTOR
15631    1   REC  MWF    11:00-11:50    RM TO BE ARR            STAFF
15632    2   REC  MWF    12:00-12:50    RM TO BE ARR            STAFF
15633    3   REC  MWF     2:00- 2:50    RM TO BE ARR            STAFF


15660    HBW    151    INTERMED HEBREW I                  3.0
   PREREQ: HBW 112 OR EQUIV
         SEC TYP  DAYS        TIME        BUILDING      ROOM    INSTRUCTOR
15661    1   REC  MWF    10:00-10:50    RM TO BE ARR            BEIZER


15690 HBW 221    ADVANCED HEBREW I                        3.0
   PREREQ: HBW 152 OR EQUIV
         SEC TYP  DAYS        TIME        BUILDING      ROOM    INSTRUCTOR
15691    1   REC  MWF     9:00- 9:50    RM TO BE ARR            BEIZER


15720    HBW    285    CLASSICAL HEBREW                   3.0
   PREREQ: HBW 221 OR PERMIS OF INSTR
         SEC TYP  DAYS        TIME        BUILDING      ROOM    INSTRUCTOR
15721    1   LEC  MWF     1:00- 1:50    RM TO BE ARR            LICHTENSTEIN


***************************** HIS COURSES *****************************

CALL#    DPT    CRS    TITLE                              CRD


15750    HIS    101    EUR HIS: PRE-INDUSTR               3.0
         SEC TYP  DAYS        TIME        BUILDING      ROOM    INSTRUCTOR
15751    1   LEC  MW     11:00-11:50    RM TO BE ARR            WELTSCH
             REC  F      11:00-11:50    RM TO BE ARR
15752    2   LEC  MW     11:00-11:50    RM TO BE ARR            WELTSCH
             REC  F      11:00-11:50    RM TO BE ARR
15753    3   LEC  MW     11:00-11:50    RM TO BE ARR            WELTSCH
             REC  F      12:00-12:50    RM TO BE ARR


15780    HIS    103    INTRO-STUDY AMER HIS               3.0
         SEC TYP  DAYS        TIME        BUILDING      ROOM    INSTRUCTOR
15781    1   LEC  TU     10:10:50       RM TO BE ARR            KAVENAGH
             REC  TH     10:00-11:50    RM TO BE ARR
15782    2   LEC  TU     10:00-10:50    RM TO BE ARR            KAVENAGH
             REC  TU     12:00- 1:50    RM TO BE ARR
15783    3   LEC  TU     10:00-10:50    RM TO BE ARR            KAVENAGH
             REC  TH     12:00- 1:50    RM TO BE ARR
15784    4   LEC  TU     10:00-10:50    RM TO BE ARR            KAVENAGH
             REC  TU     12:00- 1:50    RM TO BE ARR
15785    5   LEC  TU     10:00-10:50    RM TO BE ARR            KAVENAGH
             REC  TH     10:00-11:50    RM TO BE ARR
15786    6   LEC  TU     10:00-10:50    RM TO BE ARR            KAVENAGH
             REC  TH     12:00- 1:50    RM TO BE ARR


15810    HIS    140    PERSPECT WORLD HIS                 3.0
   PREREQ: FRESHMAN STANDING
         SEC TYP  DAYS        TIME        BUILDING      ROOM    INSTRUCTOR
15811    1   LEC  TUTH    9:30-10:45    RM TO BE ARR            WEINSTEIN
```

Table 6.5.1

entry can appear just once under the subject area heading and the reader will not be confused.

The entries corresponding to individual courses now contain only information, uncontaminated by intermixing column headings as was done previously. In order to locate an individual course, the reader can scan down the left margin, where he finds listed only the course designation codes that are in common use throughout the university. If the entry for a course must be broken, listing some sections on a following page, then the course designation is repeated there. Since the subject area defines the major groupings of courses, a boxed title identifies the beginning of each new subject area group.

Surprisingly, when the format of the report has been modified for improved readability, the amount of information that can be put on a single page is also increased, instead of decreased, although this was not part of our consideration in redesigning the format. In order to design a program to print pages of this report, none of the individual programming steps is more difficuult than those studied in the example of the last section; there are just more of them. Specifiying a program in detail is left as an exercise for the reader.

6.6 Teaching the computer to draw

With a little effort, we can have the computer print pictures for us. There are many types of graphical display devices that can serve as output devices for a computer, and draw graphs, pictures and charts as desired. However, we shall assume that the only output device available to us is a line printer, and shall start from there. The main thing to remember when you are trying to generate graphical output on a line printer is that the image to be printed must be dissected into horizontal slices, and each slice or line will have to be assembled for output in order of its appearance from top to bottom on the page. Since this line-by-line assembly is not the way we ordinarily go about generating a pencil drawing, it will cause us a certain amount of trouble. However, it is exactly the way that a television camera scans an image to generate a video signal representing a frame of a TV picture, and thinking about the formation of a picture by scanning successive lines may help us to visualize the procedure that the computer must follow.

```
++++++++++++++++++++++++++++++++++++++++++++++++++++
+                                                  +
+                 H E B R E W                      +
+                                                  +
++++++++++++++++++++++++++++++++++++++++++++++++++++
COURSE  CREDITS TITLE
    SECTION TYPE DAYS   TIME          CALL#  INSTRUCTOR

HBW 111    3          INTRODUCTORY HEBREW I
       1    REC  MWF    11:00-11:50  15631  STAFF
       2    REC  MWF    12:00-12:50  15632  STAFF
       3    REC  MWF     2:00- 2:50  15633  STAFF

HBW 151    3          INTERMEDIATE HEBREW I
    PREREQ: HBW 112 OR EQUIV
       1    REC  MWF    10:00-10:50  15661  BEIZER

HBW 221    3       ADVANCED HEBREW I
    PREREQ: HBW 221 OR EQUIV
       1    REC MWF      9:00- 9:50  15691  BEIZER

HBW 285    3       CLASSICAL HEBREW
    PREREQ: HBW 221 OR PERMIS OF INSTR
       1    LEC  MWF     1:00- 1:50  15721  LICHTENSTEIN


++++++++++++++++++++++++++++++++++++++++++++++++++++
+                                                  +
+                 H I S T O R Y                    +
+                                                  +
++++++++++++++++++++++++++++++++++++++++++++++++++++
COURSE  CREDITS   TITLE
    SECTION TYPE DAYS   TIME          CALL#  INSTRUCTOR

HIS 101    3          EUROPEAN HISTORY: PRE-INDIUSTRIAL
     1-3    LEC  MW    11:00-11:50           WELTSCH
       1    REC  F     11:00-11:50  15751
       2    REC  F     11:00-11:50  15752
       3    REC  F     12:00-12:50  15753

HIS 103    3          INTRODUCTION TO THE STUDY OF AMERICAN HISTORY
     1-6    LEC  TU    10:00-10:50           KAVENAGH
       1    REC  TH    10:00-11:50  15781
       2    REC  TH    12:00- 1:50  15782
       3    REC  TH    12:00- 1:50  15783
       4    REC  TU    12:00- 1:50  15784
       5    REC  TH    10:00-11:50  15785
       6    REC  TH    12:00- 1:50  15786

HIS 140    3       PERSPECTIVES ON WORLD HISTORY
    PREREQ: FRESHMAN STANDING
       1    LEC  TUTH   9:30-10:45  15811  WEINSTEIN

HIS 150    3       CIVILIZATION OF ISRAEL I
    REMARK: CROSSLISTED WITH INT 150
       1    LEC  HBTA               15841



                    Table 6.5.2
```

There are two distinct ways that images may be represented in a computer. The computer may hold in an array, a line-by-line replica of the image in which light and dark spots along each line are represented by binary values, 0 or 1, or possibly a scale of light values from black through shades of gray to white may be represented by a range of integer values. Each such value represents the shade of a single point of the image. The location of a point in the image is indicated by the indices of the element in the array. For instance, an image consisting of 200,000 points might be represented by an integer array,

INTEGER ARRAY IMAGE (1::500, 1::400)

In this representation, the value of the point lying in the 40th row from the top, and the 135th column from the left margin might be represented by the element IMAGE (40, 135). Many of the pictures generated on a line printer and that you see hung around the halls of every computing center are represented in the computer in this way.

Another way in which images can be represented in the computer is by parameters of mathematical formulas. We have already seen (in Example 3.5.2) how straight lines can be represented. More complicated geometric figures can also be represented using formulas of analytic geometry, or as solutions to systems of equations whose parameters are stored as values of computational variables. In these cases, the images are actually generated by computation. Most of the so-called "computer generated art", consisting of abstract patterns of geometrical figures and printed on computer-controlled plotting devices, is of this type. We shall study simple examples of each type of image representation in order to discover how to have the images printed on a line printer.

Example 6.6.1 -- Printing with large font pictorial letters

In the last section, we saw that large-font, pictorial letters are often useful in forming titles that are visually distinguishable from the surrounding text in a page of computer output. Since a line printer allows the use of only a single type font, any large letters we intend to use must be constructed as a pattern of standard, printable symbols upon a blank background. This affords us a good example of the technique of forming pictures by printing patterns of small symbols. A single line of the large font letters must extend over several actual print lines.

First of all, suppose that images of the letters that we intend to use have already been stored in the computer, presumably by reading punched cards or input from a typewriter terminal. As a standard format for the alphabet, assume that each letter is five print lines in height, and may be three, four, or five print columns in width. Since we will need spaces between letters, let each letter be preceded by a single print column of blank characters. Thus, the images we are to represent look like:

```
 XX    XXX    XXX  XXX   XXXX  XXXX   XXX
X  X   X  X   X      X    X     X    X
X  X   XXX    X      X    X  X  XXX   XXX   X XX
XXXX   X  X   X      X    X  X  X     X       X  X
X  X   XXX    XXX   XXX   XXX   XXXX  X       XXX
```

Each letter will be represented by an array consisting of five strings of six characters each. Thus the letter "A" is represented by

" XX ", " X X ", " X X ", " XXXX ", " X X ",

and these strings are read from an input device to initially store the image of our "A" in the computer. The twenty-six letters of the alphabet, plus a blank symbol five print lines high, are stored in a two dimensional array of six-character strings, declared by

```
STRING (6) ARRAY ALPHABET (0::26, 1::5)
```

In the array identifier ALPHABET(1,3), the first index picks out letter number 1, which is "A", and the second index tells that the third row of the letter is to be selected. The strings of ALPHABET whose first index is zero are all blank, and will be used to obtain spaces between words in the large print.

The elements of the array representing the "A" are:

```
ALPHABET (1, 1) = "  XX  "
ALPHABET (1, 2) = " X  X "
ALPHABET (1, 3) = " X  X "
ALPHABET (1, 4) = " XXXX "
ALPHABET (1, 5) = " X  X "
```

To print an "A" in large font pictorial type, we could execute the iterated instruction

```
FOR I := 1 UNTIL 5 DO
    WRITE (ALPHABET(1, I))
```

Since we have provided for letters of variable width, so that an "I" requires fewer print columns than an "M", the printing of a word will not look well if six print columns are allowed for each letter. In that case, the spacings between letters within the word may not be uniform. In order to overcome this difficulty, we can define a second array to keep track of the number of print columns actually required to print each letter, including an initial column of blanks to achieve separation between successive letters. This array is defined by

```
INTEGER ARRAY LETTERWIDTH (0::26)
```

The value of LETTERWIDTH(1) will be initialized to 5, allowing one column of spacing and four columns of printed symbols to form an "A". LETTERWIDTH(9) will be 4, to print an "I", and LETTERWIDTH(13) will be 6, to print an "M". Now we are ready to give an algorithm to print a whole title in large font pictorial type as we have defined it.

Suppose that the title we wish to have printed is the message "THIS IS A TITLE". In order to encode the message for printing, the input representing this message should give the index of each letter of the message, that is, should give in place of each letter the integer representing the order of that letter in the alphabet. An input record would look like:

```
20 8 9 19 0 9 19 0 1 0 20 9 20 12 5
```

in which each zero stands for a blank to separate successive words.

At this point, we have created an assemblage of interrelated data objects, called a data structure, and it may be well to pause to describe the structure by means of a diagram.

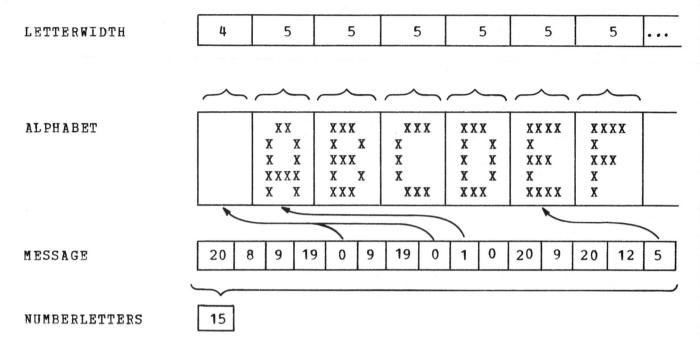

Figure 6.6.1 -- A data structure diagram

In Figure 6.6.1, the brackets are meant to indicate that the lengths of the significant portions of strings or arrays are given by the values of certain variables. The arrows indicated from some elements of MESSAGE to the boxes that have been drawn to correspond to elements of ALPHABET are to indicate that MESSAGE is used to encode a sequence of elements of ALPHABET. At each position in the sequence, the corresponding element of MESSAGE indicates which element of ALPHABET is to occupy that position. This means that a particular letter of the message to be printed would be referred to indirectly. For instance, the third line of the tenth letter of the message would be referred to by

        ALPHABET(MESSAGE(10), 3)

Frequently, by taking the time to draw a data structure diagram, one can save considerable time and effort in the formulation of an algorithm to operate on the data structure. In fact, the chance of getting the algorithm correctly designed without referring to a data structure diagram is relatively slight.

The first task of the algorithm is relatively easy; it must read data describing the indices of the letters to be printed. Then it must check that the number of columns required to print the message is not greater than the width of the paper, and finally, the message itself is to be printed, line by line. A description of the algorithm by means of an iteration graph is

read (Number_of_letters)
for I := 1 until Number_of_letters
read (Message(I))
calculate the number of print columns required to print the message, and check for overflow; calculate the indentation needed to center the message on the page
for Line := 1 until 5
start a new print line; print the indentation in blanks; print one line of all letters of the message

Most of the steps designated by the iteration graph are, if not elementary, either simple computations or are achievable by the iteration of an elementary step. Actual printing should be done by means of the WRITEON instruction, since many characters are to be printed, one at a time, on the same line. When the WRITEON instruction is used, a separate command may have to be used to specify the beginning of a new line. ALGOL W provides two ways to do this, either a WRITE (" ") instruction can be given, causing a new line to begin with a single blank character, or the command IOCONTROL(2) can be used to start a new print line, without causing any character to actually be printed. (See Sec. A10.4 of the Appendix.)

A step which is not elementary is to print one line of all letters of the message. Apparently, this step requires iteration over the number of letters of the message, but the indices of the actual letters to be printed are to be obtained from the index array, MESSAGE. According to the data structure diagram, a line of the Ith letter of the message must be referred to by

ALPHABET(MESSAGE(I), LINE)

(A common mistake is to try to refer to the Ith letter of
the alphabet, rather than to the letter indexed by the Ith
element of MESSAGE.) The specification is not yet complete,
however, for due to the fact that the large-font letters are
of differing widths, the strings of ALPHABET must be printed
one character at a time, with the number of characters to be
printed controlled by the corresponding value of
LETTERWIDTH. Thus the printing of characters in a line must
be iterated first over the number of letters, and then, for
each letter, must be iterated over the appropriate value of
the width of that letter.

Expanding the final line of the preceding iteration
graph, its action is represented by a subsidiary iteration
graph

print one line of each letter of Message:

```
┌──────────────────────────────────────────────────────┐
│ for I := 1 until Number_of_letters                    │
│   ┌──────────────────────────────────────────────────┐│
│   │ for L := 0 until Letterwidth(Message(I))         ││
│   │   ┌──────────────────────────────────────────────┤│
│   │   │ print next character                         ││
│   └───┴──────────────────────────────────────────────┘│
└──────────────────────────────────────────────────────┘
```

With some attention to detail, the iteration graph can
now be translated to an ALGOL W program. The details of
initialization of the ALPHABET are omitted.

```
BEGIN
    STRING(6) ARRAY ALPHABET (0::26, 1::5);
    INTEGER ARRAY LETTERWIDTH (0::26);
    INTEGER ARRAY MESSAGE (1::30);
    INTEGER NUMBERLETTERS, INDENT, WIDTH, PAGEWIDTH:
        .
        .
        .
    (initialization of ALPHABET, LETTERWIDTH goes here)
        .
        .
    COMMENT*********************************************
    *   PRINT LETTERS OF ALPHABET AS INDEXED BY MESSAGE, *
    *   IN LARGE-FONT PICTORIAL LETTERS                  *
    ***********************************************;
    READ (NUMBERLETTERS);
    ASSERT NUMBERLETTERS <= 30;
    PAGEWIDTH := 132;
    WIDTH := 0;
    FOR I:= 1 UNTIL NUMBERLETTERS DO
        BEGIN
            READON (MESSAGE(I));
```

```
              WIDTH := WIDTH + LETTERWIDTH(MESSAGE(I));
          END;
      IF WIDTH > PAGEWIDTH THEN
          WRITE ("MESSAGE IS TOO WIDE FOR PAGE");
      INDENT := (PAGEWIDTH - WIDTH) DIV 2;
      FOR LINE := 1 UNTIL 5 DO
          BEGIN
              IOCONTROL(2):  COMMENT***** NEW PRINT LINE *****;
              FOR L := 1 UNTIL INDENT DO
                  WRITEON (" ");
              FOR I := 1 UNTIL NUMBERLETTERS DO
                  FOR L := 0 UNTIL LETTERWIDTH(MESSAGE(I)) DO
                      WRITEON (ALPHABET(MESSAGE(I), LINE) (L|1));
          END;
  END.
```

The final WRITEON instruction in the program appears to
be quite complex. It can be read as follows. The item to
be written is a substring of length one, for the substring
selector (L|1) appears following the variable name in the
list of one argument presented for output. The variable is
an element of the string array ALPHABET, with first index
MESSAGE(I), which selects a particular letter of the
alphabet, and second index LINE, which selects one of the
constituent strings that make up the image of that letter.
The reader should notice that the data structure diagram is
a direct aid to reading or formulating expressions such as
this one.

The last example dealt with the printing of figures that
were represented by a map of their images in an array in the
memory of the computer. In an alternative representation of
figures that has been mentioned, each line is to be represented
by a parametric equation. The exact values of the parameters,
stored in the computer as the values of program variables, enable
one to determine the coordinates of points on the line by
computation. For instance, a straight line is represented by the
parametric equation,

$$ax + by + c = 0,$$

in which the values of a, b and c determine exactly which line is
represented. Sections of conic figures (circles, ellipses,
parabolas, hyperbolas) are represented by second-degree
equations,

$$ax^2 + bxy + cy^2 + dx + ey + f = 0,$$

and more complex curves by equations of higher degree. Any of these equations is of the form $F(x,y) = 0$, where F stands for some formula in two variables, and may contain a number of parameters. Every point on the curve is given by a pair of coordinates (x,y) that satisfy the equation. Points not on the curve have coordinates (x,y) for which $F(x,y)$ is not zero, but has some positive or negative value. If we were to plot a grid of the signs of the values of $F(x,y)$ on a rectangular array of points in the x-y plane, it would look something like this:

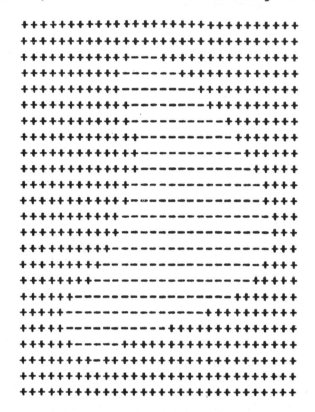

Obviously, since the values of F vary continuously with changes in x and y, points at which F is zero-valued must lie womewhere between each pair of adjacent points of the grid on which the signs differ. If we were to draw a continuous line on the grid, passing it between pairs of points of differing sign, we would have a pretty good approximation to the curve defined by the equation $F(x,y) = 0$. We can make use of this scheme in developing an algorithm to plot figures on a line printer when the equations of the figures are known.

The reason that a rectangular grid of points suggests itself is that a line printer only permits you to print at points that lie on such a grid. Each printable point must lie in a row that fixes its vertical position on the page, and in a column that fixes its horizontal position. In fact, we should not even speak of printable points but of printable areas, since each print character occupies a small, roughly rectangular area on the paper.

To give the impression that we are printing a line of characters, we can print a standard character such as "X", in each printable area that our mathematically defined curve would pass through. In order to determine whether or not the curve passes through a given area, evaluate the sign of the defining formula, F(x,y), on the points that form the corners of the rectangle. If there is a change of sign from one corner to another, then the curve must pass through the specified rectangle, and a character should be printed in it. Otherwise, that area can be left blank. Following this procedure, the print pattern determined from the grid of signs shown above would be:

```
            XXXX
           XX  XXX
           X       XXX
           XX         XX
           X            XXX
            XX            XX
             X             XX
             X              XX
              XX             XX
              X               X
               XX             XX
               X               X
                XX             X
                XX            XX
                 XX           XX
                  XXX        XXX
                   XX       XXXX
                    X      XXXXX
                    XX   XXXXXX
                     XXXXXX
                      XX
```

We can now give an example of an algorithm to print figures using the scheme described above.

<u>Example 6.6.2</u> -- Curve plotting on a line printer

Suppose that one wishes to plot the curve whose points satisfy the equation <u>f</u>(x,y) = 0, where <u>f</u> is some computable, continuous function of two variables. The height and width of the plot are assumed to be given in units of lines and print columns by the values of integer type variables,

HEIGHT and WIDTH. The value of WIDTH must be less than or equal to 132, the number of columns that can be printed on a standard line printer. Our technique will be to keep track of the sign changes of the formula $f(x,y)$ that occur upon evaluation on successive corners of an individual printable area. For this purpose, think of a printable area as a small rectangle as shown in Fig. 6.6.2. Each edge of the rectangle links two adjacent corners, so a sign change can be considered to be a property of an edge. It is not necessary to check all four edges for sign changes; either two of the edges will have sign changes or none will. (We assume that the rectangular area is very small compared with the area of the figure to be plotted, so that a boundary line of the figure can pass through an individual printable area at most once.)

The sign changes of $f(x,y)$ can be recorded for each print row. For an individual printable area, imagine that we already have stored the values of the sign of f on its upper right and lower left corners, and that we have one more piece of information, namely, whether or not the sign of f on the lower left corner is the same or different from the sign on the upper left corner. Now we shall evaluate the sign of the function on the remaining corner, the lower right. Check to see if this sign is different from that on the upper right corner. If it is, then the curve must pass through the printable area. If not, then check to see if the newly computed sign of the lower right corner differs from the sign of the lower left. That makes two sides checked. If neither shows a sign difference, we check to see if the left side of the rectangle showed a sign difference. If not, then the curve could not have passed through the rectangle, for three of the four sides have been checked.

Now the only information needed from previous computations are the signs of the function on the upper corners of the rectangle, and the sign change, if any, on the left side. The sign change on the left side can be saved from the immediately preceding computation performed on the rectangle to the left in the same row. The signs of the function on the upper corners must be saved from the computations of sign on the lower corners of rectangles in the preceding row. But notice that by this argument, it is only necessary to store a single row of sign information, and not the sign information for the entire grid of points! An algorithm to accomplish the printing of a figure follows. This algorithm is not quite a complete ALGOL W program, because the function to be plotted has not been given as an ALGOL W function (see Chapter 7) but is instead represented

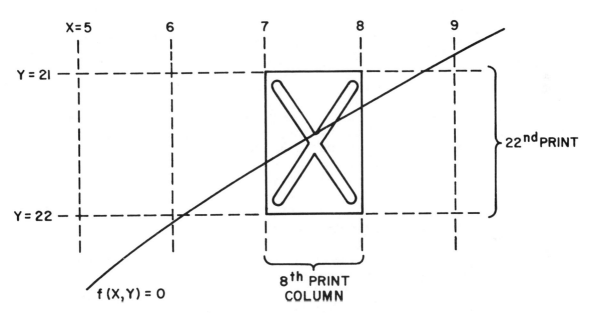

Fig. 6.6.2   An example of an individual print
rectangle through which passes the
locus f(X,Y) = 0

by the symbol $\underline{f}$, denoting any function of two integer
arguments.

```
BEGIN
    COMMENT*********************************************************
    *   PLOTS:   WILL CAUSE PLOTTING OF THE LOCUS OF f(X,Y) = 0   *
    *            WHEN f IS REPLACED BY A SUITABLE FUNCTION.        *
    *            THE VARIABLES SIGN, NEWSIGN, SIGNCHANGE ARE USED  *
    *            TO KEEP TRACK OF THE ALGEBRAIC SIGN OF THE        *
    *            FUNCTION AS EVALUATED ON DIFFERENT POINTS.        *
    *************************************************************;
    LOGICAL NEWSIGN, SIGNCHANGE;
    LOGICAL ARRAY SIGN (0::132);
    INTEGER HEIGHT, WIDTH;
    HEIGHT := 60;  WIDTH := 132;
    COMMENT*********************************************************
    *  INITIALLY, DETERMINE THE SIGN OF f AT POINTS ALONG THE    *
    *  UPPER BOUNDARY OF THE FIRST PRINT ROW.  THEN PRINT ROWS.  *
    *************************************************************;
    FOR COL := 0 UNTIL WIDTH DO
        SIGN(COL)  := f(COL, 0) >= 0;
    FOR ROW := 1 UNTIL HEIGHT DO
        BEGIN
            COMMENT*************************************************
            *  INITIALIZE A NEW PRINT ROW. DETERMINE THE CHANGE OF *
            *  SIGN ON THE CORNERS OF THE LEFT EDGE OF THE FIRST   *
            *  PRINT RECTANGLE.                                    *
            *****************************************************;
            IOCONTROL (2);
            NEWSIGN := f(0, ROW) >= 0;
            SIGNCHANGE := NEWSIGN ¬= SIGN(0);
            SIGN(0)  := NEWSIGN;
            COMMENT*************************************************
            *  FOR EACH PRINT RECTANGLE IN THE ROW, DETERMINE     *
            *  WHETHER OR NOT TO PRINT A MARK, ACCORDING TO THE   *
            *  SIGN CHANGE ALONG THE RIGHT EDGE, BOTTOM EDGE,     *
            *  AND LEFT EDGE OF THE RECTANGLE.                    *
            *****************************************************;
            FOR COL := 1 UNTIL WIDTH DO
                BEGIN
                    NEWSIGN := f(COL, ROW) >= 0;
                    IF NEWSIGN ¬= SIGN(COL) THEN
                        BEGIN
                            SIGNCHANGE := TRUE;
                            WRITEON ("X");
                        END
                    ELSE
                        BEGIN
                            IF SIGNCHANGE OR (NEWSIGN ¬= SIGN(COL-1) THEN
                                WRITEON ("X")
```

```
                ELSE
                    WRITEON (" ");
                    SIGNCHANGE := FALSE;
                END;
                SIGN(COL) := NEWSIGN;
            END;
        END;
END.
```

In the preceding example, we have assumed that the coefficients of the formula $f(x,y)$ are such that the figure to be plotted will be neither too small nor too large to be displayed on the printed page, when the units of x and y are print columns and print rows, respectively. Naturally, the scale of the figure will not be correct by accident any more than all objects of the real world can be drawn life-sized on a sheet of 8 1/2 by 11 inch paper. It is necessary to scale the plotting of figures to make sure that they will fit onto the available page, yet will not be too small for details to be seen. The same is true of architectural drawings and with photographs taken through a microscope. The problem of scaling has been ignored in the example for the reason that we will not be able to understand algorithms that do too many different things at once. We prefer the point of view that the problem of scaling requires a separate algorithm for its solution, and a scaling algorithm must be used in conjunction with the plotting algorithm in order to produce successful displays of figures. In the next two chapters, we shall see how to combine several algorithms in order to solve difficult problems, and how to separate the components of problems in order to find simple algorithms for their separate parts.

Exercises for Chapter 6

6.1 Design an ALGOL W program to print a bar chart of the U.S. cost-of-living index from 1966 to the present. The bars are to be printed vertically to a scale of 12 units per inch. Each bar should be five print columns wide, with three columns of blanks separating adjacent bars. The chart should have a title and captions indicating the year represented by each bar.

6.2

a) Design a program to print messages in large-font type, 12 print lines in height. Have it print your name and address.

b) Modify the program to have it scale the letters automatically to any size. Have the computer print an eye examination chart, using scaled letters of heights 60, 36, 24, 12, 8, 6, and 4 print lines high. At what size do the scaled letters become indistinguishable?

6.3 To print the time schedule of Section 6.5, the computer should read the information from cards, and print it in the desired format. Design a program to read cards in the format given below, and print it as shown in Fig. 6.5.2.

Card format:

<u>Columns</u>	<u>Contain</u>
1 -- 5	"H" in column 1 if the information on the card is a program or department heading; Call number if the card gives information about a particular course section
6 -- 80	Program heading, if column 1 contains "H ; <u>otherwise</u>,
6 -- 11	Three-letter department or program code and course number
12 -- 13	Number of credits
14 -- 41	course name or abbreviation
44 -- 45	Section number (if there is only a single section of the course, this

field may be left blank)

46 -- 48	Mode of instruction (LEC, REC, LAB, etc.)
49 -- 54	Days (MWF, T-Th., etc.)
55 -- 65	Hours (3:00 - 4:15, etc.)
66 -- 80	Name of instructor

6.4 Design a program to print a monthly circulation report of a college library, including the following data:

a title;
date of report;
month and year reported on;
the following statistics, both broken down by library branches, and given in aggregate form:
number of borrowers
number of volumes borrowed
number of volumes returned
number of volumes in circulation at month's end
number of volumes reported lost or missing
number of overdue notices issued
number of new volumes cataloged

6.5 Design a program to scale and print figures represented by equations of the form $f(x,y) = 0$. Plot, using the line printer, to a scale which makes the height of each figure 50 print lines,
a) a square;
b) a circle;
c) a circle with an inscribed square;
d) a square whose sides are diagonal to the edges of the paper, and containing an inscribed circle.

6.6 Have the computer print a line diagram of the daily fluctuations of the New York Times Stock Index daily closing price over a two month period. Include axes at the left side and the bottom of the diagram, print registration marks on the axes, and label the registration marks to indicate values along each of the coordinates.

NOTES

Chapter 7

COMPUTATION WITHIN COMPUTATIONS

In the course of composing a computational algorithm, it is frequently necessary to repeat an application of a part of the algorithm that has been previously developed. Or, as we have seen in previous chapters, one may need to evaluate a function for which there already exists a computational algorithm. In cases such as these, one should not have to restate the part of the program to be re-executed, for it would be wasteful of effort, would distract attention from the business of composing the new algorithm, and would make the resulting text longer and needlessly complicated to read. A better way to call for evaluation of an previously defined known portion of a program is to give it a name, and when re-evaluation is needed in the course of composing the main algorithm, to refer to the portion to be re-used by its name. In fact, we have already made use of such a device, by using the built-in functions of ALGOL W. These functions represent algorithms for which computer programs have already been generated and stored in the machine. When we wish to have the functions evaluated, we refer to them by name in our own ALGOL W text, indicating the the computer that a specific program is to be executed at that point in the computation.

The ALGOL W programming language (and most other programming languages as well) makes provision for the naming and re-use of algorithms that are composed by the user. These are called <u>procedures</u>, and the object of this chapter will be to help you to learn how to use them. Procedures are very flexible; they may be used like functions, returning a value as the result of their execution, or they may just be executable sub-algorithms having names for identification. Using procedures as sub-algorithms is very useful when programs are developed by the process of stepwise refinement. It enables us to avoid packaging too much complexity into any single segment of a program. Data may be communicated among procedures in several different ways that we shall investigate. Procedures can use program variables of their own that are privately kept within the procedure, or they can use program variables that are defined in the surrounding program text.

7.1 <u>Block structure</u>

ALGOL W employs a convention concerning the definition of identifiers or names called <u>block</u> structure. A block, very simply, is any group of statements bracketed by BEGIN . . . END and containing at least one declaration. If you look at the uses of BEGIN . . . END that we have made in the examples so far, you will see that most entire programs consist of a block, but that the use of BEGIN . . . END to bracket a group of statements under the control of an iteration clause or an if-clause is not usually a block, for it does not usually include any declarations. Such a bracketed group of statements without declarations is called a compound group.

Any object (by which is meant a constant, variable, or procedure) that is declared within a block, has the scope of its definition limited to that block and must live its whole life within the boundaries of the BEGIN . . . END that surrounds it. However, objects that are declared in the text surrounding a block are also known within the block, and so may be used there. There is one exception to this rule. An identifier that is used as the name of an object defined outside any given block can be temporarily stolen away for a different use within the block. The way this is done is simply to define a new object by means of a declaration internal to the block, giving the new object the same name as that of some object known outside the block. Then whenever that name is mentioned in a statement inside the block, the naming conflict is resolved by having the name refer to the locally defined object. When the same name is used outside the block, it will refer to the externally defined object.

Although blocks can be used anywhere in an ALGOL W program, the principal use we shall make of them will be in connection with procedures. For it will often be the case that for the algorithm represented by a procedure, we shall wish to have available some privately-owned, local variables. The part of the program that is external to the body of the procedure need not have any knowledge of these variables, nor of their values, and conversely, one would not want the use of these local variables to have any influence on the values of objects defined externally to the procedure. Block structure affords us a means of keeping locally defined values separate from those known outside a procedure. Program variables defined within a block are said to be local to a block, while variables known within a block because they are defined in the surrounding text are called global variables.

A block can be used to define a temporary variable, one which is used to store intermediate values during the course of a computation, and then not used again. For instance a temporary variable was made use of in the program segment called reorder, which was defined in connection with an algorithm to sort the elements of an array in Section 5.6. The program segment could have been given as a block, defining the variable TEMPORARY only within a localized context.

```
BEGIN
    STRING ARRAY NAME (1::1000);
        .
        .
        .
    BEGIN COMMENT***** REORDER *****;
        STRING TEMPORARY;
        TEMPORARY := NAME(J-1);
        NAME(J-1) := NAME(J);
        NAME(J) := TEMPORARY;
    END;
        .
        .
    END.
```

In the partially defined program above, the task of the segment marked by the comment as reorder is to exchange the values held by a pair of array elements. The segment consists of a block in which TEMPORARY is declared as a local, integer variable. The array NAME is global within this block. Since a local variable cannot be counted on to retain the value it might have held the last time a block was executed, a local variable must have its value initialized within the block prior to its being referenced. For a more formal definition of local and global variables, see section A8.1.1 of the Appendix.

Local and global definitions can apply not only to variables, but also to procedures themselves. This is because the definition of a procedure is itself a declaration. The declaration of a procedure is located in the text of a program in the initial section of some block, along with variable declarations. But the algorithm represented by the procedure is not executed at that point in the program. Instead, it is invoked at a point in the program at which it is referred to by its name. Most frequently, the way that a procedure will be made known for use within the body of another procedure will be by global definition.

Of course, blocks may be nested within one another. According to the rules we have stated governing the scope of definition of program objects, the innermost block of a nest of blocks will have the largest number of objects defined within it. For it will have all of its own locally defined variables plus all the variables and procedures that are defined globally, unless the names of some of them have been preempted by local redefinition.

7.2 Communicating data to procedures

The simplest way that values of program variables can be communicated to a procedure is by referencing, within the procedure body, the names of globally defined variables. However, if this were the only way to pass data to a procedure, it would be very limiting. In the case of functional notation in mathematics, the idea is that a function defines a mapping from one set of objects to another. The arguments of a function are expressions that take values from the specified set of objects. Similarly, it is convenient to allow procedures to have arguments that can be any expressions belonging to the data type declared for arguments of that function. In defining the program text that is the body of the procedure, it is necessary to have some notation by which to refer to the arguments that the procedure is to receive. The actual arguments (called actual parameters in ALGOL nomenclature) cannot be known at the time the procedure is defined, but only when it is invoked. So in the definition of the procedure, some dummy arguments are defined (known as formal parameters in the nomenclature of ALGOL). The formal parameters may be thought of as locally defined names to be used in the definition of the procedure body to represent variables or expressions that will be specified upon actually invoking the procedure.

If the arguments of a procedure are to be simple variables (that is, are neither arrays nor procedures), then we need only be concerned with passing the value of an actual parameter at the time of invocation, and possibly with returning as a result the final value that the computation has assigned to the dummy argument, to be assigned as the value of the actual parameter. ALGOL W allows one to specify this convention by its formal parameter declarations. An ALGOL W procedure heading, used to begin the declaration of a procedure, consists of the keyword PROCEDURE followed by the name to be given, followed by a parenthesized list of formal parameter declarations. In addition to declaring the data type of each formal parameter, the simple type parameters can be declared to have the attributes VALUE or RESULT, or both. When a formal parameter is given one of these attributes, it means that is is to be treated just as though it were a locally declared variable. If it has the attribute VALUE, then upon each invocation of the procedure, the local variable is initialized with the value of the actual parameter. RESULT works conversely to assign a final value of the local variable to the actual parameter. (See Section A9.3 of the Appendix.)

On the other hand, a formal parameter that is not given either of these attributes cannot be a local variable. Instead, when the procedure is invoked, the computation proceeds exactly as if the name of the actual parameter appeared in the procedure body in place of the name of the formal parameter. This type of substutution sounds simple, but is in fact sometimes tricky, and it is preferable to use formal parameters with either of the attributes VALUE or RESULT whenever possible.

We can now give some examples of procedure declarations and the invocations of procedures. An easy example to begin with will be the algorithm for finding the greatest common divisor of a pair of integers, which was given in section 4.1.

Example 7.2.1 -- A procedure for the greatest common divisor

In this example the procedure is to evaluate a function. It is to take integer-valued arguments, and is to return an integer value as the result of its execution. ALGOL W allows us to declare a simple data type for the procedure identifier itself, and to compute a value to be returned as the value of the function by evaluating an expression which appears as the last item in the procedure body. A procedure declaration for the greatest common divisor function is:

```
INTEGER PROCEDURE GCD (INTEGER VALUE M, N);
    BEGIN
        WHILE M ¬= N DO
            IF M > N THEN
                M := M - N
            ELSE
                N := N - M;
        M
    END GCD
```

The expression giving the value to be returned at the end of execution is simply the variable M, appearing just at the end of the group of statements that make up the procedure body.

We can illustrate the use of some simple procedures by considering some computations with rational numbers. A rational number can be represented by a pair of integers, interpreted as the numerator and denominator of a fraction. We shall only deal with non-negative numbers. There are a number of computations that one might wish to do with rational numbers, but we shall consider only one of the simplest -- to compare two rationals, determining if one is greater than the other.

159

Example 7.2.2 -- Comparison of two rational numbers

In this example, we are given four positive integers representing a pair of rational fractions, and we are to determine whether the first is larger than the second. The value that is to be returned is just a logical value, true if the first rational is the larger, false otherwise. If the rational numbers are a/x and b/y, then the comparison could be effected by comparing a*y with b*x. However, there is a disadvantage to this, for then the ability to compare rational fractions will be severly restricted by the size of the largest integer number that can be represented in the computer. It may be that the two denominators, x and y, contain a common factor. If so, then this factor should be extracted before multiplying the numerators by the opposite denominators, in order that the products will not be larger than is necessary to make the comparison. The common factor of the denominators can be found by using the GCD function. Assuming that the procedure GCD of the previous example has been defined globally to the procedure that we are about to write, the comparison algorithm can be given as:

```
LOGICAL PROCEDURE GREATER (INTEGER VALUE A, X, B, Y);
    BEGIN
        INTEGER G;
        G := GCD (X, Y);
        A*(Y DIV G) > B*(X DIV G)
    END GREATER
```

Here the integer variable G has been defined locally to the procedure, to hold the value of the greatest common divisor.

Another possible representation for rational numbers is by a triple of integers, the first standing for the integral part of a rational number, and the second and third for the numerator and denominator of a fractional part, as in 2 1/4. In this representation, there is a reduced form of any rational number, in which the fractional part is less than unity in value, and the greatest common divisor of the numerator and denominator of the fractional part is unity.

Example 7.2.3 -- Computing the reduced form of a rational number

A procedure to compute the reduced form of a rational number given as a triple of integers will differ from the procedures of the preceding examples, in that it does not compute a function. Instead, it computes a transformation on the triple of values it is given, yielding in its place another triple that represents the same rational value. To

accomplish this, the formal parameters of the procedure are
declared to have both the attributes VALUE and RESULT. (See
Section A9.3.4 of the Appendix.)

```
PROCEDURE REDUCE (INTEGER VALUE RESULT M, A, X);
    COMMENT***********************************
    *  IF 'A' IS NON-ZERO, EXTRACT THE INTEGRAL *
    *  PART OF THE FRACTION A/X, THEN REDUCE THE*
    *  FRACTION BY ELIMINATING COMMON FACTORS.  *
    **********************************************;
    IF A > 0 THEN
        BEGIN
            INTEGER G;
            M := M + A DIV X;
            A := A REM X;
            G := GCD (A, X);
            A := A DIV G;
            X := X DIV G;
        END REDUCE
```

Finally, we shall give as an example a complete ALGOL W program
that uses the three procedures defined in the preceding examples
to find and print in reduced form the greater of two rational
numbers that are read in the form of integer triples from an
input device.

Example 7.2.4 -- Comparing and reducing rational numbers

```
BEGIN
    INTEGER I1, A1, X1, I2, A2, X2;

    INTEGER PROCEDURE GCD (INTEGER VALUE M, N);
        BEGIN
            WHILE M ¬= N DO
                IF M > N THEN
                    M := M - N
                ELSE
                    N := N - M;
            M
        END GCD;

    LOGICAL PROCEDURE GREATER (INTEGER VALUE A, X, B, Y);
        BEGIN
            INTEGER G;
            IF (X > 0) AND (Y > 0) THEN
                G := GCD (X, Y)
            ELSE
                G := 1;
            A*(Y DIV G) > B*(X DIV G)
        END GREATER;
```

161

```
PROCEDURE REDUCE (INTEGER VALUE RESULT M, A, X);
    IF A > 0 THEN
        BEGIN
            INTEGER G;
            M := M + A DIV X;
            A := A REM X;
            G := GCD (A, X);
            A := A DIV G;
            X := X DIV G;
        END REDUCE;

COMMENT**** BODY OF THE MAIN PROGRAM STARTS HERE ****;
READ (I1, A1, X1, I2, A2, X2);
ASSERT (I1 >= 0) AND (A1 >= 0) AND (X1 > 0) AND
       (I2 >= 0) AND (A2 >= 0) AND (X2 > 0);
REDUCE (I1, A1, X1);
REDUCE (I2, A2, X2);
WRITE ("THE LARGER RATIONAL NUMBER IS");
IF (I1 > I2) OR (I1 = I2) AND GREATER (A1, X1, A2, X2)
  THEN
    WRITEON (I1, A1, "/", X1)
ELSE
    WRITEON (I2, A2, "/", X2);
END.
```

This algorithm illustrates several aspects of the use of procedures. As we progress to the consideration of more complex problems, we shall find that most of the individual algorithms that we consider will be written as ALGOL W procedures.

One further comment is in order concerning the algorithm that has been used in the example. It will only be capable of comparing rational fractions if the procucts that are formed in the logical expression at the end of the procedure GREATER remain smaller than the maximum representable integer. If we used other algorithms that did arithmetic on rationals, we sould discover that this is a serious limitation. This limitation can be avoided, but only at the cost of additional computational and programming effort.

7.3 Side effects

Since the global variables defined in surrounding blocks are available for use in the statements of a procedure, it may be that a procedure not only references the values of global variables, but also assigns new values to some of them. When this happens, it is called a side effect of the execution of a procedure, for it cannot be anticipated by looking only at the statement that invokes the procedure; one must look at the procedure declaration as well to discover possible side effects. Side effects are a prefectly legitimate function of a procedure, but since they are not always apparent from the text of an algorithm statement, one must be especially careful to document side effects by the use of comments in the ALGOL W text. The principal use of side effects is to enable procedures to manipulate the global data structures used in an algorithm. Since local variables cannot retain their values from one invocation of a procedure to the next, any data which is to exist for a longer time than does a single invocation of a procedure must be held in a data structure that is global to the procedure. Of course, other procedures or program statements can also manipulate these global data.

Conversely, if a globally defined variable is used to store temporary values needed only for a single execution of a procedure, then there is the possibility that an unintended side effect may occur. This could happen if the same variable is used to store a value in the program segment from which the procedure is invoked. After invocation of the procedure, the global variable may have had its value changed, although that fact will not be apparent by reading only the program segment in which the procedure invocation appears. This kind of side effect is undesirable and can be avoided by following a policy of using local variables whenever possible.

Another possible consequence of a side effect is that the repeated invocation of a procedure may not produce an identical result, even if it is given the same actual parameters in each invocation. An example of such a procedure is the standard ALGOL W procedure READ.

Example 7.3.1 -- Decomposition of integers into prime factors

Every integer has a unique decomposition as a product of prime factors according the the fundamental theorem of arithmetic. Let us devise an algorithm that will read successive integers from an input device and print each integer together with its factorization. For this purpose, we shall need to be able to refer to a list of prime numbers, but as we do not know in advance how many primes will be needed, we must have an algorithm to generate primes. The algorithm PRIME2 of Example 5.4.1 will accomplish this task. However, there is no necessity to recompute all of the primes previously generated, each time PRIME2 is invoked. It would be more efficient to keep a list of all primes generated by previous invocations of

PRIME2, and only generate new primes if the list needs to be lengthened. In order to do this, we shall make a procedure out of PRIME2, but shall let the list of primes (contained in the integer array PRIMES) and the variable PRIMESFOUND that gives the length of the list be global to the procedure, so that their values will be retained from one invocation of the procedure to the next.

In constructing an algorithm, the first task will be to initialize the global variables that are to be used by PRIME2. Since the algorithm is to accept a sequence of numbers as input, some means of controlling the iteration must be provided. However, our algorithm is only intended to work with positive integers, and so a means of control would be to terminate the list of data with an invalid value, that is, zero or a negative integer. An iteration graph describing this control is

```
+---------------------------------------------------------------+
| initialize global variables;                                  |
| read (Number);                                                |
+---------------------------------------------------------------+
| while Number > 0                                              |
|   +-----------------------------------------------------------+
|   | determine the prime factors of Number                     |
|   +-----------------------------------------------------------+
+---------------------------------------------------------------+
```

The task of determining prime factors will require that the prime numbers be examined, in order, to see if each one will divide Number. Whenever a prime factor is discovered, it should be extracted from Number by a division, so that the value of Number is reduced at each factorization. Finally, when the value of Number has been reduced to 1, all of its factors will have been discovered. In carrying out this strategy, we must be careful to account for possible multiple factors, by extracting as many instances of each prime as will successively divide Number, before going on to test any succeeding primes. In the following iteration graph, N is used as an index to the primes, and the Nth prime is obtained by invoking the procedure PRIME2. This strategy is summarized in the following iteration graph determine the prime factors of Number:

```
N := 1;  Nth_prime := PRIME2(1);

while Number > 1

          if Nth_prime divides Number
  then                              else

  extract Nth_prime    N := N + 1;
  as a factor from     Nth_prime :=
  Number                      PRIME2(N)
```

These iteration graphs are easily translated in an ALGOL W program:

```
BEGIN
    COMMENT*********************************************************
    *   PRIMEFACTORS:                                             *
    *      FIND AND PRINT ALL PRIME FACTORS OF A POSITIVE INTEGER *
    *      FIRST COME THE GLOBAL DECLARATIONS                     *
    ***********************************************************;
    INTEGER NUMBER, PRIMESFOUND, NTHPRIME, N;
    INTEGER ARRAY PRIMES (1::1000);

    INTEGER PROCEDURE PRIME2 (INTEGER VALUE N);
        COMMENT*********************************************************
        *   COMPUTES THE NTH PRIME NUMBER BY THE ALGORITHM OF        *
        *   EXAMPLE 5.4.1.  GLOBAL VARIABLES ARE TO BE INITIALIZED   *
        *   IN THE SURROUNDING BLOCK.                                *
        ***********************************************************;
        BEGIN
            INTEGER I, M;
            LOGICAL NOTAFACTOR;
            IF N > PRIMESFOUND THEN
                BEGIN
                    I := PRIMES(PRIMESFOUND) + 2;
                    WHILE PRIMESFOUND < N DO
                        BEGIN
                            M := 2;  NOTAFACTOR := TRUE;
                            WHILE NOTAFACTOR AND
                                (PRIMES(M)*PRIMES(M) <= I) DO
                                BEGIN
                                    NOTAFACTOR := I REM PRIMES(M) -= 0;
                                    M := M + 1;
                                END;
```

```
                    IF NOTAFACTOR THEN
                        BEGIN
                            PRIMESFOUND := PRIMESFOUND + 1;
                            PRIMES(PRIMESFOUND) := I;
                        END;
                    I := I + 2;
                END;
            END;
        PRIMES(N)
    END PRIME2;

PRIMES(1) := 2;  PRIMES(2) := 3;
PRIMESFOUND := 2;
INTFIELDSIZE := 7;
READ (NUMBER);
WHILE NUMBER > 0 DO
    BEGIN
        WRITE (NUMBER, "HAS THE PRIME FACTORS");
        COMMENT************************************************
        *   LET 'N' BE AN INDEX TO THE PRIMES.  STARTING WITH   *
        *   THE FIRST PRIME, TEST 'NUMBER' FOR DIVISIBILITY BY  *
        *   THE NTH PRIME.  IF DIVISIBLE, THEN FACTOR OUT THE    *
        *   PRIME AND PRINT IT.  DON'T ADVANCE THE INDEX 'N'     *
        *   UNTIL THE NTH PRIME IS NO LONGER A FACTOR OF         *
        *   'NUMBER' IN ORDER NOT TO MISS ANY REPEATED FACTORS. *
        ************************************************;
        N := 1;  NTHPRIME := 2;
        WHILE NUMBER > 1 DO
            IF NUMBER REM NTHPRIME = 0 THEN
                BEGIN
                    NUMBER := NUMBER DIV NTHPRIME;
                    WRITEON (NTHPRIME);
                END
            ELSE
                BEGIN
                    N := N + 1;
                    NTHPRIME := PRIME2 (N);
                END;
        READON (NUMBER);
    END;
END.
```

In this example, the procedure PRIME2 acts as a function, returning the value of the Nth prime number when it is presented with N as an argument. But it also has the responsibility of maintaining the table of previously computed primes which it does by its side effects on the global variables PRIMESFOUND and PRIMES.

7.4 Recursion

Some mathematical functions can be defined in a very concise way in terms of their own properties. For example the factorial function of a positive integer is given very neatly in terms of the factorial function of the next smaller integer,

$$\text{factorial}(N) = N * \text{factorial}(N-1)$$

The definition appears at first hand to be circular, but it is not necessarily so, for the argument of the defining expression on the right is not the same as the argument of the expression defined.   Of course, in order to complete the definition, one must also give an actual value for the function on some particular value of the argument. For the factorial function, we give

Factorial(0) = 1,
Factorial(N) = N * Factorial(N-1), for N > 0.

This defines the function for all non-negative integers.   A definition of a function in terms of its own properties is said to be recursive.

A recursive definition may also provide a means of computing values of the function, provided that one has available a programming language in which recursive computation is allowed. ALGOL W is such a language. Since the name of a procedure is an identifier defined in the block in which the procedure declaration appears, that name is automatically made known within the procedure body as a globally defined identifier. Thus, it is perfectly legal in a statement within the procedure body to re-invoke that very same procedure by mentioning its name!   The process is not so mysterious as it sounds, for each invocation of the procedure is a separate computation.

A simple illustration of a recursive computation can be furnished by giving a procedure to compute the factorial function:

```
INTEGER PROCEDURE FACT (INTEGER VALUE N);
    IF N = 0 THEN 1
    ELSE N * FACT (N-1)
```

To see how the recursion works, let us follow the computation of factorial(3) by this algorithm. We can follow the computation by substituting, on successive lines, the body of the procedure each time it is invoked with the value of its argument substituted for the formal parameter N.

```
FACT (3)                                          (first invocation)

IF 3 = 0 THEN 1 ELSE 3 * FACT (2)                 (second invocation)

IF 3 = 0 THEN 1 ELSE 3 *
    (IF 2 = 0 THEN 1 ELSE 2 * FACT (1))           (third invocation)

IF 3 = 0 THEN 1 ELSE 3 *
    (IF 2 = 0 THEN 1 ELSE 2 *
        (IF 1 = 0 THEN 1 ELSE 1 * FACT (0)))
                                                  (fourth invocation)

IF 3 = 0 THEN 1 ELSE 3 *
    (IF 2 = 0 THEN 1 ELSE 2 *
        (IF 1 = 0 THEN 1 ELSE 1 *
            (IF 0 = 0 THEN 1 ELSE 0 *            (evaluation of
                FACT (-1))))                      fourth invocation)

IF 3 = 0 THEN 1 ELSE 3 *
    (IF 2 = 0 THEN 1 ELSE 2 *                     (evaluation of
        (IF 1 = 0 THEN 1 ELSE 1 * 1))            third invocation)

IF 3 = 0 THEN 1 ELSE 3 *
    (IF 2 = 0 THEN 1 ELSE 2 * 1)                 (evaluation of
                                                  second invocation)

IF 3 = 0 THEN 1 ELSE 3 * 2                        (evaluation of
                                                  first invocation)
6
```

Although the computer does not literally expand the text of the
program in the way it has been done above, it does carry out the
procedure invocations and evaluations in exactly the order
indicated.

For the simple example of the factorial function, an
iterative algorithm equally as simple could also be given.
However, this is not always the case. Although it is always
possible to give an iterative algorithm for a function that can
be computed by a recursive procedure, there are some functions
for which the invention of an iterative algorithm will be much
more difficult than the invention of a recursive algorithm. The
converse is also true; for other functions, an iterative
algorithm will be easier to compose.

Let us examine another function that we know how to compute,
and compare recursive and iterative procedures for its
evaluation. Euclid's algorithm for the greatest common divisor
of a pair of integers was given as a procedure in Example 7.2.1.
A recursive procedure computing the g.c.d. is:

```
INTEGER PROCEDURE GCDR (INTEGER VALUE M, N);
   IF N = M THEN M
   ELSE IF N > M THEN GCDR (N-M, M)
   ELSE GCDR (N, M-N)
```

Tracing the evaluation sequence of GCDR(6,8) shows it to call for the evaluation of GCDR(6,2), which in turn calls for GCDR(4,2), which calls for GCDR(2,2). The evaluation of each of these calls is held in abeyance awaiting evaluation of the next, until upon reaching GCDR(2,2), evaluation is possible without further procedure calls. The result of evaluating GCDR(2,2) is then passed back along the line, becoming the value of GCDR(4,2), of GCDR(6,2), and finally of GCDR(6,8).

For any pair of positive integers, the results of evaluating GCDR and the iterative procedure GCD will be identical. In case one or both of the arguments are not positive, execution of GCD will loop forever on the WHILE statement, whereas GCDR will embark upon an unending sequence of recursive procedure calls, and will never return any result! In this sense, both procedures correspond to the notion of a mathematical function that is undefined on zero or negative arguments.

The following example illustrates a problem for which it is difficult to compose an iterative algorithm, but for which a recursive algorithm is not hard to find.

Example 7.4.1 -- Evaluating the determinant of a square matrix

When a system of linear equations is to be solved by computation, one of the calculations that must usually be made is of the determinant of a matrix whose elements are the coefficients of terms of the equations. The determinant is a single number defined for a square matrix of numbers, as the sum taken over all permutations of the columns of the matrix, of the products of elements appearing on the principal diagonal of the permuted matrix. The sign with which each of these terms is added to the sum is positive or negative according to whether the permutation of the columns is even or odd.

No one actually computes a determinant of a matrix larger than 3 by 3 by generating all permutations of the columns and evaluating the products of diagonals. Usually, one uses the method of expansion of cofactors. If a_{ij} denotes the matrix element in the ith row and jth column, then the cofactor of a_{ij} is the matrix obtained from the original matrix by deleting its ith row and jth column. The

169

determinant of a matrix can be evaluated by summing over the
column indices the products of the elements of any given row
with the determinants of the cofactor matrices of the
respective elements. The sign of each term of the sum is
given by $(-1)^{i+j}$, where the indices i and j are numbered
from 1 up to the dimension of the matrix. Symbolically,
this formula for evaluation of the determinant of an N by N
matrix can be written as follows:

$$\text{Det}(A) = \sum_{j=1}^{N} (-1)^{i+j} * A_{ij} * \text{Det}(\text{Cofactor}_{ij}(A))$$

where the choice of the row index, i, is arbitrary so long
as it is within the range of 1 to N. This formula is a
recursive definition of the determinant, since it gives the
determinant of an N by N matrix in terms of the determinants
of a set of N - 1 by N - 1 matrices, the matrices designated
as Cofactor(A). In order for the recursive definition to be
complete, it must have a termination condition telling
explicitly how to get the determinant for a matrix of some
fixed size. It can be completed by considering as a special
case the matrix that consists of only a single element,
specifying that

$$\text{Det}(A) = A_{11}, \quad \text{when } N = 1.$$

In designing an ALGOL W procedure to evaluate the
determinant of a square matrix of real-valued elements, we
can follow the outline of the recursive definition. This
suggests an iteration graph such as

Det (A, N)

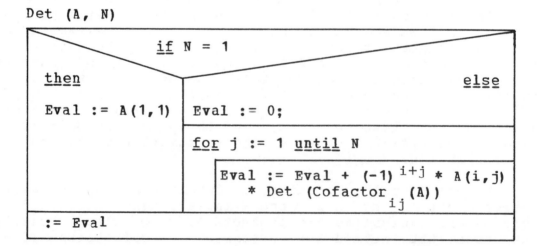

where the assignment operator on the last line designates
the value that is to be returned as the value of the

170

function procedure Det.

The part of the computation not yet specified by this
iteration graph is the formation of the cofactor matrix.
This is to be an N - 1 by N - 1 square matrix, obtained from
the matrix A by deleting one row and one column. Since the
row which is to be deleted can be selected arbitrarily, let
us choose the Nth row, letting the index i of the iteration
graph equal N. Also, since the result is independent of the
order in which summation over the column indices is done,
let us reverse the order of summation, letting j start from
N and go in steps of -1 until 1. The initial relation of the
cofactor matrix to the host matrix A is shown in the diagram
below.

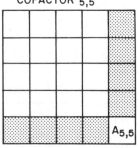

This particular choice of the order in which to iterate over
the columns of A is in no way crucial to the success of the
algorithm; it merely serves to simplify the calculation of
indices in forming the cofactor. Cofactor$_{N,N}$(A) is formed
simply by copying the first N - 1 columns of each of the
first N - 1 rows of A.

For a value of the column index that is intermediate
between 1 and N, the relationship of the cofactor matrix to
the host matrix A is as shown below

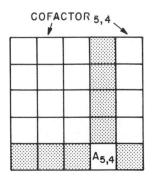

Notice that to transform Cofactor$_{N,j+1}$(A) to Cofactor$_{N,j}$(A),
only a single column of the cofactor matrix needs to be
replaced. The jth column of the cofactor matrix should be
replaced by the first N - 1 elements of the j+1st column of
A.

The final modification of the iteration graph that we
shall make is to account for the sign of the cofactor
expansion by alternation, rather than by raising -1 to an
integral power. The transformations of the original
iteration graph have altered it significantly, and we shall
redraw it before proceeding to translate it into a
procedure.

Det (A,N)

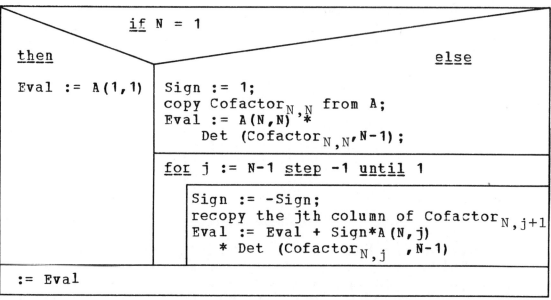

The iteration graph is translated into the procedure DET in
the following program. The procedure has been embedded in a
program block that also reads data, applies the procedure to
the data, and prints a result.

172

```
BEGIN

REAL PROCEDURE DET (REAL ARRAY A(*,*); INTEGER VALUE N);
    COMMENT************************************************************
    *    A RECURSIVE PROCEDURE TO EVALUATE THE DETERMINANT OF AN N BY N *
    *    REAL MATRIX, 'A'.                                              *
    ****************************************************************;
BEGIN
    REAL ARRAY COFACTOR (1:: N-1, 1:: N-1);
    REAL SIGN, EVAL;
    IF N = 1 THEN
        EVAL := A(1, 1)
    ELSE
        BEGIN
            FOR ROW := 1 UNTIL N - 1 DO
                FOR COL := 1 UNTIL N - 1 DO
                    COFACTOR(ROW, COL) := A(ROW, COL);
            EVAL := A(N, N) * DET (COFACTOR, N - 1);
            SIGN := 1;
            FOR J := N - 1 STEP -1 UNTIL 1 DO
                BEGIN
                    SIGN := -SIGN;
                    FOR ROW := 1 UNTIL N - 1 DO
                        COFACTOR(ROW, J) := A(ROW, J + 1);
                    EVAL := EVAL + SIGN * A(N, J) * DET (COFACTOR, N - 1);
                END;
        END;
    EVAL
END DET;

COMMENT***** PROGRAM TO TEST 'DET' *****;
    REAL ARRAY A(1::20,1::20);
    INTEGER ARRAY COLS (1::6);
    INTEGER N;
    REAL DETERMINANT;

    READ (N);
    FOR I := 1 UNTIL N DO
        FOR J := 1 UNTIL N DO
            BEGIN
            READON (A(I,J));  WRITEON (A(I,J));
            END;
    WRITE (" ");
    FOR I := 1 UNTIL N DO COLS(I) := I;
    DETERMINANT := DET (A, N);
    WRITE ("THE DETERMINANT EVALUATES TO:", DETERMINANT);
END.
```

Exercises for chapter 7

7.1 Complete the specification of the algorithm of Example 3.6.1, for finding the intersection of a pair of lines, as an ALGOL W procedure. Do not neglect to specify how the parameters giving the lines are to be passed to the procedure, and how the coordinates of any intersection which has been found are to be returned. Compose a surrounding block of ALGOL W text to enable the procedure to be tested.

7.2 When the computer reads input records on which are encoded the text of an ALGOL W program, its first task in interpreting the text is to recognize the reserved words, identifiers, and constants of the language. Compose a procedure called SCAN to perform this function. It may, of course, employ other procedures local to itself to carry out specialized tasks.

Upon each successive call, SCAN is to locate the next word or operator symbol of the text, returning the word itself as the value of a global STRING (256) variable called WORD_SCANNED. Another global integer variable, WORD_LENGTH, is to contain the number of characters in the scanned word.

The several reserved words and operator symbols of ALGOL W are to be assigned index numbers, and SCAN is to return the appropriate index number as the value of a global integer variable RESERVED_INDEX. Assign the index number values 1 for any identifier, 2 for any numerical constant, 3 for any logical constant, and 4 for any string constant. Let illegal constructions (such as 12.ABC) be given the index number 0.

The problem can be simplified significantly by adding the restriction that no 'word' is allowed to be broken across the boundary of an input record. Don't forget to allow the procedure to scan to the end of a comment.

7.3 In many computational applications, a sequence of randomly generated numbers is utilized to simulate randomly occurring events. It is, of course, impossible to generate a truly random sequence by means of a finite, deterministic algorithm, but one can generate sequences that satisfy the simplest statistical tests of randomness quite easily. Some of these generators actually produce repetitive sequences of numbers, having a long period of repetition. For example, two such generators are described by:

```
X1 := (509 + 67*X1) REM 4096

X2 := 2*X2 REM 4096 + (X2 + X2 DIV 4 + X2 DIV 2048) REM 2
```

(the second generator cannot be given initial values of 0 or 4095 for X2.)

Give ALGOL W procedures for each of these pseudo-random sequence generators (the variables X1 and X2 must be global to the procedures in order to have their values saved from one invocation to the next). Perform the following tests on both generators:

a) determine the period of repetition.
b) determine the distribution of values by counting the number of values generated in each interval of 100, from 0 to 4095, as the generator cycles through a complete period.
c) determine the mean of the values generated.
d) determine the covariance of values separated by intervals of 1, 2, and 5 in the sequence. The covariance of values separated by an interval I is given by

$$\frac{1}{N} \sum_{i=1}^{N} (x_i - mean)*(x_{i+1} - mean)$$

where N is the period of the generator.

Pseudo-random sequence generators of the first type (with with any values of the constant parameters) are called multiplicative congruence generators; those of the second type are called linear congruence generators, or shift-register sequence generators.

7.4 Give a procedure that will compute and print a calendar for any month, past or future, that is given as an argument. Note that leap year occurs every fourth year, but only every fourth whole century.

7.5 The Fibonacci function is defined by a recursion formula involving two previous values,

```
F(n) = if n = 1 or n = 2 then 1
       else F(n-1) + F(n-2).
```

If this formula is implemented directly as a recursive
ALGOL W procedure, it is needlessly inefficient in that many
computations are repeated. For instance, in the computation
of F(6), the evaluation sequence would be

```
      F(6)      compute F(5), then F(4)
      F(5)      compute F(4), then F(3)
      F(4)      compute F(3), then F(2)
      F(3)      compute F(2), then F(1)
      F(2)  =  1
      F(1)  =  1
      F(3)  =  1 + 1 = 2
   *  F(2)  =  1
      F(4)  =  2 + 1 = 3
   *  F(3)      compute F(2), then F(1)
   *  F(2)  =  1
   *  F(1)  =  1
   *  F(3)  =  1 + 1 = 2
      F(5)  =  3 + 2 = 5
   *  F(4)      compute F(3), then F(2)
   *  F(3)      compute F(2), then F(1)
   *  F(2)  =  1
   *  F(1)  =  1
   *  F(3)  =  1 + 1 = 2
   *  F(2)  =  1
   *  F(4)  =  2 + 1 = 3
      F(6)  =  5 + 3 = 8
```

Out of the 22 steps of the execution sequence, the 12 marked
with asterisks are duplications of previous steps. As the
argument of the Fibonacci function is increased the
inefficiency grows much worse.

a) Can you give a simple <u>iterative</u> procedure for computing the
   Fibonacci function, which does not needlessly repeat
   computations?

b) Can you give a recursive algorithm that does not cause
   repetition of previous computations?

NOTES

SOLVING HARD PROBLEMS

Even after one has learned to use most of the standard tools of computation, when faced with the specification of a problem to be solved it is still not easy to generate an algorithm for the solution. We often encounter the difficulty that when one starts to think of the steps required in a possible solution, he is swamped by a tidal wave of details, all seemingly interrelated, that must be taken into account. If only the problem could be reduced in its complexity by taking just one step at a time, then an algorithm might be developed by a process of orderly analysis. It is this difficulty of complexity that we are about to tackle in this chapter.

8.1 Top-down problem solving

There is one concept of dealing with problems in a large organization that says you should always start at the top. If you can get the attention of the person who has overall responsibility for the organization, and present your problem to him, he then will determine the general course of action to be taken and will delegate the responsibility for carrying out this action to appropriate second-level executives within the organization. They may, in turn, have some of the details taken care of by employees under their jurisdiction. The solution to the problem begins at the top, and details are allowed to filter down to the workers by a process of delegation.

This process works in many human organizations, and it is not a bad thing to imitate in the organization of a computational algorithm. We can make it a little more specific by giving a recursive procedure for this type of problem solving. (This is informal, not an ALGOL W procedure).

        SOLVE (Problem):
          1. Obtain a precise statement of the specifications to be
             met.
          2. Formulate a simple, iterative solution, naming as
             subproblems any trouble spots encountered along the
             way.
          3. While any subproblem remains unsolved,
               SOLVE(Subproblem).

We shall attempt to follow this procedure in generating algorithms for the examples in this chapter. You may already recognize that the ability to define procedures in a programming language is of enormous importance in carrying out this plan of attack, for the algorithm solving each identified subproblem can be given as an ALGOL W procedure.

179

Example <u>8.1.1</u> -- Printing a column of text

A computer printout is to be prepared from text submitted on punched cards. The printout is to appear as a sequence of numbered pages of text, in lines no more than 60 characters wide, with a left margin of 15 print spaces, an upper margin of 6 print lines, and up to 50 printed lines appearing on a page. Words are not to be broken at the ends of the lines, as the computer does not know all of the rules of syllabification of English. There is to be a blank line left between paragraphs, and the first line of each new paragraph is also to have an indentation of five spaces from the left margin.

The input is to be in the form of 80 character records, with words to be separated by one or more blanks, or by an end-of-paragraph character (@) optionally followed by blanks, or by an end of record. Words are not to be broken from one record to the next. A word will be any sequence of non-blank characters except for the end-of-paragraph character. Thus, if the text consists of ordinary English, the punctuation marks following any word will be treated as though part of the word, and will not be separated. If a word ends with a period, a question mark, or a colon, it is to be separated from the following word on the print line by two blank spaces, regardless of the separation that occurs in the input text. If a word ends with any other symbol, it is to be separated from the following word by a single space. Printing of the text is to continue until an end-of-text symbol (@@) is encountered.

We begin composing an algorithm according to our top-down method by giving a control program whose function is merely to identify subtasks and assign them to other procedures. This control program will also contain the declarations of global variables and procedures, but since we do not yet know what they shall be, we cannot write these declarations yet.

```
BEGIN  COMMENT*****  PRINTTEXT  *****;
    (declarations of global variables and
    procedures go here)
    INITIALIZE;
    WHILE ¬END_OF_TEXT DO
        PRINTPAGE;
END;
```

As you can see, the top-down design philosophy makes it very easy to get started. So far, the algorithm calls for some form of initialization to be performed by a procedure yet to be specified, followed by the printing of pages until some condition arises to cause the logical variable END_OF_TEXT to become false. Since we don't yet know what to initialize, our next step will be the composition of PRINTPAGE.

The task assigned to PRINTPAGE is to begin a new page of output with an upper margin of six blank lines in which is embedded a page number, then to print 50 lines of text. It must also take responsibility for updating the page number in preparation for the printing of a page that may follow. At this point, we realize that the original specification of the problem did not say how the page number should appear, so we must make that decision at this point in order to complete the specification of the task for PRINTPAGE. Let us say that the page number is to appear in a four character field, followed by two blanks, and this field is to be bracketed by dashes to set it apart, and centered on the second (otherwise blank) line from the top of the page.

There are some integer variables that must be declared globally to PRINTPAGE. One is to keep track of page numbers; call it PAGE. Others will be used to keep the values of constants; these are MARGIN, giving the width of the left margin, LINEWIDTH, the maximum width of a printed line, and PAGELENGTH, the number of printed lines on a page. Since the values of these quantities have been specified in advance to be 15, 60 and 50, respectively, one may ask why we should bother to declare variables to hold these constant values. The answer is that the values are constant for the duration of one execution of the algorithm, but may not be constant for all time if the problem specification is changed. If we anticipate that these parameters might sometime be altered, then the difficulty involved in modification of the algorithm will be minimized by declaring variables to hold the values of the parameters. The only place in the entire algorithm where these variables will have their values set will be at the initialization step, and so this will be the only point at which the program must be changed to accommodate new values of the parameters. On the other hand, if the parameter values were represented as literal data in the program, then to change a parameter value would require one to locate each instance at which it had been referenced, and change the program text at each such point. There is a good chance to make an error in such an operation.

An ALGOL W procedure to print a page is:

```
PROCEDURE PRINTPAGE;
    BEGIN
        (procedure declarations go here)
        INTEGER LINECOUNT;

        IOCONTROL (3);   COMMENT***** STARTS A NEW PRINT PAGE*****;
        WRITE (" ");   COMMENT***** BLANK LINE AT TOP OF PAGE*****;
        COMMENT*****************************************************
        *   CENTER THE PAGE NUMBER ON THE SECOND LINE, AND         *
        *   FOLLOW IT WITH FOUR MORE BLANK LINES.                  *
        ***************************************************************;
        IOCONTROL (2);   COMMENT***** STARTS A NEW PRINT LINE*****;
        FOR I := 1 UNTIL MARGIN + (LINEWIDTH - 8) DIV 2 DO
            WRITEON (" ");
        WRITEON ("-", PAGE, "-");
        WRITE (" ");   WRITE (" ");   WRITE (" ");   WRITE (" ");
        FOR LINECOUNT := 1 UNTIL PAGELENGTH DO
            PRINTLINE (LINECOUNT);
        PAGE := PAGE + 1;
    END PRINTPAGE
```

Much of the work involved in printing a page has been re-delegated to another procedure, PRINTLINE. There are special cases to be dealt with, for if the last line printed ended a paragraph, then the next line is to be left blank, unless it occurs at the top of a page. Also, the beginning of a line is to be indented if it is the first line of a paragraph. To summarize these cases, it may be useful to draw an iteration graph,

PRINTLINE:

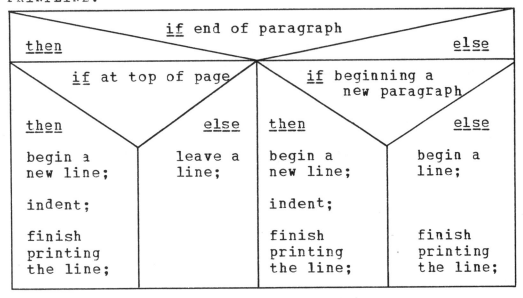

The several conditions controlling the course of execution of PRINTLINE depend on circumstances outside its area of responsibility, and must be communicated to it somehow. Determining that the line to be printed is the first on a page can be done by testing the condition LINECOUNT = 1, since LINECOUNT is a parameter whose value is passed to PRINTLINE. For the conditions of having ended a paragraph or of being ready to begin a new one, we shall introduce global, logical variables ENDPARAGRAPH and PARABEGIN. These variables will have to be declared in the outermost block, that of the control program, but part of the job of maintaining their values correctly will fall to PRINTLINE. We are now ready to compose this procedure.

```
PROCEDURE PRINTLINE (INTEGER VALUE LINECOUNT);
  IF ¬END_OF_TEXT THEN
    BEGIN
       (declarations of procedures and local variables go here)
       IF ENDPARAGRAPH THEN
         BEGIN  COMMENT***** TEST FOR TOP OF PAGE *****;
           IF LINECOUNT = 1 THEN
             BEGIN COMMENT***** START A NEW PARAGRAPH *****;
               STARTLINE;
               INDENT;
               WRITELINE;
             END
```

```
                ELSE
                    BEGIN
                        COMMENT*****************************
                        *   LEAVE A BLANK LINE AND INDICATE *
                        *   THE START OF A NEW PARAGRAPH IS *
                        *   TO FOLLOW                       *
                        ***********************************;
                        WRITE (" ");
                        PARABEGIN := TRUE;
                    END;
                    ENDPARAGRAPH := FALSE;
                END
            ELSE
                BEGIN
                    STARTLINE;
                    IF PARABEGIN THEN
                        BEGIN
                            INDENT;
                            PARABEGIN := FALSE;
                        END;
                    WRITELINE;
        END PRINTLINE
```

Again, most of the work has been left to other
procedures, STARTLINE, INDENT, and WRITELINE. We see that
the use made of the flag, PARABEGIN, has been simply to
remember, following the termination of one paragraph, that
the next line printed is to be indented to begin another
paragraph. After this action has been taken, the flag is
reset to FALSE until it is needed again. Both the flags,
ENDPARAGRAPH and PARABEGIN will have to be set in the
initialization procedure in order that PRINTLINE will work
correctly the first time that it is called.

The two procedures STARTLINE and INDENT are very simple
in function. STARTLINE is to begin the printing of a new
line, set the left margin, and initialize a variable called
RESTOFLINE that will keep track of how many characters can
be printed before the end of the print line is reached.
INDENT is to fill in the indentation space with blank
characters, and record the fact that fewer characters remain
to be printed before encountering the end of the line. The
variable RESTOFLINE, which is to be of type integer, must be
global to both of these procedures and to WRITELINE, but it
need not be known or remembered outside of a single
execution of PRINTLINE. Therefore, we can add its
declaration to the declarations local to PRINTLINE, which
are:

```
INTEGER RESTOFLINE;

PROCEDURE STARTLINE;
   BEGIN
      COMMENT*****BEGIN PRINTING ON A NEW LINE *****;
      IOCONTROL(2);
      FOR I := 1  UNTIL MARGIN DO
         WRITEON (" ");
      RESTOFLINE := LINEWIDTH;
   END STARTLINE;

PROCEDURE INDENT;
   BEGIN
      WRITEON ("      ");
      RESTOFLINE := RESTOFLINE - 5;
   END INDENT;

PROCEDURE WRITELINE;
   COMMENT*****************************************************
   *   PRINT THE NEXT WORD AS LONG AS IT WILL FIT ON    *
   *   THE PRINT LINE, UNLESS THE PARAGRAPH IS ENDED.   *
   *****************************************************;
   WHILE (WORDLENGTH <= RESTOFLINE) AND ¬ENDPARAGRAPH DO
      BEGIN
         PRINTWORD;
         SCANAWORD;
         COMMENT**********************************************
         *   WORDLENGTH MUST BE SET BY SIDE EFFECT OF    *
         *   SCANAWORD.  SCANAWORD GETS THE NEXT WORD    *
         *   FROM THE INPUT RECORD, AND MUST BE CALLED   *
         *   BEFORE WRITELINE IS FIRST EXECUTED          *
         **********************************************;
      END WRITELINE;
```

We now get down to the definition of two procedures that do most of the work. Let us consider SCANAWORD first. Its function is to obtain the next word from the input text. It must scan over blank characters if there are any, until it comes to a non-blank character. If in the process it encounters the end of one input record, then it is to call for another. When a string of non-blank characters is found, it is to scan over it, recording its length as the value of WORDLENGTH until thw word is terminated either by a blank, by the end-of-paragraph character, or by the end of an input record. It must also remember, from one instance of its execution to the next, the input record it was last working on and its position in scanning that record. It must note for the benefit of the printing procedure, the position of the beginning of the word it has found in

185

the input record. In case a word is found to be terminated by the end-of-paragraph character, it must note that fact and pass over the character. And, if a word is terminated by a punctuation mark indicating that two blank spaces are to follow it, that fact also must be noted.

The global variables needed will be a string variable, TEXT, to hold the input record, two integer variables, WP and TP, to keep track of the position in the input record where a word begins, and of how far the scan has progressed, and an integer variable NBLANKS to indicate the number of spaces that are to follow the word.

There is one additional requirement of SCANAWORD that we can discover by careful analysis of the operation of the procedures already written. The value of WORDLENGTH that it returns must never be greater than the parameter LINEWIDTH. WRITELINE will never put a word on a line if the length of the word is more than RESTOFLINE, and the largest value that RESTOFLINE can have is the value of LINEWIDTH. If too large a value of WORDLENGTH is ever set the algorithm will fail to terminate, with new lines continually being started, and WRITELINE stubbornly refusing to print anything on them because they aren't long enough. Since nothing has been said about this contingency in the original specification of the problem, we shall make an arbitrary decision that if a word is encountered whose length exceeds LINEWIDTH, it will be split into two with the first part having WORDLENGTH equal to LINEWIDTH, and the remainder will be given as the next word.

We can give an iteration graph to specify the algorithm in informal terms.

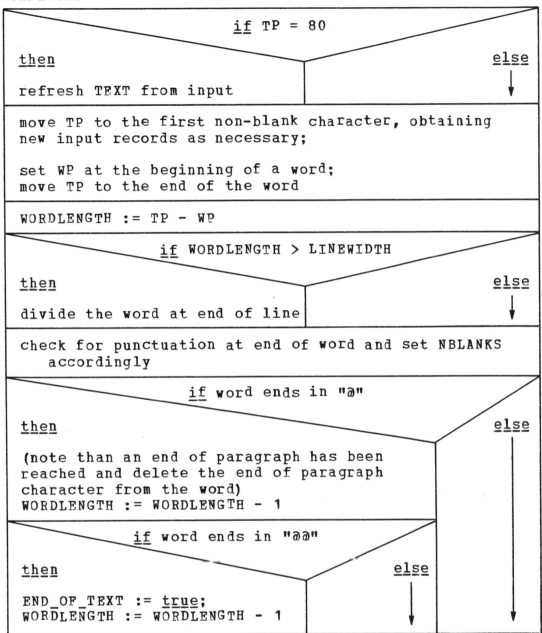

In the algorithm SCANAWORD, when the end-of-paragraph character (∂) has been found, we might have been tempted to set the flag ENDPARAGRAPH. However, the use made of ENDPARAGRAPH in previously composed procedures has been to indicate that the processing of one paragraph has been completed. SCANAWORD can know only that the end of a paragraph has been detected in the input; completion of

processing for that paragraph is outside the jurisdiction of
SCANAWORD, and so it should not be allowed to set this flag.
In particular, printing of the last word of the paragraph
will probably not have been completed when SCANAWORD detects
the terminating symbol. If SCANAWORD were allowed to
overstep its jurisdiction and set ENDPARAGRAPH to TRUE when
the symbol (@) was encountere, then WRITELINE might
terminate a line without having called PRINTWORD to print
the last word of a paragraph. That word would then appear
at the head of the following paragraph, which would be an
error.

A safe course of action is to define a new logical
variable, a flag called LASTWORD, which will be set by
SCANAWORD whenever the end-of-paragraph character is
encountered. Since this variable is to be used by other
procedures as well, it must be declared globally.

The ALGOL W text of SCANAWORD can now be given.

```
PROCEDURE SCANAWORD;
    BEGIN   COMMENT***** ADVANCE THE SCAN POINTER OVER ALL LEADING BLANKS,
                     ***** REQUESTING A NEW INPUT RECORD IF NECESSARY *****;
        IF TP = 80 THEN
            BEGIN
                READCARD (TEXT);
                TP := 0;
            END;
        WHILE (TP < 80) AND ( TEXT (TP | 1) = " ") DO
            BEGIN
                TP := TP + 1;
                IF TP = 80 THEN
                    BEGIN
                        READCARD (TEXT);
                        TP := 0;
                    END;
            END;
        COMMENT*******************************************************************
        *  MARK THE BEGINNING OF A WORD, THEN SCAN TO END OF WORD.      *
        *******************************************************************;
        WP := TP;
        WHILE (TP < 80) AND (TEXT (TP | 1) ¬= " ") DO
            TP := TP + 1;
        COMMENT*******************************************************************
        *  SET THE LENGTH OF THE WORD JUST FOUND AND CHECK THAT THE     *
        *  LENGTH DOES NOT EXCEED THE LINEWIDTH.  IF IT DOES, DIVIDE    *
        *  THE WORD.                                                    *
        *******************************************************************;
        WORDLENGTH := TP - WP;
        IF WORDLENGTH > LINEWIDTH THEN
            BEGIN
                TP := TP - (WORDLENGTH - LINEWIDTH);
                WORDLENGTH := LINEWIDTH;
            END;
        COMMENT*******************************************************************
        *  DETERMINE THE NUMBER OF BLANKS TO BE PRINTED AFTER THE WORD *
        *******************************************************************;
        IF (TEXT (TP-1 | 1) = ".") OR (TEXT (TP-1 | 1) = "?") OR
           (TEXT (TP-1 | 1) = ":") THEN NBLANKS := 2
        ELSE NBLANKS := 1;
        COMMENT*******************************************************************
        *  CHECK FOR AN END OF PARAGRAPH CHARACTER AT THE END OF THE    *
        *  WORD, AND DELETE IT FROM THE WORD IF PRESENT.                *
        *******************************************************************;
        IF TEXT (TP-1 | 1) = "ə" THEN
            BEGIN
                LASTWORD := TRUE;
                WORDLENGTH := WORDLENGTH - 1;
                IF (TP > 1) AND (TEXT (TP-2 | 1) = "ə") THEN
                    BEGIN
                        END_OF_TEXT := TRUE;
                        WORDLENGTH := WORDLENGTH - 1;
                    END;
            END;
    END SCANAWORD;
```

The other working procedure is PRINTWORD. Its task is to cause the sequence of characters beginning at index WP in the input record, and whose length is given by WORDLENGTH, to be appended to the line being printed. Also, if there is room, the word is to be followed in the print line by one or two blank characters as determined by the value of NBLANKS. The variable RESTOFLINE, which keeps track of the number of character spaces remaining in the print line, must be decremented by the length of the word printed and the number of blanks that were left. And finally, if PRINTWORD happens to print the last word of a paragraph, then the processing of that paragraph is complete, so it becomes the responsibility of PRINTWORD to set the flag ENDPARAGRAPH to TRUE in such a case. It is a straightforward matter to compose an ALGOL W procedure to accomplish this task.

```
PROCEDURE PRINTWORD;
   BEGIN
      COMMENT***************************************************
      *   PRINT THE WORD BEGINNING AT INDEX WP IN TEXT   *
      ***************************************************;
      FOR I := WP UNTIL WP + WORDLENGTH - 1 DO
         WRITEON (TEXT (I | 1));
      RESTOFLINE := RESTOFLINE - WORDLENGTH - NBLANKS;
      COMMENT***************************************************
      *   IF THERE IS ROOM IN WHICH ANOTHER WORD MIGHT   *
      *   FOLLOW IN THE LINE, PRINT BLANKS TO SEPARATE   *
      ***************************************************;
      IF RESTOFLINE > 1 THEN
         FOR I := 1 UNTIL NBLANKS DO
            WRITEON (" ");

      IF LASTWORD THEN
         BEGIN
            LASTWORD := FALSE;
            ENDPARAGRAPH := TRUE;
         END;
   END PRINTWORD;
```

All that remains is to give the initialization procedure. As a guide in determining what needs to be initialized, we can examine the use made of each of the global variables, determining whether it requires initialization, and how this is to be accomplished.

MARGIN, LINEWIDTH, and PAGELENGTH must be initialized by assignment.
PAGE must be set initially to 1.
The print field width for an integer page number should

190

be set to four characters.
LASTWORD, ENDPARAGRAPH and END_OF_TEXT must be
    initialized to FALSE;
PARABEGIN must be initialized to TRUE.
TP must be initially set to 80 by assignment, in order
    that SCANAWORD will read an input record when it is
    first called.
WP, WORDLENGTH, TEXT and NBLANKS must be set by an
    initial call to SCANAWORD, following the
    initialization of TP.

We have now specified the task of INITIALIZE.

```
PROCEDURE INITIALIZE;
    BEGIN
        MARGIN := 15;  LINEWIDTH := 60;  PAGELENGTH := 50;
        INTFIELDSIZE := 4;
        LASTWORD := ENDPARAGRAPH := END_OF_TEXT := FALSE;
        PARABEGIN := TRUE;
        TP := 80;
        SCANAWORD;
    END INITIALIZE;
```

The final step needed to complete the algorithm is to
fill in the declarations of the global variables. This step
was deferred until the end in order that we could determine
what variables were needed. The following outline of an
ALGOL W program gives the global variable declarations and
also indicates the scope of each procedure declaration.

```
BEGIN
    INTEGER MARGIN, LINEWIDTH, PAGELENGTH, PAGE, TP, WP,
        WORDLENGTH, NBLANKS;
    STRING (80) TEXT;
    LOGICAL PARABEGIN, ENDPARAGRAPH, LASTWORD, END_OF_TEXT;

    PROCEDURE PRINTPAGE;
        BEGIN

        PROCEDURE PRINTLINE (INTEGER VALUE LINECOUNT);
            BEGIN
                INTEGER RESTOFLINE;

                PROCEDURE STARTLINE;
                    .
                    .
                END STARTLINE;

                PROCEDURE INDENT;
```

```
            .
            .
        END INDENT;

        PROCEDURE PRINTWORD;
                .

        END PRINTWORD;

        PROCEDURE WRITELINE;
                .

        END WRITELINE;
            .
            .
        END PRINTLINE;
        .
        .
    END PRINTPAGE;

    PROCEDURE SCANAWORD;
            .

    END SCANAWORD;

    PROCEDURE INITIALIZE;
            .

    END INITIALIZE

COMMENT***** CONTROL PROGRAM *****;
    INITIALIZE;
    WHILE ¬END_OF_TEXT DO
        PRINTPAGE;
END.
```

In addition to its utility in composing algorithms, there is another significant benefit to the use of top-down organization in the design of a computational program. Since functional responsibility for a single task is localized, insofar as possible in a single procedure, it is usually not difficult to fix the blame for malfunction when something goes wrong. When a program does not work as anticipated, the search for an error can be limited to that segment of the program whose assigned function was not carried out properly. Of course, the top-down design philosophy demands that you pay special attention to specifying the task to be performed by each procedure, in advance of beginning the composition of that procedure. Errors in the overall program can also occur because the specification of a task is given incorrectly or incompletely.

The example we have just examined is not really a very complicated task, and you may wonder whether you might have found an algorithm more quickly by a straightforward, _ad hoc_ problem solving method instead of resorting to top-down organization with all of the individual ALGOL W procedures that it entails. In the next example you will not wonder. Although it too can be stated quite simply, if you begin to think for yourself about how you might compose an algorithm to solve it before reading on to the solution presented in the example, you will realize that this is not a trivial problem. The problem and the algorithm for its solution are due to Professor E. W. Dijkstra.

<u>Example 8.1.2</u> -- Generating an alphabetical list of permutations

Suppose that as part of a word game we want to generate all of the words that can be made by permuting a given string of letters. Also, in order to test the words that will be generated in an orderly way, say by comparing them to entries in a dictionary, we shall require the permutations to be listed in alphabetical order. Since it would be of no use to have the same word listed more than once, we only wish to generate distinct permutations. Let us now specify the task for which we want a computational algorithm. It is to read a string of characters from an input record, and to generate and print in alphabetical order (where the ordering of characters is that imposed by the EBCDIC code), all distinct permutations of the character string.

There is an obvious brute-force strategy for an algorithm to meet these specifications. That is, to read in an input string, generate and store a list of all possible permutations of the string, then sort the list into alphabetical order and print the entries on the list, skipping successive repetitions of words. However, this approach has some serious disadvantages, not the least of which is that it requires us to represent in the computer an enormous list of strings and to sort that list, an expensive operation if the list is long. And no economy can be realized from possible redundancies in repeated permutations as the brute-force strategy requires that all permutations must be generated before the distinct ones can be picked out. Thus, there would not likely be enough room in the computer to store the list of 362880 possible permutations of the string "AAAAAAAAB", although the number of distinct permutations is only 9.

So the brute-force approach has disadvantages which make us want to think further. We do not actually have an algorithm at hand to generate permutations; perhaps it is not much more difficult to generate distinct permutations in alphabetical order, than it is to generate all possible permutations in an arbitrarily chosen order. If we could do this, then there would be no necessity to store a list of the permuted strings; they could just be printed as they were generated. If such an algorithm could be invented, then an algorithm to accomplish the overall task might have the iteration graph:

```
+--------------------------------------------------+
| get a string from an input record;              |
| sort it into a string of least                  |
| alphabetical order;                             |
+--------------------------------------------------+
| while the last permutation printed              |
| was not in greatest alphabetical order          |
| +----------------------------------------------+ |
| | print the string;                           | |
| | replace the string                          | |
| | by NEXTPERMUTATION                          | |
| +----------------------------------------------+ |
+--------------------------------------------------+
```

In the informal description above, we have introduced the notion of _least_ and of _greatest_ alphabetical order. A string is in least alphabetical order if its letters satisfy the relation:

$$letter_i \leq letter_{i+1},$$

where i ranges from 1 to the length of the string minus 1, for then no permutation can precede this one in alphabetical order. Conversely, by greatest alphabetical order, we mean the permutation in which the letters satisfy the relation:

$$letter_i \geq letter_{i+1}.$$

Let us consider a concrete example in order to discover an algorithm for generating the next permutation in alphabetical order. Suppose we consider the string "LITTLE". Seeking the next permutation in order, we will need to restrict the interchange of letters to a substring as far to the right as possible. The next permutation of "LITTLE" will obviously have no change made in the initial letter, the one occupying the position of greatest significance. However, notice that the terminal substring "TTLE" is already in greatest order. Thus, there is no possible permutation of this substring alone that will increase the order of "LITTLE". Apparently then, the letter "I" in the second significant position, is the leftmost letter that must be changed in the next permutation.

What letter should replace "I" in the second position? It must be one of the letters of the substring "TTLE", since we have agreed that the letter to the left of the "I" is to be left unchanged. We must choose from the terminal substring that letter which will result in the smallest increase in the order of the permuted word. Replacing the "I" by the "E" would decrease the order, and replacing it by a "T" would increase the order more than would replacement by the "L". Suppose we now exchange the "I" with the second "L" in "LITTLE" and stop to consider what we have got. The resulting word is "LLTTIE". What we desire is the word least in order among all those permutations beginning with "LL". However, we have not got it yet, for in fact, the terminal substring "TTLE" is in greatest order, not least order. Rearranging it into least order produces "LLEITT", which is the next permutation of these letters following "LITTLE" in alphabetical order.

Let us try to generalize the steps that we followed in generating the next permutation from "LITTLE", being careful to determine what about each step is particular to the choice of the example, and what is an instance of a more general rule. We begin by stating the task to be accomplished by each step.

1) From the given string, determine the longest terminal substring that is in greatest order. Let I denote the index of the letter just to the left of this substring.
2) From the terminal substring to the right of the Ith letter, pick out the letter least among those that are greater in order than the Ith letter. Let J be the index of this letter.
3) Exchange the Ith and Jth letters in the string.
4) Reorder the substring to the right of the Ith letter so as to produce a substring in least order.

Giving names to the procedures that will carry out each of these tasks, we have an initial design for a procedure to find the next permutation:

```
PROCEDURE NEXTPERMUTATION;
    BEGIN
        INTEGER I, J;
        I := LOCATE;
        J := MINMAX (I);
        EXCHANGE (I, J);
        REORDER (I+1);
    END
```

The definition given for a string to be in greatest
alphabetical order suggests an algorithm for the first
subtask. However, we shall need some way to reference the
letters of a permuted string, and we have not yet specified
how a permuted string is to be represented. This is not a
serious problem, though. Suppose we refer to the Ith letter
of a permuted string as LETTER(I), with the declaration of
LETTER to follow. Note that this does not imply a
commitment to any particular representation as yet, for
LETTER might be an array of simple type STRING (1), or it
might be a procedure of the same type. We shall also
require a global, integer variable N, whose value will be
the string length. An ALGOL W procedure to locate the index
of the letter to the left of the maximal length substring in
greatest alphabetic order is

```
INTEGER PROCEDURE LOCATE;
    BEGIN  INTEGER K;
        K := N - 1;
        WHILE LETTER(K) >= LETTER(K+1) DO
            K := K + 1;
        K
    END LOCATE;
```

There is a hazard with the use of LOCATE as given
above. If the permuted string is already in greatest
alphabetic order, then LOCATE will continue to decrement I
until it runs right off the end of the string, with I = 0.
One cannot predict what it will do after that. In this case
the difficulty can be avoided by specifying that LETTER(0),
which is not part of the permuted string, will be defined
and will always have the value " ", which is the character
least in order of the EBCDIC code. Then it will be safe to
use LOCATE on any string that contains at least one
non-blank character.

In the procedure MINMAX, which is to perform the second task listed above, one would ordinarily be obliged to search the entire substring, LETTER(I+1) through LETTER(N), keeping track of the best candidate so far discovered in order to assure that the letter that is found satisfies the specification completely. In the algorithm NEXTPERMUTATION, however, MINMAX is always executed immediately following LOCATE, and so there is some additional information concerning the substring to be searched. It can be used to advantage. It is certain that the substring to the right of the Ith letter contains at least one letter that is greater in order than LETTER(I), for the I+1st letter is one example. Also, we know that the substring from LETTER(I+1) to LETTER(N) is in greatest alphabetic order, that is, that its letters are arrayed in non-increasing order from left to right. Therefore, a satisfactory procedure to follow in MINMAX would be to scan the substring from left to right until encountering the first letter that is less than or equal to LETTER(I) in order. This letter will be one position to the right of the letter desired.

```
INTEGER PROCEDURE MINMAX (INTEGER VALUE I);
   BEGIN
      INTEGER J;
      COMMENT***************************************************
      *   SINCE LETTER(I+1) IS KNOWN TO BE GREATER IN ORDER *
      *   THAN LETTER(I), THE SEARCH CAN BEGIN WITH         *
      *   LETTER(I+2).                                      *
      *   SEARCH PROCEEDS DOWN A STRING  OF LETTERS IN      *
      *   DECLINING ORDER UNTIL ONE IS FOUND TO BE LESS     *
      *   THAN LETTER(I).  THE PRECEDING ONE MUST THEN BE   *
      *   THE LEAST THAT IS GREATER THAN LETTER(I).         *
      *****************************************************;
      J := I + 2;
      WHILE LETTER(J) > LETTER(I) DO
         J := J + 1;
      J - 1
   END MINMAX;
```

In the form given, MINMAX also lacks a condition to guarantee termination. We can employ the same rule that was suggested for termination of LOCATE. Let us specify that LETTER(N+1) is always to be defined and shall have the constant value " ". Then if the value of J in MINMAX ever reaches N + 1, the termination condition must hold.

We shall defer giving the procedure to exchange letters in the string until after deciding how the string is to be represented. The final subtask to be performed is that of reordering the terminal substring into least order. If nothing was known about the order of the terminal substring at this point, then a sorting algorithm would be required. But once again there is additional information that can be made use of. Just prior to the exchange of the Ith and Jth letters, the terminal substring from LETTER(I+1) to LETTER(N) was known to be in greatest order. Then, one of its letters, LETTER(J) was pulled out and replaced. However, it is known that LETTER(J-1) is greater in order than the letter to be inserted in the Jth position (if LETTER(J-1) is, in fact, in the substring at all), and also it is known that the letter being inserted is not greater in order than LETTER(J+1). Therefore, the substring remains in greatest alphabetic order, even though one of its letters has been replaced. To reorder a string that is initially in greatest alphabetic order into one in least order requires only a reversal. Hence, the reordering procedure becomes:

```
PROCEDURE REORDER (INTEGER VALUE FIRST);
    BEGIN
        FOR K := 0 UNTIL (N - FIRST - 1) DIV 2 DO
            EXCHANGE (FIRST + K, N - K);
    END REORDER
```

It is now possible to state with some certainty that the only operations that are performed on the permuted word by NEXTPERMUTATION are comparisons of letters and interchanging of letters. The simplest data representation for these operations seems to be an array, and so we shall declare LETTER in the outermost block of the control program to be

```
STRING (1) ARRAY LETTER (0::81)
```

The array index bounds declared for LETTER will ensure that LETTER(0) AND LETTER(N+1) can be defined for input strings that do not exceed 80 characters.

Having given the specification of LETTER as an array of single character strings, the procedure to accomplish the interchange of a pair of characters is trivial.

```
PROCEDURE EXCHANGE (INTEGER VALUE I, J);
    BEGIN
        STRING (1) TEMPORARY;
        TEMPORARY := LETTER(I);
        LETTER(I)  := LETTER(J);
        LETTER(J)  := TEMPORARY;
    END EXCHANGE
```

All that remains now is to complete the specification of the control program. As a termination condition, it requires that the last permutation that was printed should have been in greatest alphabetic order. We could test for this condition and keep track of it, but upon a little reflection, you will see that if the permuted string contained in the array LETTER is already in greatest order when NEXTPERMUTATION is executed, that we have the unique circumstance that will cause the index I to run off the end of the string in the execution of the procedure LOCATE. Therefore, when NEXTPERMUTATION is presented with the permutation in greatest order, it will record that fact by setting the variable I to zero. All that is necessary in order to test this condition in the control program is to have the value of the index variable I, which is local to NEXTPERMUTATION, communicated to the surrounding block. For this purpose, let us define a global variable INDEX, to be initialized to 1, and allow NEXTPERMUTATION to reset INDEX by side effect. Insert into the body of NEXTPERMUTATION as its last statement the line

```
INDEX := I;
```

The control program can now be given as an ALGOL W program segment:

```
BEGIN  COMMENT*****  CONTROL PROGRAM  *****;
   STRING (80) WORD;
   READ (WORD);
   N := 0;
   WHILE WORD (N | 1) ¬= " " DO
      BEGIN
         N := N + 1;
         LETTER(N) := WORD (N-1 | 1);
      END;
   COMMENT*******************************************
   * N NOW HAS THE VALUE OF THE STRING LENGTH.     *
   * SORT 'LETTER' INTO MINIMAL ALPHABETIC ORDER.  *
   ************************************************;
   SORT;
   LETTER(0) := LETTER(N+1) := " ";
   INDEX := 1;
   COMMENT*******************************************
   * AFTER THE STRING OF MAXIMAL ALPHABETIC ORDER HAS *
   * BEEN PRINTED, INDEX WILL BE SET TO ZERO BY       *
   * NEXTPERMUTATION.                                 *
   ************************************************;
```

```
        WHILE INDEX > 0 DO
            BEGIN   COMMENT***** PRINT THE PERMUTED STRING ****;
                WRITE ("   ");
                FOR J := 1 UNTIL N DO WRITEON (LETTER(J));
                NEXTPERMUTATION;
            END;
    END
```

The sorting procedure is executed only once and on an
array of not more than 80 elements. The relatively simple
BUBBLESORT algorithm studied in Section 5.6 will be
sufficient for this purpose,

```
PROCEDURE SORT;
    FOR I := 1 UNTIL N - 1 DO
        FOR J := N STEP -1 UNTIL I + 1 DO
            IF LETTER(J-1) > LETTER(J) THEN EXCHANGE (J-1, J)
```

The scope of declaration of each of the procedures we
have defined is indicated below.

```
BEGIN
    COMMENT*****  GLOBAL VARIABLES ARE:  *****;
    INTEGER INDEX, N;
    STRING (1) ARRAY LETTER (0::81);

    PROCEDURE NEXTPERMUTATION;
        .
        .
    INTEGER PROCEDURE LOCATE;
        .
        .
    INTEGER PROCEDURE MINMAX (INTEGER VALUE I);
        .
        .
    PROCEDURE REORDER (INTEGER VALUE FIRST);
        .
        .
    PROCEDURE EXCHANGE (INTEGER VALUE I, J);
        .
        .
    PROCEDURE SORT;
        .
        .
    BEGIN   COMMENT*****  CONTROL PROGRAM  *****;
        .
        .
    END;
```

END ALPHABETICPERMUTE.

    One deficiency of a textbook as a vehicle for learning how
to design algorithms is that it makes everything look unnaturally
easy. Each step is presented as though it follows from previous
steps in a manner so logical that it is hard to conceive that the
design could have progressed in any other way. When one attempts
to design algorithms on his own, however, he immediately finds
out that this is not the case. Instead, the final design of his
algorithm is the end result of a sequence of iterations,
involving many false starts and the correction of a multitude of
errors along the way.   The process of trial and error, and of
progressive refinement of detail in successive versions of an
algorithm is a perfectly natural one, a process by which our own
perception of the problem is sharpened and the steps to be taken
in its solution are clarified. What we must do, however, is to
make this process of refinement orderly enough that it eventually
comes to a successful conclusion.

    In this respect, the process of top-down design is of great
help for it permits one to defer the consideration of details
until larger concepts have been worked out, and it enables one to
refine portions of an algorithm by trial and error without having
to scrap the entire previous effort each time an error in one
part is discovered. It is hard to overemphasize that careful and
detailed specification of the task to be performed is the key to
success in top-down design.   There is a tendency, particularly
evident in computer programmers without much experience, to let
the specification of the task be defined by the result of
designing the procedure, instead of the other way around.

8.2 Using trial and error methods

    Most complicated tasks derive their complexity from the fact
that there is a very large number of possible courses of action
to be taken. Some courses will lead to a satisfactory solution
and some will not, but at the outset, one cannot predict with any
accuracy which are the successful alternatives. When faced with
such a problem, we usually resort to trial and error methods.
This is exactly the situation that faces us in many of the games
we play for recreation. In chess or checkers for example, there
are no secrets concerning the actual state of the board at any
point.   Unlike card games, all of the raw information is right
there, staring you in the face.   But the number of possible
outcomes of a given board position is astronomical, and so one
tries in his mind various possible moves, attempting to evaluate
the relative worth of each. When he finds a move that has the
potential of improving his position (or when he can no longer

201

avoid commitment because of the timer's clock), then he goes
ahead.

In a one-person game such as solitaire, the trial and error
process can be extended from alternatives considered in the mind
to alternatives tried on the board. If a chosen course of play
turns out to yield an undesirable outcome, then the board
position is restored to its previous state, and a different move
is tried. In solitaire, this is regarded as cheating, but in
actual problem solving it can be a very useful tactic if one is
allowed the luxury of retreating to a previous position from
which to choose a less disastrous next move. In computational
algorithms there is no notion of cheating, and it is usually
possible to restore the computation to a previous state, provided
the possible need to do this has been anticipated beforehand.
The tactic is known as backup.

Of course, in designing algorithms for the solution of
complicated problems, it is necessary to try to minimize the
complexity of each individual procedure by employing top-down
design. Thus, the manager of a large organization, when faced
with the necessity to carry out a large task in which there are
many possible courses of action, will attempt to identify
subtasks corresponding to a course he wishes to try. He will
hire employees for each of the subtasks, and instruct each
employee to carry out the assigned task and report on his
success. When an employee reports success, then the manager can
proceed with his chosen course of action, discharging the
employee to await the next call to duty. If an employee reports
failure, then he is discharged and the manager is forced to
modify his original course of action. The manager himself will
report on his success to his own employer, whenever he either
succeeds through the efforts of his employees or fails, having
exhausted all courses of action open to him.

By way of analogy with the manager directing his employees
toward the accomplishment of a task, we can employ top-down
design of an algorithm to perform a computational task, using
trial and error methods. The analogy to the employee's report
will be the value of TRUE or FALSE returned by a logical-valued
ALGOL W procedure to indicate whether or not it was able to
perform its assigned task. The actual performance of the task
may be accomplished as a side effect of the procedure, that is,
by setting values of variables that are defined globally to the
procedure and not passed as arguments. This technique is
illustrated in the next example.

Example 8.2.1 -- The eight queens problem

    In the game of chess, the queen is the most powerful
single piece on the chessboard. She is allowed to move any
number of squares along any of the forward-backward or
transverse files of the chessboard, or along the 45-degree
diagonals. This suggests the following puzzle. Is it
possible, with no other pieces on the 8 by 8 chessboard, to
position 8 mutually antagonistic queens in such a way that
no queen can reach any other queen in a single move? Quite
obviously, it is impossible to position more than 8 queens
on the board without conflict, for no two queens can occupy
the same column, and there are only 8 columns. But it is
not obvious that even as many as 8 can be placed on the
board in a 'safe' disposition. This is the sort of problem
that a human can solve in a few minutes by trial and error
methods and by using his amazing powers of geometric
perception. It fascinates computer scientists to try to
enable a computer to solve problems like this, and the eight
queens problem has recieved a lot of attention. The
solution given here draws on algorithms developed by
Professors E. W. Dijkstra and N. Wirth. Both Dijkstra's
algorithm and the version given here make use of a recursive
procedure, whereas Wirth's algorithm is completely
iterative. It will be worth your time to make a trip to the
library to read about his alternate method of attack.[1]

    For the sake of elegance, we shall add to the
specification of the problem that the placement of the eight
queens, if one is found, is to be printed on a replica of a
chessboard.

    A trial and error algorithm works by generating
candidates for a solution, and testing each candidate to see
whether or not it satisfies the problem specification. The
process continues until either a satisfactory solution is
found, or all candidates for a solution have been tried and
found wanting. However, if the number of possible
configurations to be tried is very large, a little
intelligence must be applied to reduce the number of
candidates generated, by avoiding obviously unsatisfactory
configurations. For instance, there are $\binom{64}{8}$, or
4,426,165,368 possible ways to place eight queens on a
chessboard (although some of these configurations are
equivalent to one another by rotating the chessboard through

----
[1] N. Wirth, Programming by stepwise refinement, Communications
of the ACM, vol. 14, p. 221, April, 1971.

90 or 180 degrees.) But since we already know that no configuration having two or more queens in a single column can succeed, we could restrict the candidate configurations to include only those in which each queen occupies a separate column, and if a solution is to be found at all, it will be found among this set of restricted configurations. The reduction in the number of candidates is appreciable: there are only 8^8, or 16,777,216 such configurations.

Moreover, it is not even necessary to generate all of the configurations having one queen per column. A board configuration can be generated by placing the queens one at a time. A partially generated configuration, one in which fewer than eight queens have been placed, can be regarded as representing a set of candidate configurations, namely all those fully generated configurations that can be formed by placing the remaining queens. If a partially generated configuration is tested and found to be unsatisfactory, then all of the fully generated configurations that could be obtained by completing it must also be unsatisfactory. Obviously, the generation of a particular candidate configuration can stop as soon as it is discovered that one of its partial configurations is unsatisfactory.

This last concept, that of generating and testing partial configurations, suggests a recursive procedure for finding a solution to the eight queens problem. Suppose that a partial configuration has been generated, one in which J - 1 queens have been placed in non-conflicting positions. A procedure is required that will place the Jth queen in a position that does not conflict with those previously placed, and such that it will also be possible to place all of the remaining queens without conflict. A procedure to accomplish this task might undertake on its own the placement of the Jth queen. However, to determine whether or not the remaining queens can be successfully placed, it will need an answer to the same problem that it itself has been faced with, except that the number of queens remaining to be placed will be one fewer. This suggests a recursive call to the procedure. It is as if the manager has a task to delegate which requires all of the same capabilities as does his own task, except that it is slightly smaller in scope. His solution may be to hire, as the employee to perform this task, one of his college classmates, a replica of himself.

In informal notation, the control procedure will have the iteration graph

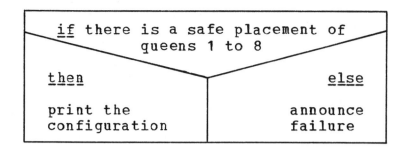

```
           if there is a safe placement of
                   queens 1 to 8

    then                              else

    print the                         announce
    configuration                     failure
```

A procedure to determine a safe placement of the Jth through
8th queens is now needed. We have determined that it should
be a recursive procedure, and a termination condition is
needed to halt the recursion. A suitable way to halt it is
to observe that after all eight queens have been
successfully placed, the procedure might be called with a
value of J greater than 8. In such a case, there is no work
to be done, and the procedure could immediately report
success, thereby halting the recursion. Let us call this
procedure PLACE, and pass to it as an argument the column
number of the next queen to be placed. The queens will be
placed in columns successively from column 1 to column 8 of
the chessboard. An iteration graph for the procedure is:

PLACE (J)

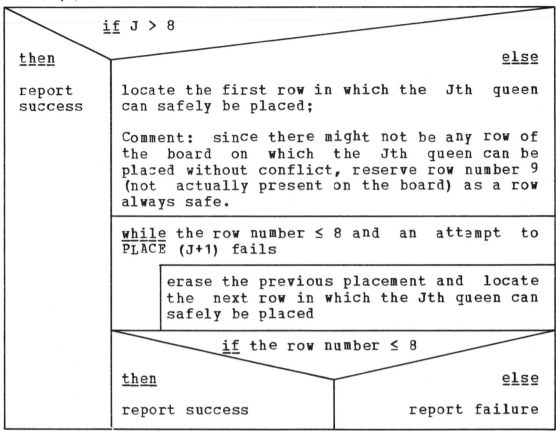

In order to locate a row in which a queen in the Jth column can safely be placed, another procedure will be needed. Since we have provided a dummy row 9 in which a queen will always be safe from attack, there is no need for this procedure to report success or failure; it can always succeed. A possible iteration graph for it is:

SAFEROW (I)

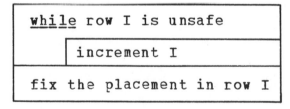

206

At this point we can avoid no longer the decision as to how to represent the data concerning the position of the queens already placed and the areas that they might reach in one move. A first thought might be to represent the chessboard by a two-dimensional array of logical variables. One could use the value TRUE to represent a position occupied by a queen already placed, and FALSE to represent a vacant square. However, we should quickly recognize that the limitation of the layout of the chessboard offers no advantage to the computer. We humans make use of our facility of visual perception to take advantage of the array of squares on a chessboard, and can immediately visualize from it the domain of influence of a queen. (If we cannot, then our chess games will be of short duration.) But for the computer to make direct use of the chessboard in order to determine whether a given square comes under the influence of a given queen, it would have to simulate the movement of the queen along one of the paths she might travel. This makes no sense at all.

Since only the occupied squares are of any real interest in this algorithm, a second representation might be to keep an array of eight integers, representing the row indices of the squares occupied by queens in each of the eight columns. Suppose such an array is named ROW. Then, to determine whether a square whose indices are (X, Y) is subject to attack by the queen in column J, one could ask the following questions.

1) Is $Y = J$?   (square in column J)
2) Is $X = ROW(J)$?   (square in the same row as the Jth queen)
3) Is $X - ROW(J) = Y - J$? (square subject to diagonal attack)
4) Is $ROW(J) - X = Y - J$? (square subject to attack on the perpendicular diagonal)

Although these questions are sufficient to determine whether or not a square is safe from attack by any single queen, what we must be able to calculate is whether a square is safe from attack by _any_ previously placed queen. Using this method of representation, the questions must be asked successively concerning every previously placed queen before the status of the square under consideration can be determined.

Another possibility, yet further in abstraction from the idea of simulating the chessboard, is to represent the domains of influence of the queens. Although each queen commands a row, a column, and two perpendicular diagonals of the board, in all there are only eight rows, eight columns, and 15 diagonals of each inclination on the chessboard. So instead of recording the domain of influence of <u>each</u> queen, one might instead record which of these lines on the board was under the control of <u>some</u> queen. The columns are already taken care of by the convention that only those partial configurations will be generated in which the queens are all in separate columns. The required information can be recorded in three logical-valued arrays, that we shall call ROW, DIAGONAL, and LANOGAID. To determine in which diagonals a given square lies, it is only necessary to take the sum and the difference of its row and column indices. To find out whether or not a square is safe we can evaluate the expression

ROW(I) OR DIAGONAL(J-I) OR LANOGAID(J+I)

where I represents the row number and J is the number of a column not yet occupied by a queen.

After developing the strategy of an algorithm in preliminary form, using informal iteration graphs to represent procedures, we are now ready to consider the detailed composition of the algorithm as an ALGOL W program. The function of the control program will be to provide global declarations of the variables in which the status of the board positions will be recorded, and to initialize these variables to correspond to an empty board. It will then call the procedures that are to do the work,

```
BEGIN
  COMMENT*****  THE GLOBAL VARIABLES ARE:  *****;
  INTEGER BOARDSIZE;
  COMMENT*******************************************************
  *  'QUEEN' IS AN INTEGER ARRAY USED TO RECORD THE ROW NUMBER *
  *  IN WHICH THE QUEEN OF COLUMN J IS PLACED.  IT WILL BE     *
  *  NEEDED BY THE PROCEDURE 'PRINTBOARD'.                     *
  *  'ROW' IS A LOGICAL ARRAY INDICATING WHICH ROWS ARE SUBJECT*
  *  TO ATTACK BY QUEENS ALREADY PLACED.                       *
  *  'DIAGONAL' AND 'LANOGAID' ARE LOGICAL ARRAYS INDICATING   *
  *  THE DIAGONALS SUBJECT TO ATTACK.                          *
  *************************************************************;
  INTEGER ARRAY QUEEN (1::8);
  LOGICAL ARRAY ROW (1::8);
  LOGICAL ARRAY DIAGONAL (-7::7);
  LOGICAL ARRAY LANOGAID (2::16);
  LOGICAL SUCCESS;
  (declarations of the procedures INITIALIZE, PLACE, and
     PRINTBOARD go here)
```

```
INITIALIZE;
INTFIELDSIZE := 2;
COMMENT****************************************************************
*   THE CONDITIONAL CLAUSE CALLS THE PROCEDURE 'PLACE', WHICH   *
*   WILL FIND A SOLUTION TO THE PROBLEM OF PLACING THE QUEENS,  *
*   IF A SOLUTION EXISTS.  THE PROCEDURE WILL SET THE PLACEMENT *
*   OF THE QUEENS IN THE ARRAY 'QUEENS' AND RETURN A TRUE VALUE *
*   IF IT SUCCEEDS, OTHERWISE IT WILL RETURN A FALSE VALUE.     *
*****************************************************************;
PLACE (1);
IF SUCCESS THEN PRINTBOARD
ELSE WRITE ("NO SOLUTION TO THE", BOARDSIZE,
            "QUEENS PROBLEM HAS BEEN FOUND");
END EIGHTQUEENS.
```

The next step is the composition of the recursive procedure that does most of the work.

```
PROCEDURE PLACE (INTEGER VALUE J);
    BEGIN
        COMMENT****************************************************
        *   THE ARGUMENT J REPRESENTS THE COLUMN NUMBER OF THE  *
        *   NEXT QUEEN TO BE PLACED.  THIS VARIABLE WILL BE     *
        *   GLOBAL TO ALL PROCEDURES DEFINED WITHIN THIS BLOCK. *
        *   'PLACEMENT' IS A TEMPORARY VARIABLE INDICATING THE  *
        *   ROW IN WHICH THE J_TH QUEEN LIES.  GLOBAL VARIABLE  *
        *   'SUCCESS' WILL HOLD THE LOGICAL VALUE TO BE RETURNED*
        *********************************************************;
        INTEGER PLACEMENT;
        (declarations of procedures SAFEROW and DELETEPLACEMENT
            go here)

        COMMENT***** THE BODY OF PROCEDURE 'PLACE' STARTS HERE *****;
        IF J > BOARDSIZE THEN SUCCESS := TRUE
        ELSE
            BEGIN
                COMMENT***** LOCATE A SAFE PLACEMENT FOR QUEEN J *****;
                PLACEMENT := SAFEROW (0);
                PLACE (J+1);
                WHILE (PLACEMENT <= BOARDSIZE) AND ¬SUCCESS DO
                    BEGIN
                        COMMENT***************************************
                        *   THE RECURSIVE CALL TO 'PLACE' IN THE    *
                        *   PRECEDING LINE HAS FAILED TO FIND A     *
                        *   SAFE CONFIGURATION FOR THE REMAINING    *
                        *   QUEENS, SO THE J_TH QUEEN MUST BE MOVED.*
                        ********************************************;
                        DELETEPLACEMENT;
                        PLACEMENT := SAFEROW (PLACEMENT);
```

```
                    PLACE (J+1);
                END;
            IF PLACEMENT <= BOARDSIZE THEN
                BEGIN
                    SUCCESS := TRUE;
                    QUEEN(J) := PLACEMENT;
                END
            ELSE SUCCESS := FALSE;
        END;
    END PLACE;
```

In order to locate a safe placement of the queen in the Jth
column, it will be necessary to scan the squares of the column,
checking to see if each square is under the influence of some
previously placed queen. When a square is found that is not
subject to attack, the row number of that square gives a safe
placement for a queen in column J.

```
    INTEGER PROCEDURE SAFEROW (INTEGER VALUE ROWNUMBER);
        BEGIN
            COMMENT***************************************
            *   THE ROW NUMBER IS INITIALLY EITHER 0 OR  *
            *   THE LAST ROW IN WHICH THE J_TH QUEEN WAS  *
            *   PLACED.  THE TASK IS TO ADVANCE TO THE    *
            *   NEXT SAFE ROW.                            *
            *********************************************;

            (declarations of procedures UNSAFE and FIXPOSITION
                go here)

            ROWNUMBER := ROWNUMBER + 1;
            WHILE (ROWNUMBER <= BOARDSIZE) AND UNSAFE DO
                COMMENT***** TRY THE NEXT ROW. *****;
                ROWNUMBER := ROWNUMBER + 1;
            IF ROWNUMBER <= BOARDSIZE THEN FIXPOSITION;
            ROWNUMBER
        END SAFEROW;
```

Finally, we have reached the point at which use must be
made of the arrays in which the status of rows and diagonals
of the board are recorded.

```
    LOGICAL PROCEDURE UNSAFE;
        ROW(ROWNUMBER) OR DIAGONAL(J-ROWNUMBER)
                        OR LANOGAID(J+ROWNUMBER);

    PROCEDURE FIXPOSITION;
        ROW(ROWNUMBER) := DIAGONAL(J-ROWNUMBER)
                        := LANOGAID(J+ROWNUMBER) := TRUE;
```

Notice that FIXPOSITION can only be applied to a square for which UNSAFE is false. Therefore, the logical values of ROW, DIAGONAL, and LANOGAID for that square are all false before FIXPOSITION is applied, and are changed to true values to place a single queen. No other queen previously or subsequently placed can lie in the row or either of the diagonals dominated by the Jth queen unless she is first moved to a different square. Therefore, to move her it will suffice to restore the truth values marking her row and diagonals to FALSE, and there is no danger that in so doing the domain of any other queen will be inadvertently affected. The procedure to delete the placement of a queen is therefore very simple.

```
PROCEDURE DELETEPLACEMENT;
    ROW(PLACEMENT) := DIAGONAL(J - PLACEMENT)
                   := LANOGAID(PLACEMENT + J) := FALSE;
```

The hard part of the algorithm is now done. It is also obvious what needs to be initialized; it is only the status of the domains of influence, and the constant value of BOARDSIZE. Although SUCCESS is also a global variable, it does not require explicit initialization, since it is always set by a call to PLACE before it is tested.

```
PROCEDURE INITIALIZE;
    BEGIN
        BOARDSIZE := 8;
        FOR I := 1 UNTIL BOARDSIZE DO ROW(I) := FALSE;
        FOR I := -BOARDSIZE + 1 UNTIL BOARDSIZE - 1 DO
            DIAGONAL(I) := FALSE;
        FOR I := 2 UNTIL 2*BOARDSIZE DO LANOGAID(I) := FALSE;
    END INITIALIZE;
```

All that remains is to print the display of the board with the final placement of the queens. This is accomplished by an iterative procedure. To print horizontal lines, one can use the underbar character "_". The vertical bar "|" can be arrayed on the paper to create vertical lines. If we choose a square of the chessboard to be five print squares wide and three print spaces high, it will come out nearly square on the output listing. A board square that is to contain a queen will have "Q" printed in its center, while other squares will be left blank.

```
PROCEDURE PRINTBOARD;
   BEGIN
      WRITE (" ");
      COMMENT*****************************************************
      *   FIRST PRINT A HORIZONTAL LINE MARKING THE TOP      *
      *   BOUNDARY OF THE BOARD.   THEN, PRINT ROWS OF SQUARES *
      *****************************************************;
      FOR J := 1 UNTIL BOARDSIZE DO WRITEON ("____ ");
      FOR I := 1 UNTIL BOARDSIZE DO
         BEGIN
            COMMENT*****************************************************
            *   PRINT THE FIRST THIRD OF THE VERTICAL LINE    *
            *   SEPARATING THE SQUARES                        *
            *****************************************************;
            WRITE ("|");
            FOR J := 1 UNTIL BOARDSIZE DO WRITEON ("    |");
            COMMENT*****************************************************
            *   PRINT THE MIDDLE THIRD OF EACH SQUARE,        *
            *   CONTAINING THE SYMBOL 'Q' IF OCCUPIED         *
            *****************************************************;
            WRITE ("|");
            FOR J := 1 UNTIL BOARDSIZE DO
               BEGIN
                  WRITEON (" ");
                  IF QUEEN (J) = I THEN WRITEON ("Q ")
                  ELSE WRITEON ("  ");
                  WRITEON (" |");
               END;
            COMMENT*****************************************************
            *   PRINT THE BOTTOM THIRD OF EACH SQUARE,        *
            *   INCLUDING THE BOUNDARY LINE AT THE BOTTOM     *
            *****************************************************;
            WRITE ("|");
            FOR J := 1 UNTIL BOARDSIZE DO
               WRITEON ("____|");
         END;
   END PRINTBOARD;
```

The resulting display will appear like this, which is the solution to the four queens problem:

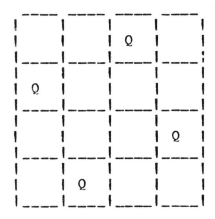

In the examples of this chapter, a methodology of computational problem-solving has been displayed. Although the methods may not yet be your methods, with time and a little more practice they can become yours. The keys to the simplification of hard problems are the choice of a suitable data representation and the decomposition of a large task into more or less independent subtasks. Top-down design of algorithms is an attempt to systematize the decomposition of a task into subtasks and the composition of subordinate algorithms to accomplish those tasks. There has not, as yet, been developed quite such a systematic approach to the definition of data representations, but a good principle to follow is to avoid committing oneself to a particular choice of representation for as long as possible. In this way, the crucial choice is made at a time when one understands the problem and the form of the intended solution better than is possible at the outset.

In the remaining chapters of this book, we shall learn more about how computers do their work and more about techniques useful in particular applications, but the basic tools and techniques of algorithm composition are already in our hands.

Exercises for Chapter 8

8.1 Design an ALGOL W program that will accept as input the text of any program written in ALGOL W, and will print a listing of the program with proper indentations of block bodies, compound groups, conditionally executed statements, the bodies of iteration loops, text of comments, etc. The linewidth and indentation should be parameters of the program. If you have done Exercise 7.2, you may find the SCAN procedure defined there to be a useful component of your program. Don't forget to provide for continuation of lines that are too long to fit on a single print line, and for resetting a left margin in case it becomes indented too near to the right margin.

8.2 Design an ALGOL W program to determine all the triangles that are formed by a finite set of line segments. Each straight line segment is defined by a pair of points which lie at its ends. Each point is given by a pair of real numbers. Three lines form a triangle if each pair intersects, and if the intersections do not all coincide. You may find the algorithm given in the example of Section 4.4 to be helpful in determining whether two line segments intersect.

Test the program on the following two sets of data:

Input for the first case consists of 12 line segments whose endpoints are

X1	Y1	X2	Y2
-50.0	-50.0	-60.0	60.0
1.0	901.0	1.0	-927.0
-837.0	1.0	843.0	-1.15
-50.5	37.0	325.0	-401.0
-51.1	-50.0999	87.3	88.3001
-6.1	6.1	6.1	-6.1
-.00001	999.0	99.0	-.0001
1.0	3.0	9.0	27.0
881.0	343.0	2.0	4.0
7.0	49.0	-8.0	-16.0
98.765	-87.654	-76.543	65.432
-999.0	0.0	999.0	0.0

214

Input for the second case consists of eight lines

X1	Y1	X2	Y2
-4.	4.	4.	4.
-4.	4.	-4.	-4.
-4.	-4.	4.	-4.
4.	-4.	4.	4.
0.0	5.656	5.656	0.0
0.0	-5.656	-5.656	0.0
5.656	0.0	0.0	-5.656
-5.656	0.0	0.0	5.656

8.3 Give a recursive procedure for generating the permutation of the elements of a vector of characters, that will immediately precede the given vector in lexical order.

8.4 In the game of poker, a hand consists of five cards dealt from a deck of 52, comprising 13 ranks in four suits. The hands are valued as follows, from best to worst:

A straight flush consists of 5 cards of the same suit, in sequence.
Four of a kind is any hand containing four cards of the same rank.
A full house is three cards of one rank, and a pair of another rank.
A flush is five cards all of the same suit, but not in sequence.
A straight is five cards in sequence, but not all of the same suit.
Three of a kind is any hand containing three (but not four) cards of the same rank, and two other cards not a pair.
Two pair is a hand containing two distinct pairs of the same rank (but the ranks of the pairs differ).
One pair is a hand containing one pair of the same rank, but no other pair.
No pairs is a hand containing no two cards of the same rank, but not in sequence nor all of one suit.

Within each category given above, hands are ordered by the rank of the largest tuple (four, three, pair), then by the ranks of the largest single card, then the second largest single, etc. The number of distinct hands possible in each of the major categories is:

Straight flush[1]	36
Four of a kind	624
Full house	3,744
Flush	5,112
Straight[1]	9,180
Three of a kind	54,912
Two pair	123,552
One pair	1,098,240
No pair	1,303,560

Design an ALGOL W program to accept as input the description of up to seven poker hands, all presumably dealt from the same deck, to check the hands for validity (names of rank and suit must be valid, and no two cards in the deal can be identical), print a description of each hand along with the category to which it belongs, and tell which hand (or hands) is the best of those dealt.

8.5   The knight's tour.
In the game of chess, there are several different sorts of playing pieces that are allowed different moves on the 8 by 8 grid of squares that constitutes a chessboard. The piece having the most interesting move pattern is the knight, whose move allows him to advance exactly two squares along a horizontal or vertical file and exactly one square along a perpendicular file. The possible moves of a knight on an open board can be represented as ordered pairs, whose elements give the number of squares advanced along rows and columns of the board. The eight possible moves are: (1,2), (2,1), (2,-1), (1,-2), (-1,-2), (-2,-1), (-2,1), (-1,2).

An old problem, one reputedly solved by the German mathematician Gauss at age four, is to find a sequence of moves of the knight, starting from a given square on the board, that will eventually visit every square exactly once. That is, no square previously visited in the sequence is to be reoccupied. Compose an ALGOL W program that, when given the coordinates of an initial square, will find a knight's tour from that square if one exists.

8.6   The stable marriage problem.
Suppose there are two finite sets, each of N elements, and that we are to make a one-to-one assignment or correspondence between elements of one set and elements of the other. Such an assignment we shall call, by way of analogy, a marriage. Let us call the sets M and F, for want

----

[1] In sequences, the ace is taken as the highest card only.

of better names. Note that what we mean here by a marriage is a multiple assignment of N pairs, not just a single pairing.

To complicate matters, let there be associated with each element a vector of integers indicating the relative affinity of that element for each element of the opposite set. The affinity is indicated by an integer from 1 to N, and all affinities of a given vector must be distinct numbers. By convention, let 1 stand for the greatest affinity, N for the least. Thus for instance, if N = 10, the affinity vector for element M(5) might be (3,10,5,6,2,9,1,8,7,4), indicating that the greatest preference of M(5) is for F(7), the least is for F(2).

We can now define some plausible notions of a stable marriage, subject to the affinities expressed by the vector elements.

a) M-stability: We shall define stability by the absence of instability. If the marriage contains pairs (i,j) and (k,l) for which both

M(i) prefers F(l), who is the spouse of M(k), to F(j), his own spouse,

and

M(k) prefers F(j) to his own spouse, F(l),

then the marraige assignment is said to be M-unstable. If no such condition occurs, then it is said to be M-stable. Obviously, the notion of M-stability takes no notice of the preferences of the elements of set F; hence it is only a model of marriage rules in certain societies. Give an algorithm for finding an M-stable marriage assignment.

b) F-stability: A marriage is said to be F-unstable if the marriage contains pairs (i,j) and (k,l) for which

M(i) has greater affection for F(l), the spouse of M(k), than does M(k) himself

and

M(k) finds M(i)'s spouse, F(j) more attractive than M(i) does.

A marriage is F-stable if it contains no F-unstable pairs. This notion of stability also depends only on the affinity vectors of set M, but F-stability and M-stability are nevertheless independent; one does not necessarily imply the other. Give an algorithm for F-stable marriage assignment.

c) M-F stability: A notion of stable assignment that utilizes both sets of affinity vectors is the following. A marriage is said to be M-F unstable if there are pairs (i,j) and

(k,l) in the marriage such that both
          M(i) prefers F(l) to his own spouse,
and
          F(l) prefers M(i) to her own spouse.
A marriage assignment is said to be M-F stable if it
contains no M-F unstable pairs. Obviously M-F stability is
independent of either M or F stability since it depends on
additional affinity data. It is also somewhat more
difficult to produce an M-F stable assignment algorithm.
Give an algorithm for M-F stable marriage assignment.

8.7   When a message is transmitted over a communications system,
      the format of the message must ordinarily be checked to
      ensure that it observes the protocol required for proper
      functioning of the system. You are to design, write, and
      test an ALGOL W program to check messages and compute their
      cost on the simulated telegraph system described below.
          A message is any sequence of 200 or fewer words,
      preceded by a header and followed by the unique terminating
      string "STOPSTOP".
          A header is a message prefix consisting of a type (one
      of "STANDARD", "URGENT", or "NITE MAIL") and two zones (a
      zone is an integer between 1 and 20), regarded as the origin
      and destination of the message.
          A word is a sequence of one to sixteen alphabetic
      characters, other than the terminating sequence "STOPSTOP".

          An input message that contains punctuation marks is not
      to be rejected, but the punctuation marks are to be replaced
      by words,
          "." = STOP
          "," = COMMA
          "?" = QUESTNMARK

          Any word in the message regarded (by you) as profanity
      is to be replaced by a nonsense word.

          The maximum message length of 200 words applies only to
      NITE MAIL. STANDARD type messages are limited to 100 words,
      URGENT to 50.

          Cost is calculated by the following formulas. For
      STANDARD type messages, within the same zone (origin equals
      destination)) $3.00 for the first 20 words, $0.10 for each
      additional word. For crossing zones, there is a surcharge
      of $0.01 per word for each zone crossed. An URGENT type
      message is charged 300% of the cost of a STANDARD type
      message. For NITE MAIL, the cost is 75% of the cost for
      STANDARD type.

Your program is to read telegrams in succession, print the type, zones and cost of each, and print the edited version of each message. Each telegram is to appear on a new output page.

Chapter 9

SIMULATING THE REAL WORLD

So far, the problems that have been studied have been sufficiently simple that one could think in terms of directly composing an algorithm to give a solution. The most difficult problem yet encountered was the eight queens problem of section 8.2, for there we were forced to use trial and error methods to grope toward a solution, retracing steps whenever it was discovered that a false start had been made. There are worse problems. There are some situations in which our understanding of the process at work is so incomplete that there seems to be no recourse open to us, in order to predict an outcome, other than to perform an experiment to see how the result will turn out. Of what use can computation be in dealing with a problem like that?

It sometimes is the case, in dealing with very complex problems that doing an actual experiment is unfeasible, because of danger, cost, time limitations, or possible catastrophic outcome in case a wrong choice is made in choosing the initial parameters. In such cases, we would like to be able to simulate the conditions of a real experiment, but to do the simulation under conditions of comparative safety, at low cost, in a reasonably short time, and without having to bear the consequences of an unfavorable outcome. This is where the computer can help. For if the underlying laws governing the actual process are known with sufficient precision, then the computer can be used to model the dynamic behavior of the process, calculating the state of the model from one instant to the next as the process unfolds from beginning to end. If the computer model has been carefully made, and no important details left out, then the conclusions drawn from the simulated experiment will also apply to the real world situation that generated the original problem.

9.1 Simulating deterministic processes

The easiest processes to simulate are those in which the outcome is deterministic, that is, there is no unpredictable event, or element of chance, that enters into the laws that govern the process. Examples of such processes are the orbital motions of planets or of space vehicles, the flow of water past the hull of a moving ship, and the transformation of one chemical isotope into another by a process of radioactive decay. One might think that in such problems, mathematical analysis would be able to provide formulas from which solutions could be directly calculated, and that there would be no need to simulate the process in order to predict its outcome. Although this is often possible, it also happens that for many deterministic processes the mathematical description is so complicated that mathematical analysis is not a very attractive way to get a solution. For instance, in studying the orbital motion of planets, in a system in which the gravitational attraction of three or more bodies must be considered simultaneously, mathematical analysis becomes extremely difficult, but computational simulation is not complicated in any profound way by increasing the number of bodies beyond two. In the following example, we consider a relatively simple problem, one for which a fairly sophisticated mathematical analysis could provide an answer. However, simulation will also provide an answer, and very little mathematics will be required.

Example 9.1.1 -- A pursuit problem

On his way to school each day, a farmer's son must pass by a rectangular fenced field, as shown in the diagram of Fig. 9.1.1. His route can either take him around a corner of the field, or he can climb through the fence and walk diagonally across it. If he goes around the field, outside the fence, he must cross a swampy area near the corner, and he always steps in water over his boot tops. On the other hand, if he crosses the field, his feet stay dry, but the field is inhabited by a very large and ill-tempered bull, who will certainly try to run him down. So on each schoolday, the farmer's son must observe the position at which the bull is grazing in the field, and estimate his chances of crossing the field that day without being caught. Can you help him?

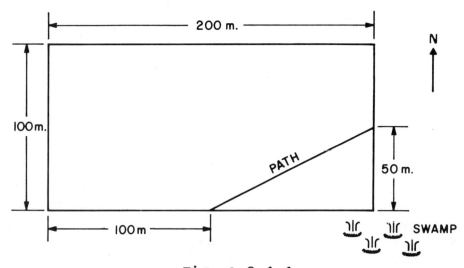

Figure 9.1.1

222

The details of the problem specification are as follows. The field is 100 meters wide from north to south, and 200 meters wide from east to west. The path that the farmer's son uses has its starting point in the middle of the south side, 100 meters from the southwest corner, and its end on the middle of the east side, 50 meters from the southeast corner. The boy can run at at a rate of 5.5 meters per second, carrying his school bag, and the bull has a top speed of 7.5 meters per second. The bull, not being very bright, never anticipates the boy's route to try to cut him off, but instead runs straight at the boy, at each instant that he is within the boundaries of the fence. We shall neglect the time that it takes for either the bull or the boy to accelerate to full running speed, and further assume that if the bull gets to within 2 meters of the boy's position at any instant, that the bull's attack is successful. (At the least, the boy will have to abandon his school bag.)

Let us measure distances from the southwest corner of the field, letting any point in the field be designated by an ordered pair (x,y) denoting meters north and east of the reference point, respectively. The problem we wish to solve is this: Given an initial location (x_0, y_0) of the bull in the field, if the boy began to run across the path, would the bull's attack succeed?

In any simulation one must have some uniform measure of the evolution of the simulated process. Very often, this uniform measure is best provided by a time scale. The state of the simulated process can be evaluated at discrete, equal intervals of time, and once evaluated, the data of the state at one instant form the basis for the evaluation of the state of the process at the succeeding instant. Selection of the uniform time interval is an important, and often critical decision to be made in setting up a simulation. The time interval must be small enough that the change in the state of the process during a single interval is small, relative to the total change expected to occur during the lifetime of the process. On the other hand, very little additional accuracy is ordinarily gained by making the interval smaller than is needed, and the cost of running the simulation will be inversely proportional to the time interval selected.

In the example we are dealing with here, a suitable time interval can be guessed at by examining the physical capabilities of the participants in the chase. The boy is expected to run in a straight line at a constant speed, and so his trajectory is completely insensitive to the interval chosen. On the other hand, the bull's trajectory is unknown, but will ordinarily be some curved path. His path will be approximated by a series of straight line segments, each segment being the distance he will have run in a single interval of time. If the length of the bull's stride in full gallop is about two meters, we might guess that he cannot change his direction very abruptly in any shorter distance, and so approximating his path by a succession of two-meter straight line segments should be quite satisfactory. Since he moves at a speed of 7.5 meters/second, it will take him 0.26667 seconds to cover two meters, and in this way we arrive at a reasonable time interval.

The next step is to formulate a system of simple equations that tell how to make the transition in the state of the process from one time interval to the next. Such a system of equations is very easy to give in vector notation. Let P_1 and P_2 be vectors (in this case, ordered pairs) denoting[1] the positions of the boy and the bull, respectively. Let V_1 and V_2 be vectors denoting their respective velocities, and let $\triangle t = .26667$, the time interval in seconds. Then

$$P_1(t+1) = P_1(t) + V_1(t) * \triangle t,$$

$$P_2(t+1) = P_2(t) + V_2(t) * \triangle t.$$

The equations given in this notation illustrate the general nature of simulation equations; values for the next time instant depend on values previously calculated for the present time.

Since the time intervals are constant, the velocities of the boy and of the bull can be multiplied by the constant time interval to convert them into positional increment. The equations then become

$$P_1(t+1) = P_1(t) + \triangle P_1(t),$$

$$P_2(t+1) = P_2(t) + \triangle P_2(t).$$

The positional increment for the boy is the ordered pair $(\triangle x, \triangle y)$ giving the distance he has moved in .26667 seconds in components of direction norhtward and eastward, respectively. From his path, it is easy to see that the northward and eastward components of his progress must be in the ratio of 1 to 2, and from his running speed and the time interval, it is also evident that the total distance covered must be 1.4667 meters. Since the geometry of a right triangle tells us that the total distance covered is the sum of the squares of the perpendicular components, the vector positional increments of the boy's position is given by

$$\Delta P_1 = 1.4667*(1/\sqrt{5}, 2/\sqrt{5}) = (2.4597, 4.9193).$$

The positional increment traversed by the bull in any time interval is not quite so easy to obtain, for although he moves a constant distance of two meters, his direction may change from one instant in time to the next. In fact, his direction will always be that of a line drawn from his own position to that of the boy. This line has a northward component of $x_1 - x_2$ and an eastward component of $y_1 - y_2$, as shown in Figure 9.1.2 -

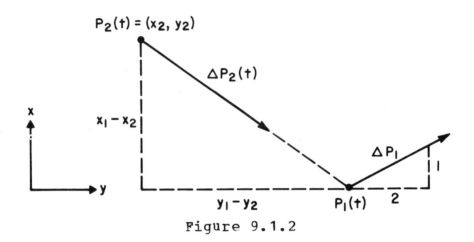

Figure 9.1.2

Its total length is $Dist = \sqrt{(x_1-x_2)^2 + (y_1-y_2)^2}$, where the x's and y's are the components of the two position vectors at some instant of time. The positional increment of the bull in the next interval of time will be $2 *((x_1-x_2)/Dist, (y_1-y_2)/Dist)$. With this amount of preliminary analysis out of the way, we are prepared to begin the composition of an algorithm for simulation. An iteration graph describes informally the steps to be carried out.

```
┌─────────────────────────────────────────────────┐
│   initialize the positions of the              │
│   boy and the bull;                             │
│   compute the initial DISTANCE                  │
│   between them;                                 │
├─────────────────────────────────────────────────┤
│   while DISTANCE > 2 meters                     │
│       and the boy has not                       │
│       reached the east fence                    │
│   ┌─────────────────────────────────────────────┤
│   │   advance the bull's position;             │
│   │   advance the boy's position;              │
│   │   compute DISTANCE between them;           │
├───┴─────────────────────────────────────────────┤
│       if the position of the boy               │
│          is beyond the east fence              │
│   ┌──────────────────────┬──────────────────────┤
│   then                   │                 else │
│                          │                      │
│   report the            │   report the bull    │
│   boy escaped;          │   caught the boy;    │
└──────────────────────────┴──────────────────────┘
```

A translation of the iteration graph into an ALGOL W program is:

```
BEGIN
    COMMENT*********************************************************
    *   SIMULATION OF A BULL PURSUING A BOY ACROSS A PASTURE.   *
    *   (X1, Y1) ARE COORDINATES OF THE BOY'S POSITION          *
    *   (X2, Y2) ARE COORDINATES OF THE BULL'S POSITION         *
    *   THE SIZE OF THE PASTURE IS 100 BY 200 METERS.  THE BOY  *
    *   ALWAYS STARTS FROM A POINT 100 METERS ALONG THE SOUTH   *
    *   BOUNDARY AND RUNS TO A POINT 50 METERS ALONG THE EAST   *
    *   BOUNDARY.  THE TIME INTERVAL IS THE TIME THAT IT TAKES  *
    *   THE BULL TO TRAVEL TWO METERS.                          *
    *************************************************************;
    REAL X1, Y1, X2, Y2, BOYS_MOVE_NORTH, BOYS_MOVE_EAST;
    REAL DISTANCE, BOYS_SPEED, BULLS_SPEED, TIME_INTERVAL;
    REAL LENGTH_OF_BULLS_STRIDE;

    BOYS_SPEED := 5.5;
    BULLS_SPEED := 7.5;   COMMENT*** METERS PER SECOND ***;
```

```
LENGTH_OF_BULLS_STRIDE := 2.0;  COMMENT*** METERS ***;
TIME_INTERVAL := LENGTH_OF_BULLS_STRIDE / BULLS_SPEED;
BOYS_MOVE_NORTH := BOYS_SPEED * TIME_INTERVAL / SQRT(5);
BOYS_MOVE_EAST := 2*BOYS_MOVE_NORTH;
READ (X2, Y2);  COMMENT*** INITIAL POSITION OF BULL ***;
WRITE ("THE INITIAL POSITION OF THE BULL IS", X2, Y2);
ASSERT (X2 >= 0) AND (X2 <= 100) AND (Y2 >= 0) AND (Y2 <= 200);
DISTANCE := SQRT ((X1-X2)**2 + (Y1-Y2)**2);
WHILE (DISTANCE > LENGTH_OF_BULLS_STRIDE) AND (Y1 < 200) DO
    BEGIN
        COMMENT*****************************************************
        *   ADVANCE THE POSITION OF THE BULL FIRST, SINCE THIS *
        *   COMPUTATION MUST UTILIZE THE PREVIOUS POSITION OF  *
        *   THE BOY.                                           *
        ******************************************************;
        X2 := X2 + LENGTH_OF_BULLS_STRIDE * (X1-X2) / DISTANCE;
        Y2 := Y2 + LENGTH_OF_BULLS_STRIDE * (Y1-Y2) / DISTANCE;
        X1 := X1 + BOYS_MOVE_NORTH;
        Y1 := Y1 + BOYS_MOVE_EAST;
        DISTANCE := SQRT ((X1-X2)**2 + (Y1-Y2)**2);
    END;
    IF Y1 >= 200 THEN WRITE ("THE BOY ESCAPES THE BULL.")
    ELSE WRITE ("THE BOY IS CAUGHT AT", X1, Y1);
END.
```

9.2   Growth of Populations

One of the intriguing uses to which simulation can be put
is the study of the growth of populations of man or other
species. Various phenomena, such as changes in the availability
of food supply, predators, epidemics, the effect of population
density on mating patterns, and the reduction of fertility in
birds due to DDT poisoning can be introduced into the simulation
model to determine the effect on population growth. Upon first
consideration, it is not clear that a population model is a
deterministic one, and indeed it is not if the behavior of
individuals must be simulated, as would be the case in very small
populations. But when one is dealing with large populations, one
need not consider individuals at all; one can rely on the
statistics of group behavior. For example, the school board of a
large city does not ordinarily feel it necessary to send out
queries to all women residents of childbearing age, asking them
whether or not they anticipate having new children within the
year, in order to anticipate the probable size of the enrollment
in first grade classes six years hence. Instead, it can obtain
an estimate that is probably equally reliable by simply counting
the number of women of childbearing age, and multiplying by the
current birth rate for the community. The contribution of any
individual, only weakly predictable in any case, is unimportant

when averaged with that of a large number of similar individuals.

Example 9.2.1 -- Growth of a rabbit population

Everyone knows that rabbits are capable of impressive rates of reproduction, for as long as the lettuce holds out, so a rabbit population may provide a good model for studying growth. Suppose that on the average, each pair of rabbits produces four surviving offspring per year. With such a phenomenal rate of growth, we shall calculate the replacement rate on a monthly basis,as

4 (offspring) / 2 (parents) / 12 (months) =
.167 new rabbits per adult per month.

Life is not all eating and reproducing for a rabbit, however. It has its hazards. Let us suppose that the toll taken by owls, foxes, weasels, and shotguns is 50 rabbits per 1000 of population per month. With these data, we can write a small simulation program to study the growth for a rabbit population for a year. The logic of an elementary simulation program is often quite simple, as illustrated by the following iteration graph

```
+-------------------------------------------------+
| initialize the population;                      |
+-------------------------------------------------+
| for each successive month, up to               |
|       the duration of the simulation            |
|    +-------------------------------------------+ |
|    | calculate the number of                   | |
|    | individuals added, the                    | |
|    | number lost, and the                      | |
|    | total population                          | |
|    +-------------------------------------------+ |
+-------------------------------------------------+
```

A program to carry out the simulation is:

```
BEGIN
    COMMENT*****************************************************
    *   A SIMULATION OF GROWTH IN A POPULATION HAVING A CONSTANT *
    *   REPLACEMENT RATE OF .167 PER INDIVIDUAL PER MONTH, AND   *
    *   A CONSTANT LOSS RATE OF .05 PER INDIVIDUAL PER MONTH.    *
    ***********************************************************;
    INTEGER POPULATION_SIZE, NUMBER_ADDED, NUMBER_LOST, DURATION;
    REAL REPLACEMENT_RATE, LOSS_RATE;

    REPLACEMENT_RATE := .167;
    LOSS_RATE := .05;
    POPULATION_SIZE := 1000;
```

```
        DURATION := 12;
        INTFIELDSIZE := 10;
        WRITE ("A SIMULATION OF GROWTH OF AN INITIAL POPULATION OF",
              POPULATION_SIZE);
        WRITE ("INDIVIDUALS, WITH REPLACEMENT RATE =",
              REPLACEMENT_RATE, "AND LOSS RATE =", LOSS_RATE);
        WRITE (" ");
        WRITE ("       MONTH    POPULATION      ADDED        LOST");
        WRITE (" ");
        FOR MONTH := 0 UNTIL DURATION DO
            BEGIN
                NUMBER_ADDED := ROUND (REPLACEMENT_RATE *
                                        POPULATION_SIZE);
                NUMBER_LOST := ROUND (LOSS_RATE * POPULATION_SIZE);
                POPULATION_SIZE := POPULATION_SIZE + NUMBER_ADDED
                                            - NUMBER_LOST;
                WRITE (MONTH, POPULATION_SIZE, NUMBER_ADDED, NUMBER_LOST);
            END;
END RABBIT_SIMULATION.
```

The function ROUND referred to in the calculation of NUMBER_ADDED and NUMBER_LOST is a predefined procedure of ALGOL W. It rounds the real number given it as an argument to the nearest whole integer. Upon executing this small program, the computer prints the following table:

A SIMULATION OF GROWTH OF AN INITIAL POPULATION OF   1000
INDIVIDUALS, WITH REPLACEMENT RATE = .167 AND LOSS RATE = .05

MONTH	POPULATION	ADDED	LOST
0	1000	167	50
1	1117	186	56
2	1247	208	62
3	1393	232	69
4	1556	259	78
5	1737	289	87
6	1939	323	97
7	2165	361	108
8	2418	403	121
9	2700	450	135
10	3015	503	151
11	3360	560	168
12	3752	625	188

As is often the case when we try to make simplified models of real world processes, the model of the preceding example is sure to be criticized. For it tacitly assumes that newborn bunnies spring to maturity in a period of one month, immediately ready to participate in the procreation of young, and it similarly ignores the fact that the mortality rate of young rabbits is greater than that for adults.

Nevertheless, the model serves to illustrate the nature of population growth when birth and death rates are not in balance. The rate at which a population increases is proportional to some constant times the population itself, at least until some environmental or behavioral factors act to alter the birth or death rates. For the values of replacement and loss rates assumed in the model, you can see that the rabbit population will have doubled in approximately 6-1/2 months, and furthermore it will continue to double again in each 6-1/2 month period, unless the growth rates should change. You may recognize this law of expansion, for it is the same law that governs the growth of capital given compound interest, as well as many other natural phenomena.

In the next example, we shall refine a population growth model to take into account the fact that birth and death rates vary with the age of individuals. A new factor then enters into the population study. How many individuals will there be in each age group of a population? The exact distribution of ages cannot be easily predicted by mathematical analysis, but it can be found as a result of simulation.

Example 9.2.2 -- Distribution of ages in a human population

Unlike animals of most other species, humans require a relatively long period of time, nearly 20% of a life span, to reach sexual maturity. On the other end of the time scale, humans tend to outlive their prime reproductive years by 25 to 40 years. Also, since humans have few predators (other than fellow humans), the rate of loss of individuals is not nearly uniform with respect to age, but tends to be much higher among older members of a population than among younger. Thus, the use of a constant replacement rate, the number of births per year per 1000 individuals, and a constant death rate ignoring the distribution of individuals by ages, provides a very crude model by which to simulate the growth of a human population. A somewhat better model can be obtained if birth rate and death rate are given by age bracket.

Suppose that we are given birth and death rates by ten-year age brackets for a human population. However, the age distribution, or relative number of individuals in each case of these age brackets is unknown. This distribution will actually be determined from the simulation, and remarkably, it will be substantially independent of the assumed age distribution of the initial population!

If the simulation proceeds with time intervals of one year, then the number of individuals of age k years will be determined by the number of individuals who were of age k-1 in the preceding year, less the number of that age who were lost during the year. The replacement of individuals occurs entirely at age 0, however. The number entering the population as infants is given by the sum over all ages, of births produced by each age group during the preceding year.

As results of the simulation, let us ask for the population growth rate, the expected doubling time, and the final distribution of population by ages. Since the number of individuals finally calculated is not of primary interest, let us obtain the final distribution in ten-year age brackets, normalized to a sample population of 1000. Similarily, let the initial population be given by specifying numbers of individuals at ages of whole decades, since we do not expect to gain much precision by any more detailed specification. With these requirements given, the simulation algorithm can be designed.

The constants governing population growth will be birth and death rates. Since these are needed for ten-year age brackets between 0 and 99 years, ten-element vectors will be provided to hold these constants.

    REAL ARRAY BIRTH_RATE, DEATH_RATE (0::9).

In order to access the correct birth rate rate for a population sample whose age is given by the value of an integer variable AGE, and lies between 0 and 99, the index can be calculated by dividing AGE by 10, as in
    BIRTH_RATE (AGE DIV 10).

Internal to the algorithm, the number of individuals of each age from 0 to 99 will be kept by an array,

    INTEGER N (0::99).

We shall also need an integer variable to record the NUMBER_BORN in each year.

231

At the heart of the simulation algorithm must be a program segment that gives the distribution of individuals in each age group, by calculating the number of survivors from the year before. It must also accumulate the number of new births. This calculation requires an iteration over the ages 0 to 99. However, since the computation of N(AGE) will depend on the value of N(AGE-1) from the previous year, we should not compute a new value of N(AGE-1) until a new value of N(AGE) has been first evaluated. The easiest way to impose this ordering on the sequence of computation of elements of an array will be to iterate over the array indices from greatest to least. The following program segment will accomplish the task.

```
COMMENT**** INITIALIZE NUMBER_BORN FOR THE YEAR ****;
NUMBER_BORN := 0;
FOR AGE := 99 STEP -1 UNTIL 1 DO
    BEGIN COMMENT**** CALCULATE BIRTHS FROM PARENTS(AGE) ****;
        NUMBER_BORN := NUMBER_BORN +
                     ROUND (BIRTH_RATE(AGE DIV 10) * N(AGE));
        COMMENT**** CALCULATE SURVIVORS FROM PREVIOUS YEAR ****;
        N(AGE) := ROUND (N(AGE-1) * (1 - DEATH_RATE((AGE-1)
                                    DIV 10)));
    END;
N(0) := NUMBER_BORN;
```

In the program segment, the ALGOL W built-in function ROUND( ) has been used to round the number of individuals born or surviving to the nearest whole number. This rounding will not adversely affect the simulation so long as the assumption of a population large enough that the individual behavior is unimportant is justified.

Note, however, that if the population were to be chosen so small that it became essential to simulate the behavior of individuals, then this algorithm would fail completely. For instance, suppose the value of the birth rate is given to be .1 births per year per individual (which is already fairly high, given that only half of the individuals can bear children). Then if the simulation was begun with an initial population of 2 (Adam and Eve), the value of ROUND (.1 * 2) would always be zero, denying the existence of any progeny.

To obtain a complete simulation program, all that remains is to provide means of iterating the above program segment over a number of one year intervals, and of reading in and printing out the required data.

```
BEGIN
   INTEGER ARRAY N (0::99);
   REAL ARRAY BIRTH_RATE, DEATH_RATE (0::9);
   INTEGER TOTAL_NUMBER, NUMBER_LAST_YEAR, NUMBER_BORN,
         DURATION, NORMALIZATION_COEFFICIENT;
   FOR I := 0 UNTIL 9 DO READON (BIRTH_RATE(I));
   FOR I := 0 UNTIL 9 DO READON (DEATH_RATE(I));
   COMMENT*********************************************
   *   CLEAR POPULATION VECTOR TO ZERO, AND           *
   *   READ INITIAL DISTRIBUTION OF WHOLE DECIMAL AGES *
   ***************************************************;
   FOR I := 0 UNTIL 99 DO N(I) := 0;
   FOR AGE := 0 STEP 10 UNTIL 90 DO READON (N(AGE));
   READ (DURATION);
   WRITE (" S I M U L A T E D   P O P U L A T I O N   G R O W T H");
   WRITE(" ");  WRITE(" ");  WRITE(" ");
   INTFIELDSIZE := 6;
   WRITE ("        AGE              0-9    10-19    20-29    30-39",
         "  40-49    50-59    60-69    70-79    80-89    90-99");
   WRITE(" ");
   WRITE ("BIRTH_RATE          ");
   FOR I := 0 UNTIL 9 DO WRITEON (ROUND (1000*BIRTH_RATE(I)));
   WRITE(" ");
   WRITE ("DEATH_RATE          ");
   FOR I := 0 UNTIL 9 DO WRITEON (ROUND (1000*DEATH_RATE(I)));
   WRITE(" ");
   WRITE ("INITIAL POPULATION   ");
   FOR AGE := 0 STEP 10 UNTIL 90 DO WRITEON (N(AGE));
   WRITE(" "); WRITE(" "); WRITE(" ");
   WRITE ("PROGRESS OF SIMULATION");
   WRITE(" ");
   WRITE ("          YEAR        POPULATION           BIRTHS          ",
         "DEATHS");
   INTFIELDSIZE := 14;
   WRITE(" ");
   COMMENT***** INITIALIZE THE SIMULATION FOR YEAR ZERO *****;
   TOTAL_NUMBER := 0;
   FOR AGE := 0 STEP 10 UNTIL 90 DO
      TOTAL_NUMBER := TOTAL_NUMBER + N(AGE);
   WRITE (0, TOTAL_NUMBER);
   FOR YEAR := 1 UNTIL DURATION DO
      BEGIN
         NUMBER_LAST_YEAR := TOTAL_NUMBER;
         TOTAL_NUMBER := NUMBER_BORN := 0;
         FOR AGE := 99 STEP -1 UNTIL 1 DO
            BEGIN
               NUMBER_BORN := NUMBER_BORN +
                  ROUND (BIRTH_RATE(AGE DIV 10) * N(AGE));
               N(AGE) := ROUND(N(AGE-1)*(1-DEATH_RATE((AGE-1) DIV 10)));
               TOTAL_NUMBER := TOTAL_NUMBER + N(AGE);
```

```
            END;
         N(0)  := NUMBER_BORN;
         TOTAL_NUMBER := TOTAL_NUMBER + NUMBER_BORN;
         WRITE (YEAR, TOTAL_NUMBER, NUMBER_BORN,
                    NUMBER_LAST_YEAR - TOTAL_NUMBER + NUMBER_BORN);
      END;

   WRITE(" "); WRITE(" "); WRITE(" "); INTFIELDSIZE := 6;
   WRITE ("THE RATE OF POPULATION GROWTH IS",
               (100 * (TOTAL_NUMBER/NUMBER_LAST_YEAR -1)),
         "PER CENT PER YEAR");
   WRITE ("THE POPULATION WILL DOUBLE IN",
         ROUND (LOG(2) / (TOTAL_NUMBER/NUMBER_LAST_YEAR -1)),"YEARS.");
   WRITE(" "); WRITE(" ");
   WRITE ("THE FINAL DISTRIBUTION OF POPULATION BY AGES, ",
         "NORMALIZED TO A SAMPLE POPULATION OF 1000, IS:");

   WRITE(" ");
   WRITE("    AGE        0-9     10-19     20-29     30-39     40-49     50-59",
         "    60-69    70-79    80-89    90-99");
   WRITE(" ");
   WRITE ("NUMBER    ");
   COMMENT************************************************************
   *   ACCUMULATE THE DISTRIBUTION IN TEN-YEAR AGE BRACKETS; *
   *   NORMALIZE TO A POPULATION OF 1000,                    *
   *   AND PRINT THE NORMALIZED DISTRIBUTION.                *
   ************************************************************;
   FOR AGE := 0 STEP 10 UNTIL 90 DO
      FOR I := 1 UNTIL 9 DO  N(AGE) := N(AGE) + N(AGE+I);
   NORMALIZATION_COEFFICIENT := (TOTAL_NUMBER + 500) DIV 1000;
   FOR AGE := 0 STEP 10 UNTIL 90 DO
      WRITEON (ROUND (N(AGE) / NORMALIZATION_COEFFICIENT));
END.
```

You may have noticed that the model for the simulation program given above takes no account whatsoever of centenarians. This is based on the assumption that so few reach the age of 100 that they will have no effect on the statistics of the population as a whole. Alternatively, we might say to those who are interested in the statistics of longevity, that our model, which cannot account for distinctions between individuals, is not sufficiently refined to yield meaningful results about the small segment of the population over 100 years old.

If the program is now run with a set of data as given below:

Birth rates: 0 .030 .124 .005   0   0   0   0   0   0

Death rates: .004 .003 .003 .005 .010 .018 .030 .050 .075 .100

Initial
population: 0   0 1000   0   0   0   0   0   0   0

Duration   200

then final results that will be printed are:

THE RATE OF POPULATION GROWTH IS   2 PERCENT PER YEAR
THE POPULATION WILL DOUBLE IN   14 YEARS.

AGE	0-9	10-19	20-29	30-39	40-49	50-59	60-69	70-79
NUMBER	267	208	162	126	94	66	42	23

80-89	90-99
10	3

It is seen that the final distribution of population bears no resemblance whatsoever to the assumed initial population of 1000 20-year olds. If the final distribution of population obtained in the first run of the simulation is now used as initial data, with the birth and death rates remaining the same as before, and the simulation is re-run, the final output is:

THE RATE OF POPULATION GROWTH IS   2 PERCENT PER YEAR
THE POPULATION WILL DOUBLE IN   14 YEARS.

And the final distribution by ages is virtually the same as it was before, to within rounding errors

AGE	0-9	10-19	20-29	30-39	40-49	50-59	60-69	70-79
NUMBER	265	206	161	124	94	66	42	23

80-89	90-99
10	3

We see that the final results are not much affected by the initial choice of a population distribution, so long as the initial population is young enough to reproduce itself.

An interesting use that can be made of the population growth model of the preceding example is to study the composition (by age) and growth rate of a population in case birth and death rates should change. As you might anticipate, a reduction in birth rates tends to produce not only a slower rate of population growth, but a population containing a higher percentage of old people. See Exercise 9.3 for some examples.

There are many applications other than the one we have studied in which simulation is used to predict the outcomes of possible courses of action. Simulations are used to anticipate the possible effects of changes in predator-prey populations in wild species, and to investigate strategies for control of population sizes of wild game species by establishing hunting quotas. They are also used to model such phenomena as the migration of families from cities to suburbs, the effects of government economic policies on a national economy, and to plan effective strategies for the use of capital and industrial capacity in commerce.

9.3 Probabilistic simulations

In all of the simulation examples considered so far, we have assumed that we know accurately the relations between elementary data and dependent quantities. In the case of population models, although it is not possible to predict with certainty when a single pair of individuals will produce offspring, our models relied on measurable average birth rates that could be used with confidence when the total number of individuals in the population was large.

However, there are some simulation problems in which, although only statistics for the population as a whole are desired as answers, the behavior of individuals cannot be ignored. In the example that follows, the statistics of individual behavior in an unconstrained environment are assumed to be accurately known. However, when constraints are placed on the environment, the consequences of individual behavior can no longer be predicted accurately from a knowledge of his average behavior. It is not satisfactory to apply the constraints to average behavior; it is necesary to take an average over constrained behavior. Exactly what is meant by this last sentence should become clear from the example.

236

Example 9.3.1 -- <u>The drunken sailors</u>

The navy of the Republic of Inebria has a single naval vessel. Each year, when the navy holds exercises, the vessel puts to sea for several days, making a stop at the port of Firewater, in the Booze Islands. The sailors are there given shore leave, during which they invariably visit the local bars and become intoxicated. Upon returning to their ship, they must walk the length of a dock, at the end of which the ship is moored.

If sober, this would be no problem, but an intoxicated Inebrian sailor is not in complete control of his faculties, and when he is trying to walk forward in a straight line, he sometimes staggers one step to either side, or one step backwards. The ship's physician has gathered extensive statistics on drunken Inebrian sailors, and has concluded that the probability that a drunken sailor's next step will be forward is .7, that it will be backward is .1, and that the probabilities are .1 that it will be to either side. Also, he determined that the length of a sailors stride is uniformly one yard.

The dock at Firewater harbor is 20 yards long and four yards wide. In walking the dock, a sailor's path can deviate from the center line of the dock by as much as two yards to either side, but if he goes further off line than two yards, he will fall off the dock. Also, a sailor who backs off the dock into the street will decide to spend the rest of the night in town, and will be A.W.O.L. Only those sailors who traverse the entire length of the dock without first falling into the water or going A.W.O.L. will successfully return to the ship. Our problem is to determine, for a drunken sailor who arrives at the entrance to the dock, on its center line, with the intention of returning to his ship, what are his relative chances of successfully returning, of falling off the dock, or of going A.W.O.L.

A first, naive approach to the problem might be to determine the average behavior of a sailor, and apply it to the problem. Since the probability of deviating from a straight path to the right is the same as that of deviating to the left, the average path followed by a large population of sailors on open ground will be down the middle. Also, since the probability of moving forward is higher than that of moving backward, the average path will be straight forward. If this average path were to be applied to try to answer the question posed above, the conclusion would be that a sailor is certain to return to his ship

237

successfully.   However,   we know that this answer does not
make sense, for in truth, almost no individual sailor will
follow the average path.

        Thus we are forced to consider the actual paths that
different sailors might follow, and to determine the outcome
of each, following such a path. After examining the fate of
a large number of individual sailors, we can determine
approximately the probability of each of the three outcomes
by taking the quotient of the number of experiments that
ended in each outcome with the total number of trials of the
experiment. But how is an actual path traversed by a
drunken sailor to be computed? One way that is available to
us is to simulate the behavior of a sailor. This can be
done by keeping track of his position as he takes one step
after another. At each position, we must stop and made a
random choice, governed by the probabilities established by
the ship's physician, of the direction of the sailor's next
step.

        How does one get a deterministic computer to make a
'random' choice?   In this case, what we mean by a random
choice is one in which the relative frequency of occurence
of each choice in a long series of trials is consistent with
the probabilities given, and such that in any sequence of
choices, there is no discernible rule by which the next
choice can be predicted from the result of the several most
recently past choices.   We can use the computer to generate
a sequence of choices that will satisfy this weakened notion
of randomness.   In order to obtain the desired probability
of making each choice, let us use the computer to generate a
sequence of decimal digits, such that each digit from 0 to 9
will occur equally often in a long sequence.   Then we can
equate the various choices with the occurence of various
digits, as follows:

        0 -- step to the left,
        1 -- step backward,
        2 -- step to the right,
        3-9 -- step forward.

        It is easy to obtain a generator of a sequence in which
each digit occurs equally often. For instance, the
following generator, in which N is a global variable, used
to record the state of the sequence generator from one call
to the next, will satisfy the stated requirement   on
distribution of values:

```
INTEGER PROCEDURE DIGIT_SEQUENCE;
  BEGIN
    N := N + 1;
    N REM 10
END.
```

Successive calls to this generator, begun with an initial
value of N = 0, will produce the sequence

    1 2 3 4 5 6 7 8 9 0 1 2 3 4 5 6 7 8 9 0 1 2 ...

As you can see, this sequence does not satisfy our second
criterion for randomness, as it is easy to predict the next
element from the preceding one. This is hardly surprising,
since the rule used by the generator to obtain the next
digit depended only on the previous one. How could we
obtain a sequence in which the next digit depended on more
than just the immediately preceding one?

   It is useful for our purpose to consider a number
simply as a sequence of digits. The operation of
multiplying the number by 10 then just shifts the whole
sequence one place left, putting a zero in the rightmost
place, and the operation DIV 10 moves the sequence right one
place. Also, if N is any integer, N REM 10000 represents
the sequence of the four least significant digits of
N. Suppose we let ABCD stand for some four-digit
sequence. If we want to obtain a new digit, depending on
the digits of ABCD, one way would be to take a linear
combination of these digits, as

    $(c_1*A + c_2*B + c_3*C + c_4*D)$ REM 10,

where c_1 through c_4 are constant coefficients. The final
operation, REM 10, just selects the least significant digit
of the linear combination as the result. Let us adopt this
strategy for generating a new digit.

   What are we to do with the digits of the previous
sequence? We should save them, except for the greatest
significant digit, which can be discarded. Accordingly, to
save the three least significant digits and discard the
fourth, we could take

    10 * (ABCD REM 1000).

producing the sequence BCD0. Upon combining the newly
formed digit with the ones saved, we get a new four-digit
sequence, whose computational formula is

$$10 * (ABCD \text{ REM } 1000) + ((c_1*A + c_2*B + c_3*C + c_4*D) \text{ REM } 10)$$

The sequence ABCD can be called a <u>predictive</u> sequence, for it is used to determine the next digit of the longer, pseudo-random sequence in which it appears.

In the following sequence generator N_RAND is a global integer variable that is used to represent the predictive sequence of digits as a number. It must be global to the procedure in order that its value will be retained from one invocation of the procedure to the next.

```
INTEGER PROCEDURE RANDOM_DIGIT;
   BEGIN
     INTEGER D;
     D := (N_RAND + 7*(N_RAND DIV 10) + 7*(N_RAND DIV
  1000))
          REM 10;
     N_RAND := 10*(N_RAND REM 1000) + D;
     D
   END RANDOM_DIGIT;
```

Upon calling RANDOM_DIGIT successively, with an initial value of N_RAND = 0001, the following squence of digits is generated

1 8 5 8 0 2 7 7 6 9 0 2 4 1 9 0 1 8 8 4 7 1 6 ...

Although it is not evident from such a short sequence that the digits are generated with equal probability, this fact can be confirmed by the generation of longer sequences. The sequence does not show any discernable regularity, although it will actually repeat itself regularly. Notice that this generator will not work at all if the initial value of N_RAND is set to any sequence in which all digits are zeros or fives (0000, 5555, 5050, etc.).

With the RANDOM_DIGIT generator available as a tool, we can now return to the problem of simulating the staggering footsteps of a drunken sailor. Let us record the position of the sailor by a pair of coordinates, (X, Y), whose values are given in units of yards. Suppose that the end of the dock at the street is represented by the line X = -10, the ship is at the end represented by X = 10, and the two sides of the dock are bounded by the lines Y = 2. The sailor is to begin his walk at the dock entrance, X = -10, Y = 0. We shall follow his journey until he leaves the dock by one of its four sides, and then record the outcome of his journey by printing the result and by incrementing one of the counts NUMBER_AWOL, NUMBER_SHIPPED, or NUMBER_DROWNED. The

simulation of a single sailor is given as a procedure, with
the intent that it may be executed several times by a
control program that seeks to accumulate statistics by
performing independent trials of the sailor's walk.

```
PROCEDURE DRUNKEN_SAILOR;
   BEGIN
      INTEGER X, Y, N, CHOICE;
      X := -10;
      Y := 0;
      N := 0;
      WHILE (ABS X <= 10) AND (ABS Y <= 2) DO
         BEGIN  COMMENT**** CHOOSE THE SAILOR'S NEXT STEP ****;
            CHOICE := RANDOM_DIGIT;
            IF CHOICE > 2 THEN X := X + 1
            ELSE IF CHOICE = 1 THEN X := X - 1
            ELSE Y := Y + CHOICE - 1;
            N := N + 1;
         END;
      IF X < -10 THEN
         BEGIN  COMMENT***** INCREMENT THE NUMBER_AWOL *****;
            NUMBER_AWOL := NUMBER_AWOL + 1;
            WRITE ("    THE SAILOR HAS GONE A.W.O.L.");
         END
      ELSE IF X > 10 THEN
         BEGIN  COMMENT***** INCREMENT THE NUMBER_SHIPPED *****;
            NUMBER_SHIPPED := NUMBER_SHIPPED + 1;
            WRITE ("    THE SAILOR RETURNED TO HIS SHIP");
         END
      ELSE
         BEGIN  COMMENT***** INCREMENT THE NUMBER_DROWNED *****;
            NUMBER_DROWNED := NUMBER_DROWNED + 1;
            WRITE ("    THE SAILOR FELL OFF THE DOCK");
         END;
      WRITEON (" IN", N, "STEPS.");
   END DRUNKEN_SAILOR;
```

   Now that we know how to simulate the path taken by one
sailor, how can the paths taken by several be simulated? We
are accustomed to procedures that will yield the same result
upon successive executions.   However, notice that in this
case there is a hidden global variable that controls the
choices made at each step of the way. This is the variable
N_RAND that is used to remember the previous four digits
from the pseudo-random sequence.   Two executions of
DRUNKEN_SAILOR will only yield the same result for certain,
if the values of N_RAND are the same when the procedure is
invoked in the two trials. This suggests a way to make the
successive trials of the sailor's walk independent of one
another. If the period in which the sequence generated by

RANDOM_DIGIT repeats itself is long enough, then a
succession of trials of DRUNKEN_SAILOR can be run letting
the final value of N_RAND at the end of one trial be the
initial value for the next. There may not be a repetition
of N_RAND that would force a repetition in the behavior of
DRUNKEN_SAILOR during the course of a fixed number of
trials.

Assuming that the period of the pseudo-random sequence
is long enough to permit 100 trials to be run without a
forced repition of outcome, the control program that governs
the repition of the experiment and the summary of the
outcomes is:

```
BEGIN
    COMMENT********************************************************
    *  DETERMINE THE RELATIVE NUMBERS OF INEBRIAN SAILORS WHO   *
    *  ARE ABLE TO RETURN ALONG THE DOCK TO SHIPBOARD, WHO FALL *
    *  OFF THE DOCK ALONG THE WAY, OR WHO LEAVE THE DOCK BY THE  *
    *  SHORE END, GOING A.W.O.L.                                 *
    ************************************************************;
    INTEGER N_RAND, N_TRIALS, NUMBER_AWOL, NUMBER_SHIPPED,
            NUMBER_DROWNED;
    (declarations of procedures RANDOM_DIGIT and DRUNKEN_SAILOR
        go here)
    N_RAND := 1;
    NUMBER_AWOL := NUMBER_SHIPPED := NUMBER_DROWNED := 0;
    READ (N_TRIALS);
    INTFIELDSIZE := 6;
    WRITE (N_TRIALS, "DRUNKEN SAILORS RETURN FROM SHORE LEAVE.");
    WRITE (" ");
    FOR I := 1 UNTIL N_TRIALS DO DRUNKEN_SAILOR;
    WRITE (" ");
    WRITE ("OF THE", N_TRIALS,  "SAILORS,",
            NUMBER_AWOL, "WENT A.W.O.L.",
            NUMBER_SHIPPED, "RETURNED TO THEIR SHIP, AND",
            NUMBER_DROWNED, "DROWNED.");
END.
```

All that remains to do is to check the assumption that
the period of the pseudo-random sequence generator is
sufficient. Since the path to the ship will require at
least 20 paces, but it will probably require less than that
many to fall into the water, one might assume that 20 paces
will approximate the length of a walk on the dock. Since
100 trials are to be run, the period of repetition of the
pseudo-random sequence should be greater than 20*100, or
2000. To determine the period of the sequence generator
that has been developed above, one might run the following

test.

```
BEGIN
    INTEGER N_RAND, N_INITIAL, COUNT;
    (declaration of RANDOM_DIGIT must be inserted here)

    N_RAND := N_INITIAL := 1;
    COMMENT***** CALL THE GENERATOR ONCE TO MODIFY  *****
            ***** THE VALUE OF N_RAND                *****;
    RANDOM_DIGIT;
    COUNT := 1;
    WHILE N_RAND ¬= N_INITIAL DO
        BEGIN
            RANDOM_DIGIT;
            COUNT := COUNT + 1;
        END;
    WRITE ("THE PERIOD OF THE SEQUENCE GENERATOR IS", COUNT);
END MEASURE_PERIOD.
```

When this test program is run with the sequence generator RANDOM_DIGIT, it gives the result that the period is 4369. This period considerably exceeds the number of steps anticipated in 100 trials of the simulation. Obtaining a generator with a long period of repetition usually involves a certain amount of trial and error to select suitable coefficient values.

When the simulation is run for the Inebrian navy. The conclusions yielded by the program are

```
OF THE    50 SAILORS,    10  WENT A.W.O.L.,
20 RETURNED TO THEIR SHIP, AND    20  DROWNED.
```

On the basis of this simulation, it is apparent that the captain of the ship has a problem on his hands!

The example above, while not terribly realistic, does at least serve to introduce you to one important class of simulation problems in which individual behavior must be modeled in order to obtain statistics for a group. Such simulations are widely used in such problems as the study of traffic flow on highways. Many of the more realistic examples require greater knowledge of the mathematics of probability and statistics than has been assumed of readers of this book.

Exercises for chapter 9

9.1 Recode the simulation of example 9.1.1 as a procedure. Use it in a program that will determine the boundary between safe and unsafe initial positions of the bull in the field, and plot the boundary on an image of the field as the program output.

9.2 Modify the assumptions of example 9.1.1 to account for the limited agility of an old bull. Suppose that the bull can change his direction by at most 30° at any single 2-meter stride. Also modify the criterion for successful attack to be

DISTANCE < 2 meters and required change of direction < 30°.

Include in the simulation the capability to plot a map of the field, indicating by printed numerals the successive positions of the boy and the bull. Choose a few initial positions of the bull that were unsafe under the original conditions of example 9.1.1, and repeat the simulations using the modified assumptions about the bull's agility.

9.3 Investigate the effects of various social factors on population growth and distribution by ages, using the simulation program of example 9.2.2.

   a) Suppose that the average age at which people marry is advanced, altering the birth rates to:

AGE	0-9	10-19	20-29	30-39	40-49	50-59	60-69 ...
BIRTH_RATE	0	.010	.112	.036	.006	0	0 ...

   b) Suppose the free availability of contraceptives would affect the birth rate as follows:

AGE	0-9	10-19	20-29	30-39	40-49	50-59	60-69 ...
BIRTH_RATE	0	.020	.100	.010	.001	0	0 ...

   c) Suppose that a combination of conditions a) and b) yields the following birth rates:

AGE	0-9	10-19	20-29	30-39	40-49	50-59	60-69 ...
BIRTH_RATE	0	.003	.085	.018	.001	0	0 ...

   d) In societies in which medical care for infants is inadequate, infant mortality rates are often high. Rerun the simulation using the birth rates of example 9.2.2, except that the death rate for ages 0-9 is altered to 0.040.

244

9.4 The life cycle of the salmon is an unusual one among saltwater fish. Salmon fry are hatched from eggs in the headwaters of streams and rivers, live their first year in fresh water, descend as yearlings to the sea, and grow to maturity at sea during the next two or three years. Then they return to the same rivers and streams from which they were hatched, swim upstream to the headwaters, spawn their eggs and die. Suppose that the following survival rates are known for salmon:

Age:	1 mo.-1 yr.	1-2 yrs.	2-3 yrs.	3-4 yrs.
Rate of survival:	20%	50%	70%	70%

Furthermore, suppose that of the surviving three-year olds, 10% mature and attempt to spawn at that age, while 90% remain at sea. All four-year olds are mature and attempt to spawn. Spawning is a hazardous endeavor, and only 80% of those adult fish that attempt it will live long enough to succeed. A successful female will drop 100,000 eggs.

The highest loss occurs from the time the eggs are dropped until the fry have hatched and reached one month of age. If the supply of eggs is abundant, then it attracts an extra supply of predators to dine on salmon eggs and fry. If the supply of eggs is scanty, then predators are not attracted, and the percentage that hatch and grow to one month is actually higher. An oversimplification of this phenomenon is given as follows. Suppose that for each river there is a fixed, limiting number of salmon fry that can be hatched and survive to one month; a maximum capacity of the stream to hatch salmon, if you will. Suppose that the number of fry who survive to one month, N_f, is given as a function of the capacity, C, and the number of eggs laid, N_e, by the function

$$N_f = \frac{.005 \, N_e C}{\sqrt{.000025 \, N_e^2 + C^2}}$$

a) For $C=1000$, determine the number of salmon that will enter the mouth of a stream to spawn each year.

b) If a natural disaster occurred in 1973 to eliminate the entire batch of salmon fry from the stream in that year, in which of the years 1977, 1981, 1985, 1989,... will the number of salmon returning to the mouth of the river to spawn have returned to 90 percent of normal?

c) Coastal salmon fishing usually harvests the mature fish as they return to the mouths of the rivers preparatory to swimming upstream to spawn. Determine the size of the annual catch, for the stream having C = 1000, if the fishermen take 20 percent of the adult fish. What will be the catch if 50 percent are taken? 80 percent? 90 percent?

d) Determine the percentage of adult fish that should be taken each year to assure the largest size catch on a continuing basis.

9.5   In example 9.3.1, suppose that the ship's captain puts up a rope along each side of the dock, so that the probabilities of a sailor's sideways motion are altered at the edge of the dock.

probability	forward	backward	left	right
at Y = -2	.7	.1	.02	.18
Y =-1,0, or 1	.7	.1	.1	.1
Y = 2	.7	.1	.18	.02

Can you determine the effectiveness of the captain's safety measure?

9.6   A statistical knight's tour. In the knight's tour (Exercise 8.5) the task was to determine a sequence of moves to be made by the knight on a chess board that would take him to every square on the board exactly once. Suppose we consider a knight who chooses his next move randomly with equal probability from the eight possibilities afforded him. For this knight, we define a tour to be a sequence of moves that does not leave the board and does not repeat any position previously visited. The tour ends when the knight's random selection results in a next move that would violate one of these conditions.

For a knight starting at square (4,4) determine the average length of his tours. Also, have the computer plot a bar chart showing the relative frequency of tours of each length, found in a series of 100 independent trials.

NOTES

Chapter 10

NUMERICAL COMPUTATION

Most of the computation done by scientists, including social scientists, and by engineers involves computing with numbers. The largest and fastest digital computers have been designed in order to make possible the numerical solution of some extraordinarily large systems of equations, such as the meteorological equations governing the movement of air masses, and whose solutions are used in long range weather forecasting. The same basic techniques are used in designing algorithms for numerical computation as in other types of applications, but there are also some special considerations related to the limits of precision with which real numbers can be represented in a computer. The design of numerical algorithms relies heavily on the tools of mathematical analysis, and in this chapter, you will have to make greater use of your mathematical knowledge than has been required in previous chapters.

When we talk about numerical computation, we usually mean that the computation is to be carried out with real (or sometimes complex) numbers, as distinguished from computation that can be done solely on integers or rationals. This is because in scientific applications we very often deal with continuously varying quantities: position, temperature, chemical concentrations and the like. Because of the relative imprecision with which we are able to measure physical quantities in the real world (even the velocity of light is only known to a precision of about three parts in 10^9 and this is one of the most precisely known physical constants), for most of our purposes a finite approximation to real numbers, having only six to eight significant decimal digits, is sufficient. However, the range of numbers that must be represented is truly enormous. For example, the size of the universe is estimated to be of the order of 5 billion light years -- approximately 10^{25} meters, whereas the diameter of the nucleus of a helium atom is approximately 10^{-15} meters. In order to meet these requirements, the numbers used in a computer to approximate real numbers are the so-called floating point numbers. The notation was adapted from that used by scientists to represent values of physical quantities.

10.1 Computing with floating-point numbers

In scientific notation, a number is represented as a fixed-point decimal, followed by a multiplier which is a positive or negative power of ten. This notation saves the trouble of writing long strings of trailing zeros to represent a large number, or of zeros following a decimal point to represent a very small number. Equally important, it allows the scientist to indicate in a very simple way the precision with which the quantity represented by the number is known. This is indicated by the use of a fixed point decimal having no surplus digits; if the scientist is honest, he lists just those digits of which he is certain. Thus a precisely measured interval of time might be given as $1.03622*10^3$ seconds, a distance measured by a survey as 753.1 meters, a voltage read from a portable voltmeter as 124 volts, and a concentration of mercury ion in water as $2*10^{-11}$.

The number of significant digits used in representing the mantissa, or fixed point portion of a number, is called the precision of the representation. In some computers the precision of number representation can easily be controlled by the programmer, but most machines allow only a choice between one or two predetermined levels of precision. There are two things to keep in mind when the numerical precision is arbitrarily set, rather than being set by the demands of the particular application. One is, that no matter how many significant figures can be printed on the computer output, the precision of an answer cannot be better than the precision of the input data. Too often, novices at scientific computation will present an answer given to the limit of numerical precision of the computer, such as a velocity of $2.74460*10^2$ meters per second, although the input data on which the computation is based may only be known with a precision of two or three decimal digits. The extra decimal digits of the answer, while printed by the computer, are completely meaningless in such a case.

The other danger in the use of fixed precision arithmetic is that although the precision of the number representation may be sufficient to cope with the input data, that accuracy can be lost in an intermediate step of the computation. Since this is a process that can occur without the knowledge of the programmer, it is particularly dangerous, and we shall investigate it in some detail.

First, let us see how floating-point numbers are represented in a computer. As an example, we shall use the representation in the IBM 360 and 370 series machines. The memory of these machines is divided into individually addressable units, called words. A word is a string of 32 bits, and in representing a floating point number they are used as follows: the rightmost 24 bits represent the mantissa as a fraction in radix 2 arithmetic. That is, the binary point is assumed to lie immediately to the left of these 24 bits. It is not necessary, therefore, to waste any of the precious bits to represent the point. The leftmost bit is used for the algebraic sign of the number. The remaining seven bits, those in positions 2 through 8, counting from the left end of the word, are available to represent the exponent. Now there appears to be a problem, however. With seven bits, one can only represent numbers from 0 to 127, or if one bit is used for the sign of the exponent, then the magnitude of the exponent can only be as large as 63, which is 2^6-1. If our floating point number is expressed in radix 2 arithmetic, then an exponent of 63 will only suffice to represent a multiplier of 10^{19}, in round figures. Although this is indeed a large number, it may not be large enough for all purposes. A way out of this problem is to sacrifice a few bits of precision for the sake of the ability to represent larger multipliers. The way that this has been done on the IBM machines is to treat the mantissa as though it were a fraction in radix 16 arithmetic, rather than radix 2 arithmetic. The bit patterns remain exactly the same except that some fractions will require one, two, or three leading zeros following the radix point, in radix 16 representation. The advantage gained is that each of the precious units of the exponent now represents a power of 16, rather than a power of two, and the exponent of 63 can stand for a multiplier of approximately 10^{76}, which should be sufficient for almost any purpose. The sacrifice in precision is only three bits, slightly less than one decimal place.

To give you some feel for the representations of the mantissa, here are a few fractions in their various representations:

rational fraction	fixed decimal	radix 2 with exponent	radix 16 bit pattern
1/2	.5000	.1000000000000000 E 0	.1000000000000000 E 0
1/4	.2500	.1000000000000000 E-1	.0100000000000000 E 0
1/16	.0625	.1000000000000000 E-3	.0001000000000000 E 0
1/64	.0078125	.1000000000000000 E-5	.0100000000000000 E-1
3/4	.7500	.1100000000000000 E 0	.1100000000000000 E 0
1/10	.1000	.1100110011001100 E-3	.0001100110011001 E 0
1/3	.3333...	.1010101010101010 E-1	.0101010101010101 E 0

The fractions 1/10 and 1/3 cannot be exactly represented by a finite length binary expansion, and have been truncated in the representations above.

In the course of ordinary arithmetic, the operations commonly performed on the exponent of a floating point number are addition, subtraction, and multiplication or division by a power of 2. It turns out, for reasons we shall not go into here, that the representation of the exponent as a signed magnitude is not advantageous for these operations. In fact, it is not even necessary to represent a zero exponent by a string of binary zeros. It is equally satisfactory to regard the string of 7 bits of the exponent as a positive integer between 0 and 127, and to choose a middle value, 64, as representing an exponent of zero. Thus, in order to get the actual power of 16 that is to be the multiplier of the mantissa, one takes the integer represented by the seven bits, and subtracts 64 from it. This operation is easily done by the hardware of the computer itself.

In the convention outlined above, the representation of the number 125.1 would be found as follows. The integer part, 125, has the binary representation 1111101. The fractional part, .1 has the binary representation .0001100110011001100110011... . Putting the two together gives the binary fixed point number
1111101.0001100110011001100110011... .

However, this number is in unnormalized form, that is, the binary point does not appear at the left side of it. To normalize it in binary arithmetic, we would slide the whole bit pattern to the right seven places with respect to the decimal, and record the multiplier of 2^7. But since the normalization is required to be with respect to radix 16 arithmetic, the only acceptable multipliers are powers of 16. Sliding the bit pattern one more place to the right, so that a leading zero appears between the point and the leftmost 1, will accomplish the task, and the multiplier will then be 2^8, or 16^2. The normalized mantissa is then
.0111110100011001100110011001100110011... .

There are only 24 bits allocated for the representation of the mantissa, so the string of bits will have to be truncated. The easiest way to do this is to chop the string off after the 24th bit, yielding .011111010001100110011001. Some computers do this, but it is not the most accurate way to abbreviate a number, as it introduces systematic error; every time that a number must be truncated, the value is made slightly smaller. A better way, which does not introduce systematic error, would be to round the number up or down to the nearest representable number. In binary representation this is very easy to do, for you simply test the first bit that is to be thrown away. If that bit is a 1, then add 1 in the least significant position of the number that is to be kept, otherwise simply chop it off. The IBM 360 and 370 machines do rounding, and the mantissa that will be retained will be .011111010001100110011010, since the first bit of the string thrown away was a 1. Finally, the floating point representation of 125.1, in the machine, will be a word having the bit pattern

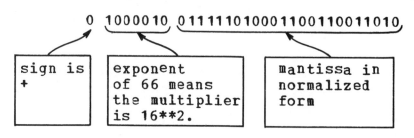

| 0 | 1000010 | 011111010001100110011010 |

| sign is + | exponent of 66 means the multiplier is 16**2. | mantissa in normalized form |

252

The limit of precision in the normal floating-point representation of the IBM computers is about 2^{-25} in absolute terms. However, because some numbers have three leading zeros in the bit positions of the mantissa, the precision can be as poor as 2^{-22}; approximately one part in four million is susceptible to loss. Where the loss of accuracy due to the limitations of precision has its most obvious effect is in the comparison of numbers. When one asks whether or not two numbers are the same, he must be prepared to believe that they may be the same if they agree to within one part in two million. Similarly, in evaluating a sum, the accuracy of the result will obviously be limited by the precision with which the sum can be represented, but if the terms being summed are not all of one sign, then the accuracy of the sum may be further reduced by having subtracted quantities of like magnitudes.

For instance, in the algorithm of Example 3.5.2, a test to find out whether two lines are parallel consists of inquiring if the determinant of a two by two matrix of coefficients is zero. The determinant is of the form A1*B2-B1*A2, where the variables are of type REAL, and take values that are floating point numbers. Given the limitations of a finite precision representation, one cannot ask simply whether the determinant evaluates to zero, but should ask whether it is smaller than one part in two million of one of the component terms. The test should be

      IF DETERMINANT <= .5'-6 * A1*B2 THEN . . .

It often happens in scientific computation that one could safely avoid any loss of accuracy of one's result due to accumulated errors in rounding numbers if the precision of the internal representation were only twice as great. After all, a possible error of one part in 10^{12} is quite a bit smaller than one part in 10^6, and allows much more margin of safety before the accumulation of errors can affect a result whose precision is only required to, say, one part in 10^4. ALGOL W allows the programmer to specify his need for greater precision by declaring variables of the data type LONG REAL. These variables are then represented in the computer by a pair of words in the memory, with the entire string of bits of the second word devoted to extending the length of the mantissa of the floating point number. Thus the precision is more than doubled when LONG REAL is used in preference to REAL. The price payed for the added precision is essentially only that more memory locations are used; it takes the computer very little extra time. Unless the computation is one that requires an enormous amount of storage of intermediate results in the computer, there will be more than enough memory locations available anyway, and the use of extended precision computation will cost essentially nothing.

10.2 Evaluation of functions

There are many functions of analysis that recur frequently in the equations governing natural phenomena, and one of the primary tasks of numerical computing is the evaluation of these functions. During the 1930's, the U.S. National Bureau of Standards employed an army of mathematicians to evaluate many of the more commonly occuring functions, using desk calculators. From the results of their labors, tables of values were published, and the use of these tables was for many years the standard means of determining values of these functions when they were needed in scientific calculations. Today, tables are hardly used any more, at least by scientists who have access to a digital computer. Instead of publishing tables of values, people now publish computational algorithms for the evaluation of functions. It is less work to recompute a value, using an efficient algorithm, than it is to look up a value in a table and use an interpolation formula if the desired argument lies between a pair of argument values listed in the table.

Typical of the mathematical functions we have in mind are the exponential function, the natural logarithm, trigonometric functions, Bessel functions, and various distribution functions used in statistics. There are, of course, many more that have not been mentioned. Most of these are functions of one argument, although they may have one or more parameters as well. Only a few can be evaluated by a finite polyomial formula; more typically, they can most easily be defined in terms of an infinite series in ascending integral powers of the argument. Typical of these, in fact the quintessential power series, is that for the exponential function:

$$e^x = 1 + x + \frac{1}{2}x^2 + \frac{1}{6}x^3 + \frac{1}{24}x^4 + \frac{1}{120}x^5 + \ldots = \sum_{n=0}^{\infty} \frac{x^n}{n!}$$

This power series is as well-behaved as one could wish for; it is uniformly convergent for all values of x. In case you have forgotten what this means, its implication is, that should you desire the value of the series for some fixed value of x to be given to any specified accuracy, say to within an absolute error of 10^{-6}, that there exists some fixed, finite number of terms of the series that must be summed. The rest can be thrown away, for although there are infinitely many of them, they are so small that their total contribution is less than the specified limit of error. Now this fact makes a definition in terms of infinite series really useful, for all we are ever interested in is an evaluation to within some finite error, such as the limit of precision of our number representation.

For example, consider the special case when x = 1. Then

$$e = 1 + 1 + \frac{1}{2} + \frac{1}{6} + \frac{1}{24} + \frac{1}{120} + \frac{1}{720} + \frac{1}{5040} + \frac{1}{40320} + \frac{1}{362880} + \ldots$$

Suppose we wish to evaluate the transcendental number e to a precision of six significant decimal digits. The first 10 terms of the series given above will be sufficient. We shall prove this by giving a convincing demonstration. Let us expand each of the fractions, rounding the sixth digit to the right of the decimal. We get the sum:

```
        1.000000
        1.000000
        0.500000
        0.166667
        0.041667
        0.008333
        0.001389
        0.000198
        0.000025
        0.000003
        2.718282
```

Rounding the sum to six significant figures gives the value of e to the specified precision, 2.71828.

But what about the terms that have been omitted? Each has a positive value, how can one be sure that the accumulation of these values will not have a large effect on the result? Note that the first term omitted has the value of the last term divided by 10, the next term is further divided by 11, and so on. Thus the remainder of the series is of the form

$$.000003 * (\frac{1}{10} * (1 + \frac{1}{11} * (1 + \ldots)))$$

This is certainly less than if each denominator of the continued fraction were 10, but in that case, the sum would be

$$.000003 * (\frac{1}{10} * (1 + \frac{1}{10} * (1 + \frac{1}{10} * (1 + \ldots))))$$

$$= .000003 * .11111111\ldots$$

$$= .00000033333333 \ldots$$

So we discover that there is a bound on the value of the discarded portion of the infinite sum, and that the bound is too small to affect the value of the sum, to the precision that we have required.

255

It might appear then, that there are no computational problems involved in evaluation of the exponential function by using the power series. This might be a true statement if computers used infinite precision real arithmetic, but it is not true of computations done in finite precision floating point arithmetic. Suppose that the exponent is negative, say -10, and the desired precision of the result is six decimal digits. Fifty terms of the series will more than suffice to limit the error in the sum to the precision specified, if the remaining terms are simply neglected. However, the first few terms of the series are found to be

$$e^{-10} = 1 - 10 + 50 - 166.6667 + 416.6667 - 833.3333$$
$$+ 1388.889 - 1984.127 + 2480.159 - 2755.732$$
$$+ 2755.732 - 2505.211 + \ldots$$

The terms increase in magnitude until they reach $-10^9/9!$. The term that follows that one is $10^{10}/10!$, the same in magnitude, and from then on, successive terms are smaller in magnitude. However, the fact that such large numbers must be accumulated and subtracted means that, if our computer can retain only seven decimal digits in a floating point number (roughly the equivalent of a 24-bit mantissa), whereas the result to be computed is actually .00004540, that no significant digit of the result can be computed by this method! The difficulty has nothing at all to do with the convergence of the series, but has to do with the fact that the discrepancy in size between the largest individual terms in the alternating series and the result to be computed is some eight orders of magnitude. Thus, the computational error made in rounding off one of the large terms to the precision of the internal number representation will be greater than the magnitude of the final result.

One way around the difficulty would be to use extended precision arithmetic, by declaring the variables in an ALGOL W program to be of type LONG REAL. With a 56-bit mantissa available, one could compute e^{-10} by direct evaluation of the series, but could not compute e^{-20}. There is, however, a better way, a different algorithm, which we shall study in the following example.

Example 10.2.1 -- Evaluating the exponential function

Our task is to formulate an algorithm that will compute the exponential function for any real argument, yielding a result with six significant decimal digits of accuracy.

It has already been demonstrated that accuracy can be lost when we try to sum a series whose terms alternate in sign. Furthermore, the number of terms of the power series that must be included in the sum in order to attain the desired accuracy of the result is strongly dependent on the magnitude of the argument. And yet, if the exponent is an integer, and the value of the constant e is known, the exponential function can be evaluated by a sequence of multiplications or divisions with no degradation in accuracy. Suppose that one was to write the argument of the exponential function as the sum of two parts.

$$x = \text{integer part} + \text{fractional part};$$

where the fractional part is between zero and one, and the integer part is a positive or negative integer. Then since

$$e^x = e^{\text{integer part}} * e^{\text{fractional part}}$$

the two components can be evaluated separately, and one need not even use the same algorithm for the two evaluations. To compute the exponential of an integer argument, we can use iterated multiplication, while the exponential of a positive fractional argument can be evaluated by summing the first few terms of the power series.

An obvious way to raise a number to an integral power is by repeated multiplication (or division if the power is negative). This suggests as a first version of an algorithm to compute the exponential function of an integer:

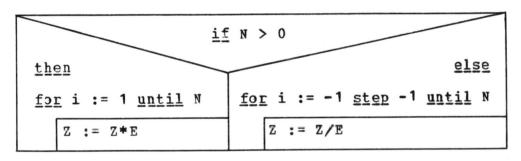

However, this naive procedure is not one that you would want to advertise for public use. First of all, negative powers of e can be treated in the same way as are positive powers, by selecting 1/e as the constant multiplier. Secondly, the naive algorithm uses unnecessarily many multiplications, in the general case. By way of illustration, consider the representation of e^{15} as

$$e^{15} = e*e*e*e*e*e*e*e*e*e*e*e*e*e*e$$

257

An alternate representation is

$$e^{15} = e^8*e^4*e^2*e$$

Instead of requiring 14 multiplications, it appears that three will be sufficient if the second representation is used. However, there is a bit of cheating going on, for in the representation given above, it is assumed that the values of e raised to powers of two are freely available. But if these values are not known, it will require additional multiplications to determine them. The potential for saving computation lies in the observation that the values e, e^2, e^4, e^8, need only be obtained in succession, so that they can be computed by the formulae

$$e^2 = e*e,$$
$$e^4 = e^2*e^2,$$
$$e^8 = e^4*e^4.$$

This sequence adds only three more multiplications to the process, making it possible to evaluate e^{15} by using only 6 multiplications. (To evaluate e^{16} is easier, requiring only 4 multiplications.) Incorporating this into an algorithm, we can give the iteration graph (for positive N only)

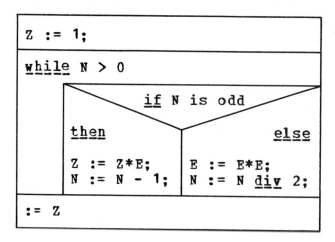

To translate this into a procedure, we need only make provision for negative values of N.

```
REAL PROCEDURE INTEXP (INTEGER VALUE N);
    COMMENT***** EVALUATES EXP(N) *****;
    BEGIN
        REAL E, Z;
        Z := 1;
        E := IF N >= 0 THEN 2.718282 ELSE .3678794;
        N := ABS N;
        WHILE N > 0 DO
            IF ODD(N) THEN
                BEGIN
                    Z := Z*E;
                    N := N - 1;
                END
            ELSE
                BEGIN
                    E := E*E;
                    N := N DIV 2;
                END;
        Z
    END INTEXP;
```

In the procedure to evaluate the exponential of the
fractional part, we already know a bound on how many terms
of the series will need to be summed. The exponent must be
smaller than one, but if it were one, then ten terms of the
series would suffice to give the required accuracy.
We have a choice: we can either take ten terms of the
series in all cases, or we can test the size of successive
terms, halting the computation when the size has vanished to
insignificance. The first course of action is simpler,
while the second will be more efficient in most cases. We
choose the second.

```
REAL PROCEDURE FRACTEXP (REAL VALUE X);
    BEGIN COMMENT***** SUM A SERIES OF TERMS OF THE FORM:
                 *****       X**I / FACTORIAL(I) *****;
        REAL TERM, SUM, I;
        I := TERM := SUM := 1;
        WHILE TERM > 1'-7 DO
            BEGIN
                TERM := TERM * X/I;
                SUM := SUM + TERM;
                I := I + 1;
            END;
        SUM
    END FRACTEXP;
```

Now the two procedures need only to be put together in a control procedure that will separate the exponent into its integer and fractional parts.

```
REAL PROCEDURE EXPONENTIAL (REAL VALUE X);
    BEGIN
        INTEGER INTPART;
        REAL FRACTPART;
        (declarations of the procedures INTEXP and FRACTEXP
                        go here)
        INTPART := ENTIER (X);
        FRACTPART := X - INTPART;
        INTEXP (INTPART) * FRACTEXP (FRACTPART)
    END EXPONENTIAL;
```

Other computational problems arise in the evaluation of functions whose series do not converge so rapidly. Consider for example, an infinite power series representation for the natural logarithm,

$$\ln(x) = -\sum_{i=1}^{\infty} \frac{(1-x)^i}{i}$$

When x = 0, the sum is

$$- (1 + \frac{1}{2} + \frac{1}{3} + \frac{1}{4} + \frac{1}{5} + \frac{1}{6} + \frac{1}{7} + \frac{1}{8} + \frac{1}{9} + \ldots)$$

It is well known that this sum does not converge, for no matter what finite number of terms you might take as an approximation to the sum, there is no bound to the value of the sum of the terms remaining. This is true in spite of the fact that the magnitude of the individual terms approaches a limit of zero as the index of the terms approaches infinity.

On the other hand, for x = 2, one obtains a series whose terms have the same magnitudes as those of the series above, but whose signs alternate:

$$\ln(2) = 1 - \frac{1}{2} + \frac{1}{3} - \frac{1}{4} + \frac{1}{5} - \frac{1}{6} + \frac{1}{7} - \frac{1}{8} + \frac{1}{9} - \ldots$$

This sum converges to the value .693147 in the sense that there is a limit of the partial sums. However, in a very real sense, the sum cannot be computed. For instance, suppose one attempts the computation in a straightforward manner by means of the ALGOL W program

```
BEGIN
    REAL SUM;
    INTEGER I;
    SUM := 0;
    FOR I := 1 UNTIL 10000000 DO
        SUM := 1/I - SUM;
END
```

where the result is to be the magnitude of the final value of
SUM.   In spite of having summed ten million terms of the series,
the accuracy of the answer will be only three significant decimal
digits.   It is easy to see what happens if we consider successive
pairs of terms to be added to the sum.   When I becomes as large
as 2^{12}, or 4096, then the difference between 1/I and 1/(I+1) will
be less than 2^{-24}. Thus, when these terms are added to the sum,
whose magnitude is about .6, the addition of successive terms is
like

$$.6......$$
$$.0002441\ 40625$$
$$-.\underline{0002440\ 81035}..$$

However, with approximately seven decimal digits of precision,
the computer will round these numbers, and evaluate
$$.6......$$
$$.0002441$$
$$-.\underline{0002441}$$

so that the successive pairs of terms 1/4096 and -1/4097 actually
contribute nothing to the computation!   One might just as well
sum from I = 1 until 4096, which obviously cannot yield better
than three place accuracy.

It may have occurred to you that the above algorithm is not
the right one to use, and that one would be better off to combine
adjacent terms of the series algebraically, so as to obtain a new
series whose terms are all of one sign.   In general, this is a
good strategy to follow.   In this case, the series would become

$$\ln(2) = \frac{1}{2} + \frac{1}{12} + \frac{1}{30} + \frac{1}{56} + \frac{1}{90} + \frac{1}{132} + \cdots$$

An algorithm to sum this series would be

```
BEGIN
   REAL SUM;
   INTEGER I;
   SUM := 0;
   FOR I := 1 STEP 2 UNTIL 4096 DO
      SUM := SUM + 1/(I*(I+1));
END
```

The sum is carried out until the individual terms have become
smaller than 2^{-24}. Beyond that point, terms can no longer be
added using floating-point arithmetic with a 24-bit mantissa.
However, the result will still only be correct to three
significant decimal digits! The reason is that the terms that
have been thrown away, although small, do not decrease in size
fast enough, and their total contribution is of the order of
1/4096, or .00024.

How then, is one to evaluate the natural logarithm of 2? One
way would be to use the algorithm above, but to use extended
precision arithmetic. Then, by summing approximately 2^{24} terms
of the series, one could obtain a result accurate to seven
decimal digits. This could require several minutes of
computation time, and one is forced to suspect that there may be
a better way.

If we turn our attention once more to the power series for the
natural logarithm, we can see that the series must converge more
rapidly, the nearer the argument of the logarithm is to 1. For
when the magnitude of 1 - x is smaller than 1, successively
higher powers assume decreasing values. Thus it should be easier
to compute the logarithm of $2^{(1/2)}$ than to compute the logarithm
of 2, using the power series. This is indeed the case. It
requires only 17 terms of the series to calculate the logarithm
of $2^{(1/2)}$ to seven digit accuracy, and the easy way to evaluate
ln(2) is by taking $2*\ln(2^{(1/2)})$. This idea forms the basis for
the algorithm of the following example.

Example 10.2.2 -- Evaluating the natural logarithm

We wish to compose an algorithm to evaluate the natural
logarithm of a positive real argument, yielding accuracy
commensurate with the precision of the floating point number
representation. In this algorithm, we shall assume that the
number representation is that used in the IBM 360 and 370
series machines, with a 24-bit mantissa in normal precision
arithmetic, and each unit of the exponent representing a
power of 16. The only significant way in which this
information is used is in deciding on convenient
multiplicative constants. With this type of number
representation, multiplication or division by 16 affects

262
```
```

only the exponent of a floating point number, and so there is no reduction in accuracy due to rounding of the mantissa.

The strategy of the algorithm is to bring an arbitrary positive number into the range of values $1/(2^{(1/2)})$ to $2^{(1/2)}$ by multipling or dividing it by powers of $2^{(1/2)}$. Each time there is a multiplication or division by $2^{(1/2)}$, the constant value of $\ln(2^{(1/2)})$ is added to or subtracted from the result. In order to expedite matters if the number is very large or very small, powers of 16 and powers of 2 are first factored out. When the number, shorn of all integral powers of $2^{(1/2)}$, is within the desired range, its logarithm is evaluated by the following procedure, and added to the result.

```
REAL PROCEDURE LOGSUM (REAL VALUE X);
    BEGIN
        COMMENT*****************************************
        *   X IS A NUMBER WHOSE MAGNITUDE LIES     *
        *   BETWEEN THE SQUARE ROOT OF 2 AND ITS   *
        *   RECIPROCAL.  THE NATURAL LOGARITHM     *
        *   OF X IS TO BE EVALUATED BY SUMMING     *
        *    THE SERIES OF TERMS -(1-X)**I / I     *
        ***********************************************;
        REAL I, PRODUCT, SUM;
        I := 1;
        PRODUCT := SUM := 1 - X;
        WHILE ABS(PRODUCT) > 1'-6 DO
            BEGIN
                PRODUCT := (1 - X) * PRODUCT;
                I := I + 1;
                SUM := SUM + PRODUCT/I;
            END;
        -SUM
    END LOGSUM.
```

The main procedure consists almost entirely of a sequence of tests to determine the range in which the argument lies, and to add or subtract the appropriate constants to the result.

```
REAL PROCEDURE NATLOG (REAL VALUE X);
    BEGIN
        REAL L; COMMENT***** L IS TO ACCUMULATE THE RESULT *****;
        L := 0;
        IF X <= 0 THEN
            WRITE ("CANNOT TAKE THE LOGARITHM OF ",
                "ZERO OR A NEGATIVE NUMBER")
```

```
ELSE
   BEGIN
      REAL ROOT2, LR2, L2, L16;
      COMMENT********************************
      *    ROOT2 IS THE SQUARE ROOT OF 2.       *
      *    LR2 IS THE LOGARITHM OF THE SQUARE *
      *        ROOT OF 2.                       *
      *    L2 IS THE LOGARITHM OF 2.            *
      *    L16 IS THE LOGARITHM OF 16.          *
      ********************************************;
      ROOT2 := 1.414214;
      LR2 := .3465736;
      L2 := .6931472;
      L16 := 2.7725887;
      IF X > 1 THEN
         BEGIN
            WHILE X >= 16 DO
               BEGIN
                  X := X/16;
                  L := L + L16;
               END;
            WHILE X >= 2 DO
               BEGIN
                  X := X/2;
                  L := L + L2;
               END;
            IF X >= ROOT2 THEN
               BEGIN
                  X := X/ROOT2;
                  L := L + LR2;
               END;
         END
      ELSE
         BEGIN
            WHILE X <= .0625 DO
               BEGIN
                  X := 16*X;
                  L := L - L16;
               END
            WHILE X <= .5 DO
               BEGIN
                  X := 2*X;
                  L := L - L2;
               END;
            IF X <= 1/ROOT2 DO
               BEGIN
                  X := ROOT2*X;
                  L := L - LR2;
               END;
         END;
```

```
COMMENT*******************************************
   *  THE REMAINING PART OF THE LOGARITHM IS TO *
   *  BE EVALUATED BY SUMMING THE POWER SERIES  *
   *********************************************;
   L := L + LOGSUM(X);
 END;
L
END NATLOG
```

The examples of this section have illustrated some of the common computational problems involved in the evaluation of mathematical functions. Many of the more subtle problems that one can encounter require a substantial knowledge of mathematical analysis in order to develop good algorithms.

10.3 Finding roots of equations

In the mathematical problems that arise out of science, it very commonly happens that the desired answer can be expressed as the root of an equation of one variable, also depending on one or more parameters. For example, the radius of a circular orbit of an earth satellite is given by the solution of the equation

$$r^3 - \left(\frac{T}{2\pi}\right)^2 m_e g = 0$$

where r stands for the unknown radius, and the parameters T, m_e, and g refer to the period of the orbit, the mass of the earth, and the gravitational constant, respectively. In some cases, one wishes a solution to be given in analytic form as a specific function. Then, the behavior of the solution as the parameters are varied can be inferred from the mathematical properties of the function. However, it is also often the case that the solution cannot be given analytically as a simple function of the parameters. Polynomial equations furnish a good class of examples. Although there is a simple analytic formula for the solution to a quadratic equation in terms of its coefficients, the analytic formulas for cubic and quartic equations are so cumbersome that they are almost never used, and polynomial equations of higher degree than quartic do not admit analytic solutions in terms of algebraic formulas.

On the other hand, equations can be solved numerically even when the algebraic complexity of the formulas seems overwhelming. All that is required is that the component formulas of the equation are themselves computable, continuous functions of the unknown variable. In order to standardize the problem somewhat, all of the terms of the equation are collected together on one side of the equals sign, so that we can give this collection of terms a name, call it f(x). Roots of the equation are those values of x for which f(x) = 0. A numerical solution consists in searching out those values. This does not require that any explicit, analytical solution of the equation ever be found.

There are two more or less distinct parts of the problem of root-finding. First, one must locate an interval of values of the variable, x, within which one can be certain that a root is to be found. The second part is the exact location of the of the root within that interval, to the accuracy desired.

In order to locate an interval in which a root is certain to be found, one must by some means acquire some knowledge of the behavior of f(x). There are several possible ways this might be done. One might know some properties of the function from mathematical analysis or from knowledge about a scientific problem from which the equation arose. Or one might plot the function to determine the approximate locations of its roots. The fundamental idea is that if (x1,x2) is an interval for which f(x1) and f(x2) differ in algebraic sign, then there is at least one root of the equation f(x) = 0 within the interval. For, since f is a continuous function of x, the curve representing f(x) has to cross the zero axis somewhere between the two endpoints, as indicated in Fig. 10.3.1a. In fact, it is possible that there is more that one root of the equation within such an interval, as is shown in Fig. 10.3.1b.

The converse of this assertion is false. In an interval (x1,x2) for which f(x1) and f(x2) are of the same sign, one cannot be sure there is no root of f(x). In Fig. 10.3.2 are shown plots of three quadratic equations over the interval (0,2). In each case, f(0) = f(2), so the signs of the endpoint values agree, yet in the first case f(x) has two roots in the interval, in the second case a double root at x = 1, and in the third case none. Double roots, that is, two roots which coincide on a single point, are particularly difficult to locate accurately by purely computational methods, and we shall ignore them in the discussion that follows.

If one wishes to locate intervals in which there can be no more than one root of an equation f(x) = 0, one can first locate the points at which f takes maximum and minimum values, that is, the points at which the curve of f(x) changes slope from positive to negative, or vice versa. In any interval between a maximum point and the next minimum point, f(x) must have negative slope. Therefore, if it also happens to pass through zero in that interval, this zero crossing will be the unique root of the equation within the interval, as depicted in Fig. 10.3.3. By dividing the interval of values of x that is to be searched for roots into sub-intervals between adjacent maximum and minimum

266

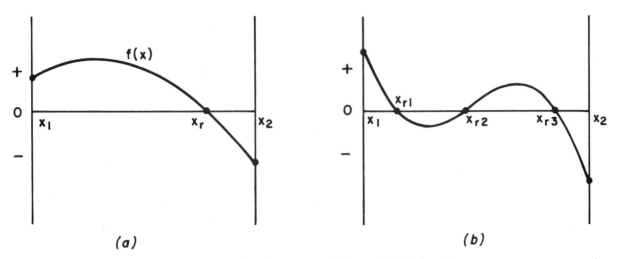

(a)   *(b)*

Figure 10.3.1 -- Roots of the equation $f(x) = 0$ are zero crossing points of the curves.

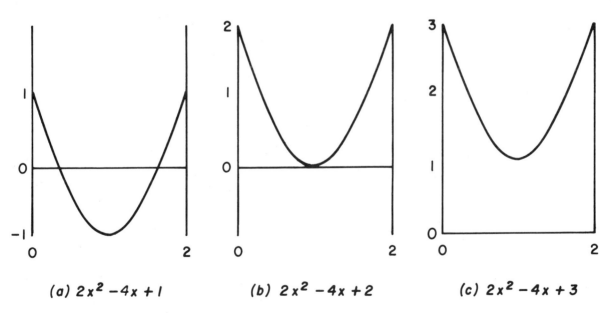

(a) $2x^2 - 4x + 1$ (b) $2x^2 - 4x + 2$ (c) $2x^2 - 4x + 3$

Figure 10.3.2 -- When the function has the same sign at both endpoints, there may or may not be any roots of the equation within the interval.

points of f(x), and applying to each sub-interval the test that determines whether it contains at least one root, a set of intervals each containing a single root of the equation can be found. We shall not dwell further on the process of locating intervals, except to mention that an algorithm for locating maximum and minimum points of a function can be found in Forsythe, Keenan, Organick and Stenberg, Computer Science: A First Course, John Wiley and Sons, New York, 1969.

Instead, let us concentrate on studying a computational method for locating a root precisely within an interval over which the function f(x) changes sign. A very simple algorithm suggests itself. Divide the interval in some way into two sub-intervals. Choose from the sub-intervals that one in which there is still a sign change of the function from one end point to the other. Continue the process until the desired accuracy has been obtained. There are two important refinements of this sketchily-defined procedure that must be made. One is to tell precisely how the division into sub-intervals is to be made, and the other is to determine a criterion to apply to tell us when to stop the process.

Since the function f(x) must be repeatedly evaluated in the process of searching for a root, it might seem reasonable to use, as a criterion for having located the root, the condition that f(x) is small, say less than 10^{-6} times its value at one of the endpoints of the original interval. There is an objection to be raised to such a condition, however. The precision that is specified in that condition is not a precision on the accuracy of location of the root, but on the value of the function at the approximately located root. These quantities will be related, but how they are related depends on special knowledge about the function, and in general, we will not have that knowledge. In some problems, such as finding a square root, which involves solving the equation $x^2 - N = 0$, the relation will be a direct one and the condition that f(x) should be small is a satisfactory way to determine an accurate location of the root. In other cases the accuracy may not be as good, and it will be preferable to specify the desired precision of root location directly.

One way to accomplish this is to continue subdividing the interval that contains the root until the interval size itself is within the desired precision. This precision may be given as a fraction of the original interval, or might be given in absolute terms, as a numerical interval.

On the other question, the method by which the interval is to be divided into sub-intervals, we could, if no better way suggests itself, simply divide the interval in half at each iteration. This is known as the bisection method, for obvious

268

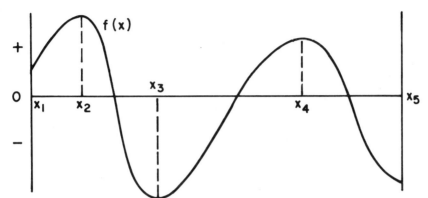

Figure 10.3.3 -- Single roots of the equation f(x) = 0 lie in each of the intervals (x₂, x₃), (x₃, x₄), and (x₄, x₅).

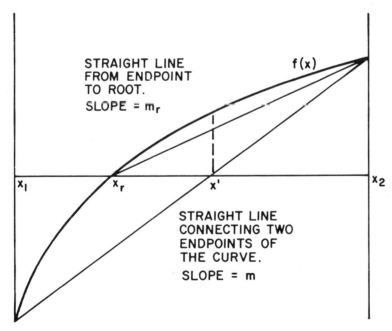

Figure 10.3.4 -- Division of an interval by linear interpolation. The interval from x_1 to x_2 will be replaced by the smaller interval from x_1 to x' in the next iteration.

reasons. Another method, which we shall call division by linear interpolation, begins by taking the values of the function at the endpoints, f(x1) and f(x2), as points on a graph of the function. Although we do not know as yet precisely what the function looks like between these endpoints, we know that it must cross the zero axis somewhere between them. As a very crude approximation to the function, we might connect the two known points on the graph of the function by a straight line. Solving for the point at which this straight line crosses the zero axis gives an estimate for the zero-crossing point of the actual function. To iterate the approximation, the interval is divided in two at the estimated zero crossing point, the actual function is evaluated at that point, and one of the two sub-intervals is selected for further searching.

The method of division by linear interpolation sounds as if it may produce better estimates of the root location, in fewer iterations, than will the method of bisection, for it utilizes more of the available information, namely the relative magnitudes of the values of the function at the endpoints of an interval. But in fact, it will only produce better estimates for functions that can be approximated to some degree by straight lines. For a more detailed analysis, let us refer to the graph of Figure 10.3.4. In this graph, you can see that the distance between the approximate root and the actual root is (1 - m(r)/m) times the distance of the actual root from the endpoint, where m and m(r) are the slopes of the two lines indicated in the diagram. In very many cases, the slopes of the two lines will be nearly the same, and the process will converge rapidly to an accurate estimate. However, if the slope of the curve at the actual root is nearly zero, as indicated in Fig. 10.3.5, then the process will converge to an accurate estimate more slowly than will the method of bisection.

In addition to its simplicity, the method of bisection assures us of a uniform rate of convergence to a root, independent of the details of the behaviour of the function near its root. The uncertainty in the root location, which is the interval width, is always 2^{-N} times the width of the original interval after N iterations of the bisection method. For this reason the bisection method is often to be preferred over the method of division by linear interpolation, even though the latter method yields more rapid convergence to a root in many typical problems.

A combination of the two methods can yield the advantages of both, however. Linear interpolation provides a good estimate of a root location in an interval in which the actual function can be well approximated by a straight line. For smoothly varying functions, which are most frequently encountered in the description of continuous systems, any function is well

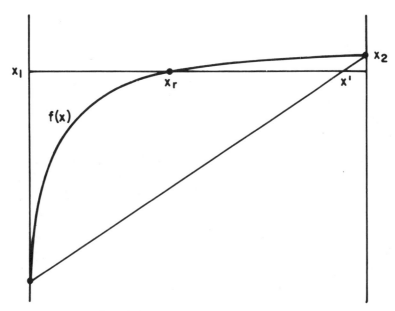

Figure 10.3.5 -- Illustrating a case for which division by linear
interpolation does not move the endpoint much
closer to the root.

approximated by a straight line over a sufficiently narrow interval. Since the aim of the bisection method is to define a narrow interval in which the root of an equation must lie, this suggests application of the method of linear interpolation to further refine a root estimate, after the interval has been narrowed by the bisection method. Using linear interpolation as a final step makes it possible to save half the number of iterations of the bisection method that would be required to obtain comparable accuracy without the use of interpolation.

Example 10.3.1 -- Finding a root by bisection

The specifications for our root-finding program are that when it is given as arguments the endpoints of an interval, and a function whose values at these endpoints differ in sign, it will attempt to find the root of the equation $f(x) = 0$ by dividing the interval 10 times. This may produce an estimate of the root accurate to one part in 2^{10}, if the numerical accuracy of evaluation of the function is good enough. Following the estimate of the root by iterated bisection, linear interpolation will be applied to further refine the estimate.

Since only the sign of the function at the endpoints of the interval is of interest, the sign is the only information that needs to be recorded. An ALGOL W program for locating roots of equations is:

```
BEGIN
    COMMENT**** FUNCTION WHOSE ROOT IS TO BE FOUND ****;
    REAL PROCEDURE F (REAL VALUE X);
        X*(X*(X+3.5)-3.5)-6.0;

    REAL END_1, END_2, MIDDLE;
    INTEGER SIGN_1, SIGN_2, SIGN_MID;

    READ (END_1, END_2);
    WRITE ("BETWEEN", END_1, "AND", END_2);
    SIGN_1 := IF F(END_1) < 0 THEN -1 ELSE 1;
    SIGN_2 := IF F(END_2) < 0 THEN -1 ELSE 1;
    ASSERT SIGN_1 ¬= SIGN_2;
    FOR K := 1 UNTIL 10 DO
        BEGIN
            MIDDLE := (END_1 + END_2) / 2;
            SIGN_MID := IF F(MIDDLE) < 0 THEN -1 ELSE 1;
            IF SIGN_MID = SIGN_1 THEN
                END_1 := MIDDLE
            ELSE
                END_2 := MIDDLE;
        END;
    COMMENT***** REFINE THE FINAL ESTIMATE OF THE ROOT *****
            ***** BY LINEAR INTERPOLATION                *****;
    MIDDLE := END_1 + (END_2 - END_1) * ABS F(END_1) /
                        ABS(F(END_1) - F(END_2));
    WRITE ("THERE IS A ROOT OF F(X) AT X =", MIDDLE);
END.
```

10.4 Solving systems of linear equations

There are many problems in the physical sciences which lend
themselves to formulation in terms of a set of simultaneous,
linear equations in several variables. This is the analytical
technique used in systems involving several variables, and the
physical world is full of such systems. For instance, the
description of motion in three-dimensional space can be given in
such a system. A very important computational problem is to
obtain the solution of a system of N linear, simultaneous
equations in N variables. Since this is a very old problem,
there is a standard method for its solution, originally
attributable to Gauss. It involves only the linear operations of
addition and multiplication by a constant, but the objects
subjected to these operations are the equations themselves.

Let the N equations each be written in a standard form,
illustrated for the ith equation,

$$a_{i1}x_1 + a_{i2}x_2 + a_{i3}x_3 + \ldots + a_{in}x_n + b_i = 0$$

where the a_{ij}'s are coefficients and the x_j's are the variables. Since the right hand side of each equation is equal to zero, the system of equations will have exactly the same solutions if any equation is replaced by a constant multiple of itself. That is, if each coefficient a_{ij} of the ith equation, (including the coefficient b_i) is replaced by $C*a_{ij}$, where C is any non-zero constant. Also, the solutions will remain unchanged if any equation is replaced by the sum of itself and another one of the equations. To sum the ith and jth equations, the coefficients of common variables in the two equations are added. Finally, these two operations, multiplication by a constant and addition of equations, can be composed without affecting the solutions. Thus the ith equation could be replaced by

$$(a_{i1} + C*a_{j1})*x_1 + ((a_{i2} + C*a_{j2})*x_2 + \ldots + (b_i + C*b_j) = 0$$

How can these operations be used to derive a simpler, but equivalent set of equations from the system originally given? First, let us observe one particular form that such a system might take, in which a solution can be found directly. In order to study this form, it will be most convenient to represent the equations by a matrix of their coefficients,

$$
\begin{matrix}
a_{11} & a_{12} & a_{13} & \cdots & a_{1N} & b_1 \\
a_{21} & a_{22} & a_{23} & \cdots & a_{2N} & b_2 \\
\vdots & \vdots & \vdots & \vdots & \vdots & \vdots \\
a_{N1} & a_{N2} & a_{N3} & \cdots & a_{NN} & b_N
\end{matrix}
$$

In the matrix representation, we have omitted writing the plus signs, the variables, and the right hand sides of the equations. All these are understood. Now if all of the coefficients to the left of the term a_{ii} in the ith equation happened to be zero, and this were the case for every equation so that the matrix looked like this

$$
\begin{matrix}
a_{11} & a_{12} & a_{13} & \cdots & a_{1N} & b_1 \\
0 & a_{22} & a_{23} & \cdots & a_{2N} & b_2 \\
\vdots & \vdots & \vdots & \vdots & \vdots & \vdots \\
0 & 0 & 0 & \cdots & a_{NN} & b_N
\end{matrix}
$$

then the equations could be solved directly, provided that none of the coefficients a_{ii} was zero. The solution procedure would start with the Nth equation, which is independent of the others.

$$a_{NN}x_N + b_N = 0$$

After this equation is solved, the value $-b_N/a_{NN}$ can be substituted for the variable x_N in each of the remaining equations. But when this has been done, then the N-1st equation is also susceptible to direct solution, and so the solution proceeds, one equation after the other, until all of the variables have been evaluated. This form, in which the non-zero coefficients lie in a triangle, is one we would be justified in regarding as a simplification.

Returning to the business of replacing equations in the system by linear combinations of themselves and other equations, we now have some motivation to ask, is there some linear combination of the first equation with the ith that will have zero as the coefficient of the first variable? Suppose that we multiply the first equation by $-a_{i1}/a_{11}$, and add the result to the ith equation. We will get the row of coefficients

$$(a_{i1} - \frac{a_{i1}}{a_{11}}a_{11}) \quad (a_{i2} - \frac{a_{i1}}{a_{11}}a_{12}) \cdots (a_{iN} - \frac{a_{i1}}{a_{11}}a_{1N}) \quad (b_i - \frac{a_{i1}}{a_{11}}b_1)$$

of which the first one is seen to be zero. In fact, if we were to apply a similar operation to each equation following the first, choosing a constant multiplier appropriate to each, then the whole first column of coefficients in the matrix would be zero, except for the first one. At this point, the matrix of coefficients would look like

$$
\begin{array}{ccccccc}
a_{11} & a_{12} & a_{13} & \cdots & a_{1N} & b_1 \\
0 & a'_{22} & a'_{23} & \cdots & a'_{2N} & b'_2 \\
\vdots & \vdots & \vdots & \vdots\ \vdots & \vdots & \vdots \\
0 & a'_{N2} & a'_{N3} & \cdots & a'_{NN} & b'_N
\end{array}
$$

where the primes over some of the coefficients indicate only that they are different from those of the original system of equations.

In the matrix above, the 2nd through Nth equations can be solved independently of the first. Ignoring the first equation for the time being, we see that the procedure for putting columns of coefficients to zeros can be applied recursively to the system of equations 2 through N. When the whole process has finished, we shall have a system of equations whose matrix is in triangular form. Most importantly, it will be equivalent to the original system, provided that none of the diagonal coefficients that appeared in the denominator of any coefficient was zero. In order to see more explicitly the form that a computational algorithm will take, let us compose an ALGOL W procedure.

Example 10.4.1 -- Solution of simultaneous linear equations by Gaussian elimination

The procedure that we wish to construct will take as its arguments a two-dimensional array containing the coefficients of the equations that are to be solved, a one-dimensional array into which the answers are to be written, and an integer value which is the number of equations and variables. When arrays are passed as arguments to a procedure in ALGOL W, it is not necessary to declare the dimension of the array in the formal parameter declaration. Instead, the number of dimensions of the array is indicated by substituting an asterisk for the position of each subscript in the parentheses following the array identifier (see section A9.2.1 of the Appendix). Recall that the matrix of a system of N equations in N unknowns will have N + 1 columns, the extra column containing the constant term of each equation.

```
PROCEDURE GAUSS (REAL ARRAY A(*,*); REAL ARRAY X(*);
                INTEGER VALUE N);
    COMMENT**************************************************
    *  THE ARRAY 'A' HOLDS THE COEFFICIENTS OF THE       *
    *  EQUATIONS TO BE SOLVED.  EXECUTION OF THE PROCE-*
    *  DURE WILL CAUSE THE ORIGINAL COEFFICIENTS TO BE *
    *  LOST, REPLACING THEM WITH VALUES COMPUTED DURING*
    *  THE COURSE OF SOLVING THE EQUATIONS.  THE SOLU- *
    *  TION FOR THE VARIABLES WILL BE RETURNED IN THE   *
    *  ARRAY 'X'.  'N' GIVES THE NUMBER OF EQUATIONS    *
    *  TO BE SOLVED.                                    *
    ***************************************************************;
BEGIN
    (declarations of procedures SUBTRACTEQUATION
       and SUM go here)

    COMMENT***** TRIANGULARIZE THE MATRIX *****;
    FOR I := 1 UNTIL N - 1 DO
       FOR J := I + 1 UNTIL N DO
          SUBTRACTEQUATION (I, J);
    COMMENT***** SOLVE FOR THE UNKNOWNS *****;
    FOR I := N STEP -1 UNTIL 1 DO
       X(I) := -SUM(I) / A(I,I);
END GAUSS;
```

276

The procedure to subtract equations is to determine a constant coefficient by which to multiply the first equation, so that when subtracted from the second equation, the coefficient of the Ith variable will be zero. The subtraction is then carried out, one column at a time. Notice that it is not actually necessary to carry out the step of setting the coefficient of the Ith variable to zero, for it will never be used again in the course of the remaining computations. We can save an unnecessary step by beginning the subtractions at the coefficient of the I+1st variable.

```
PROCEDURE SUBTRACTEQUATION (INTEGER VALUE I, J);
    COMMENT*********************************************
    *   DETERMINE A CONSTANT MULTIPLIER THAT WILL     *
    *   MAKE THE ITH COEFFICIENT IN THE ITH EQUATION  *
    *   EQUAL TO THE ITH COEFFICIENT IN THE JTH       *
    *   EQUATION.                                      *
    *   THEN SUBTRACT THIS MULTIPLE OF THE ITH EQUA-  *
    *   TION FROM THE JTH EQUATION.                    *
    ***************************************************;
BEGIN
    REAL C;
    C := A(J,I)/A(I,I);
    FOR K := I+1 UNTIL N+1 DO
        A(J,K) := A(J,K) - C*A(I,K);
END SUBTRACTEQUATION;
```

The final procedure required has the task of summing, in the Ith equation, the products of the coefficients with the variables already found. These are the I+1st through the Nth variables. The constant coefficient A(I, N+1) must also be added.

```
REAL PROCEDURE SUM (INTEGER VALUE I);
    COMMENT*********************************************
    *   SUM THE PRODUCTS OF COEFFICIENTS WITH VARI-   *
    *   ABLES ALREADY EVALUATED.                      *
    ***************************************************;
BEGIN
    REAL ROWSUM;
    ROWSUM := A(I, N+1);
    FOR K := I+1 UNTIL N DO
        ROWSUM := ROWSUM + A(I,K) * X(K);
    ROWSUM
END SUM;
```

10.1 Compose an ALGOL W procedure to compute the sine function for an argument given in radians. Test the procedure on argument values of 0, .1, 1, 10, 100, and 1000 radians. Compare the results with those yielded by the built-in function SIN( ).

10.2 Evaluate the following finite sum, for n = 45 and n = 50

$$\sum_{r=1}^{n} \frac{n!\,(n-2r)\,(-1)^{r}}{(n-r)!\,r!}$$

Can it be evalutated for n = 1200?

10.3 Conventional earth-based navigation utilizes the solution of triangles. If only one fixed reference point can be located, then compass directions to that reference point, taken from two ends of a line whose length has been measured will enable the positions of the ends of the line to be determined relative to the known position of the reference point. The determination involves setting up and solving a pair of simultaneous algebraic equations. Similarly, compass observations of a pair of known, fixed reference points, made from a single observation point provide sufficient information from which to calculate the position of the observation point. (To obtain a pair of equations that are to be solved, you must apply the techniques for solution of triangles that you have learned in high school trigonometry.)

a) Design an ALGOL W program to give the coordinates of the two observation points when one reference point is observed, and the distance between the observation points is known.

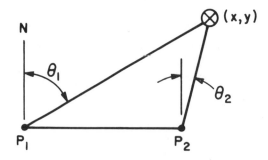

b) Design an ALGOL W program to give the coordinates of an observation point from which two known reference points are observed.

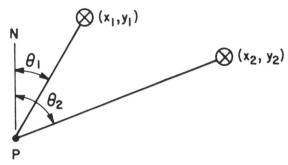

c) Modify the program of part b) to give the coordinates of the vertices of the smallest polygon enclosing all of the estimates of the observation point, when compass sightings to N fixed reference points are made, for N > 2.

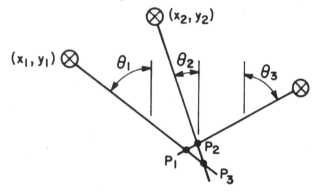

10.4 In studying the physical properties of a simple crystalline compound having a cubic cell, such as NaCl, it is of interest to calculate the binding energy of a single interior ion due to electrostatic attraction and repulsion by all of its neighbors, both near and far. After all of the constants have been factored out of the equation for the energy, it turns out to depend on a mathematical constant (called Madelung's constant) whose value can be expressed by the following triple summation

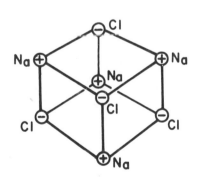

$$M = \sum \sum \sum \frac{(-1)^{k+m+n}}{\sqrt{k^2 + m^2 + n^2}}$$

where the sum is to be carried out over all values of k, m,

and n, both positive and negative, excepting the single combination k = m = n = 0.

Quite obviously, the summation can not be done over all terms, but must be approximated by a finite number of them. The approximation will be better, the more terms are included. A careful analysis will show that many terms can be evaluated without recalculation of the square root function, however. For instance, the contributions of the terms for k = 1, m = 0, n = 1 and for k = 1, m = 0, and n = -1 are identical; each contributes $1/\sqrt{2}$.

Calculate the best approximation to Madelung's constant that you can obtain in 15 seconds of computing time. (Test the builtin ALGOL W function TIME(1) to limit your execution time. But don't test it too often, for the test will cost you some extra time.)

10.5 Often one wishes to calculate the area of a plane geometrical figure, but lacks an explicit formula for that area. In such a case, one can compute the area approximately by dividing the figure into narrow bands, computing the area of each band, and summing all of the partial contributions to obtain the total area.

Two simple strategies for estimating the area of a band suggest themselves immediately. Suppose the boundary of the figure lies between the line y = 0 and the curve y = f(x), and that a typical band is bounded by the lines x = x1 and x = x2. One method of estimating area, called the midpoint rule, is to approximate the area by

$$M = (x2-x1)*f\left(\frac{x2 + x1}{2}\right)$$

Another, called the trapezoid rule is given by

$$T = (x2-x1)*\left(\frac{f(x2) + f(x1)}{2}\right)$$

From the two diagrams below, you can see that for a concave figure, the area estimated by the midpoint rule tends to be too large, while that estimated by the trapezoid rule tends to be too small.

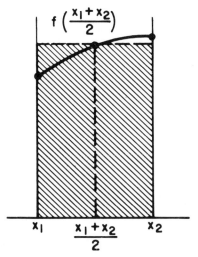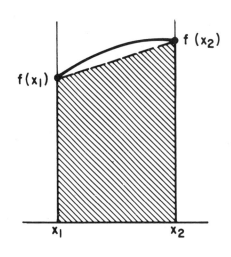

Write an ALGOL W program to compute the area of a figure using all four of the following rules:
  i) the midpoint rule;
 ii) the trapezoid rule;
iii) the average of midpoint and trapezoid estimates, (M+T)/2;
 iv) Simpson's rule, the weighted average given by (2/3)M + (1/3)T.

Use the program to estimate the areas of

   a) a parabola, $y = 1 - x^2$;

   b) a sinusoid, $y = \text{cosine}(\pi x/2)$;

   c) a semicircle, $y = \sqrt{1-x^2}$;

each extending from $x = 0$ to $x = 1$. Vary the widths of the strips, using widths of .1, .01, and .001 to determine the effect of the width on the accuracy.

Compare the results with the exact areas obtained by the use of calculus,
   (a) = 2/3, (b) = $2/\pi$, (c) = $\pi/4$.
To obtain a valid comparison, have the computer evaluate the exact values to seven significant decimal places.

NOTES

Chapter 11

HOW DOES THE COMPUTER WORK?

Up to now, we have been dealing with the computer as a device that is capable of interpreting instructions given in ALGOL W and carrying out the computations directed by those instructions. It accepts input in the form of patterns of small, rectangular holes punched in 3-1/4 by 7-3/8 inch paper cards, delivered to one of its card reading machines, and it generates output by printing messages in capital letters on long sheets of paper folded into a zig-zag stack.

A first-hand visual inspection of a computer does not tell us much more than we already know. It consists of a collection of metal cabinets, commonly painted in shades of gray, blue, or coral, and having a few switches and neon indicator lights on the front, and large electrical cables issuing from the back. Some of the cabinets contain spools on which magnetic tapes are mounted, some contain stacks of discs vaguely reminiscent of coin-operated juke boxes, and some do not. If you should happen to see one of these cabinets with its covers open, you are liable to see panels of circuit boards and an elaborately organized birds-nest of fine wires. Obviously, you are not going to find out very much about a computer by looking at it.

11.1 Organized complexity

One thing that a look inside a computer should do is to dispel you of any notion you might have had that a modern computer is designed along similar lines as is the human brain. From what is known of biological information processors, it appears that the organization of current computers is quite dissimilar. Nor is there a close parallel between the basic elements. The basic element of the human brain is the neuron, or neural cell, which is in itself an enormously complex unit whose physiology is still not completely understood. The basic element of a computer is an electronically controlled switch, usually realized by one of the many variant forms of a transistor. The physics of these switches is quite well understood, and an individual switching element is simplicity itself. A single computer may contain some number of these switching elements between several thousand and several millions, but it is still a far cry from the estimated ten billion cells that constitute an adult human brain.

It is apparent just from the numbers of basic elements involved that both the human brain and the digital computer are structures of potentially enormous complexity. But since relatively little is known, in detail at least, about how the brain is organized, and the organization of a digital computer is entirely known and documented, we shall cease speculation about the brain as a model and look at the organization of a hypothetical computer. Because of the potential for complexity, one should not attempt to understand the functioning of a whole computer on the level of the operations of its primitive switching elements. We shall approach the computer by looking at successive levels of refinement of details, just as we have learned to approach the design of computational algorithms.

Let us begin by considering the organization of a very simple computer, shown in Figure 11.1.1. It consists of three interconnected boxes. The function of the input/output unit is to translate input given in the form of holes in a punched card, or impulses on the keys of an electric typewriter into electrical signals acceptable to the electronics of the computer. Conversely, it translates a set of these signals delivered to it to activate a printing device. The function of the memory unit is to store for future reference information that is delivered to it in the form of electrical signals. The locations of various items of data can be referred to also by a coded signal, which can itself be thought of as a type of data item. The information stored might be the value of data, or an encoded instruction for the computer, or the encoded address within the memory unit where another piece of data or instruction is to be found. The function of the central processing unit is to decode the instructions it receives, to generate memory addresses at which data or additional instructions are to be found, and to carry out the primitive computational steps called for by the instructions. The connections between the various units in Figure 11.1.1 represent bundles of cables along which signals representing data, memory addresses, orders, and replies are sent.

Each of these units is interesting in its own right, but since we must limit our objectives, let us look only at a very simple central processing unit (CPU) in more detail. Upon ripping off the cover, figuratively speaking, its contents are organized as shown in Figure 11.1.2. They are divided by function into a control unit and an arithmetic unit. It is the job of the control unit to decode instructions and issue orders. In the course of issuing orders for the execution of an instruction, it will have to assemble two addresses -- code words identifying specific locations in the vast space of the memory unit -- one of which will tell where to find the data required for the execution of the instruction, and one of which will tell where the following instruction is to be found. The control unit must have some temporary memory in which to store these two addresses. The temporary memory is provided by a pair of _registers_ (about which more will be said later) called the instruction address register and the data address register. There must be connections from these two registers to the memory unit, in order that the code

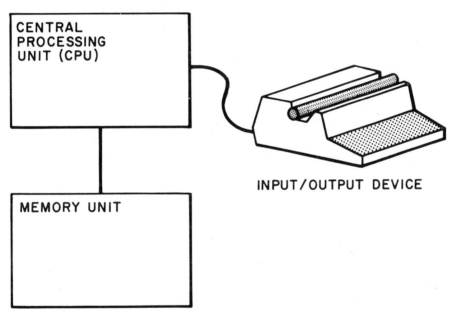

CENTRAL
PROCESSING
UNIT (CPU)

MEMORY UNIT

INPUT/OUTPUT DEVICE

Figure 11.1.1   Organization of a simple computer

words they contain can be used by the memory unit to index the contents of the desired memory locations. In addition, the instruction decoder must have a connection to the memory unit by which it receives the code word representing the next instruction to be executed. It must also have connections to the arithmetic unit and to the input/output unit so that it can send them orders and receive their replies.

The arithmetic unit also contains a visible register called the accumulator, and usually a not-so-visible register as well, here called the second operand register. There is in addition some special purpose control circuitry that we call the arithmetic logic control. Connections are required between the arithmetic unit and the control unit, to receive orders and send back replies, and to the memory uniit, to exchange data between the arithmetic unit and the memory location designated by the code word residing in the data address register.

You can see from the description outlined above, that the organization of even a simple computer is rather complex, but not really mind-boggling. At this point it may be well for us to stop and follow the course of exectution of a short sequence of instructions. Suppose that an ALGOL W program contains the statement

        A := B + C

where A, B, and C have been declared to be scalar integer variables. This ALGOL W statement might have been translated into the following sequence of instructions for the simple computer:

    LOAD B,   meaning load the value of A into the accumulator
              register,

    ADD C,   meaning add the value of B to the number already in
              the accumulator,

    STORE A, meaning store the value now in the accumulator into
              the memory location corresponding to the variable
              C.

Actually, this sequence of primitive intructions could not be presented to the computer in this form. The name that a programmer gives to a scalar variable will not have any meaning for the electronics of the simple computer; the signals that it 'understands' can more easily be represented by numbers. The reason is that the transistor switches deliver one of two possible voltage levels onto their attached wires, each of which defines a binary (two-valued) condition, one that can be represented by a numeral 1 or 0. Let 1 represent the condition

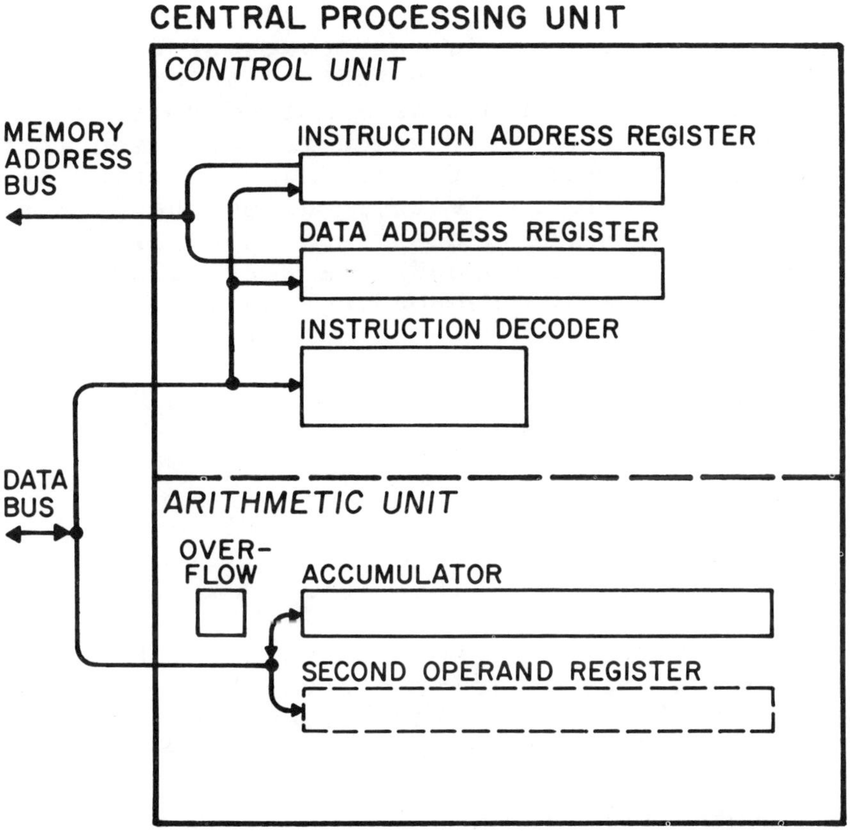

CENTRAL PROCESSING UNIT

CONTROL UNIT

MEMORY
ADDRESS
BUS

INSTRUCTION ADDRESS REGISTER

DATA ADDRESS REGISTER

INSTRUCTION DECODER

DATA
BUS

ARITHMETIC UNIT

OVER-
FLOW   ACCUMULATOR

SECOND OPERAND REGISTER

Figure 11.1.2   Contents of the CPU.   Internal
connections among the various
registers and the instruction
decoder exist, but are not shown.

that one voltage appears, and 0 represent the condition that the other voltage appears. The actual value of the voltage is quite irrelevant to us (although not to the electronics); what is of signifiance is the fact that there are just two meaningful conditions. Now if these wires are arrayed in a linear order, the linear array of numerals corresponding to the conditions of voltages on the individual wires forms a binary representation of an integer number. Hence, we claim that the signals understood by the electronics of a computer are quite naturally represented by integer numbers.

To get back to the question of how to represent program variables, the function of a program variable is to store a value for later reference. The computer can store values in its memory unit. The memory unit consists of a large physical array of memory cells, each implemented by some type of electronic or magnetic device, and each of these cells is distinguished from its neighbors by an address. In the commonest types of "random access" type of memory unit, the addressing of a memory cell is realized by encoding the address as a set of voltages on a bundle of wires called the address bus, which is connected to the memory unit, and the electronics of the memory unit responds by connecting annother set of wires, called the data bus, to the particular memory word whose address was specified. A program variable is made to correspond to a particular memory cell by giving the variable a corresponding address. Suppose the following correspondence has been established:

A EQU 001001

B EQU 001002

C EQU 001003

where EQU stands for 'is equivalent to'.

The electronics will also not accept English words as the codes of the operations it is to carry out, so the instructions seen by the electronics have numbers substituted for these words as well. Suppose that the codes are:

LOAD   EQU 60

STORE EQU 61

ADD   EQU 71

Finally, the program itself will be stored in the computer's memory unit, so the address at which each instruction is to be found must be specified. The stored instructions will look something like this, in numerical representation

Memory location	Instruction Stored here	Interpretation
000100	60 001002	Load the contents of memory location 001002 (corresponding to the variable B) into the accumulator, erasing its previous contents.
000101	71 001003	Add to the contents of the accumulator, the contents of memory location 001003 (which corresponds to the program variable C).
000102	61 001001	Store the contents of the accumulator into memory location 001001 (which represents the program variable A), in place of its previous contents.

Now let us see what the computer we have described will do with one of these instructions. Suppose the machine is started in the following state

instruction address register

    000100

data address register

    XXXXXX

accumulator

    XXXXXXX

memory unit

address:	000100	000101	000102	...	001001	001002	001003
contents:	60001002	71001003	61001001	...	00000000	00000048	00000120

where the string of X's indicated for some registers indicates that their contents are undefined or irrelevant. When we start the machine, it will seek the first instruction and attempt to execute it. Upon starting, the instruction address, 000100, will be placed on the address bus, activating the electronics of the memory unit, which will then connect the data bus to memory cell 000100. The contents of that cell, 60001002, will then appear on

289

the data bus.   Next, the rightmost six digits of the number
presented to the control unit on the data bus will be loaded into
the data address register for future reference.   The leftmost two
digits will be accepted by the instruction decoder for immediate
processing.   The registers of the CPU now look like this, at the
end of the fetch phase for this first instruction:

instruction address register

```
000100
```

data address register

```
001002
```

accumulator

```
XXXXXXX
```

In the next stage or "execution" phase of the first
instruction, the contents of the data address register are put
onto the data bus, and the electronics of the memory unit decodes
this address and connects the data bus to memory cell 001002.
Meanwhile, the instruction decoder has found out what is meant by
the operation code 60. It therefore sends an order to the
accumulator to clear itself of any previous held data, and accept
new data from the data bus. It also signals the instruction
address register to increment its current value by one, since the
instruction being executed did not explicitly specify a different
instruction address. After these operations are completed, the
registers of the CPU look like this:

instruction address register

```
000101
```

data address register

```
XXXXXX
```

accumulator

```
00000048
```

The machine is now ready to begin a new instruction fetching
cycle.

It may seem a rather complicated job to design electronics that will accomplish all of these functions, and will synchronize each activity with the others so that the functions are carried out in the right order. It is a complicated job, but computer engineers approach it by using very systematic design procedures, and by breaking down tasks of great complexity into subtasks of manageable proportions.

You may also have noticed that much of the activity in a computer involves shipping small amounts of data from one register to annother. This is also true in real computers of conventional design, even very large ones of much greater complexity than has been described here. Let's see how a computer does arithmetic in one of these registers.

11.2 Shift registers

In the simple computer we are describing, all arithmetic operations are done in the accumulator. In this example, (typical of early computers), the accumulator incorporates a "shift register". By a register, we mean merely a set of identical elements, each capable of holding a single binary bit, that is, a zero or one value, and which can be tested or set. The addressable elements of the memory unit are therefore registers. The individual binary elements that make up a register are indexed in a linear order, so that one can refer to the bits held by a register according to their position in sequence. The bits, taken in sequence, form a binary representation of an integer number. Usually, all the registers in which data is to be held will contain the same fixed number of binary elements, and this length is called the word size (in bits) used in the machine.

A shift register has, in addition to the capability to store a sequence of bits, the capability to shift the pattern of bits that it holds one position to the right or left, upon receiving a signal to do so. At first, this does not sound like a very significant ability, but remember that in the binary representation of a number, a shift of the bit pattern one position toward the left represents a multiplication by two; one position to the right, a division by two. Shifting is also useful when data are to be shipped off in packages other than the entire register contents.

It may not be helpful to describe the operation of a shift register in terms of electronics (this will depend on your previously acquired knowledge of electronics) but we can describe a shift register that can be contructed by you and your friends, if you can follow instructions. The basic element will be a human being. The shift register consists of several such elements, seated or standing in a line, side by side. As a shift register element, you have two possible states, 0 (left arm at your side) or 1 (left arm raised above your head). Most of the time, you do nothing except to remain in a constant state, but upon a given signal (when someone nudges you in your left side) you may change states, according to a fixed rule, and signal the shift register element to your right (by nudging him with your right elbow). The rules for this important activity are also very simple:

a) Upon receiving a signal (being nudged in the left side), inspect the shift register element on your left, and remember his state. Pass the signal (nudge) along to the shift register element on your right.

b) Upon receiving a second signal from your left, assume the state that you remembered as the state of the element to your left when you got the first signal, and pass the nudge on to your right. Get ready to obey instruction (a) again.

To test this shift register, you will need a control element who stands to the left of the leftmost shift register element. The control element can clear the register by nudging repeatedly while his left hand is lowered, until all shift register elements have assumed the 0 state. Then, if he raises his left hand, nudges once, then lowers his left hand and nudges repeatedly, the 'pattern' of a single 1 state will be passed steadily through the length of the shift register from left to right. If you try a few such experiments though, you will probably discover that the reliability of humans as shift register elements is not very great. Electronic devices are better.

One problem that may occur in the shift register described above is that if the control element gives nudges too quickly in succession, trying to force the shift register to act more quickly, there is a very great likelihood that errors will occur. Also, following the initiation of a signal by the control element, it takes quite a little time for the sequence of nudges to propagate from the first shift register element to the last. Similar problems can occur in the electronics of a computer. There is a design alternative that is sometimes adopted; the use of a cadence caller, or clock, to synchronize the activities of the individual elements. Suppose we introduce this modification into our experimental shift register.

Add a person whose job it is to call out, alternatively, 'Ready' and 'Shift' at two-second intervals. Also change the rules for a shift register element to eliminate nudging as a means of relaying a signal. The new rules are:

a) Upon hearing the call 'Ready', inspect the element to your left, and remember his state (1 if his left hand is raised, 0 if it is down);

b) Upon hearing the call 'Shift', assume the state you have remembered from a).

The role of the control element is as before, to initiate a pattern by raising or lowing his hand in sequence with the cadence, but he does not now have to set the cadence himself by the frequency of his nudging. The modified shift register will very likely be more reliable than the former design.

In the computer, each shift register element has a particular input on which it accepts the cadence count, or clock signal, and the role of the control element is played by an input line, or in some cases by a constant voltage line. Often, shift registers are designed so that the input line to each element, which normally inspects the state of its left neighbor upon a 'Ready' signal, can optionally be switched to inspect the state of its right neighbor for right-to-left shifting operations, or can be switched to inspect a specific line of the input data bus, in order to load the shift register from the memory unit.

11.3 The accumulator

Our accumulator is a shift register having the capabilities of left and right shifting and of being set from the data bus, and in addition it can add, complement itself by having every one of its elements simultaneously change state, and can do the logical operations AND and OR. Obviously, quite a lot of electronic circuitry is required to build such an accumulator. When electronic circuitry was expensive, up until a few years ago, many computers were designed with only a single accumulator, as is the hypothetical one we are now describing in this chapter. Since integrated circuit technology has now made electronics cheap, many newer computers have a dozen or more accumulators. The most complicated of the functions that an accumulator may perform is addition, so we shall attempt to reassemble our human shift register and give its elements the necessary instructions to become adders. All of you shift register elements, line up!

The basic operation that a shift register element needs is the ability to add 1 to his present state number modulo 2. We shall first tell him how to do this, and then tell him when to do it. Whenever you are instructed to HALFADD 1, do the following.

HALFADD: If you are in state 0, then change your state to 1, else if you are in state 1, then change your state to 0 and signal the element to your left by nudging him.

The 'nudge' used to signal the next element to the left represents a carry. One plus one modulo two is indeed 0, but if the numbers larger than one are to be represented, a carry bit must be passed along to be added into the next higher binary numeral position. Thus the adder instructions should certainly include the following:

a) Whenever you receive a carry bit (nudge) from the element to your right, HALFADD 1.

Normally, the number to be added to the accumulator will appear on the lines of the data bus. Each element of the accumulator will have to add to its binary value, the value of the input on the corresponding line of the data bus. Let us represent the data bus by recruiting another line of humans to sit in front of the shift register elements, and set some constant pattern of bits on the data bus by instructing each of its members to hold his left hand in a fixed (raised or lowered) position. Now we can give a second instruction to our shift register elements.

b) Upon shifting a signal from the cadence caller, inspect the state of the data bus line represented by the person in front of you. If that state is 1, then HALFADD 1.

Now, however, if we attempt a trial of our adder, setting one pattern of bits into the accumulator and another on the data bus, and have the cadence caller give an instruction 'Start' to simultaneously activate all of the accumulator elements, chaos will probably ensue. If the bit pattern initially in the accumulator contained a lot of 1's, then the HALFADD instructions given by rule b) are going to coincide with those given by rule a) at some accumulator elements, who will not know what to do, since they were not told to stack up simultaneously arriving HALFADD instructions. Perhaps it was not such a good idea to try to initiate addition simultaneously over all of the accumulator elements.

Suppose the accumulator elements are numbered from one up to the length of the accumulator, beginning at the rightmost element. Then, if the cadence caller signals each accumulator element individually, by calling his number in turn, and allows enough time between successive signals for all the HALFADD instructions generated by carries under rule a) to be completed, no simultaneous HALFADD instructions will be received by any element, and the accumulator will be able to add. In electronic accumulators too, there must be sufficient time lag between the additions of successive bit positions to the accumulator to allow the propagation of carries to be completed.

On most accumulators, the register is equipped with an additional binary element, whose logical position is to the left of the highest order bit. This element is not used is shifting operations, nor in OR or AND, but it is used in addition. In case the sum of two numbers, each representable by the number of bits contained in the accumulator, is a number too large to hold in the accumulator, the addition will generate a carry bit from the leftmost element of the normal accumulator, a carry bit that has no place to go. The extra accumulator element provides a place in which to put it. The problem remains, that the sum is still too large to represent in the fixed-length registers of the machine, but at least that problem can be detected, by testing the extra element of the accumulator. The extra bit is called the overflow bit, and when your ALGOL W programs produce a carry into the overflow bit during the course of adding two positive integers or two negative integers, you receive an error message which says INTEGER OVERFLOW.

11.4 Other arithmetic operations

We shall not go into the operations of floating-point arithmetic, but can take a look at other operations of integer arithmetic. Most of them turn out to depend on addition. But before we look at subtraction, for instance, it is necessary to say a little more about number representation. If the accumulator of our machine is N bits long, not counting the overflow bit, then it seems that we should be able to represent integers modulo 2 , and to represent a positive integer as large as $2^N - 1$. But one must not forget about negative integers as well, and it is going to require one bit of information to represent the sign of a number. There are many possible ways to represent negative numbers in a computer; we shall describe just one. The highest order bit is set aside to represent the sign of a number, with 0 standing for plus and 1 standing for -. This having been decided, you can see that the largest positive integer that can represented is only $2^{N-1} - 1$, since the Nth bit must be zero for every positive number. It would seem then, that the representation is fully decided, the highest bit giving the algebraic sign, and the remaining bits giving the magnitude in binary radix representation.

To do subtraction of numbers that are given in this sign-magnitude representation, one must use an algorithm such as that we are taught in elementary school, subtracting digit-by-digit and generating a carry in the number being subtracted or a borrow from the number from which the subtraction is being done. However, with a little ingenuity and a change in the way of representing negative numbers, the algorithm for subtraction becomes exactly that for addition, plus an inexpensive preparation of one of the two numbers before the addition is carried out.

Observe that, when there are just N bits to work with, a complementation of the bit pattern of any positive number gives you a representation of some negative number. For instance, suppose the register length is six bits. Then the number ten is represented as
         001010
Taking its complement gives
         110101
which we know to be the representation of some negative number, because the leftmost bit, that we have designated the sign bit, is 1. If we should add these two together, ten and its complement, their sum is
         111111.
Moreover, this last result is no coincidence, for taking any six-bit pattern and summing it with its complement produces the same result. Would the complement of a positive number make a good candidate for the representation of the negative of that number? Certainly it is a possible representation, for it is unique; one can go back and forth between a number and its complement without losing any information. But one drawback is the fact that the complement of zero gets a different representation than does zero itself; zero is 000000, but the complement of zero is 111111.

The representation we shall adopt for negative numbers is called two's-complement representation. It is commonly used in computers, although it is certainly not the only representation in use. To obtain the negative of a number, one takes the complement of its binary representation and adds one. Thus the two's complement of zero is

```
    111111
  + 000001
    000000
```

with a carry generated into the overflow bit. The negative of
ten is

```
    110101
  + 000001
    110110
```

and when the negative of minus ten is taken

```
    110101
  + 000001
    001010
```

the result is again seen to be ten. To do subtraction, A - B, in
two's-complement representation, one first takes the complement
of the binary representation of B, adds one, and then adds A. The
only capabilities needed by an accumulator are the capacity to
add and to complement a number.

   Multiplication is a little harder   than   addition   or
subtraction. Of course, multiplication can be accomplished by
repeated additions of the same number, but if the multiplier may
be large, this seems inefficient. The algorithm we have learned
in elementary school is more efficient. It forms a product by
taking the sum of partial products, shifted to the left by the
number of places that the individual multiplier digit appears
from the rightmost place in the multiplier. This algorithm is
even simpler when the numbers are represented in binary form, for
each partial product is either the shifted multiplicand or is
zero. For example, the product of ten and six would be written
as

```
        001010
        000110
        000000
       001010
      001010
     000000
    000000
   000000____
      111100
```

To modify this algorithm slightly for the computer, the sum of
the partial products will be accumulated as the algorithm
progresses, rather than saving all partial products to be added
together at the end. The multiplicand will be kept available on
the data bus throughout the multiplication operation.   Initially
the accumulator is set to zero, the multiplier is entered in the
second operand register, and the multiplicand appears on the data
bus.   The steps of the multiplication shown above, for a six-bit
accumulator, would be as follows.

First step: test the leftmost bit of the second operand
    register.   Since it is zero, no addition of a partial product
    is required.

            accumulator   second operand register   data bus
            000000   000110   001010

Second step: the contents of the accumulator and the second
    operand register are both shifted left one position, and the
    leftmost bit of the second operand register is again   tested.
    Again, no addition is called for

            accumulator   second operand register   data bus
            000000   001100   001010

Third step: the accumulator and second operand registers are
    shifted left one position. No addition is called for.

            accumulator   second operand register   data bus
            000000   011000   001010

Fourth step: the accumulator and second operand registers are
    shifted again.   Since the leftmost bit of the second operand
    register is now a one, the contents of the data bus are added
    to the accumulator.

            accumulator   second operand register   data bus
            001010   110000   001010

Fifth step: an additional shift of accumulator and second
    operand register indicates another addition of the data bus to
    the shifted accumulator.

            accumulator   second operand register   data bus
            011110   100000   001010

Sixth step: accumulator and second operand register are shifted
    once more to the left, but no further addition to the
    accumulator is indicated.

            accumulator   second operand register   data bus
            111100   000000   001010

The algorithm terminates after a number of steps equal to the
length of the second operand register. In this example, we have
ignored the sign bit, but if it is included, a very similar
algorithm succeeds with both positive and negative numbers in
two's-complement representation. When both multiplier and
multiplicand are of the same sign, a one in the sign bit of the
product indicates overflow, not a negative product.

Implementing the division algorithm in the arithmetic unit is slightly more complicated than is multiplication, although it too can be done by using only the accumulator, the second operand register, and the data bus. However, by now you should have some idea as to how the arithmetic unit functions, on the level of register operations if not in terms of electronic circuits, and there are some further topics that should be looked into.

11.5   How the computer communicates with the outside world

So far, our discussion of the operation of a simple computer has avoided mentioning of the third principal functional unit, the input/output device. Each input/output device also contains within itself a register, and the connection between CPU and the register of the input/output device is a bundle of wires called the I/O bus. Communicating with an input/output device is merely another case of doing transfer between registers, using a bus. Communication on the I/O bus does pose some special problems, however, for the reason that the input/output device is usually much slower than is the CPU. Therefore it is not practical to synchronize its activity with that of the CPU by using the same cadence caller that synchronizes activity between the CPU and its memory unit.[1] Instead, synchronization is accomplished by sending messages back and forth between the CPU and the register of the input/output device, using lines of the I/O bus that are specially designated for this purpose.

Many input/output devices are designed to handle information in units of individual characters. However, since the electronics of the computer will not recognize characters directly, they are encoded in the form of a sequence of binary bits, using the EBCDIC or some other code. A sequence of bits of the length required to encode a single character is called a byte. In most computers, certainly all but the smallest ones, the length of a register (in bits) is greater than one byte, often two to eight times greater. Thus, it is common that information stored in the memory unit in the form of characters will be stored with several bytes occupying each addressable memory register. In order to transmit a single byte to the input/output device to be printed, it is necessary to load into the accumulator the contents of the memory location in which the byte is stored, to shift the contents of the accumulator until the sequence of bits constituting the desired byte occupies the low-order bit positions of the accumulator (those from which connections can be made to the I/O bus), and finally, to connect

----

[1] In some computers, even transactions between the CPU and the memory unit are not synchronized by a cadence caller, but are handled as are input/output transactions.

299

the accumulator to the I/O bus.

Returning to the question of synchronization, the CPU must have some way to know when the input/output device is ready to receive a new byte to be printed (or in the case of input, when it is ready to transmit a new input byte). And the input/output device must have some way to know when a byte is to be printed. In Figure 11.4.1 the connections of the I/O bus to the accumulator are shown. Along with the data lines, which carry the data to be transmitted in either direction, and the order lines, which carry an instruction code to the input/output device, there is another line called the ready line which is used to pass a synchronization signal. The ready line connects a pair of one-bit registers, one in the CPU and one in the input/output device. When the line is in state 0 it indicates that there is no activity in progress on the I/O bus. In state 1 it indicates that there is an input or an output transaction in progress. It is the responsibility of the CPU to initiate input/output transactions, and so it has the duty to set the ready line to state 1 whenever it wishes to start such a transaction. It is the responsibility of the input/output device to complete these transactions, and so it is obligated to clear the ready line to state 0 when it completes a transaction. Whenever the input/output device is not actually busy processing an I/O transaction, it must sit obediently testing the state of the ready line, waiting upon the event that the CPU will set the state to 1, indicating the start of a new request for action by the input/output device.

As for the CPU, when it receives a sequence of instructions to output a byte, it will first be told to load the accumulator with the contents of a memory register in which the byte is located. Then, if the byte is not initially located in the low-order bits of the register, the next instruction in the program will tell the CPU to shift the contents of the accumulator some number of bit positions to the right. Upon decoding the next instruction of the program, the CPU will be directed to put the code for a 'print' order onto the order lines of the I/O bus, to connect the low order bit positions of the accumulator in which the byte is located to the data lines of the I/O bus, and to set the ready line to state 1. Responsibility for completion of the output transaction now rests with the input/output device, and the CPU must wait until it is done. To do this, the next instruction of the program may be one which instructs the CPU to loop on that instruction, not changing the contents of the instruction address register until a test of the ready line shows its state to be 0.

CENTRAL PROCESSING UNIT

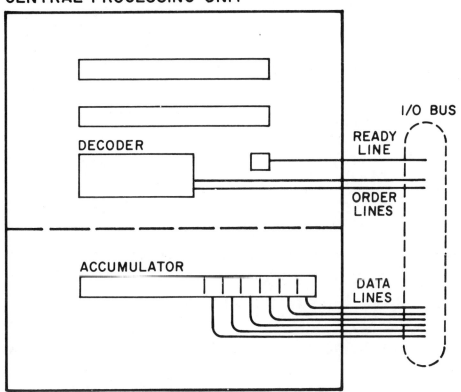

Figure 11.4.1   Connections of the I/O bus
to registers of the CPU

Now it frequently is the case, particularly in large, fast computers, that the CPU could be put to other work instead of waiting while the print ball of an electric typewriter is spun into the correct position and impacted against a carbon ribbon, paper, and platen. That action may require a very short time on the temporal scale of human activities, but it is long when compared with the time in which the CPU executes an instruction.

The situation can be compared to that of a small businessman who operates a grocery store. He employs a boy with a three-wheeled cycle to make deliveries for him. Each time he assigns the boy a a delivery to make, he wants to know when the task has been completed. One way to do this would be to send the boy off, then stand at the front door of the grocery until the boy returned. However, this is wasteful of the grocer's time, and so he will occupy himself with other work, such as stocking shelves, marking prices (up), or filling an order for another customer. In order to be notified when the delivery boy has completed his assigned task, the grocer may rely on the telephone, telling the boy 'Call me when you have finished'. The grocer in this case will be making a commitment to respond at the request of his employee, interrupting his other activity, important though it may be, to pick up the telephone. He agrees to do this because he knows that the telephone transaction with his employee will be short in duration, and it will be more convenient for him to have the opportunity to keep busy with other work while the boy makes deliveries, even at the risk of a short interruption than it would be to waste his own time while awaiting the boy's return.

By analogy, the CPU has the same problem as does the grocer, with the input/output unit playing the role of the delivery boy. In order to adopt the grocer's solution two requirements must be fulfilled by the electronics. The input/output device must be equipped with a register that can deliver or accept data from the I/O bus in a short interval of time, so as not to cause the CPU to have to wait. The register of the input/output device can then hold the value of the data item for as long as is required to complete the I/O transaction, without requiring that the accumulator hold the value on the data lines of the I/O bus during that time. Also, there must be an additional line on the I/O bus, called the interrupt line, to correspond to the bell of the grocer's telephone. Unlike the treatment given to any other line of the I/O bus, the electronics of the CPU must cause it to interrupt execution of a sequence of instructions when a signal appears on the interrupt line so that it can briefly pay attention to an I/O transaction.

With an interrupt line, the course of an output transaction
is slightly different than before. When the CPU receives
instructions to output a byte, it will store in a predetermined
memory location that we shall call BREAK_ADDRESS, the location of
the first instruction of a sequence that will load the desired
byte into the accumulator, shift it, and connect the accumulator
to the I/O bus. Having done this, the CPU sets the ready line to
state 1, indicating to the input/output device its desire to put
it to work. The CPU then goes on to another job, if it has any
to do.

The input/output device sits as before, inspecting the ready
line to see if there is an assignment for it. If it has
completed its last assigned task and finds the ready line again
set to state 1, it clears the ready line to state 0 and
simultaneously issues an interrupt signal on the interrupt line.
Shortly thereafter, it will expect to receive an instruction on
the order lines and data on the data lines, signifying the new
task it is to carry out.

When the CPU receives an interrupt, it is allowed to
complete execution of the instruction in progress, but then is
obliged to store the contents of the instruction address register
(containing the address of the next instruction in the sequence
it has been executing) into a predetermined location we shall
call RESUME_ADDRESS, and reload the instruction address register
with the contents of memory location BREAK_ADDRESS. It is all of
a sudden in the business of executing the instruction sequence of
the output transaction! When the output transaction has been
communicated to the input/output device via the I/O bus, the last
instruction of the output transaction sequence will tell the CPU
to clear the interrupt line back to state 0 and load the
instruction address register with the contents of the memory
location we have called RESUME_ADDRESS. Now it is back at
executing the normal sequence of instructions that it was doing
before receiving the interrupt, just as though nothing had
happened. What has happened though, is that a byte of data has
been shipped accross the I/O bus to the input/output device,
which is now busily at work operating the electric typewriter.
As a further development in many computers, the input/output
devices may communicate a whole sequence of bytes directly to the
memory, bypassing the CPU altogether, once the CPU has given a
general permission to begin.

In these last illustrations, of doing output transactions,
you may have noticed that the division between functions done by
electronics and functions that must be programmed is becoming
fuzzy. It is very difficult, in the case of a malfunction, to
tell whether it is due to faulty electronics or a faulty
program. Although the interrupt system is made available by the

use of electronics, its correct use to synchronize the activities of the CPU and the input/output device depends as much on the segment of he program that handles the details of the output transaction, clears the interrupt line, and recovers the interrupted instruction sequence, as it does on the electronics. For this reason, these program segments are designed by experts, standardized, and made available for use by all users of a computer. Such critical programs form a package known as the operating system of a computer. The computer user is no more welcome to alter these programs than he would be to tinker with the electronics.

11.6   Managing the computer

When you use a large computer, either in batch mode, submitting punched cards to a card reader, or in interactive mode, sitting at a typewriter keyboard, you don't get a chance to see how the operations of the computer are managed. That there is some complex management going on is more apparent when you do interactive computing, because you know that the computer is simultaneously serving several customers at once, although you are usually not made aware of the fact by the responses of your own terminal. Even in batch mode computing however, a large computer will serve several users at once, in the sense that it may not complete the execution of one's user program before it commences the execution of another's. The reason that is desirable is that it allows the computer to make more efficient use of its CPU. As we saw in the last section, it is possible for the CPU to do other work, if it has any to do, while waiting for the completion of an I/O transaction by an input/output device. A large computer, like a grocery store, may have several employees in the form of input/output devices and secondary memory units, and it can keep all of them busy at peak business hours by simultaneously servicing the orders of many customers. The CPU, which is much faster than the other employees, divides its time among the several customer's jobs, and also manages the entire enterprise.

It would be possible, in principle at least, to employ a human to manage the activities of a large computer. But while the human manager was deciding which customer to service next, and furiously typing his directives on the keyboard of the computer console, the machine would probably have completed all other input/output, all computing, and be quietly resting in a dormant state, awaiting the directive from the tired fingers of its human manager. The solution to this problem is to fire the human and train the computer to manage its own activities. The 'training' is accomplished by designing a package of programs that instruct the computer on how to make decisions covering every forseeable contingency. This package of programs is called the operating system, or executive, and is a vital part of a successful computer system. The reliability of the system depends in good measure on how astute were the designers of the operating system in forseeing all contingencies. If a condition occurs for which the operating system does not have an algorithm to tell it how to make a decision, then the computer usually stops, and human intervention is required to sort out the difficulty.

11.7 Compilers

There is probably another gap in your knowledge of how computers work that may trouble you at this point. In the earlier sections of this chapter there were given some examples of how the computer executes primitive instructions by moving data from its memory unit to its accumulator, by executing arithmetic and logical operations on the bit sequence there, and by input/output transactions. But you do not compose algorithms as sequences of the primitive instructions understood by the electronics of a computer, you write ALGOL W programs instead. How does the computer interpret your programs?

Before the computer can execute one of your programs, it must first read it. When your ALGOL W program is read by the card reader, it enters the computer as a sequence of characters, each stored as a byte in the memory unit of the computer. The interpretation of an ALGOL W program begins by analysis of this character string, utilizing techniques such as were described in Example 9.1.1 to determine the identities of constants, reserved words, and the identifiers that are the names that you have given to program variables and procedures. ALGOL W is a grammatical language, and so the organization of its words and punctuation marks into sentences is described by a grammar. An ALGOL W program is decomposed into individual phrases, such as statements or expressions. Associated with many of the types of phrases are fixed rules for their interpretation. The parameters to be included in these interpretations can be values of constants, memory addresses that have been associated in the course of the analysis with program variables, or the interpretations that have been made of other phrases of the program. There is a great deal of information that is generated during the analysis phase of the interpretation and that must be referred to in the synthesis phase, when the interpretation finally results in the formation of a list of the primitive instructions that are comprehensible to the machine. (And only to the machine!)

This task, of interpreting ALGOL W programs and generating a list of primitive machine instructions that can be executed, is directed by a large computer program called a compiler. It gets its name because its function is to compile a list of machine instructions, but it could just as well be called a translator (from ALGOL W into machine language) or an interpreter. Compilers are very interesting programs in their own right, and you may someday wish to learn more about them, but that will have to be left to other books.

NOTES

NOTES

APPENDIX

by Ronald L. Davis[*]

A1. Formal Language Description of ALGOL W

ALGOL W is a programming language which was developed to permit the expression of algorithms in a structured and concise manner. In any language, certain phrases and sentences formed from words of the language are designated as being grammatically correct while other combinations are designated as being grammatically incorrect. This designation of correct and incorrect forms is called the <u>syntax</u> of the language and is described formally by a grammar.

The process of parsing a sentence or diagramming its grammatical structure is a familiar one. We recognize that the sentence "the hungry boy ate the cake" is a grammatically correct sentence of the English language. The following diagram provides a formal description of the sentence:

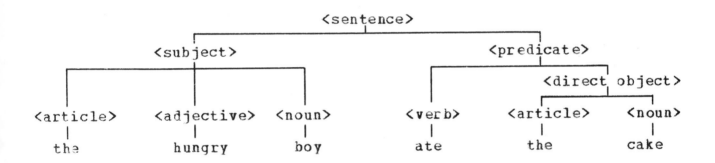

Figure A1.1

A diagram like the one shown above is called a <u>syntax tree</u>.

It is clear that the sentences "the brave boy rescued the king" and "the clever rabbit eluded the fox" are also syntactically correct English sentences and have syntax trees identical to that of Figure A1.1. It should be noted that the sentence "the hungry rabbit ate the king" is <u>syntactically</u> correct even though it describes a rather fanciful situation. We would agree that "boy the hungry the ate cake" is not syntactically correct since it is impossible to construct a syntax tree for this sentence.

Evidently the concepts of syntactic correctness and syntax trees are closely related. Let us examine more closely how syntax trees can be used to construct the syntactically correct sentences of a language.

----

* Portions of the Appendix have been excerpted, with permission, from the <u>ALGOL W Reference Manual</u>, by Richard L. Sites, Stanford University Dept. of Computer Science, Report STAN-CS-71-230, February, 1972.

We begin with the symbol <sentence>, replace it by the symbols
<subject><predicate>, and represent this substitution as

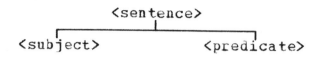

Figure A1.2

Next we replace <subject> by <article><adjective><noun> and replace
<predicate> by <verb><direct object>. Thus we arrive at

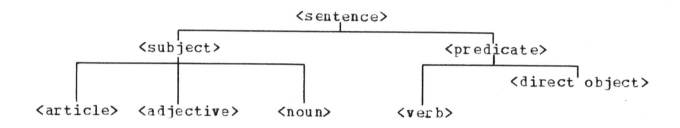

Figure A1.3

Our next step is to replace <direct object> by <article><noun> giving us

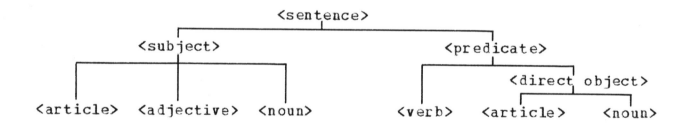

Figure A1.4

Our final substitutions are to replace <article> by "the", <adjective>
by "hungry", <verb> by "ate", the first occurence of <noun> by "boy" and
the second occurence of <noun> by "cake". This completes the
construction of the syntax tree of Figure A1.1.

There is a vocabulary associated with syntax trees which we shall
introduce at this time. Those symbols for which replacements may be
made during the construction of a syntax tree are called nonterminal
symbols. We have represented nonterminal symbols by enclosing them in
pointed brackets. Those symbols for which no replacements may be made
such as "the" are called terminal symbols. The distinguished
nonterminal which is the root of any tree and with which the
construction begins (<sentence> in Figure A1.1) is called the start
symbol or goal symbol . Those rules which define the permissible
substitutions which may be made, for example replacing <sentence> by

310

<subject><predicate>, are called productions.

The essential information conveyed by the construction of a syntax tree can also be represented linearly by a series of successive substitutions called a derivation. A derivation corresponding to the syntax tree of Figure A1.1 is given below.

```
<sentence> ==> <subject><predicate>
          ==> <article><adjective><noun><verb><direct object>
          ==> the hungry boy ate <article><noun>
          ==> the hungry boy ate the cake
```

At each step of the derivation we have made appropriate substitutions for nonterminal symbols until we eventually arrived at a sequence of terminal symbols.

With the preceding discussion as motivation, we can now give a precise definition of a grammar and of a syntactically correct sentence with respect to a given grammar. A grammar G is a quadruple G = (N, T, S, P) where N is a set of nonterminal symbols, T is a set of terminal symbols which is disjoint from N, S (the start symbol) is a distinguished element belonging to N, and P is a set of productions or permissible substitution rules. A sequence of terminal symbols is said to be syntactically correct with respect to the grammar G if there is a derivation which begins with the start symbol S and using the substitution rules of P eventually produces the given sequence. The set of all syntactically correct strings which can be produced from a given grammar is said to be the language defined by that grammar.

Specific grammars are often described in a notation known as Backus Normal Form (BNF). Let us provide a BNF description of a grammar in which we can derive the English language sentences we have previously accepted as being syntactically correct.

Nonterminal symbols will be enclosed in pointed brackets. The productions or substitution rules are to be understood as follows: if a nonterminal occurs in a syntax tree or derivation, find the production having that nonterminal as its left part. Replace the nonterminal in the tree or derivation by those symbols found on the right part of the production. The BNF symbol ::= should be read as "may be replaced by" or "is an instance of". The vertical bar appearing on the right parts of the last three productions may be read as "or" and indicates several distinct possibilities of replacement. Thus any occurence of <adjective> may be replaced by either "hungry" or "brave" or "clever".

```
<sentence> ::= <subject><predicate>
<subject> ::= <article><adjective><noun>
<predicate> ::= <verb><direct object>
<direct object> ::= <article><noun>
<article> ::= the
<adjective> ::=  hungry | brave | clever
<noun> ::= boy | king | rabbit | fox
<verb> ::= ate | rescued | eluded
```

Figure A1.5

The reader should convince himself that by varying the replacements
for the symbols <adjective>, <noun>, and <verb> it is possible to
generate 144 different sentences from the grammar of Figure A1.5. Some
of these sentences may seem less appropriate and meaningful than others,
but each is syntactically correct with respect to the grammar.

It is reasonable to ask whether or not one can define an infinite
language by a grammar which has only a finite number of nonterminals,
terminals, and productions. The answer to this question is affirmative,
and as an example, the following grammar generates the positive and
negative integers.

```
<integer> ::= <number> | <sign><number>
<number> ::= <digit> | <digit><number>
<sign> ::= + | -
<digit> ::= 0 | 1 | 2 | 3 | 4 | 5 | 6 | 7 | 8 | 9
```

Figure A1.6

The first production allows us to make the prefixing of a sign
optional. It is the second production which allows the language to
become infinite; the symbol <number> occurs in both the left and right
parts of the production. The grammar is said to be _recursive_ in the
symbol <number>. The interpretation of this production is that a digit
standing alone is an instance of a number and that once a number has
been formed, a new number may be formed by prefixing it with a digit.
We illustrate this by constructing a syntax tree for the integer -123.

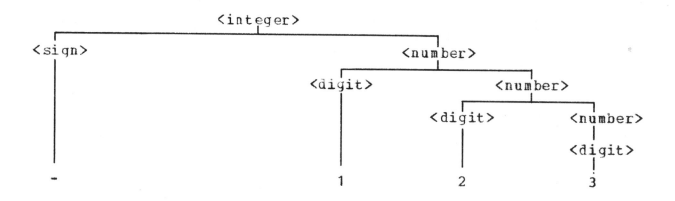

Figure A1.7

312

Notice that if a grammar is to define an infinite language then the grammar **must** be recursive.

We are now ready to explain the relation between the formal language theory we have developed and the study of the programming language ALGOL W. Many of the programs you write will be read by other persons and many will be executed on a digital computer. This necessity of communicating both with human beings and with machines requires that certain conventions of language be followed in the writing of ALGOL W programs. In particular,, machines are quite intolerant of grammatically (syntactically) incorrect sequences.

It would clearly be impossible to enumerate all the correct and incorrect constructions of ALGOL W since each individual programmer will combine the elements of the language in many diverse ways. A solution is to define the syntactic structure of ALGOL W by a grammar written in BNF notation. The question of whether or not a particular construction is a syntactically correct one can then be resolved by determining whether or not a syntax tree for the construction exists in the defining grammar. A standard computer program called the ALGOL W compiler checks and translates an ALGOL W program into an equivalent sequence of elementary instructions which can be performed by the hardware of the computer. The compiler maintains a copy of a grammar for ALGOL W, and during the checking and translation process its decisions are determined by the success or failure of attempts to construct a syntax tree for the text which has been submitted as an ALGOL W program.

In the following sections when a construction of ALGOL W is introduced, we shall provide an explanation of the use of that construction, the appropriate subset of the ALGOL W grammar which defines it, and examples of its use.

A2. Identifiers

```
    <identifier> ::= <letter> | <identifier><letter>
                   | <identifer><digit>
                   | <identifier><underscore>

    <letter> ::= A | B | C | D | E | F | G | H | I
               | J | K | L | M | N | O | P | Q | R
               | S | T | U | V | W | X | Y | Z

    <digit> ::= 0 | 1 | 2 | 3 | 4 | 5 | 6 | 7 | 8 | 9

    <underscore> ::= _
```
                        Figure A2.1

The names given to variables, formal parameters, and control identifiers which are referenced by an algorithm written in ALGOL W must be distinguishable one from another. The names chosen for these quantities are called _identifiers_. The choice of an identifier is subject to the following three rules:

1. An identifier begins with a capital letter A-Z;
2. An identifier consists only of capital letters,
   numerical digits, and the underscore character;
3. An identifier contains at least one character.
The reader will notice that these conditions are exactly those expressed
in the BNF productions of Figure A2.1. In subsequent sections we shall
often omit lengthy explanations of ALGOL W constructions and instead
direct the reader to the appropriate BNF description.

There is another restriction on identifier choices. Certain words
have special significance in ALGOL W and may not be chosen by the
programmer for his own use. These words are referred to as reserved
words. All the reserved words in ALGOL W are listed in the Reserved
Word Index.

In addition, there are several identifiers which have special uses
and, in general, should not be chosen as identifiers by the programmer.
The most important among these are

```
READ          READON          READCARD
WRITE         WRITEON
```

The programmer is urged to choose meaningful identifiers such as
LENGTH, WIDTH, AREA rather than X, Y, Z. The underscore character should
be used to improve readability so that one would write MEDIAN_INCOME
rather than MEDIANINCOME.

Every identifier used in a program must be defined. This is
achieved through
1. its explicit mention in a declaration (A5);
2. its occurence in a formal parameter list (A9.2);
3. its occurence following the symbol FOR in an
   iteration statement (A8.2.2);
4. its implicit declaration in the language. Standard
   procedures (A10) and predeclared variables (A4) may
   be considered to have been declared in a block
   containing the program.

A3. Data Types

ALGOL W provides the facilities to represent many types of data of
both a numerical and non-numerical nature. We shall explain the use of
each simple data type (see Chap. 5, Sec. 5.1) and then show how one
may construct compound data types (Sec. 5.2) for specialized
programming tasks from these simple types. The name of each data type
below is a reserved word.

A3.1 Simple Data Types

1. INTEGER -- the value may be only a positive or negative
   number which does not contain a fractional part

2. REAL -- the value is a positive or negative real single-precision floating point number

3. LONG REAL -- the value is a positive or negative real double-precision floating point number

4. COMPLEX -- the value is a complex number composed of a pair of numbers of type _real_

5. LONG COMPLEX -- the value is a complex number composed of a pair of numbers of type _long real_

6. LOGICAL -- the value is either of _true_ or _false_

7. BITS -- the value is a sequence of 32 bits (binary digits)

8. STRING -- the value is a sequence of at most 256 characters and is used primarily for processing non-numeric or textual information

9. REFERENCE -- the value is a reference or pointer to an object defined by a RECORD class (A3.2), or else is NULL.

A3.2 Compound Data Types

1. ARRAY -- the value is an indexed set of values all of _identical_ simple type. A one-dimensional array implements the notational device of single subscripting, e.g., X1, X2,.....,XN. A two-dimensional array implements the double subscripting

$$
\begin{array}{llll}
X11 & X12 & ..... & X1N \\
X21 & X22 & ..... & X2N \\
\multicolumn{4}{c}{.................} \\
XM1 & XM2 & ..... & XMN
\end{array}
$$

Higher dimensional arrays are defined in a similar manner. Examples of the use of one-dimensional arrays occur in the examples of Sec. 5.4 and in Example 6.6.1. Two dimensional arrays are used in Examples 7.4.1 and 10.4.1.

2. RECORD -- the value is an ordered set of simple type variables which need not all be of the same type. A record is used to group together data which have a logical inter-relationship. For example, an employee's name (_string_), social security number (_integer_), and hourly wage rate (_real_) can be viewed as a single entity descriptive of an employee. Variables of simple type REFERENCE are necessary to access the data items which constitute a _record_.

315

A4. Constants and Predeclared Variables

A4.1 Constants

ALGOL W has constants of each of the simple types described in Section A3.1. Constants are specified for known quantities in a computation and are used to initialize the values of certain variables before a computation begins. We shall explain the notation and, where necessary, the meaning of these constants.

1. INTEGER -- Integer constants are positive and negative numbers which do not contain a fractional part. The values are denoted by a plus (+) or minus (-) sign followed by a sequence of decimal digits. If a sign is not specified the value is assumed to be positive. The maximum integer value allowed by ALGOL W is 2147483647 and the minimum integer value is -2147483648.

examples   48   0   -89
           -176   1985671   0234

2. REAL -- Real values may contain a fractional part which is represented by digits following a decimal point. There are two notations for real values which correspond to the common and scientific representations in use. In standard mathematical notation one may write either 101.78 or $1.0178 * 10^2$. In ALGOL W these two forms would be written as 101.78 and 1.0178'2 where the apostrophe (') stands for "times 10 to the power of". In the first form the decimal point (.) must be present. In the second form the number preceding the apostrophe may be an integer or a real number of the first form (or may be absent, in which case it is assumed to be 1). The number following the apostrophe must be an integer and may be preceded by a plus (+) or minus (-) sign. If no sign is present, a + is assumed. The following forms of the real number 101.78 are equivalent:

101.78 = 1.0178'2 = 1.0178'+2 = 10178'-2

examples   0.0   .387   1'+5   1.0'5   '5
           1.   -78.65   -1'-5   .1'-8

3. LONG REAL -- The precision of single-precision floating point numbers seems very adequate for most scientific and engineering purposes, being at the level of seven decimals. However, a considerable number of computations require still more precision in the middle in order to come out with ordinary accuracy at the end. LONG REAL constants may specify a precision greater than that obtainable with REAL constants. The proper use of long real values requires an understanding of the meaning of significant digits in a computation as well as a knowledge of the degree of accuracy with which the data is known.

A long real constant is denoted by appending the letter L to an integer or real value, without an intervening space. All other rules for denoting real values remain valid.

316

If a number is written in one of the decimal forms without an L at the end, it will be chopped to single-precision, no matter how many digits are set down. Thus 3.1415926535897932 will be immediately chopped to single-precision in the program and all the superfluous digits are lost at once.

Also, since the internal number representation is not decimal, simple decimal fractions are not always exactly represented. Thus the single-precision representation of .1 is not exactly the same as the extended precision representation of .1L (see Chapter 10 for further explanation).

examples   4L   -0.5'-3L   -7.8L   3.L   0.1L

4. COMPLEX -- Complex constants in ALGOL W require the specification of imaginary numbers. To write an imaginary constant, an integer or real constant must be followed, without a space, by the letter I. The character I is used only as a notational device and has no mathematical properties. That number whose square is -1 is denoted in ALGOL W by 1I.

examples   5I   8.5I   7.8'5I.

In order to form complex numbers which have a non-zero real part or which have a negative imaginary part, the usual rules of forming sums and differences in arithmetic expressions must be followed (A7.1).

examples   4 + 5.6I   -12.2 + 0.4I   38.6 - 5.85I
            -585.3I   -1.21 -0.82I

Complex numbers appearing on data cards may specify both a real and imaginary part. A zero real part need not be indicated. These numbers have the form of the expressions in the preceding examples except that no spaces are permitted within a complex constant on a data card. For example, 4 + 5.6I would have to appear as 4+5.6I on a data card. The reason for this restriction is that blank spaces are used to separate individual data items on a data card.

5. LONG COMPLEX -- The attribute long may be given to complex values. Long complex constants are written by following the name of complex constants immediately by the letter L. All other details concerning long complex arithmetic are the same as for complex arithmetic.

examples 8.765IL   4IL   2'3IL

Because ALGOL W interprets a complex number as the sum of a real constant and an imaginary constant, some care must be taken in view of the rules concerning the type of resulting values from arithmetic expressions (A7.1). When a long complex value which is the sum or difference of a real constant and a complex constant is written, both the real constant and the imaginary constant must have the attribute long.

examples   8.6L - 8.6IL   3.8'2L+4IL
            -1.0L + 1.5IL   0.04L-'8IL

6. LOGICAL -- The only logical constants are <u>true</u> and <u>false</u> both of which are reserved words.

7. BITS -- Bit constants represent a sequence of 32 binary digits. The necessity of writing long strings of binary digits is alleviated by expressing a sequence of four bits as a hexadecimal (base 16) digit as shown in the table below:

Decimal	Binary	Hexadecimal	Decimal	Binary	Hexadecimal
0	0000	0	8	1000	8
1	0001	1	9	1001	9
2	0010	2	10	1010	A
3	0011	3	11	1011	B
4	0100	4	12	1100	C
5	0101	5	13	1101	D
6	0110	6	14	1110	E
7	0111	7	15	1111	F

Each <u>bits</u> constant is denoted by a pound sign (#) followed by from one to eight hexadecimal digits. If less than eight hexadecimal digits are specified, additional zeros are implicitly assumed between the pound sign and the hexadecimal digits present.

<u>examples</u> #5A73BD24 = 01011010011100111011110100100100
         #4C   = 00000000000000000000000001001100

8. STRING -- A string constant consists of any sequence of (at most 256) characters enclosed by ", the string quote. If the string quote is to appear in the sequence of characters, it must be immediately followed by a second string quote which is then ignored. The number of characters in a string is said to be the <u>length</u> of the string.

<u>examples</u> "ABC" is a string of length 3
         """" is the string of length 1 consisting of
              the string quote itself

9. REFERENCE -- The only <u>reference</u> constant is the reserved word NULL which indicates that a reference variable with that value does not point to any record.

A4.2 Predeclared Variables

The following variables are to be considered declared and are initialized in the conceptual block enclosing the entire ALGOL W program. The values indicated for <u>real</u> and <u>long real</u> quantities are to be understood as decimal approximations to the actual machine-format values provided. The only one of these variables whose value you may wish to redefine in a program will be INTFIELDSIZE.

<u>integer</u> INTFIELDSIZE -- initialized to 14; controls the
         width of the field for integers (A10.3.3);

<u>integer</u> MAXINTEGER -- initialized to 2147483647; the maximum
         positive integer allowed by the implementation;

318

real EPSILON -- initialized to 9.536743'-07; the largest
     positive real number provided by the implementation
     such that 1 + ϵ = 1;

long real LONGEPSILON -- initialized to 2.220446049250031'-161;
          the largest positive long real number
          provided by the implementation such that 1 + ϵ = 1;

long real MAXREAL -- initialized to 7.23700557733226'+75L;
          the largest positive long real number provided
          by the implementation;

long real PI -- initialized to 3.141592653589790L.

A5. Declarations

```
<declaration> ::= <simple variable declaration>        (A5.1)
                | <array declaration>                  (A5.2)
                | <record class declaration>           (A5.3)
                | <procedure declaration>              (A9.1)
```

Declarations serve to associate identifiers with the quantities
used in the program, to attribute certain permanent properties to these
quantities (such as type or structure), and to determine their scope.

Upon exit from a block, all quantities declared or defined within
that block lose their value and become inaccessible (A8.1.1).

A5.1 Simple Variable Declarations

```
<simple variable declaration> ::= <simple type><identifier list>

<simple type> ::= INTEGER | REAL | LONG REAL | COMPLEX
                | LONG COMPLEX | LOGICAL | BITS | BITS(32)
                | STRING | STRING(<integer number>)
                | REFERENCE(<record class identifier>)

<identifier list> ::= <identifier>                                  (A2)
                    | <identifier list>,<identifier>
```

examples INTEGER MAX, MIN;
         REAL HOURLY_WAGE, WITHOLDING TAX;
         LONG COMPLEX Z, VECTOR;
         LOGICAL IS_POSITIVE;
         BITS SET_A, SET_B, SET_C;
         STRING(20) FIRST_NAME, LAST_NAME;
         REFERENCE (PERSON) JACK , JILL

Each identifier of the identifier list is associated with a variable which is declared to be of the indicated type. If a variable is declared to be of a certain type, then this implies that only values which are assignment compatible with this type can be assigned to it (A8.1.2.2).

A variable of type bits is always of length 32 whether or not the declaration specification is included.

A variable of type string has a length equal to the unsigned integer in the declaration specification. If the simple type is given only as string, the default length of the variable is 16 characters.

A variable of type reference may refer only to an instance of the record class whose identifier is specified in the reference declaration.

Simple variable declarations first appear in Examples 3.6.1 and 4.5.1 in the book.

A5.2 Array Declarations

    <array declaration> ::= <simple type> ARRAY <identifier list>
                            (<subscript bounds list>)

    <subscript bounds list> ::= <lower-bound upper-bound pair>
                              | <subscript bounds list>,
                                <lower-bound upper-bound pair>

    <lower-bound upper-bound pair> ::= <lower bound>::<upper bound>

    <lower bound> ::= <integer expression>

    <upper bound> ::= <integer expression>

examples   INTEGER ARRAY HEIGHT(1::100);
            REAL ARRAY TEMPERATURE (-80::150, 0::2);
            LOGICAL ARRAY A,B (1::M, 1::N);
            STRING(12) ARRAY STREET, TOWN, CITY (J::K+1)

To each identifier of the identifier list there corresponds an array of the simple type specified before the reserved word ARRAY and of the dimension specified by the subscript bounds list. The dimension of an array is the number of lower-bound upper-bound pairs in the subscript bounds list.

Every element of an array is identified by a list of indices (subscripts) equal in number to the dimension of the array. Each index is one of the integers between and including the values of the corresponding lower bound and upper bound. For example, the array defined by the declaration

                INTEGER ARRAY A(-1::1, 2::3)

has dimension two and has six elements which are identified as

```
A (-1,2)   A (-1,3)
A (0,2)    A (0,3)
A (1,2)    A (1,3)
```

Notice that negative values may appear in a lower-bound upper-bound pair.

A lower-bound upper-bound pair may involve expressions. Thus the size of arrays in a program may depend dynamically on program conditions. Every expression in the subscript bounds list is evaluated exactly once upon entry to the block in which the array declaration occurs. Therefore any variables or procedures occuring in an expression must have been declared in a surrounding block and _not_ in the block in which the array declaration itself occurs.

In order to be valid, for every lower-bound upper-bound pair, the value of the lower bound must not be greater than the value of the upper bound.

Examples of the use of arrays are to be found in Examples 5.4.1, 5.4.2, 6.6.1 and in subsequent chapters.

A5.3 Record Class Declarations

   <record class declaration> ::= RECORD<identifier>(<field list>)

   <field list> ::= <simple variable declaration>
            | <field list>;<simple variable declaration>

examples RECORD PERSON (STRING NAME; INTEGER AGE; LOGICAL MALE)
        RECORD LIST_ITEM (INTEGER ID_NUMBER; REFERENCE(LIST_ITEM) LINK)

A record class declaration serves to define the structural properties of records belonging to the class. The principal constituent of a record class declaration is a sequence of simple variable declarations which associate identifiers with the individual fields and give their types.

Record classes and _reference_ variables are not treated in the examples of this book.

A6. Comments

The reserved word COMMENT followed by any sequence of characters not containing semicolons, followed by a semicolon, is called a comment. A comment has no effect on the meaning of a program and is ignored during execution of the program.

example COMMENT THIS PROGRAM SORTS A LIST OF N ITEMS;

characteristic error: Failure to include a semicolon at the end of a comment will result in all program text up to the next semicolon being considered as the remainder of the comment; declarations or statements may be ignored by the compiler.

An identifier immediately following the basic symbol END is also regarded as a comment. The reserved word COMMENT need not appear.

example
```
        BEGIN
            <statements>
            BEGIN
                <statements>
            END INNERBLOCK
        END OUTERBLOCK
```

characteristic error: Failure to separate statements properly by means of a semicolon can cause a statement or part of a statement to be interpreted as a comment. The sequence
```
        BEGIN
            .
            .
            .
        END
        A := B;
```

will be interpreted as an identifier comment, A, followed by a syntactically incorrect string :=B and will result in a compiler-generated syntax error. A semicolon placed after the keyword END to separate the compound statement from the assignment statement that follows it would correct the error.

An error which is even more subtle and difficult to detect occurs in the sequence
```
                    .
                    .
                    .
                END
                PROC_NAME;
```

where PROC_NAME is intended as a procedure statement. The sequence is syntactically correct but during program execution the procedure will never be executed since PROC_NAME is interpreted as a comment.

The presence of errors resulting from the misinterpretation of statements as comments can be detected by running a program with the $DEBUG,2 option (A11.1). The listing provided by this option is called an execution flow summary, and all program comments are deleted from it. Any statement which has been interpreted as a comment will not appear in the summary.

A7. Expressions

Expressions are rules which specify how new values are computed from existing ones. These new values are obtained by performing the operations indicated by the operators on the values of the operands. The operands are either constants, variables or function designators, or other expressions, enclosed by parentheses , if necessary. The evaluation of operands other than constants may involve smaller units of action such as the evaluation of other expressions or the execution of statements. A constant or a single variable can also constitute an instance of an expression.

A7.1 Arithmetic Expressions

An arithmetic expression is a rule for computing a number. According to its simple type it is called an integer expression, real expression, long real expression, complex expression, or long complex expression (cf. Figures A7.1 through A7.7).

Arithmetic expressions first appear in this book in Example 2.1.1.

A7.1.1 The binary operations and symbols for forming arithmetic expressions are

addition   +
subtraction   -
multiplication *
division   /

A7.1.2 The operator "-" standing as the first symbol of a simple expression denotes the unary operation of sign inversion. The type of the result is the type of the operand. The operator "+" standing as the first symbol of a simple expression denotes the unary operation of identity.

A7.1.3 The operator DIV is mathematically defined as A DIV B = the integer quotient obtained upon dividing A by B. A and B must both be integer expressions. See Figure A7.4. Use of the DIV operator is illustrated in Examples 7.2.2, 7.2.3, and 7.3.1.

A7.1.4 The operator REM is mathematically defined as A REM B = the integer remainder obtained upon dividing A by B. A and B must both be integer expressions. See Figure A7.4. Use of the REM operator is illustrated in Examples 5.4.1, 7.2.3, and 7.3.1.

A7.1.5 The operator ** denotes exponentiation of the first operand to the second operand. The exponent must always be of type _integer_. The type of the result is given in Figure A7.5. Expressions using the exponentiation operator first appear in the book in Sec. 2.3.

If the value of the exponent, N, is positive, then the first operand is multiplied by itself N times; if N is negative, the expression is evaluated as 1/(first operand ** ABS N); if N is zero, the result is always 1. If the first operand is zero and the second operand is negative, then division by zero will result. To force I**J (where I>=0 and J>=0) to be an integer, use TRUNCATE(I**J).

A7.1.6 The unary operator ABS yields the absolute value or modulus of the operand, which may be any of the types _integer_, _real_, _long real_, _complex_, or _long complex_.

A7.1.7 The unary operator LONG changes the precision of an expression from single-precision to double-precision (Figure A7.6). The unary operator SHORT changes the precision of an expression from double-precision to single-precision (Figure A7.7).

Operators + | -

	integer	real	long real	complex	long cmplx
integer	integer	real	long real	complex	long cmplx
real	real	real	long real	complex	complex
long real	long real	real	long real	complex	long cmplx
complex	complex	complex	complex	complex	complex
long cmplx	long cmplx	complex	long cmplx	complex	long cmplx

Figure 7.1

Operator *

	integer	real	complex
integer	integer	long real	long cmplx
real	long real	long real	long cmplx
complex	long cmplx	long cmplx	long cmplx

Figure 7.2

Operator /

	integer	real	long real	complex	long cmplx
integer	long real	real	long real	complex	long cmplx
real	real	real	real	complex	complex
long real	long real	real	long real	complex	long cmplx
complex	complex	complex	complex	complex	complex
long cmplx	long cmplx	complex	long cmplx	complex	long cmplx

Figure 7.3

Table of values for DIV and REM operators

I	J	I DIV J	I REM J
10	2	5	0
11	2	5	1
10	-2	-5	0
11	-2	-5	1
-10	2	-5	0
-11	2	-5	-1
-10	-2	5	0
-11	-2	5	-1

Figure 7.4

Operator **

	integer
integer	long real
real	long real
long real	long real
complex	long complex
long complex	long complex

Figure 7.5

Operator <u>long</u>

integer	=>	long real
real	=>	long real
long real	=>	long real
complex	=>	long complex
long complex	=>	long complex

Figure 7.6

325

Operator short

integer	=>	real
real	=>	real
long real	=>	real
complex	=>	complex
long complex	=>	complex

Figure 7.7

A7.1.8 For the evaluation of complicated expressions it is necessary to define a precedence or order in which operations will be carried out. The operator precedence in ALGOL W from highest to lowest is

```
            ABS  LONG  SHORT
            **
            *  /  DIV  REM
            +  -
```

Operations of higher precedence are performed first. operations on the same line have equal precedence and are performed from left to right within an unparenthesized expression. To modify the order of evaluation, parentheses may be included in an expression.

Evaluation of parenthesized expressions has priority. Because of the precedence rules, the unparenthesized expression A*B+C indicates that the product of A and B is to be added to C; insertion of parentheses to form A*(B+C) will result in the sum of B and C being multiplied by A.

The reader should verify that the value of -3**2+1*10/5 is 11.00000. This example should convince one that a careful use of parentheses is quite helpful.

examples   C + A(I) * B(I)
       (-B + SQRT(B**2 - 4*A*C))/(2*A)
       ABS(X-Y)/X

A7.2 Relations

ALGOL W allows the programmer to compare the values of two expressions. Comparisons are indicated by the following two classes of operators:

```
        <relational operator> ::= < | <= | > | >=
        <equality operator> ::= = | ¬=
```

The relational operators applied to real, long real , and integer types denote inequalities and reflexive inequalities, less than, less than or equal, greater than, greater than or equal. They also apply to values of string type, in which case the ordering is lexical order, as in a dictionary, but with the 'alphabet' extended to include all characters of the EBCDIC code (Table A10.5.1). The relative order among individual characters is that specified by the EBCDIC code. If two strings of unequal length are compared, the shorter one is first extended to the right with blank characters until their lengths agree.

326

Two references are equal if and only if they both refer to the same record or if they are both __null__.

Relations are used to form expressions of __logical__ type.

```
<relational expression> ::=
                <expression><relational operator><expression>
              | <expression><equality operator><expression>
```

A relational expression yields the logical value __true__ if the relation is satisfied for the values of the two expressions; __false__ otherwise.

Relational expressions occur in Example 3.2.1 and subsequent examples.

The following table indicates the pairs of expression types that may be compared by relational operators (R) and equality operators (E).

	INTE-GER	REAL	LONG REAL	COM-PLEX	LONG CMPLX	LOGI-CAL	BITS	STRNG	REFER-ENCE
INTEGER	E,R	E,R	E,R	E	E				
REAL	E,R	E,R	E,R	E	E				
LONG REAL	E,R	E,R	E,R	E	E				
COMPLEX	E	E	E	E	E				
LONG COMPLEX	E	E	E	E	E				
LOGICAL						E			
BITS							E		
STRING								E,R	
REFERENCE									E

Figure A7.8

__examples__   X <= Y
                      "AB" < "ABC"
                      BROTHER(JACK) ¬= NULL

Relational expressions comprise a subset of logical expressions which are the subject of Section A7.3.

A7.3 Logical Expressions

Logical expressions are constructed by combining relations, logical variables, logical function designators, and (occasionally) logical constants using the logical operators ¬(not), AND, OR.

```
<logical expression> ::= <simple logical expression>
                       | <relational expression>                    (A7.2)
                       | ¬<logical expression>
                       | <logical expression> OR <logical expression>
                       | <logical expression> AND <logical expression>
                       | <conditional logical expression>       (A7.7)

<simple logical expression> ::= <logical constant>
                              | <logical variable>
                              | <logical function designator>
                                                              (A8.1.4.1)
                              | (<logical expression>)
```

examples (A <= B) OR (C = 0)   ¬A AND ¬B
          (C =0) OR TRUE

The precedence of the logical and relational operators from highest to lowest is

                    ¬
                    AND
                    OR
                    <, <=, >, >= , = , ¬=

Therefore ¬A OR B AND C is equivalent to (¬A) OR (B AND C). The programmer is urged to explicitly indicate precedence by the use of parentheses.

The operators ¬, AND, OR operating on logical values are defined by the following table.

if values of			then values of	
P	Q	¬P	P AND Q	P OR Q
are:		are:		
TRUE	TRUE	FALSE	TRUE	TRUE
FALSE	TRUE	TRUE	FALSE	TRUE
TRUE	FALSE	FALSE	FALSE	TRUE
FALSE	FALSE	TRUE	FALSE	FALSE

Figure A7.9

The value of a complex logical expression is determined by the values of its constituent parts and Figure A7.9.

example Suppose A = -1, B = 0, and C =1.

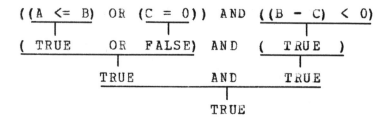

328

There is a problem of precedence in determining the meaning of expressions combining arithmetic, logical, and relational operators. The complete precedence from highest to lowest is given in Figure A7.10. Operators appearing on the same line have equal precedence. Parentheses should be used to resolve the meaning of expressions including operators of equal precedence.

```
ABS, LONG, SHORT
**
¬
AND, *, /, DIV, REM
OR, + , -
<, <= , > , >= , = , ¬=
```

Figure A7.10

Special care should be used when mixing logical and relational operators. The relational expressions should be enclosed in parehtheses. A < B OR C < D is not a well-formed expression in ALGOL W. The expression should be written as (A < B) OR (C < D). The reason is that the relational operators have the lowest precedence. In order to force the comparisons to be done before the OR operator is applied, parentheses are required.

Logical expressions occur in Example 3.2.1 and in subsequent examples.

A7.4 Bit Expressions

```
<bit expression> ::= <simple bit expression>
                   | ¬<bit expression>
                   | <bit expression> OR <bit expression>
                   | <bit expression> AND <bit expression>
                   | <conditional bit expression>          (A7.7)

<simple bit expression> ::= <bit constant>
                          | <bit variable>
                          | <bit function designator>      (A8.1.4.1)
                          | (<bit expression>)
```

example A AND #80000000

A bit expresssion is a rule for computing a bit sequence. The operators ¬, AND, OR may be used in forming bit expressions. The precedence of the operators from highest to lowest is

```
    ¬
    AND
    OR
```

The unary operator ¬ changes all 0's in a bits quantity to 1's and all 1's to 0's. The operators AND and OR operate bit by bit on corresponding bits of the two operands. Below is given a complete example of all bit combinations.

A	B	¬A	A AND B	A OR B
1100	1010	0011	1000	1110

There is an interesting correspondence between the operators ¬, AND, OR as applied to <u>bits</u> expressions and the set-theoretic operations of complement, intersection , and union. Consider a set S with four elements x1, x2, x3, x4. Any sequence of four bits represents a subset T of S if we interpret the ith bit being 1 to mean x is a member of T and the ith bit being 0 to mean x is not a member of T. Clearly the sequence 1111 represents the set S itself. In Figure A7.11, the value of A represents the subset (x1, x2) while the value of B represents (x1, x3). Evidently, ¬A represents the complement of A with respect to S, A AND B represents the intersection of the sets represented by A and B, and A OR B represents the union of these sets.

A7.5 String Expressions

```
<string expression> ::= <simple string expression>
                      | <substring designator>
                      | <conditional string expression>        (A7.7)
```

```
<simple string expression> ::= <string constant>
                             | <string variable>
                             | <string function designator>    (A8.1.4.1)
                             | (<string expression>)
```

```
<substring designator> ::= <string variable>(<integer expression>|
                           <integer constant>)
```
(The | stands for the vertical bar character "|".)

<u>examples</u>   S(0|3)   STR(X + Y|3)
          NAME(5)(LAST|6)   ELEMENT(ROW, COLUMN)(I| 1)

In a <u>string</u> variable, the position of each character is numbered sequentially, starting from 0 at the leftmost position.

In the definition of <u>substring designator</u> given above, the integer expression specifies the position number in the host string of the first character of the substring. The integer constant following the vertical bar specifies the length of the substring, and must have a value greater than 0. The sum of the values of the integer expression and the integer constant must be greater than 0 but not greater than the length of the string variable. See Section 6.2 or Example 6.4.1 for examples of use of substring designators.

Suppose that the variable S has been declared as STRING(6) S; and initialized to the value "ABCDEF". Then the substring designator S(3|2) denotes the value "DE".

The string variable in a substring designator may be an element of a string array. See, for instance, Example 6.6.1.

A7.6 Reference Expressions

```
<reference expression> ::= <simple reference expression>
                         | <conditional reference expression>

<simple reference expression> ::= NULL
                                | <reference variable>
                                | <reference function designator>
                                | <record designator>
                                | (<reference expression>)

<record designator> ::= <record class identifier>
                      | <record class identifier>(<expression list>)
```

example PERSON (JANET, 20, FALSE, NULL)

A reference expression is a rule for computing a reference to a record.

The declaration of a record class (A5.3) does not cause the creation of any records of that class. Record creation must be done explicitly by the programmer (A8.1.2).

The value of a record designator is the reference to a newly created record belonging to the designated record class. If the record designator contains an expression list, then the values of the expressions are assigned to the fields of the new record. The entries in the expression list are taken in the same order as the fields in the record class declaration, and the simple types of the expressions must be assignment compatible with the simple types of the record fields.

There are no examples of the use of reference expressions in this book.

A7.7 Conditional Expressions

A7.7.1 IF-expression

```
<if expression> ::= <if clause><first expression>
                    ELSE <second expression>

<if clause> ::= IF <logical expression> THEN
```

example IF A < 0 THEN B ELSE C + 1

The IF-expression causes the selection of and evaluation of an expression on the basis of the current value of the logical expression. If this value is true, the expression following the <if clause> is selected and its value becomes the value of the IF-expression. If the value of the conditional expression is false, the expression following ELSE is selected. If the first expression and second expression are of simple type string, the shorter expression will be padded on the right with blanks to make it the length of the longer one.

The type of an IF-expression is determined by the type of <first expression> and <second expression>. If <first expression> and <second expression> are both arithmetic types (INTEGER, REAL, LONG REAL, COMPLEX, LONG COMPLEX), the following table defines the type of the IF-expression given the types of <first expression> and <second expression>.

	INTEGER	REAL	COMPLEX
INTEGER	INTEGER	REAL	COMPLEX
REAL	REAL	REAL	COMPLEX
COMPLEX	COMPLEX	COMPLEX	COMPLEX

The IF-expression has the attribute long if either both <first expression> and <second expression> have that attribute or if one has that attribute and the other is integer. If either <first expression> or <second expression> is one of the non-arithmetic types (LOGICAL, BITS, STRING, REFERENCE) then both expressions must be of that type and the IF-expression itself is of that type. The mixing of arithmetic and non-arithmetic expressions will result in an improper combination of types error during compilation.

An IF-expression may be embedded as a part of any expression of the same type, or its value may be assigned to a variable. When an IF-expression is embedded as a part of a larger arithmeteic, logical, or bits expression, the IF-expression must be enclosed by parentheses.

The IF-expression is different from the IF statement (A8.3.1). For examples of IF-expressions, see Sec. 3.1 or Example 3.7.1.

A7.7.2 CASE-expression

<case expression> ::= <case clause>(<expression list>)

<case clause> ::= CASE <integer expression> OF

examples   CASE I OF (3.14, 2.78, 448.9)
            CASE J + K OF (X**2, Y - 1, Y + 1)

The CASE-expression causes the selection of the expression whose ordinal number in the expression list is equal to the current value of the integer expression contained in the case clause. In order that the case expression be defined, the current value of the integer expression must be the ordinal number of some expression in the expression list. The integer expression contained in the case clause is called the case selector. If this expression assumes a value which is negative, zero, or greater than the number of expressions in the expression list, evaluation of the case expression will result in a case selection indexing error and program execution will be terminated.

String expressions in the expression list will be padded on the right with blanks to make all alternatives the length of the longest one.

The CASE-expression is different from the CASE statement (A8.4.2). There are no examples of CASE-expressions in this book.

A8. Statements

The basic unit of computational action in an ALGOL W program is the statement. The execution of a statement means the performance of this unit of action, which may in turn call for the evaluation of expressions or the execution of other statements. An execution sequence of a program segment is a sequence of the statements actually executed when the program is run with some initial data. Many distinct execution sequences of a single program may be possible if the program contains conditional or iterative statements.

Statements allow modification of the values of variables and control of the execution sequence of a program.

Using BNF notation, we can give an economical description of what constitutes an ALGOL W program.

<program> ::= <statement>.

```
<statement> ::= <unconditional statement>          (A8.1)
              | <conditional statement>            (A8.3)
              | <iterative statement>              (A8.2)
              | <assert statement>                 (A11.3)

<unconditional statement> ::= <block>              (A8.1.1)
              | <assignment>                       (A8.1.2)
              | <empty statement>                  (A8.1.3)
              | <procedure statement>              (A8.1.4)
```

(Note: the terminating period is optional.)

A8.1 Unconditional Statements

A statement which does not test the value of a variable or expression to determine the control of execution is called an unconditional statement.

A8.1.1 Blocks

```
<block> ::= BEGIN <statement list> END
          | BEGIN <declaration list>;<statement list> END

<statement list> ::= <statement>                   (A8.1)
                   | <statement list>;<statement>
```

```
<declaration list> ::= <declaration>                                    (A5)
               | <declaration list>;<declaration>
```

A block permits a programmer to group together a sequence of
statements which are then viewed as one compound statement and hence a
unit of action.

The semicolon is used within a block to separate statements or
declarations in a list. The semicolon is not used to mark the
termination of a statement; in fact there are statements in ALGOL W
which cannot be followed by a semicolon such as the statement preceding
the symbol ELSE in an IF-statement (A8.3).

If certain variables are required only within a given block and not
outside of it, these variables may be declared within that block.
Declarations must precede any statements of the block.

Upon block entry, new variables are created with uninitialized
values. Upon block exit, those variables disappear and their values are
no longer accessible, even if the textual block is re-executed at some
later time.

A program may contain many blocks, and blocks may be nested one
within another. Furthermore it is possible to declare variables with
names identical to those of variables declared within another block
(this practice may occasionally be useful but is not recommended in
general). The question of which variables are available to use at
various positions in the program arises.

The scope of a variable refers to the blocks in which the variable
may be used or is accessible. Scope is divided into two categories,
local and global. A variables is local to a block if it is declared in
that block. A variables is global to a block (1) if the variable is
local to the block which immediately surrounds the given block and the
same identifier is not declared in the inner block or (2) if the
variable is global to the surrounding block and the same identifier is
not declared in the inner block.

The scope rules for variables also apply to procedures.

Within a given block the program may access any variable which is
local or global to that block. In the case that a local variable is
declared to have the same identifier as has been used to name a variable
in a surrounding block, only the local variable can be accessed within
the inner block. Upon exit from the inner block, the identifier is
again bound to the variable declared in the surrounding block.

For examples of the use of blocks see Sec. 3.6, Example 4.5.1, or
one of the examples of Sec. 5.4.

A8.1.2 Assignment Statement

```
<assignment statement> ::= <left part><expression>
                         | <left part><assignment statement>

<left part> ::= <variable identifier>:=                    (A2)
```

(note: The ALGOL W assignment symbol (:=) is not related in any way to the similar symbol (::=) of BNF notation.)

examples
```
                A := 2.8
                X := X + 1
                X := Y := Z := 0
                P := IF X > 0 THEN TRUE ELSE Q
                R := CASE I OF (-1, 0, 1)
                PTR := DATA("JANET", 20, FALSE)
                B(3) := X
```

The assignment statement provides the mechanism for storing the value of an expression or constant in a variable. A variable holds the last value assigned to it. Until some value is explicitly assigned to a variable, the value of that variable is undefined. Failure to initialize variables properly often leads to errors during the execution of a program.

In assignment of _string_ types, if the length of the string expression to the right of the assignment operator is less than the length declared for the string variable to which it is being assigned, then the shorter string is first extended to the right with blanks until the lengths are equal.

A8.1.2.1 Creating Instances of a Record Class

The record declaration (A5.3) does not cause the creation of a record. Records are created by means of the assignment statement. Suppose a program contains the declaration

```
RECORD DATA(STRING(20) NAME; INTEGER AGE; LOGICAL MALE);
REFERENCE (DATA) PTR
```

the following statement will cause the creation of one record of the record class DATA and will cause PTR to reference that record; however the values of the fields of the record will be undefined.

```
                PTR := DATA
```

The fields of the record can be initialized by including an expression list in parentheses following the record class identifier.

```
                PTR := DATA("JANET", 20, FALSE)
```

Of course a reference variable may be assigned the reference constant _null_ or the value of another reference variable.

A8.1.2.2 Assignment Compatability

A simple type T1 is said to be __assignment compatible__ with a
simple type T0 if either
    (1) the two types are identical (except that if T0 and T1
        are STRING, the length of the T0 variable must be greater
        than or equal to the length of the T1 expression or
        assignment)
  or (2) T0 is REAL or LONG REAL, and T1 is INTEGER,
        REAL, or LONG REAL
  or (3) T0 is COMPLEX or LONG COMPLEX, and T1 is INTEGER,
        REAL, LONG REAL, COMPLEX, or LONG COMPLEX.

In assignment of __reference__ types, the reference variable on the
left of the assignment operator must be bound to the same record class
as is the reference expression on the right.

A8.1.2.3 Multiple Assignment Statement

In a multiple assignment statement such as X := Y := Z := E the
assignments are performed from right to left. Thus the value of
expression E is assigned to the variables X, Y, and Z in that order.
For each variable to which assignment is made, the simple type of the
expression or assignment variable immediately to the right must be
assignment compatible with the simple type of that variable. Multiple
assignments are often used to initialize several variables to a common
value.

__example__ A(I) := I := 2

Following the right-to-left rule, this multiple assignment is
equivalent to
     I := 2;
     A(2) := 2

A8.1.3 Empty Statement

According to the BNF description of an ALGOL W block (A8.1.1), the
statement immediately preceding the word END need not be terminated by a
semicolon. If a semicolon precedes an END, an __empty statement__
consisting of no characters is assumed to follow the semicolon. The
empty statement may be used anywhere a statement is allowed.

A8.1.4 Procedure Statement

      <procedure statement> ::= <procedure identifier>
                | <procedure identifier>(<actual parameter list>)

      <actual parameter list> ::= <actual parameter>
                | <actual parameter list>,<actual parameter>

Every procedure has an identifier associated with it either by
means of a procedure declaration (A9.1) or by virtue of being a standard
procedure (A10). A __procedure statement__ is the mention of this identifier
as a statement in a program and causes execution of the corresponding

procedure. If a procedure declaration involves formal parameters in its definition, the procedure statement must provide corresponding actual parameters (A9.2). A procedure statement is said to _invoke_ or **call** its associated procedure.

Examples of procedure statements are found in Examples 7.2.3, 8.1.1, 8.2.1, and 9.3.1.

A8.1.4.1 Function Designators

<function designator> ::= <function identifier>
| <function identifier>(<actual parameter list>)

A function designator declares a procedure whose execution will evaluate a function of the arguments that are passed to it. A function procedure is invoked by mention of its name in an expression. The value that its invocation produces is the value of the expression which constitutes or appears at the end of the body of the function procedure associated with the <function identifier> (A9.1). If the function procedure declaration involves formal parameters in its definition, the function designator must provide corresponding actual parameters (A9.2).

The simple type of a function designator is the simple type provided in the corresponding function procedure declaration.

Function designators are used in Examples 7.2.2, 7.2.3, 7.3.1, 7.4.1 and several subsequent examples.

A8.1.4.2 Partial Arrays as Parameters

A complete array may be passed to a procedure by specifying the name of the array if the number of subscripts of the actual parameter equals the number of subscripts of the corresponding formal parameter. Occasionally algorithms are designed to operate on subarrays of an array. For instance, if it were desired to sum the elements of each row of a two-dimensional array, the operation could easily be performed row by row. In such a case it would be appropriate to write an algorithm which summed the elements in a one-dimensional array.

```
REAL PROCEDURE ROWSUM(REAL ARRAY X(*); INTEGER VALUE N);
   BEGIN REAL SUM;
      SUM := 0;
      FOR I := 0 UNTIL N DO SUM := SUM + X(I);
      SUM
   END
```

Suppose an array has been declared as REAL ARRAY A(1::10, 1::10). To sum the Ith row of the array we would call upon ROWSUM(A(I,*),10); subscripts which are fixed (row number) are specified by an integer expression while subscripts which vary (column number) are specified by an asterisk (*).

If the actual array parameter has more subscripts than the corresponding formal parameter, enough subscripts must be specified by integer expressions so that the number of *'s appearing in the subarray designator equals the number of subscripts of the corresponding formal parameter. The subscript positions of the formal array designator are matched with the positions with *'s in the subarray designator in the order they appear.

A8.2 Iterative Statements

Iteration is the programming technique of calling for the repeated execution of a statement, subject to control by testing a designated logical expression. ALGOL W provides two iteration statements, the WHILE statement and the FOR statement.

A8.2.1 WHILE Statement

      <while statement> ::= WHILE <logical expression> DO <statement>

      examples   WHILE (J > 0) AND (CITY(J) ¬= S) DO J := J - 1;

```
            WHILE N > 0 DO
               BEGIN FACT := FACT * N;
                     N := N - 1
               END
```

The statement following the reserved word DO is said to be controlled by the WHILE clause. In execution, the logical expression in a WHILE statement is first tested, and if its value is _true_, then the statement it controls is executed and the process is repeated, commencing with a re-evaluation of the logical expression. When the value of the logical expression is found to be _false_, execution of the WHILE statement terminates without an additional execution of the controlled statement. Notice that if the logical expression is found to be _false_ upon its initial evaluation, then the controlled statement will not be executed at all.

WHILE statements are used in Examples 4.1.1, 4.4.1, 4.5.1, 5.4.1, and several subsequent examples.

A8.2.2 FOR Statement

There are three forms of the FOR statement in ALGOL W:

(1)   FOR <control identifier> := <list of integer expressions> DO
       <statement>

(2)   FOR <control identifier> := <integer expression> UNTIL
       <integer expression> DO <statement>

(3)   FOR <control identifier> := <integer expression> STEP
       <integer expression> UNTIL <integer expression> DO <statement>

examples   FOR MULTIPLIER:= 1,10,100 DO
           IF MULTIPLIER*X > 1 THEN

```
        WRITEON (TRUNCATE(MULTIPLIER * X) REM 10)


   FOR K:=1 UNTIL M DO A(K) := A(K) + 1


   FOR I:=100 STEP -2 UNTIL 0 DO
      BEGIN A(I) := FALSE;
            B(100-I) := TRUE
      END
```

The use of the FOR statement is also illustrated in Examples 4.4.1, 4.5.1, 5.4.3, 6.5.1, 6.6.1, and in Sec. 5.6.

The control identifier is not declared in an explicit variable declaration; its appearance in a FOR statement constitutes an _implicit_ declaration of an integer variable whose scope is limited to the FOR statement (including the controlled statement) in which it appears. Outside of this statement the control variable is not accessible. For additional explanation of the restriction of the scope of declaration of the control identifier, see Sec. 4.4.

In the first form of the FOR statement, the control variable takes, in a succession of assignments, the value of each of the expressions appearing in the list that precedes the reserved word DO. The controlled statement is executed once for each of these assignments to the control variable.

In the second and third forms of the FOR statement, the control variable takes a succession of values as specified by a range of integers. The integer expressions appearing in the FOR clause are first evaluated, and these values determine the _initial_ element of the range, the _increment_ value, and the value of a _limit_ on the range. In the second form the increment value is taken to be 1, while in the third form it is the value of the expression following the reserved word STEP. The increment may be positive or negative, but must not be zero.

1. If the value of the increment is _positive_ and the value of the control variable is less than or equal to the value of the limit, the controlled statement is executed. If the value of the control variable is _greater_ than the value of the limit, the controlled statement is not executed and execution of the program continues following the FOR statement.

2. If the value of the increment is _negative_ and the value of the control variable is greater than or equal to the value of the limit, the controlled statement is executed. If the value of the control variable is _less_ than the value of the limit, the controlled statement is not executed and execution of the program continues following the FOR statement.

If the controlled statement is executed, the value of the control variable is then replaced by its previous value plus that of the increment. Step 1 or 2 is repeated until the limit is reached.

It is possible that the controlled statement will not be executed at all. This happens if the initial value of the range exceeds the limit with a positive value of the increment , or is less than the limit, with a negative increment (cf. Figure A8.1). Also the value of the limit and the increment are calculated only once at the entry to the FOR block. Their values cannot be changed by execution of the controlled statement.

Example FOR statement	Values I takes on
FOR I := 1 STEP 2 UNTIL 10 DO	1, 3, 5, 7, 9
FOR I := 1 STEP 2 UNTIL 1 DO	1
FOR I := 1 STEP 2 UNTIL -10 DO	none
FOR I := 1 STEP -2 UNTIL 10 DO	none
FOR I := 1 STEP -2 UNTIL 1 DO	1
FOR I := 1 STEP -2 UNTIL -10 DO	1, -1, -3, -5, -7, -9
FOR I := 1 STEP 0 UNTIL 10 DO	1, 1, 1, 1, 1, 1, 1, . . .
FOR I := 1 STEP 0 UNTIL 1 DO	1, 1, 1, 1, 1, 1, 1, . . .
FOR I := 1 STEP 0 UNTIL -10 DO	none

Figure A8.1 -- Table of results for various FOR statements

A8.3 Conditional Statements

```
<conditional statement> ::= <if statement>
                         | <case statement>
```

A8.3.1 IF Statement

```
<if statement> ::= <if clause><statement>
      |<if clause><unconditional statement> ELSE <statement>

<if clause> ::= IF <logical expression> THEN
```

examples   IF X = Y THEN Z := 0

```
IF X < Y THEN FLAG := TRUE ELSE FLAG := FALSE

IF X < Y THEN  U := X
ELSE IF Y < Z THEN U := Y
ELSE BEGIN V := Z;
          N := N + 1
     END
```

The execution of an IF statement causes controlled statements to be executed or skipped, depending on the value of a logical expression.

An IF statement of the form <if clause><statement> is executed as follows: The logical expression in the if clause is evaluated. If the result of the evaluation is <u>true</u>, then the controlled statement following the if clause is executed. Otherwise no action is taken, and control passes to the next statement in the program.

An if statement of the form <if clause> <unconditional statement> ELSE <statement> is executed as follows: The logical expression in the if clause is evaluated. If the result of the evaluation is <u>true</u>, then the unconditional statement following the if clause is executed. Otherwise the statement following the ELSE is executed. Following execution of one or the other of the controlled statements, control passes to the next statement in the program.

IF-STATEMENTS APPEAR IN EXAMPLES 3.3.1, 3.4.1, 3.6.1, 4.1.1, AND IN MANY SUBSEQUENT EXAMPLES.

A8.4.2 CASE Statements

> <case statement> ::= <case clause> BEGIN <statement list> END
>
> <statement list> ::= <statement>
> | <statement list>;<statement>
>
> <case clause> ::= CASE <integer expression> OF

<u>examples</u>
```
        CASE I OF
        BEGIN
            X := X + Y;
            Y := Y + Z;
            Z := Z + X
        END

        CASE J OF
          BEGIN
            H(I) := -H(I);
            BEGIN H(I-1) := H(I-1) + H(I); I := I-1 END;
            BEGIN H(I-1) := H(I-1) * H(I); I := I-1 END;
            BEGIN H(H(I-1)) := H(I);  I := I-2 END
          END
```

The case statement is executed as follows: The expression of the case clause is evaluated. The controlled statement whose ordinal number in the statement list is equal to the value of the expression is executed. Only this statement is executed from among the controlled statement list. Following its execution the <u>case</u> statement is completed, and control passes to the next statement in the program. In order that the case statement be defined, the current value of the expression in the case clause must be positive but not greater that the number of controlled statements in the statement list.

Notice that if a semicolon occurs just before the END of a case statement list, it designates an empty statement in the list (A8.1.3).

There are no examples of the use of CASE-statements in this book.

A9. Procedures

A **procedure** is a sub-algorithm which performs a specific task such as sorting a list and may be called upon to perform this task at any time during the execution of a calling program. Also a procedure may initiate a sub-computation such as computing a square root which returns a value to the calling program. Procedures which have a value associated with them (computing a square root) are called **function procedures** while procedures with no such associated value (sorting a list) are called **proper procedures**.

In addition to procedures written by the programmer, a program may access a library of procedures which perform many standard mathematical and data-handling functions. Such procedures are called **standard procedures** (A10).

A9.1 Procedure Declarations

```
<procedure declaration> ::= <procedure heading>;<statement>
                          | <function procedure heading><expression>
                          | <function procedure heading><function block>

<function block> ::= BEGIN <statement list>;<expression> END
        | BEGIN <declaration list>;<statement list>;<expression> END

<function procedure heading> ::= <type><procedure heading>

<procedure heading> ::= PROCEDURE <identifier>
                      | PROCEDURE <identifier>(<formal parameter list>)
                                                              (A9.2)
```

A9.1.1 Proper Procedure Declarations

The procedure heading specifies the identifier which is to be associated with the procedure and describes the parameters, if any, which are used in the definition of the procedure.

The statement which follows the procedure heading is called the **procedure body** and is the ALGOL W code for the algorithm which the procedure is to perform.

Although proper procedures may be written without parameters, parameters provide more flexible use of the procedure concept. Frequently, parameterless procedures must depend on global variables in order to operate correctly. If the procedure is moved to another program or elsewhere in the same program, these global variables must still be accessible. When parameters are used the procedure may be made completely independent of global variables.

Examples of procedure declarations occur in Chapters 7 through 10.

A9.1.2 Function Procedure Declarations

The function procedure heading differs from the proper procedure heading in that a type for the resulting value of the procedure must be indicated before the word PROCEDURE. The procedure body may be either an expression or a function block.

The first form of the procedure body is an expression whose type is assignment compatible with the declared type of the function. The value of the expression is the resulting value of the function procedure.

example

```
        REAL PROCEDURE MAX (REAL X, Y);
          IF X < Y THEN Y ELSE X;
```

The second form of the procedure body is a modified block. It is just like a block except that the last statement in the block must be followed by a semicolon (;) and the expression which is the value of the procedure is placed before the word END. This expression followed by the END terminates the procedure. The expression may never be followed by a semicolon .

example

```
        INTEGER PROCEDURE FACTORIAL (INTEGER VALUE N);
            BEGIN INTEGER FACT;
                FACT := 1;
                FOR I:=2 UNTIL N DO FACT := FACT * I;
                FACT
            END
```

The function procedure call may occur anywhere in the program where an expression of the same type as the function may occur. The form of the function procedure call is the same as that of proper procedures and does not depend on which of the two forms of the function procedure declaration is used.

Examples of function procedure declarations occur in Chapters 7 through 10.

A9.2 Parameters

Procedures may require the use of formal parameters in their definition. Formal parameter specifications define identifiers which are local to the procedure body and merely indicate what to do with the arguments, or actual parameters, that are supplied when the procedure is called. The following definition of a procedure to interchange the values of two integer variables specifies two formal parameters, X and Y. (The variable SAVE is a temporary working variable. Such variables may be introduced by means of local variable declarations.)

```
PROCEDURE SWAP (INTEGER X, Y);
      BEGIN INTEGER SAVE;
            SAVE := X;
            X := Y;
            Y := SAVE
      END
```

During the execution of a program one might wish to interchange the values of two integer variables, FIRST and LAST. They would be specified as actual parameters in a call to the procedure of the form SWAP(FIRST, LAST).

A9.2.1 Formal Parameter Specification

The formal parameters specified in a procedure declaration may be simple variables, arrays, or procedures. Because much of the information about the use of the variables may come from the actual parameters, somewhat less information needs to be specified in the formal parameter specifications than in declarations.

Simple parameter specifications have the same form as simple variable declarations (A5.1).

            INTEGER FIRST, SECOND, THIRD
            REAL VELOCITY

Additional information which may increase the efficiency of a procedure and provide protection from inadvertently changing the values of global variables may be provided when simple variables (but not arrays or procedures) appear in a formal parameter specification list (A9.3).

Array parameter specifications do not indicate the bounds on the array. Instead of the lower-bound upper-bound pairs, an asterisk must be used in place of each dimension of the array to indicate the number of dimensions.

            INTEGER ARRAY A, B(*)
            REAL ARRAY C (*,*)

Array parameters are illustrated by Examples 7.4.1, 10.4.1.

Procedure parameter specifications give only the name and function type (if any) of formal procedure parameters.

It may not be obvious to the reader why one would use a procedure as a parameter. Suppose we have developed a procedure AREA to calculate the area bounded by the curve y = f(x) and the lines x = a and x = b. A procedure heading for declaration of this function procedure could be

            REAL PROCEDURE AREA (REAL A,B; PROCEDURE F)

This would be followed by instructions for some numerical computation of the area under a graph of an arbitrary function F (cf. Exercise 10.5). To calculate the area bounded by the curve y = sin x between x = 0 and x = $\pi/2$, this procedure would be called by AREA(0, PI/2, SIN).

344

A9.3 Parameter Calling Conventions

A9.3.1 Name Parameters

In the procedure SWAP (A9.2) the formal parameters X and Y stood for the names of the actual parameters which were to be supplied at the time the procedure was called. Such formal parameters are called name parameters. Execution of the procedure may be thought of as being done by textual substitution in which each occurence of a formal parameter in the procedure body is replaced by the corresponding actual parameter.

Whenever a name parameter is encountered, execution returns to the place of the procedure call to evaluate the actual parameter. This action is often unnecessary as well as inefficient. Furthermore, the procedure may change the value of an actual parameter if its corresponding formal parameter appears on the left side of an assignment in the procedure body.

Unless the programmer specifies one of the formal parameter attributes VALUE, RESULT, or VALUE RESULT defined below, the default action of the compiler is to treat a parameter as a name parameter. The compiler lists a warning for the programmer's information specifying each parameter which is a name parameter. In order to minimize the inefficiencies involved in handling procedures, ALGOL W provides alternate ways of treating formal parameters for simple variables, although not for arrays or procedures.

A9.3.2 VALUE Parameters

When the attribute VALUE is specified for a simple variable parameter, the formal parameter represents a variable local to the procedure body. This parameter is assigned as an initial value, at the time of a procedure call, the value of the corresponding actual parameter. This means that the actual parameter is evaluated once when the procedure is called, and that subsequent assignments to the formal parameter do not directly affect the actual parameter. Everywhere the formal parameter occurs, the local variable is used. Call by value may be used whenever only the value of an actual parameter is needed as an argument.

To specify that a parameter is to be a VALUE parameter, the type of the parameter in the formal parameter declaration should be followed by the word VALUE.

INTEGER VALUE A, B, C;
REAL VALUE MASS

Suppose a procedure specifies VALUE formal parameters FP_1, FP_2,.....,FP_LAST and is called with actual parameters AP_1, AP_2,.....,AP_LAST. One can then think of the procedure as being contained within an implicit surrounding block in which the formal parameters are locally declared and the statements

FP_1 := AP_1;
FP_2 := AP_2;
FP_LAST := AP_LAST
immediately precede the procedure body.

If a formal parameter is specified by VALUE then the simple type of the actual parameter must be assignment compatible with the formal type.

procedure declaration with VALUE parameters occurs in Example 7.2.1.

A9.3.3 RESULT Parameters

When the attribute RESULT is specified for a formal simple variable parameter, the formal parameter is made a variable local to the procedure, as is the case for a VALUE parameter. Instead of the value of the formal parameter being initialized, the final value held by the formal parameter is assigned to the corresponding actual parameter upon return from the procedure body. This means that until a value is assigned to the formal parameter in the procedure, its value is undefined. Second, the corresponding actual parameter must be a variable which can be assigned to. And third, the type of the formal parameter must be assignment compatible with the type of the actual parameter.

In order to specify call by result, the type of the formal parameter must be followed by the word RESULT.
                    INTEGER RESULT A, B, C;
                    REAL RESULT MASS

Suppose a procedure specifies RESULT formal parameters FP_1, FP_2,....,FP_LAST and is called with actual parameters AP_1,AP_2,....,AP_LAST. One can think of the procedure as being contained within an implicit surrounding block in which the formal parameters are locally declared and in which the statements
                    AP_1 := FP_1;
                    AP_2 := FP_2;
                    AP_LAST := FP_LAST
immediately follow the procedure body.

When the RESULT attribute is specified for a formal parameter, that parameter must be assigned a value within the procedure body; otherwise the value that is returned to the actual parameter upon completion of the procedure will be undefined.

A9.3.4 VALUE RESULT Parameters

The effects of both call by value and call by result may be gained by using call by VALUE RESULT. This form of parameter is specified by the two words VALUE RESULT. Their order may not be interchanged.

                    INTEGER VALUE RESULT A, B, C;
                    REAL VALUE RESULT MASS

The actual parameter is only evaluated once at the procedure call. The value is assigned to a local variable which is used whenever the parameter is referred to. When execution of the procedure body is completed, the value of this parameter is assigned to the actual parameter. This means that the actual parameter must be a variable which may be assigned to and the types of the actual and formal parameters must be assignment compatible in both directions.

A procedure declaration using VALUE RESULT parameters occurs in Examples 7.2.3, 7.2.4.

A9.4 Recursive Procedures

A procedure which calls itself or which invokes a second procedure which in turn calls the first is said to be a recursive procedure. The possibility of circularity or a closed loop of procedure calls is avoided by including within each recursive procedure a conditional statement which specifies a termination condition (see Sec. 7.4).

Recursive procedures are illustrated by examples in Sec. 7.4 and by Example 8.2.1.

A10. Standard Procedures and Standard Functions

A10.1 The Input/Output System

Standard procedures are provided in ALGOL W for the purpose of communication with the input/output system. These standard procedures differ from explicitly declared procedures in that the number and type of actual parameters need not be identical in every instance in which the procedure is invoked.

In ALGOL W both the input stream and the output stream are conceived of as sequences of records, each record consisting of a character sequence of fixed length. The input stream has the logical properties of a sequence of cards in a card reader; records consist of 80 characters. The output stream has the logical properties of a sequence of lines on a line printer; records consist of 132 characters, and the records are grouped into logical pages. Each page consists of at least one and at most 60 lines.

In the remainder of this section we shall often refer to input records as cards and to output records as print lines.

A10.2 Standard Input Procedures

A10.2.1 READ(<variable list>)

Scanning for data items begins with the first character of the next card. Data items are separated by one or more blanks and leading blanks are ignored. Constants in the input stream must be of a type which is assignment compatible with the variables to which they are being assigned; in particular, string constants must be enclosed in the string quote (").

If the data card being scanned contains fewer data items than are specified in the varaible list, a new card is obtained with position 80 of one card considered to be immediately followed by position 1 of the next card. Therefore if the last character of a number appears in column 80, the character in column 1 of the succeeding card must be blank.

If the data card being scanned contains more data items than are specified in the variable list, scanning will stop when the last variable in the variable list has received a value. If the next input statement encountered in the program is a READ statement, the excess data items will be lost since scanning will begin with the first character of the next card. It is possible to continue reading data on the same card at a subsequent time by means of the READON statement.

The READ statement appears in Sec. 2.4 and in subsequent examples in the book.

A10.2.2 READON(<variable list>)

The READON statement is similar in all respects to the READ statement except that scanning of data continues from where the last reading terminated. If fewer data items are found than are specified in the variable list, a new card is obtained.

A10.2.3 READCARD(<variable list>)

The READ and READON statements perform an editing function as they scan the input stream interpreting data items as numbers, bit sequences, strings, or logical values according to the type of the corresponding variable in the variable list.

It may be more convenient to read a data card as a string of characters without having to use the string quotes to delimit it. The READCARD statement accomplishes this purpose.

The word READCARD is followed by a list of string variable identifiers, each of which must have a declared length of 80 or greater. A new card is read for each string variable within the parentheses. If a variable is longer than 80 characters, each extra character to the right is assigned the blank character.

The READCARD statement is illustrated by example in Sec. 6.2.

A10.3 Standard Output Procedures

A10.3.1 WRITE(<list of expressions>)

The WRITE statement causes initiation of a new print line. In addition to constants and variables, the WRITE statement may contain expressions whose values are to be printed.

Character strings are frequently desired in printed output in order to identify the meaning of the values. A sequence of characters may be printed by enclosing the sequence in quote (") marks. If a quote mark occurs within the sequence of characters it must be followed by a second quote mark. The following is an example of output labeling:

```
WRITE("SIDE_1=", A, "SIDE_2=", B, "HYPOTENUSE=", SQRT(A**2 + B**2))
```

A10.3.2 WRITEON(<list of expressions>)

The WRITEON statement permits the programmer to continue printing values on the same line which the last WRITE or WRITEON statement used. If there is insufficient space on the line, a new line is begun.

The WRITEON statement is illustrated in Example 6.4.1 and in subsequent examples.

A10.3.3 Format of Output

Output items are automatically edited. Data is automatically converted to character sequences and placed in fields according to the simple type of each item as described below.

Simple Type	Field Description
INTEGER	right justified in a field containing the number of characters specified by the current value of INTFIELDSIZE (initialized to 14 but may be changed anywhere in the program to any positive integer value, cf. A4.2) and followed by 2 blanks
REAL	right justified in a field of 14 characters and followed by 2 blanks
LONG REAL	right justified in a field of 22 characters and followed by 2 blanks
COMPLEX	two adjacent _real_ fields
LONG COMPLEX	two adjacent _long real_ fields
LOGICAL	right justified in a field of 6 characters followed by 2 blanks
STRING	placed in a field exactly the length of the string
BITS	right justified in a field of 14 characters and followed by 2 blanks

A10.4 Input/Output Control Statements

IOCONTROL(N) is a standard procedure which affects the state of the input/output system. The arguments for which it is defined and their effects are given below.

N=	Action

1   Subsequent input scanning will begin in the next card column 1 available. Does nothing if the next column is column 1. IOCONTROL(1) can be used in conjunction with the READON procedure when one wants to commence reading from the next input card.

2   Subsequent output printing will begin at position 1 of a line. Does nothing if the next position is position 1. IOCONTROL(2) can be used in conjunction with the WRITEON procedure when one wants to cause printing to begin on a new line. Its use is illustrated in Sec. 6.2 and in subsequent examples.

3   Like IOCONTROL(2) except that the new line is also caused to begin a new output page. Does nothing if already positioned at the first character at the top of a page.

4   ALGOL W automatically prints only 60 lines to a page. IOCONTROL(4) suppresses this feature, causing page boundaries to be ignored.

5   Undoes IOCONTROL(4).

72   Subsequent use of READ and READON are to use only the first 72 characters of a card; the last eight are ignored. Used when reading data from cards punched by the computer with sequence numbers in columns 73-80. READCARD still reads all 80 characters.

80   Undoes IOCONTROL(72).

A10.5 Standard Transfer Functions

Certain function for conversion of values from one simple type to another are provided. These functions are predeclared; the corresponding implicit declaration headings are listed below:

    integer procedure TRUNCATE (real value X);
        comment the integer i such that
        |i| <= |X| < |i| + 1 and i*X >= 0;

    integer procedure ENTIER (real value X);
        comment the integer i such that
        i <= X < i + 1;

    integer procedure ROUND (real value X);
        comment the value of the integer expression
        if X < 0 then TRUNCATE(X - 0.5) else TRUNCATE(X + 0.5);

    integer procedure EXPONENT (real value X);
        comment 0 if X = 0, otherwise the largest integer i such that
        i <= log[base 16] (|X|) + 1.
    This function obtains the exponent used in the internal representation of the real number in the IBM 370 computers;

```
real procedure ROUNDTOREAL (long real value X);
    comment the properly rounded value of X;

real procedure REALPART (complex value Z);
    comment the real component of Z;

long real procedure LONGREALPART (long complex value Z);

real procedure IMAGPART (complex value Z);
    comment the imaginary component of Z;

long real procedure LONGIMAGPART (long complex value Z);

complex procedure IMAG (real value X);
    comment the complex number 0 + Xi;

long complex procedure LONGIMAG (long real value X);

logical procedure ODD (integer value N);
    comment the logical value
        N rem 2 = 1;

bits procedure BITSTRING (integer value N);
    comment two's complement representation of N;

integer procedure NUMBER (bits value X);
    comment integer whose two's complement representation is X;

integer procedure DECODE (string(1) value S);
    comment EBCDIC numeric code for the character S;

string(1) procedure CODE (integer value N);
    comment character whose EBCDIC code is
        abs (N rem 256);
```

A10.6 Standard Functions of Analysis

The following functions of analysis are provided. These functions are predeclared. For a discussion of the use of function procedures, see section A.9.

```
real procedure SQRT (real value X);
    comment the positive square root of X,
        domain: X >= 0;

long real procedure LONGSQRT (long real value X);
    comment the positive square root of X,
        domain: X >= 0;

real procedure EXP (real value X);
    comment e ** X,
        domain: X < 174.67;
```

```
long real procedure LONGEXP (long real value X);
    comment e ** X,
        domain: X < 174.67;

real procedure LN (real value X);
    comment logarithm of X to the base e,
        domain: X > 0;

long real procedure LONGLN (long real value X);
    comment logarithm of X to the base e,
        domain: X > 0;

real procedure LOG (real value X);
    comment logarithm of X to the base 10,
        domain: X > 0;

long real procedure LONGLOG (long real value X);
    comment logarithm of X to the base 10,
        domain: X > 0;

real procedure SIN (real value X);
    comment sine of X in radians,
        domain: -823550 < X < 823550;

long real procedure LONGSIN (long real value X);
    comment sine of X in radians,
        domain: -3.537'+15 < X < 3.537'+15;

real procedure COS (real value X);
    comment cosine of X in radians,
        domain: -823550 < X < 823550;

long real procedure LONGCOS (long real value X);
    comment cosine of X in radians,
        domain: -3.537'+15 < X < 3.537'+15;

real procedure ARCTAN (real value X);
    comment arctangent in radians of X,
        range: -PI/2 < ARCTAN(X) < PI/2;

long real procedure LONGARCTAN (long real value X);
    comment arctangent in radians of X,
        range: -PI/2 < ARCTAN(X) < PI/2;
```

A10.7 The Time function

The ALGOL W environment includes a clock which measures elapsed time since the beginning of program execution. The resolution of the clock is 1/60 second. A predeclared function is provided for reading the clock.

<u>integer procedure</u> TIME (<u>integer value</u> N);
<u>comment</u>   <u>Argument Result units</u>
                 -- time of day--
        -1   seconds/60
               -- elapsed execution time --
         0   minutes/100
         1   seconds/60
         2   seconds/38400
The result for any other argument is not defined;

A11. Debugging Facilities

A11.1 $DEBUG,n(m)

ALGOL W provides extensive facilities to aid the programmer in detecting and correcting logical errors ("bugs") in his program. The tracing, statement counting, and post-mortem dump facilities of ALGOL W are activated by insertion of the following card into the deck between a %ALGOL and the next % card

$DEBUG,n(m)

where the $ sign occupies the first column of the card, and no spaces are left between characters.

The single digit n specifies the following actions.

n=   action

0   no tracing is done

1   a post-mortem dump of all the programs's variables if execution
        terminates abnormally, otherwise nothing (cf. A11.4)

2   (1) plus a paragraphed listing of the program with all comments
        deleted. Each statement is preceded by a count of how many times
        that statement was executed. This listing is called an <u>execution
        flow summary</u>. Use of the $DEBUG,2 option adds almost nothing to
        the cost of running an ALGOL W program and provides information
        that can be enormously useful in analysis of the execution of the
        program.

3   (2) plus a statement-by-statement trace of each value stored

4   (3) plus a statement-by-statement trace of each value fetched

If tracing is specified ($DEBUG,3 or $DEBUG,4) and the standard procedure TRACE is not used (A11.2), then each ALGOL W statement will be traced in symbolic form the first m times it is executed. Each time a statement is traced it produces at least two lines of output which are included in the run-time limit. The default provided when no $DEBUG card is included in the deck is equivalent to $DEBUG,1 -- post mortem dump but no statement counting or tracing.

The following abbreviated control cards are acceptable:
```
$DEBUG             for $DEBUG,4(2)
$DEBUG,x           for $DEBUG,x(2)  where X is either 3 or 4
(no $DEBUG card)   for $DEBUG,1
```

A11.2 TRACE Standard Procedure

The number of times each source statement is traced by the debugging facilities (as specified on the $DEBUG card, cf. A11.1) can be modified by the standard procedure TRACE.

This procedure has the following implicit declaration heading:

```
procedure TRACE (integer value N);
    comment changes the upper bound for statement tracing:
    if N > 0 then N becomes the bound,
    if N = 0 then tracing is suspended,
    if N < 0 then the $DEBUG card value (m)
    becomes the bound;
```

TRACE has no effect unless the $DEBUG option digit is 3 or 4.

A11.3 ASSERT Statement

<assert statement> ::= ASSERT <logical expression>

example ASSERT (X > 0)

the ASSERT statement causes evaluation of the logical expression and termination of the program if this value is false; if the expression has the value true then program execution continues. The ASSERT statement can be used both as a debugging aid (asserting conditions which should be true, but may not be if a bug exists), and as a program documentation aid.

A11.4 Details of Post-mortem Dump

The post-mortem dump begins with => TRACE OF ACTIVE SEGMENTS, then the complete call chain is printed starting with the procedure which was active at the point of termination and working back to its caller, etc. For each procedure, the following information is printed:

a) The name of the procedure. The outermost procedure is called "(MAIN)" and a simple BEGIN block is named "<BLOCK>".

b) The names and values of the local variables in the procedure. Uninitialized values print as "?". Local copies of parameters are named with primes. Strings are printed with a single quote added on each end, but quotes within the string are not doubled. At most eight values are printed from an array, usually the first seven and the last one. Reference values are printed as Recordclass.#, where # is a unique number (in order of allocation). The control variables in FOR statements are all distinct even if they are spelled the same way. So if I is used in many FOR statements, it will be dumped many times.

c) The name of the calling routine and the coordinate of the call. For name parameters, a procedure may be re-entered (environment re-established) to evaluate the corresponding argument.

Table A10.5.1 Character Encodings

The following table gives the correspondence between the printable character set and the EBCDIC codes, which are given as integer numbers. This encoding establishes the ordering relation on characters and thus on strings. The characters in parentheses are not available on most line printers. Unlisted integer codes do not correspond to any established character.

64	space	129	(a)	193	A	240	0
74	(¢)	130	(b)	194	B	241	1
75	.	131	(c)	195	C	242	2
76	<	132	(d)	196	D	243	3
77	(	133	(e)	197	E	244	4
78	+	134	(f)	198	F	245	5
79	|	135	(g)	199	G	246	6
80	&	136	(h)	200	H	247	7
90	(!)	137	(i)	201	I	248	8
91	$	145	(j)	209	J	249	9
92	*	146	(k)	210	K		
93	)	147	(l)	211	L		
94	;	148	(m)	212	M		
95	¬	149	(n)	213	N		
96	-	150	(o)	214	O		
97	/	151	(p)	215	P		
107	,	152	(q)	216	Q		
108	%	153	(r)	217	R		
109	_	162	(s)	226	S		
110	>	163	(t)	227	T		
111	?	164	(u)	228	U		
122	:	165	(v)	229	V		
123	#	166	(w)	230	W		
124	@	167	(x)	231	X		
125	'	168	(y)	232	Y		
126	=	169	(z)	233	Z		
127	"						

NOTES

NOTES

INDEX

INDEX BY PROGRAMMING TERMINOLOGY

In this index, references beginning with A denote sections of the Appendix; numbered references denote page numbers in the main text. Underlined references indicate definitions or explanations; page references not underlined indicate the first examples of use in the text.

actual parameter	A9.2, 160
algorithm	2
array	A3.2, 87, 96, 98
assignment compatability	A8.1.2.2
assignment statement	A8.1.2, 20
block	A8.1.1, 48, 111
Backus normal form (BNF)	A1
comment	47, 48, 54
compound statement	48, 51
conditional expression	A7.7, 33, 35
conditional statement	A8.3, 39, 43
constant	A4.1
controlled statement	A8.2, A8.3, 39
correctness	65, 81, 109
data representation	87, 95, 198, 207
data type	83
declaration	A5, 85, 51
dimension	A5.2
efficiency	7, 111
empty statement	A8.1.3
execution flow summary	A6, A11
execution sequence	A8, 176
expression	A7, 20, 21, 34, 39, 105
flag	37, 51, 92
formal parameter	A9.2, 158, 159
(called by name)	A9.3.1, 173
(called by value)	A9.3.2, 158, 159
(returned by result)	A9.3.3, 161
function designator	A8.1.4.1
function procedure	A9, $A9.1.2, 159
global definition	A8.1.1, 156, 164
grammar, formal	A1
identifier	A2, 19
index, array	A5.2, 94, 96
input	23, 26, 104, 120, 121, 299
iteration	A8.2, 61, 62, 68, 72
iteration graph	38, 39, 61, 62
local definition	A8.1.1, 156, 157
output	23, 34, 125, 128, 299

precedence of operators   A7.1.8, A7.3
                        A7.10, 22
predeclared variables   A4.2
proper procedure   A9, A9.1.1, 162
relational expression   A7.2, 34, 35
recursive grammar   A1
recursive procedure   A9.4, 167, 169
reserved word   A2
scope of declaration   A8.1.1
semicolon   A8.1
statement   A8
subscript   A5.2
syntax   A1
type   A3, 83
unconditional statement   A8.1
variable   A2, 19

ABS   A7.1.6
AND   A7.3, A7.4
ARRAY   A3.2
    declaration   A5.2
ASSERT   A11.3, 77
BEGIN   A8.1.1
BITS   A3.1
    constant   A4.1
    declarations   A5.1
    expression   A7.4
CASE
    expression   A7.7.2
    statement   A8.4.2
COMMENT   A6
COMPLEX   A3.1
    constant   A4.1
    declaration   A5.1
    expression
A7.1 DIV   A7.1.3, 160
DO   A8.2.2
ELSE   A7.7.1, A8.3.1
END   A8.1.1
FALSE   A4.1
FOR   A8.2.2, 68
IF
    expression   A7.7.1, 33
    statement   A8.3.1, 39
INTEGER   A3.1
    constant   A4.1
    declaration   A5.1
    expression   A7.1
LOGICAL   A3.1
    constant   A4.1
    declaration   A5.1
    expression   A7.3, 34, 35
    variable   37, 51
LONG   A7.1.1
NULL   A4.1
OR   A7.3, A7.4
PROCEDURE   A9
REAL   A3.1
    constant   A4.1
    declaration   A5.1
    expression   A7.1
RECORD   A3.2
    record class declaration   A5.3
REFERENCE   A3.1

constant	A4.1
declaration	A5.1
expression	A7.6
REM	A7.1.4, 93
RESULT	A9.3.3
SHORT	A7.1.7
STEP	A8.2.2
STRING	A3.1
constant	A4.1, 24
declaration	A5.1, 104
expression	A7.5, 104
length	A4.1.8
substring designator	A7.5, 105
THEN	A7.7.1, A8.3.1
TRUE	A4.1
UNTIL	A8.2.2
VALUE	A9.3.2
WHILE	A8.2.1

INDEX BY APPLICATIONS AREA

accounting calculations   27, 29, 57
binary search   7, 272
binomial coefficients   98, 114
classification   116, 215
decision-making   9, 35, 38, 40, 203
division algorithm   5
evaluation of functions   70,256,262,278,
                          279
interest calculations   31, 73, 79
intersection of lines   49,56,174,214,278
limits of sequences   78, 80
matching of lists   15, 56, 58, 116, 216
numerical algorithms   5,62,70,78,87,98,
        159,163,169,175,256,262,272,276
permutations   193, 213
polynomials   95, 115
population growth   228, 230, 244-5
printing figures   139, 147
printing tables   128,135,139,152,153,175
pseudo-random sequences   174, 237
pursuit simulation   222, 244
random walk   237, 246
roots of algebraic equations   272, 276
sequential search   6, 53, 104
sorting a list   106, 115, 200
tax computation   20, 40, 52
text processing 103,115,121,128,135,139,
                 174,180,193,214,218